GRIMMY™: THE REVENGE OF GRIMMZILLA

BY MIKE PETERS

TOR®

A TOM DOHERTY ASSOCIATES BOOK
NEW YORK

This is a work of fiction.
All the characters and events portrayed in this book are either fictitious
or are used fictitiously.

GRIMMY: THE REVENGE OF GRIMMZILLA

TM and Copyright © 2000 by Grimmy, Inc.

A Tor Book
Published by Tom Doherty Associates, LLC
175 Fifth Avenue
New York, NY 10010

www.tor.com

Tor® is a registered trademark of Tom Doherty Associates, LLC.

ISBN: 0-312-87324-7

First Edition: July 2000

Printed in the United States of America

0 9 8 7 6 5 4 3 2 1

To my best friend, my love, my wife: Marian

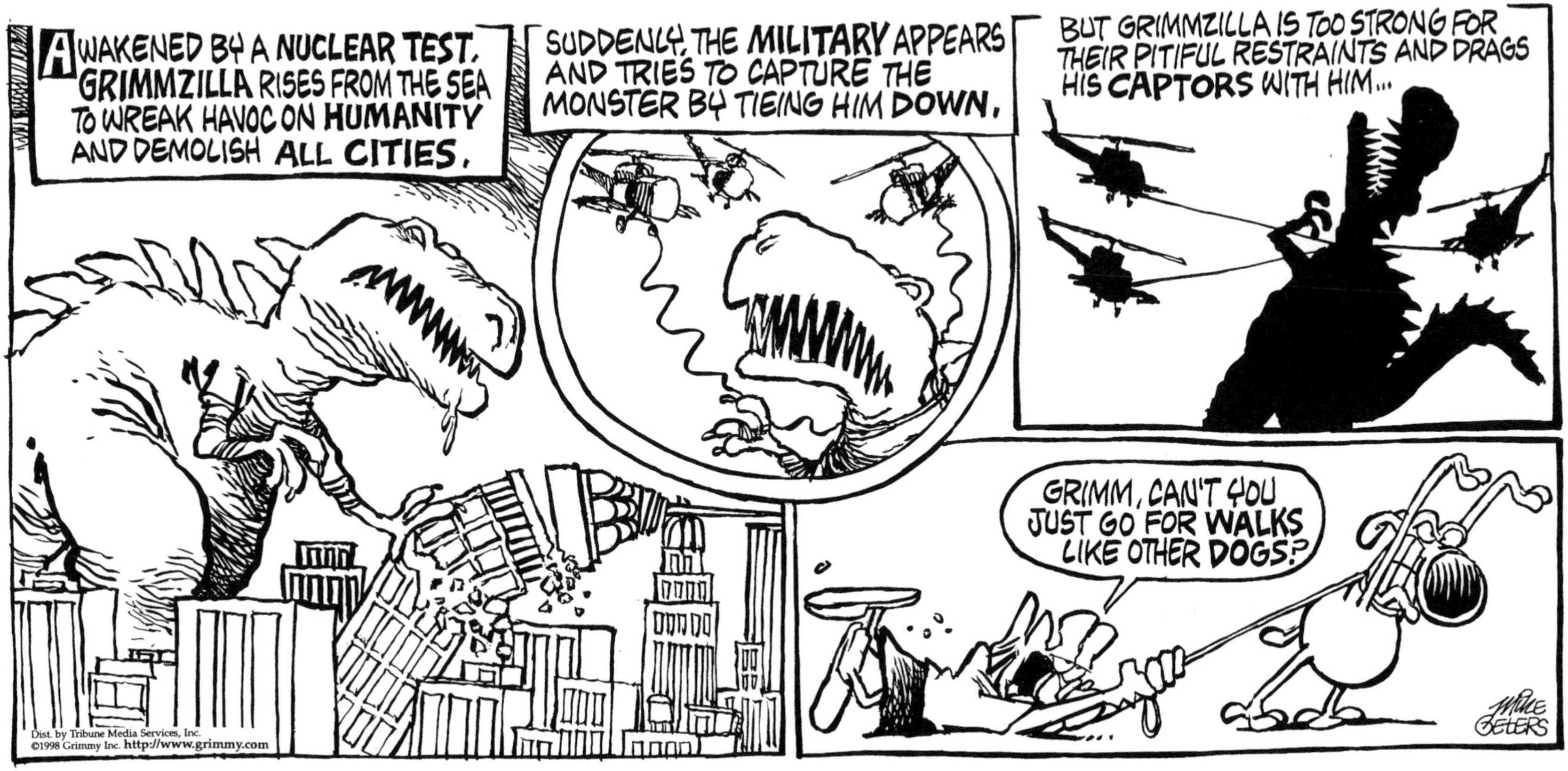
AWAKENED BY A NUCLEAR TEST, GRIMMZILLA RISES FROM THE SEA TO WREAK HAVOC ON HUMANITY AND DEMOLISH ALL CITIES.
SUDDENLY, THE MILITARY APPEARS AND TRIES TO CAPTURE THE MONSTER BY TIEING HIM DOWN.
BUT GRIMMZILLA IS TOO STRONG FOR THEIR PITIFUL RESTRAINTS AND DRAGS HIS CAPTORS WITH HIM...
GRIMM, CAN'T YOU JUST GO FOR WALKS LIKE OTHER DOGS?
Dist. by Tribune Media Services, Inc.
©1998 Grimmy Inc. http://www.grimmy.com
MIKE PETERS

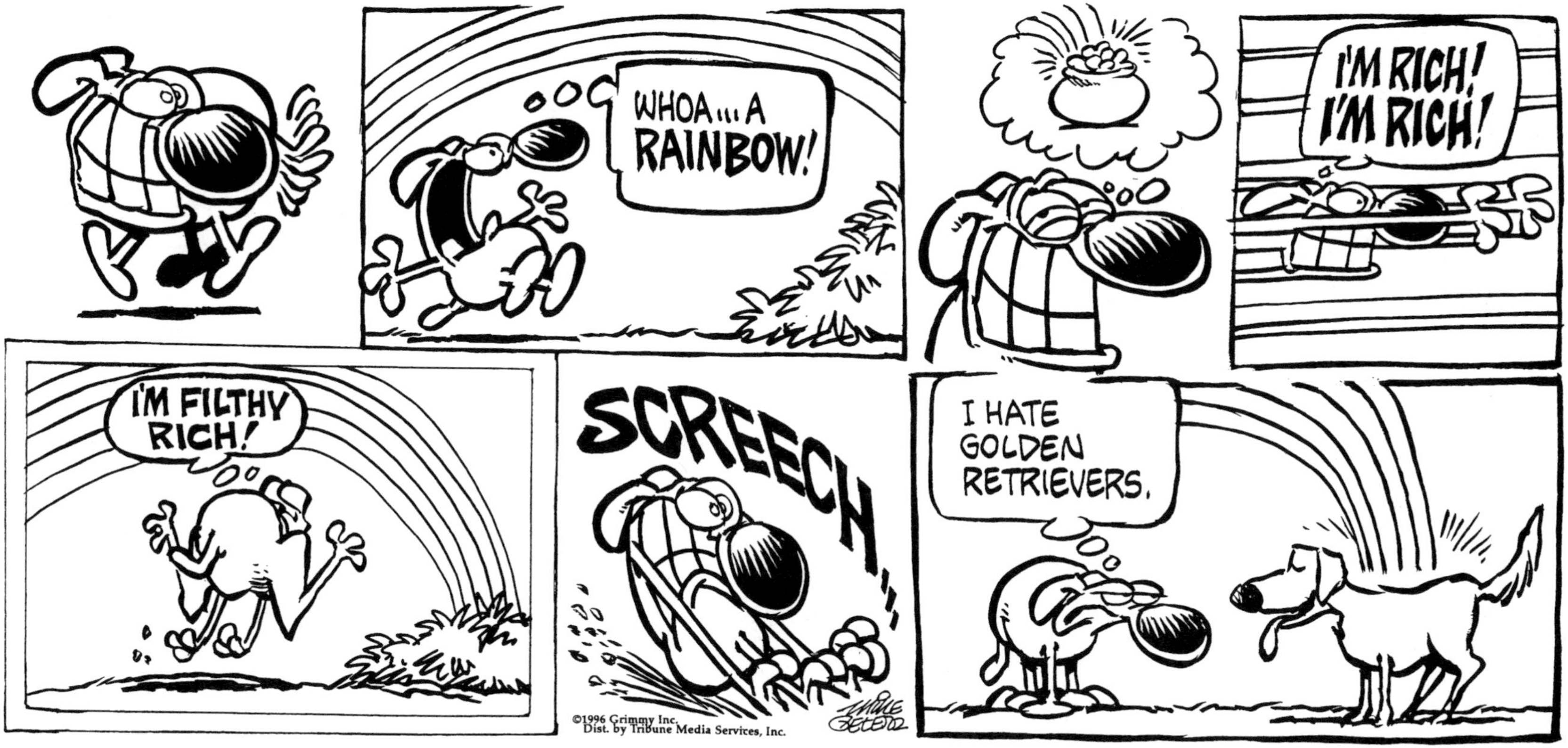
WHOA... A RAINBOW!
I'M RICH! I'M RICH!
I'M FILTHY RICH!
SCREECH...
I HATE GOLDEN RETRIEVERS.
©1996 Grimmy Inc.
Dist. by Tribune Media Services, Inc.

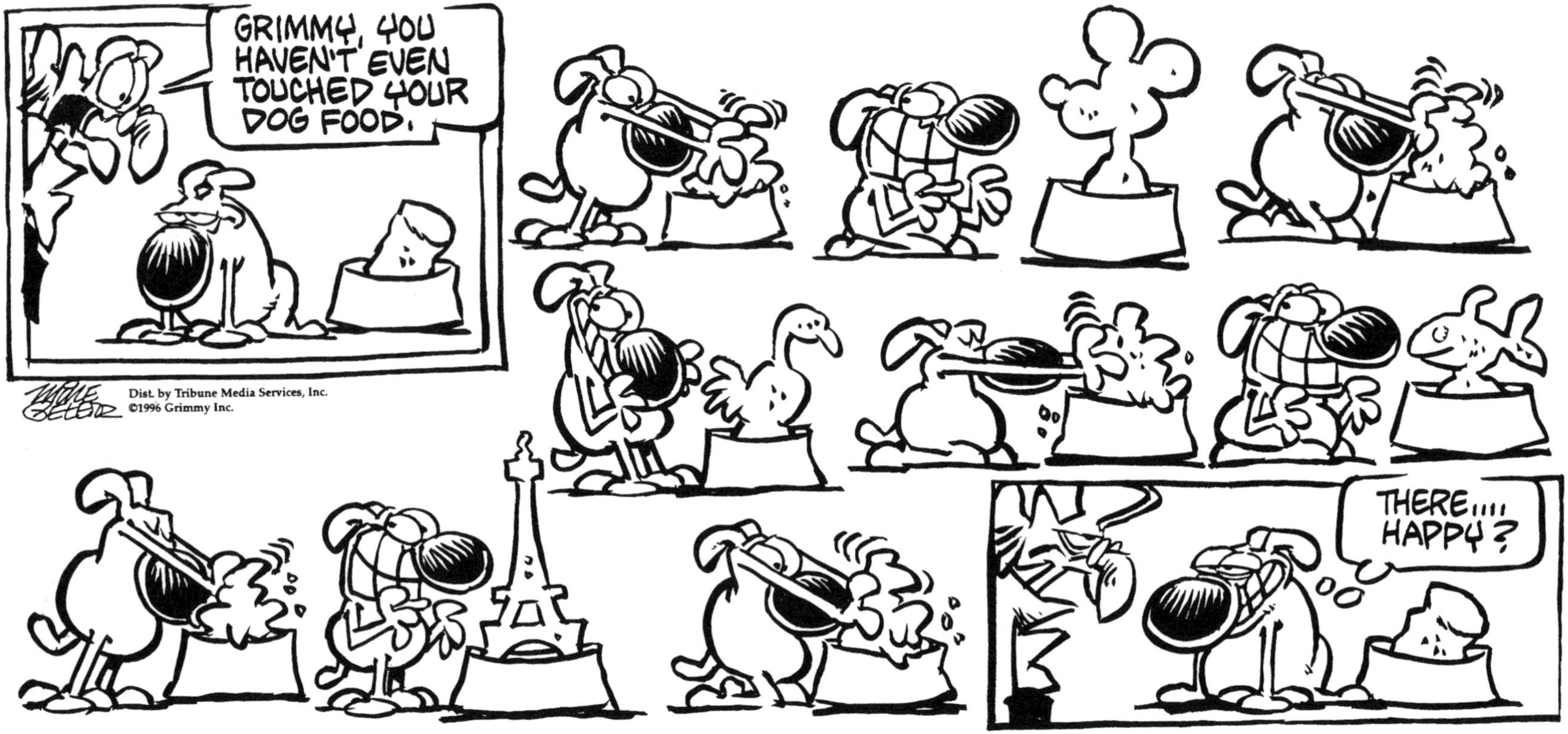
GRIMMY, YOU HAVEN'T EVEN TOUCHED YOUR DOG FOOD.
THERE.... HAPPY?

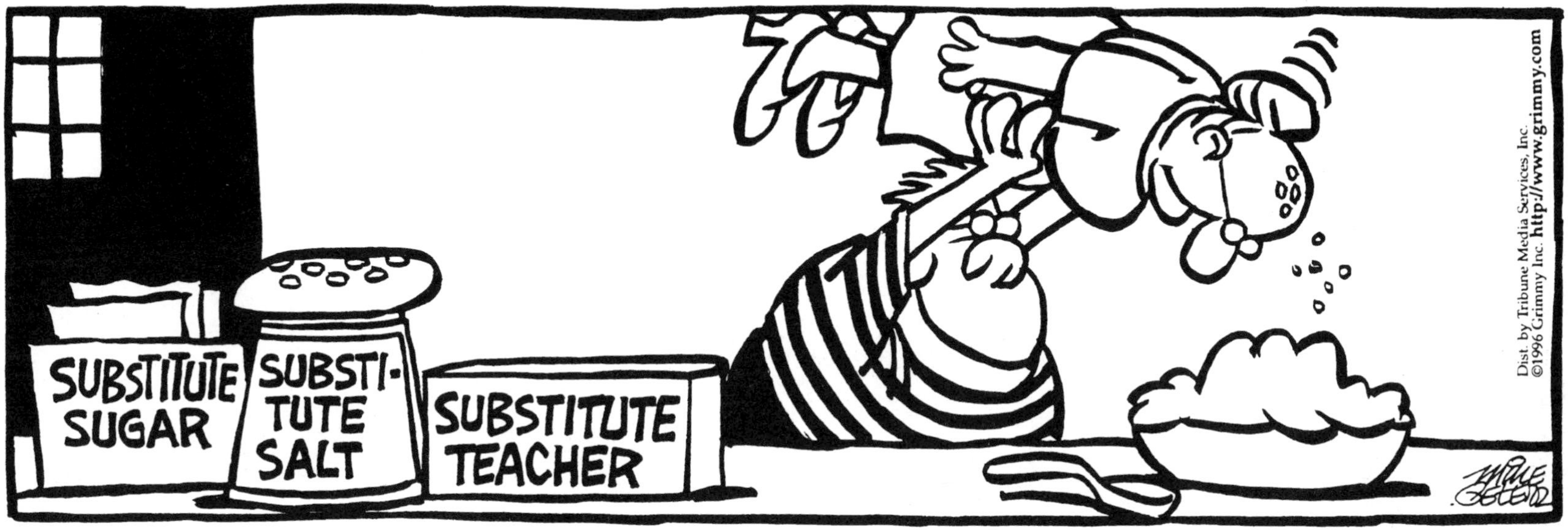
SUBSTITUTE SUGAR
SUBSTI-TUTE SALT
SUBSTITUTE TEACHER
Dist. by Tribune Media Services, Inc.
©1996 Grimmy Inc. http://www.grimmy.com

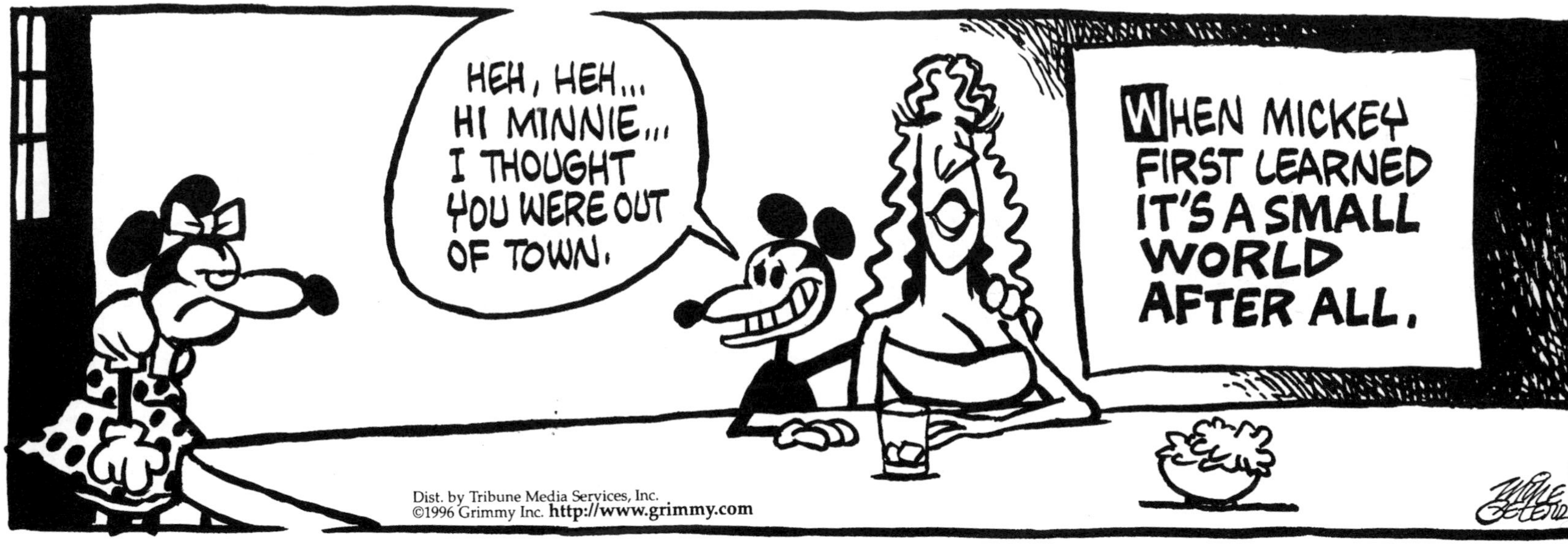
HEH, HEH... HI MINNIE... I THOUGHT YOU WERE OUT OF TOWN.
WHEN MICKEY FIRST LEARNED IT'S A SMALL WORLD AFTER ALL.
Dist. by Tribune Media Services, Inc.
©1996 Grimmy Inc. http://www.grimmy.com

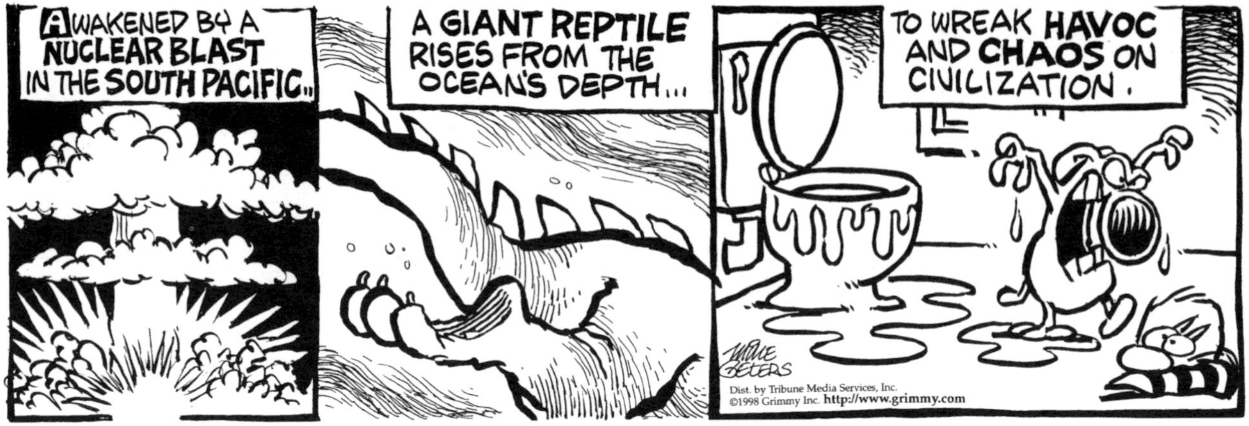
AWAKENED BY A NUCLEAR BLAST IN THE SOUTH PACIFIC...
A GIANT REPTILE RISES FROM THE OCEAN'S DEPTH...
TO WREAK HAVOC AND CHAOS ON CIVILIZATION.
MIKE PETERS
Dist. by Tribune Media Services, Inc.
©1998 Grimmy Inc. http://www.grimmy.com

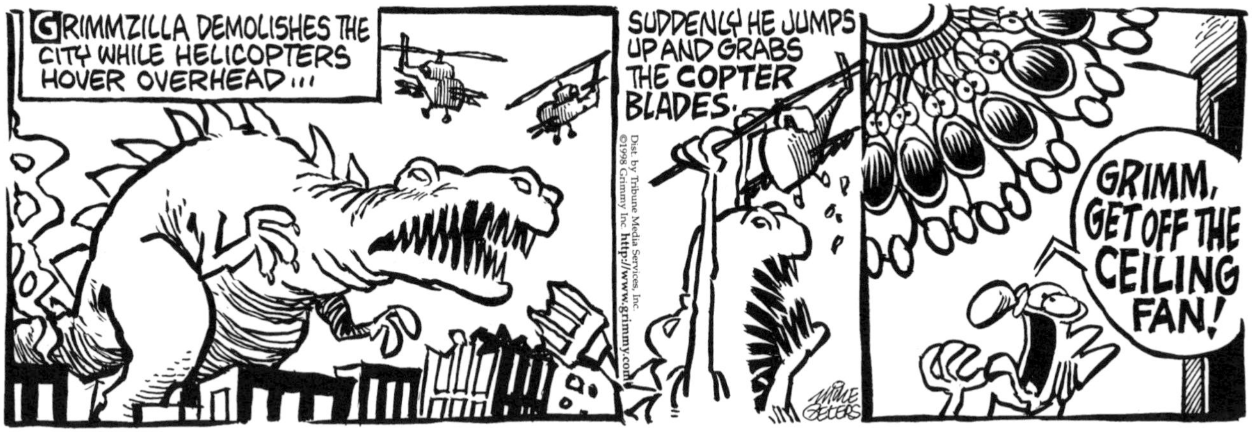
GRIMMZILLA DEMOLISHES THE CITY WHILE HELICOPTERS HOVER OVERHEAD...
Dist. by Tribune Media Services, Inc.
©1998 Grimmy Inc. http://www.grimmy.com
SUDDENLY HE JUMPS UP AND GRABS THE COPTER BLADES.
MIKE PETERS
GRIMM, GET OFF THE CEILING FAN!

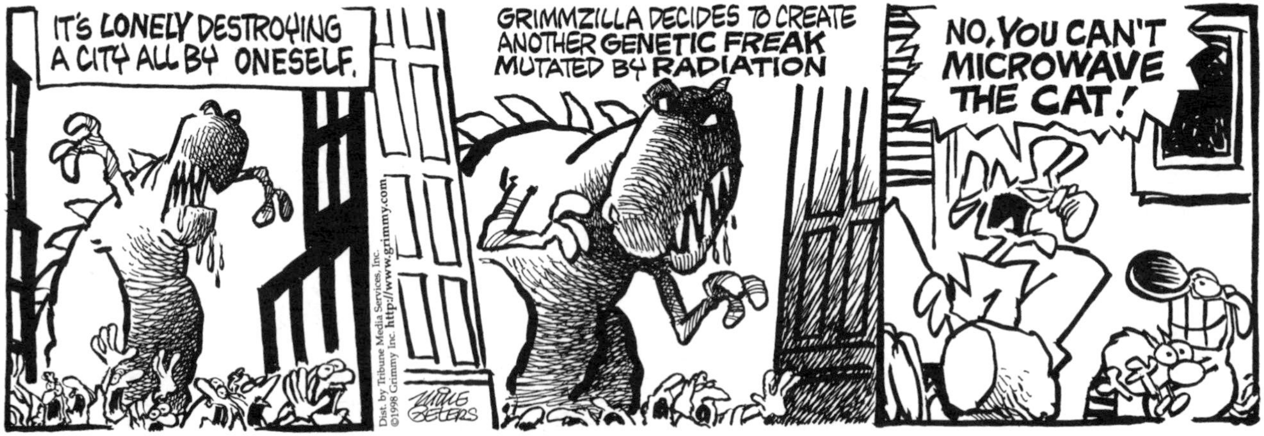
IT'S LONELY DESTROYING A CITY ALL BY ONESELF.
Dist. by Tribune Media Services, Inc.
©1998 Grimmy Inc. http://www.grimmy.com
MIKE PETERS
GRIMMZILLA DECIDES TO CREATE ANOTHER GENETIC FREAK MUTATED BY RADIATION
NO, YOU CAN'T MICROWAVE THE CAT!

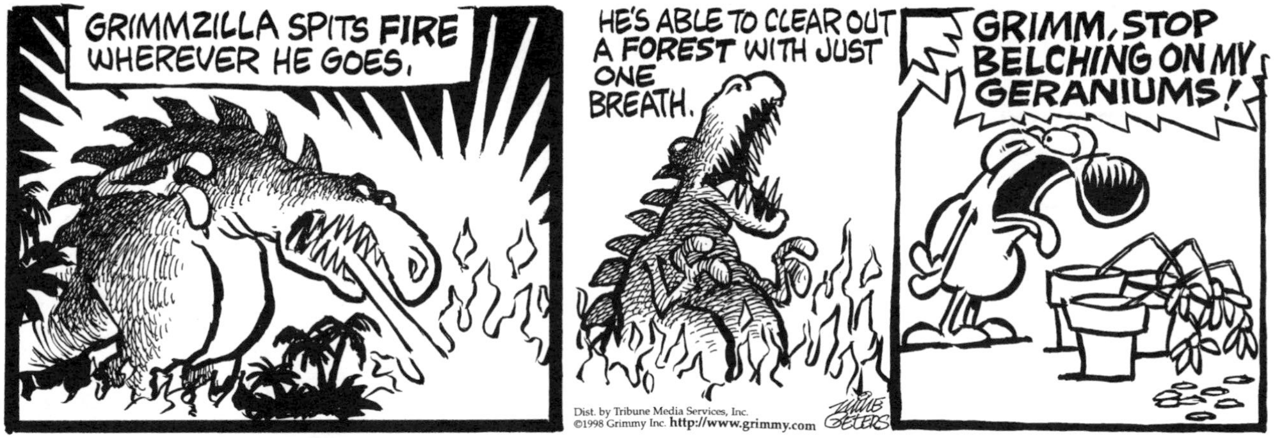
GRIMMZILLA SPITS FIRE WHEREVER HE GOES.
HE'S ABLE TO CLEAR OUT A FOREST WITH JUST ONE BREATH.
GRIMM, STOP BELCHING ON MY GERANIUMS!
Dist. by Tribune Media Services, Inc.
©1998 Grimmy Inc. http://www.grimmy.com
MIKE PETERS

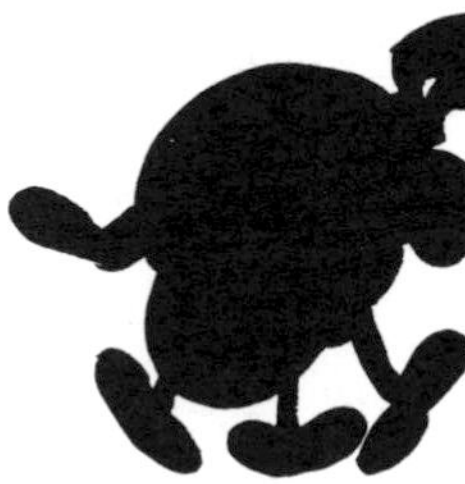

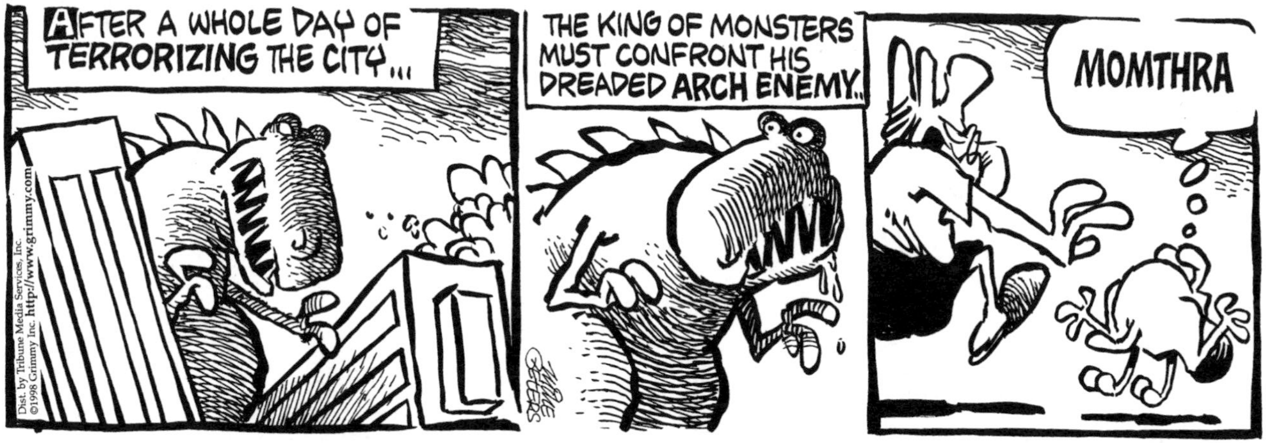
AFTER A WHOLE DAY OF TERRORIZING THE CITY...
THE KING OF MONSTERS MUST CONFRONT HIS DREADED ARCH ENEMY...
MOMTHRA
Dist. by Tribune Media Services, Inc.
©1998 Grimmy Inc. http://www.grimmy.com
MIKE PETERS

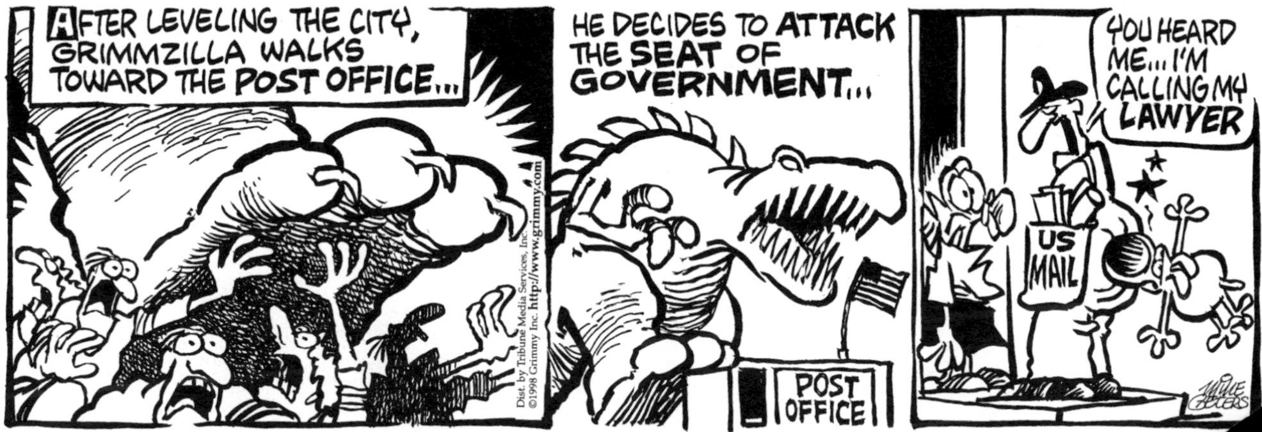
AFTER LEVELING THE CITY, GRIMMZILLA WALKS TOWARD THE POST OFFICE...
HE DECIDES TO ATTACK THE SEAT OF GOVERNMENT...
POST OFFICE
YOU HEARD ME... I'M CALLING MY LAWYER
US MAIL
Dist. by Tribune Media Services, Inc.
©1998 Grimmy Inc. http://www.grimmy.com
MIKE PETERS

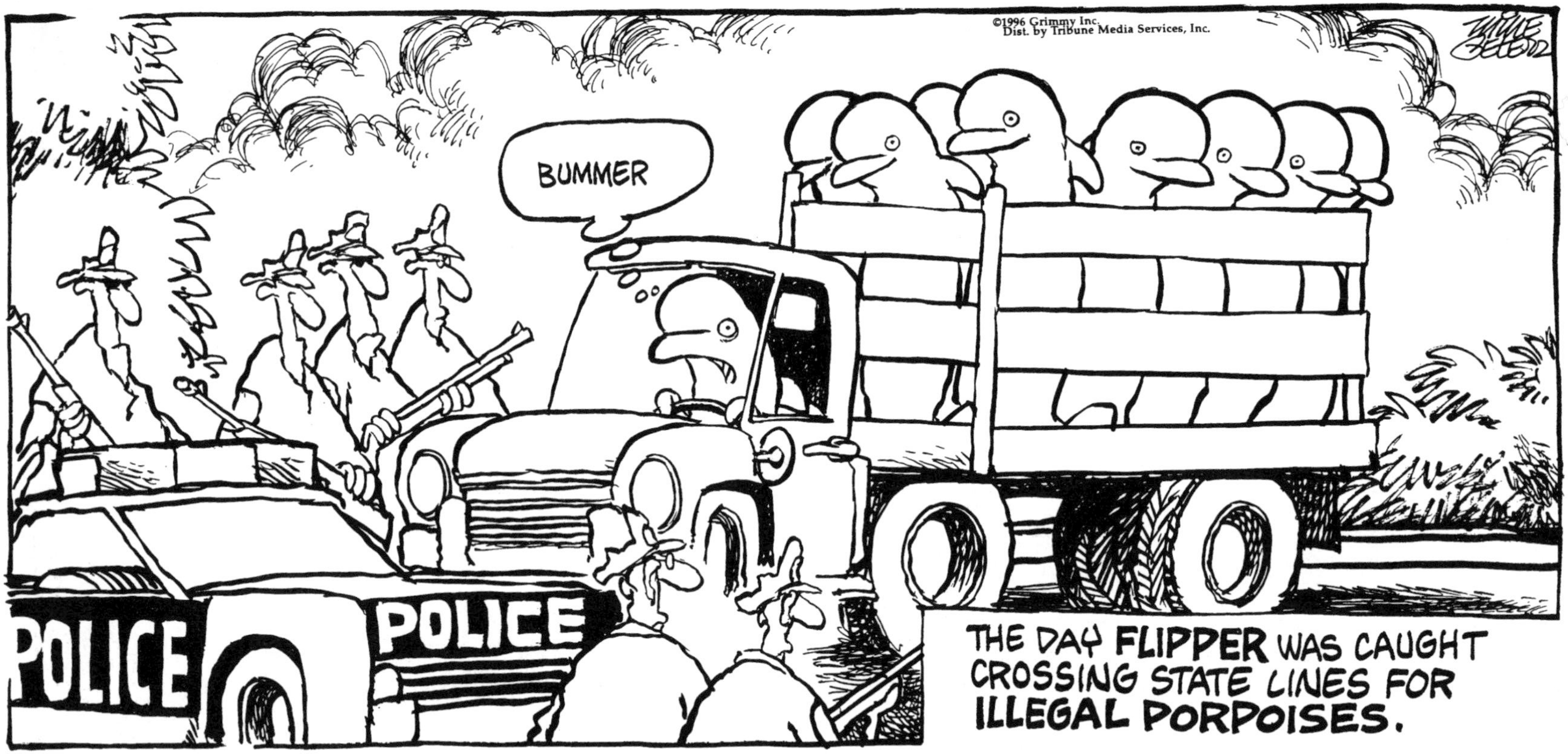
©1996 Grimmy Inc.
Dist. by Tribune Media Services, Inc.
BUMMER
POLICE
POLICE
THE DAY FLIPPER WAS CAUGHT CROSSING STATE LINES FOR ILLEGAL PORPOISES.

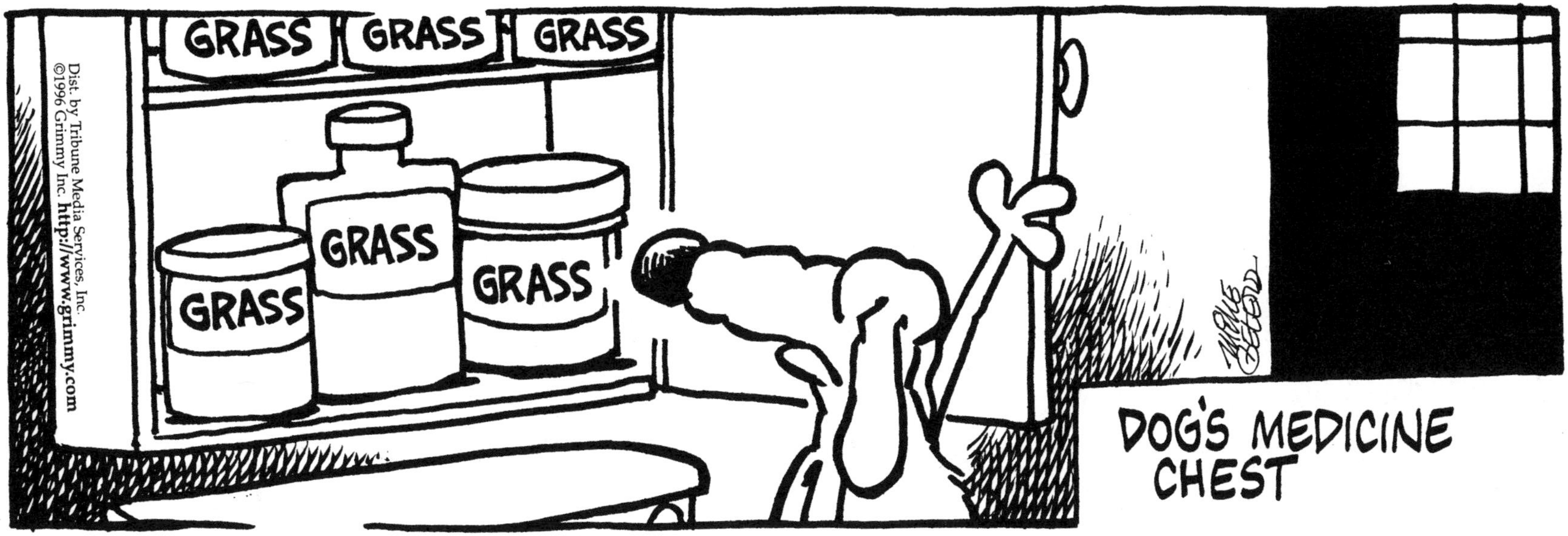
GRASS GRASS GRASS
GRASS
GRASS
GRASS
DOG'S MEDICINE CHEST
Dist. by Tribune Media Services, Inc. ©1996 Grimmy Inc. http://www.grimmy.com

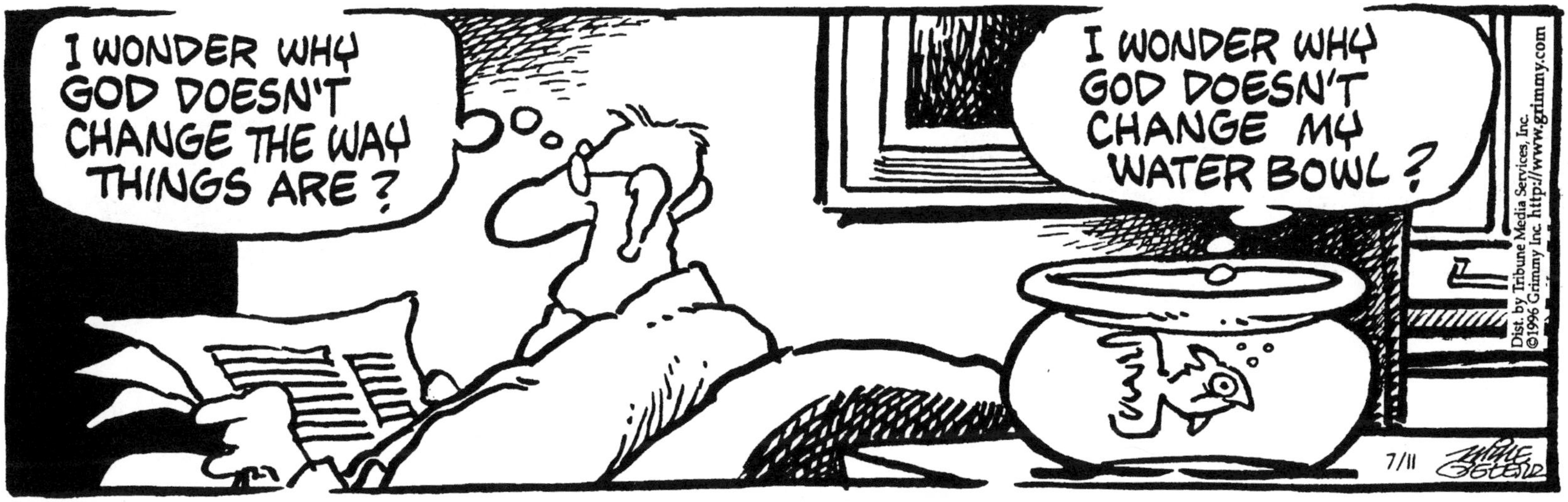
I WONDER WHY GOD DOESN'T CHANGE THE WAY THINGS ARE?
I WONDER WHY GOD DOESN'T CHANGE MY WATER BOWL?
Dist. by Tribune Media Services, Inc. ©1996 Grimmy Inc. http://www.grimmy.com
7/11

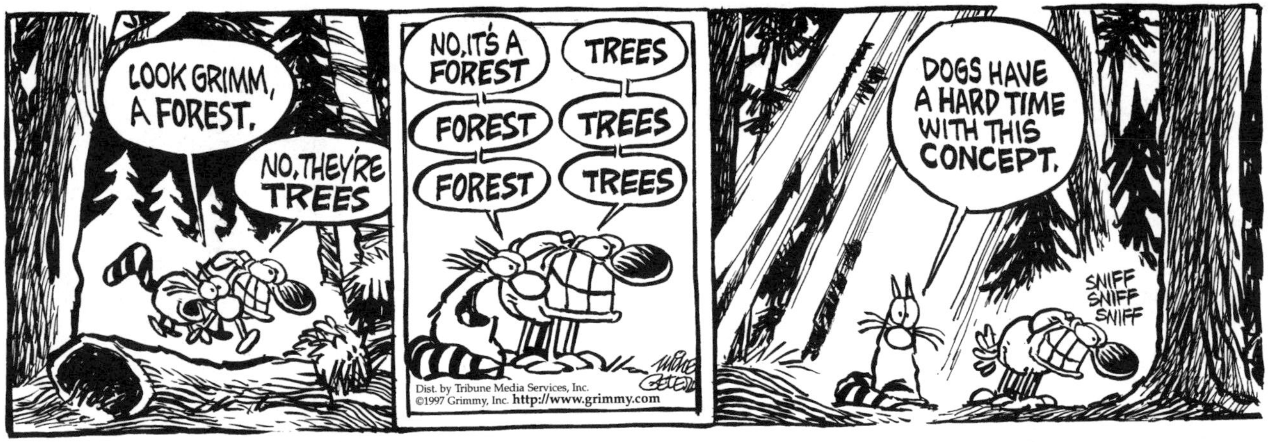
LOOK GRIMM, A FOREST.
NO, THEY'RE TREES
NO, IT'S A FOREST
TREES
FOREST
TREES
FOREST
TREES
DOGS HAVE A HARD TIME WITH THIS CONCEPT.
SNIFF SNIFF SNIFF
Dist. by Tribune Media Services, Inc.
©1997 Grimmy, Inc. http://www.grimmy.com

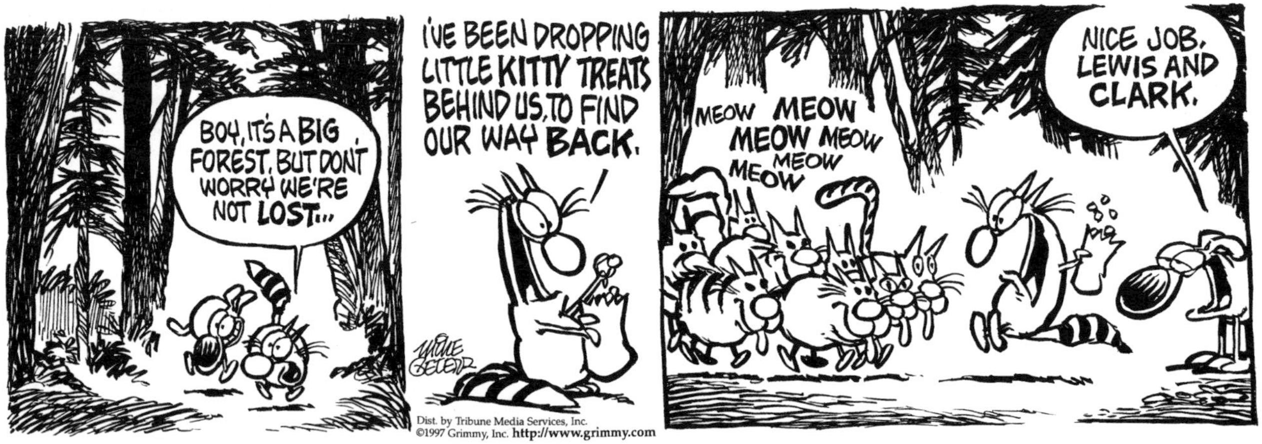
BOY, IT'S A BIG FOREST, BUT DON'T WORRY WE'RE NOT LOST...
I'VE BEEN DROPPING LITTLE KITTY TREATS BEHIND US, TO FIND OUR WAY BACK.
MEOW MEOW
MEOW MEOW
MEOW
MEOW
NICE JOB, LEWIS AND CLARK.
Dist. by Tribune Media Services, Inc.
©1997 Grimmy, Inc. http://www.grimmy.com

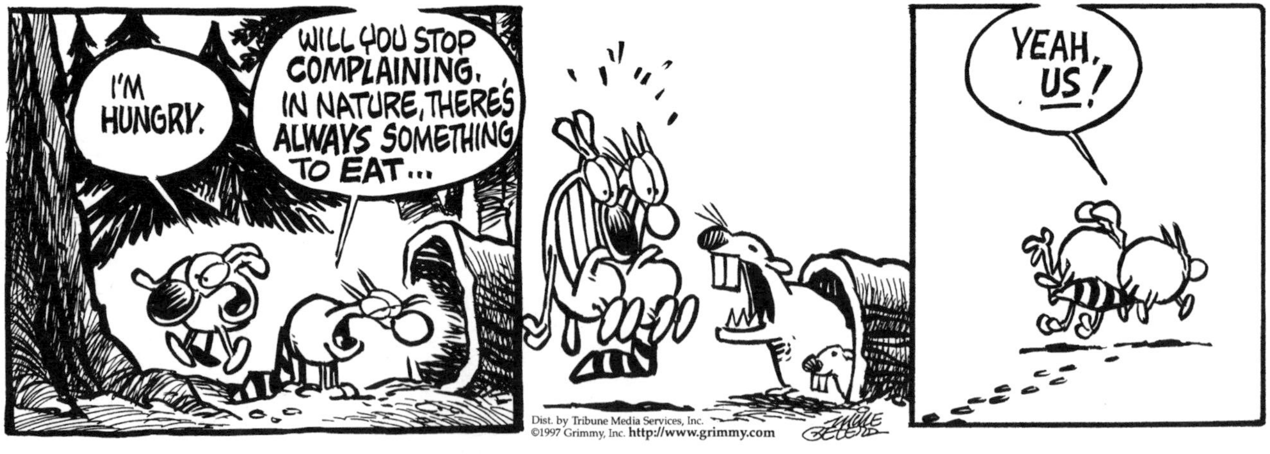
I'M HUNGRY.
WILL YOU STOP COMPLAINING. IN NATURE, THERE'S ALWAYS SOMETHING TO EAT...
YEAH, US!
Dist. by Tribune Media Services, Inc.
©1997 Grimmy, Inc. http://www.grimmy.com

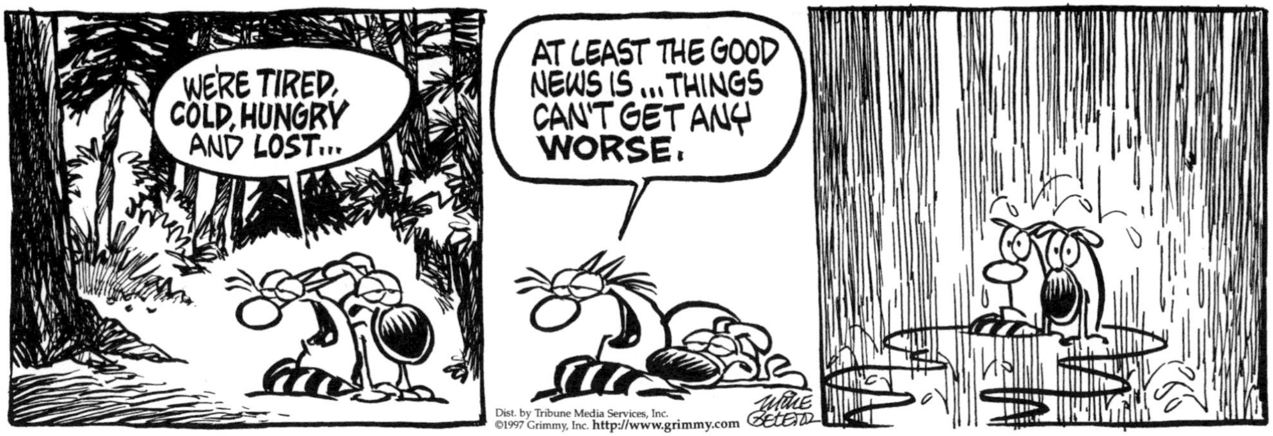
WE'RE TIRED, COLD, HUNGRY AND LOST...
AT LEAST THE GOOD NEWS IS ... THINGS CAN'T GET ANY WORSE.
Dist. by Tribune Media Services, Inc.
©1997 Grimmy, Inc. http://www.grimmy.com

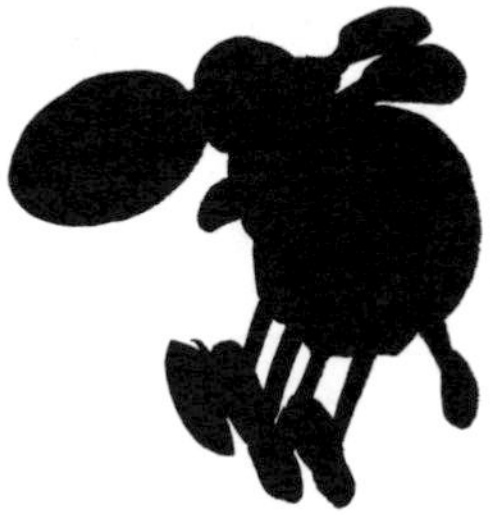

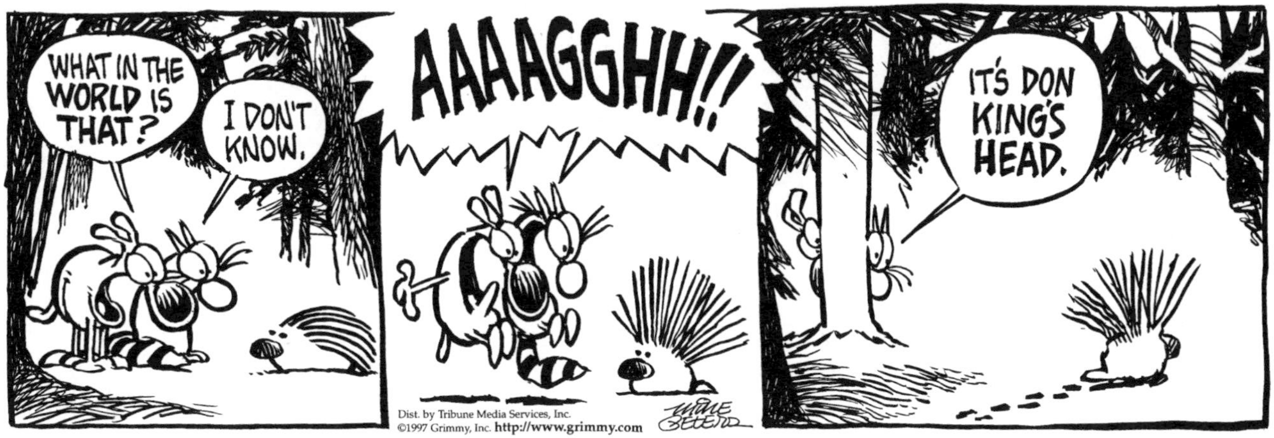
WHAT IN THE WORLD IS THAT?
I DON'T KNOW.
AAAAGGHH!!
IT'S DON KING'S HEAD.
Dist. by Tribune Media Services, Inc.
©1997 Grimmy, Inc. http://www.grimmy.com

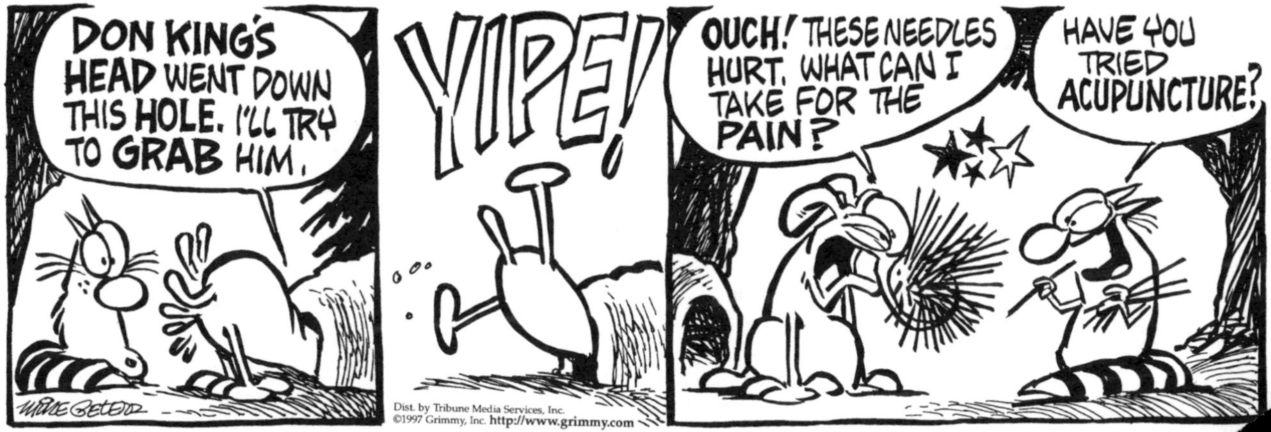
DON KING'S HEAD WENT DOWN THIS HOLE. I'LL TRY TO GRAB HIM.
YIPE!
OUCH! THESE NEEDLES HURT. WHAT CAN I TAKE FOR THE PAIN?
HAVE YOU TRIED ACUPUNCTURE?
Dist. by Tribune Media Services, Inc.
©1997 Grimmy, Inc. http://www.grimmy.com

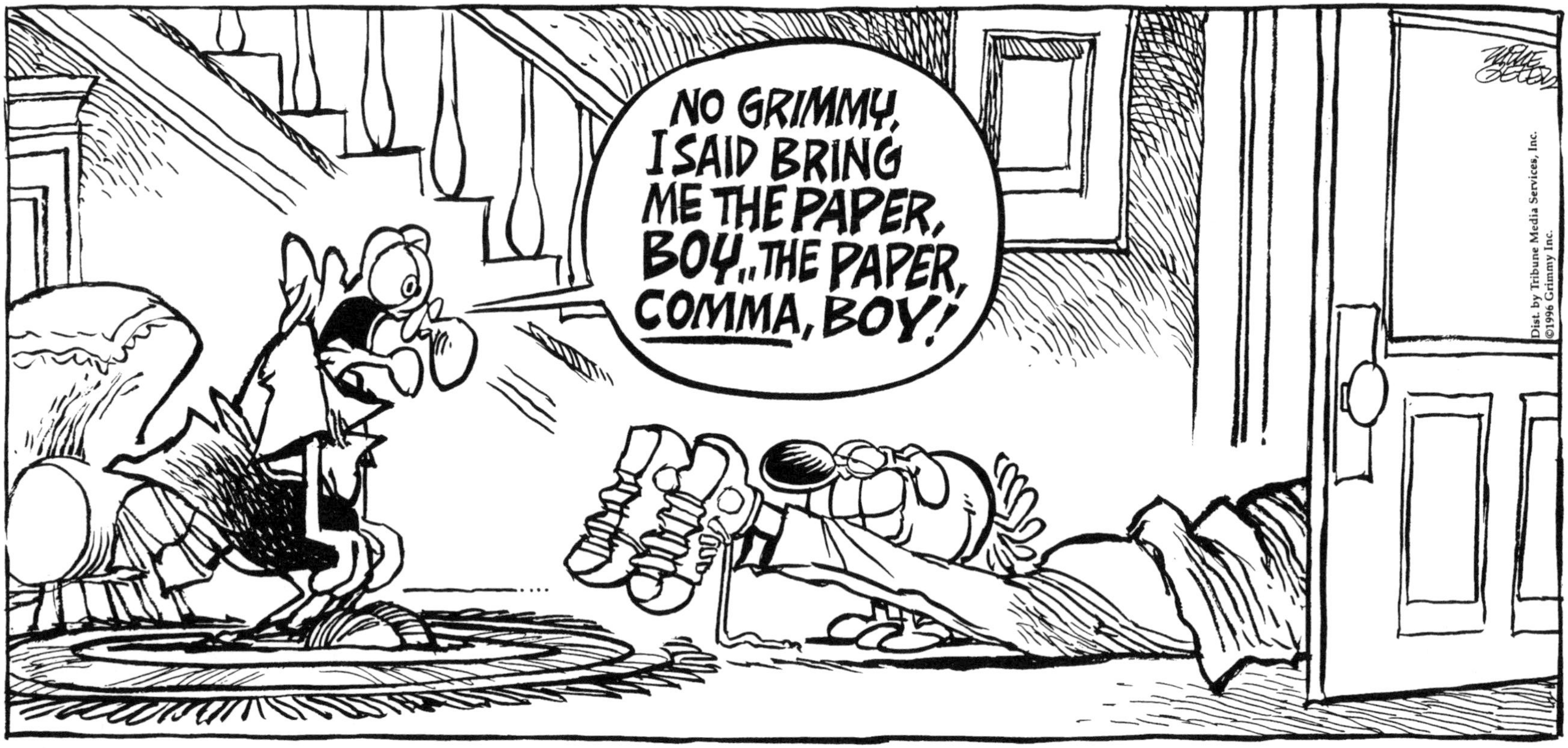
NO GRIMMY, I SAID BRING ME THE PAPER, BOY.. THE PAPER, COMMA, BOY!

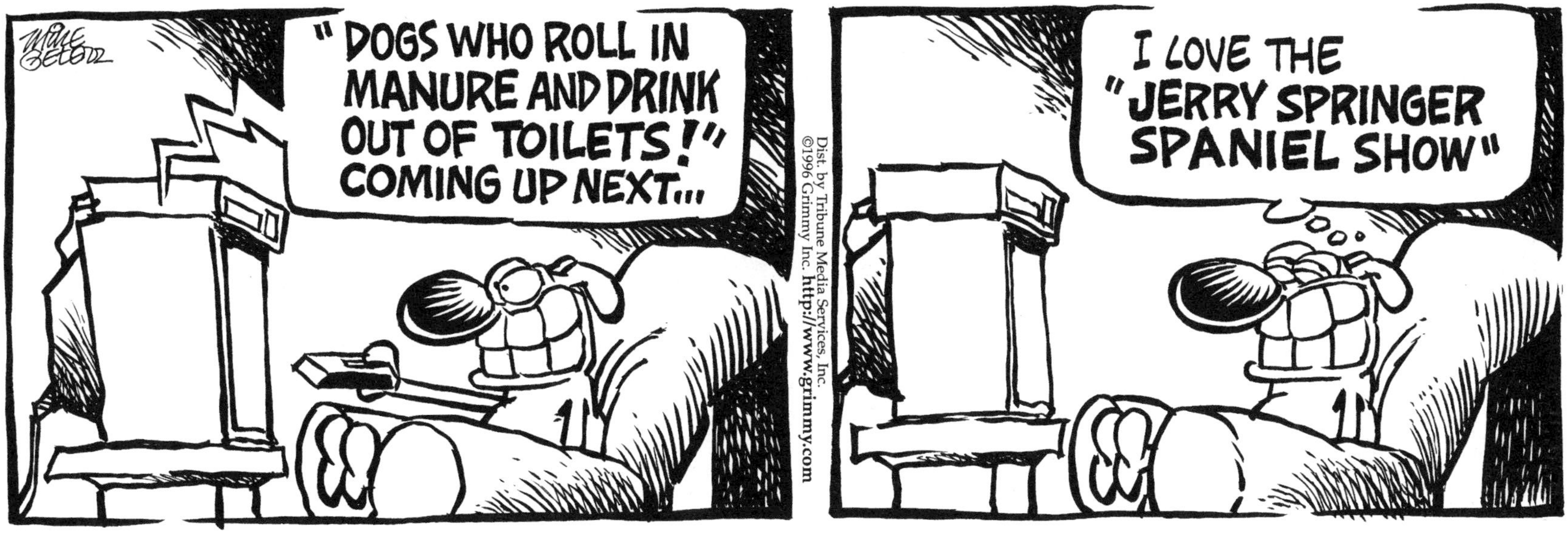
"DOGS WHO ROLL IN MANURE AND DRINK OUT OF TOILETS!" COMING UP NEXT...
Dist. by Tribune Media Services, Inc. ©1996 Grimmy Inc. http://www.grimmy.com
I LOVE THE "JERRY SPRINGER SPANIEL SHOW"

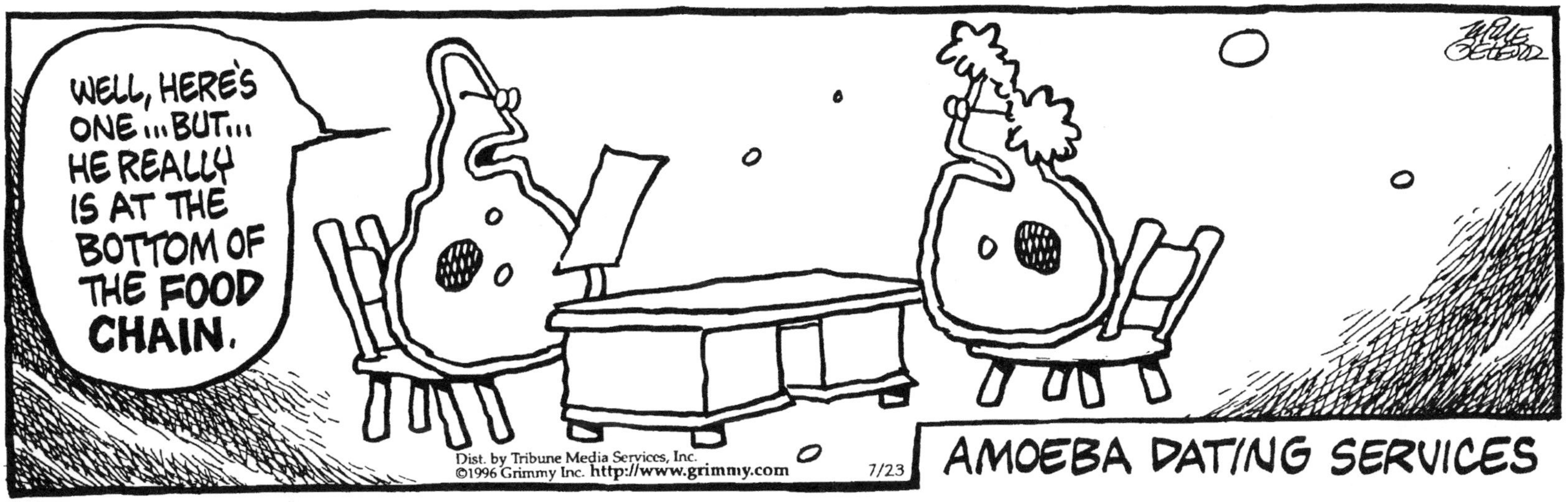
WELL, HERE'S ONE... BUT... HE REALLY IS AT THE BOTTOM OF THE FOOD CHAIN.
Dist. by Tribune Media Services, Inc. ©1996 Grimmy Inc. http://www.grimmy.com
7/23
AMOEBA DATING SERVICES

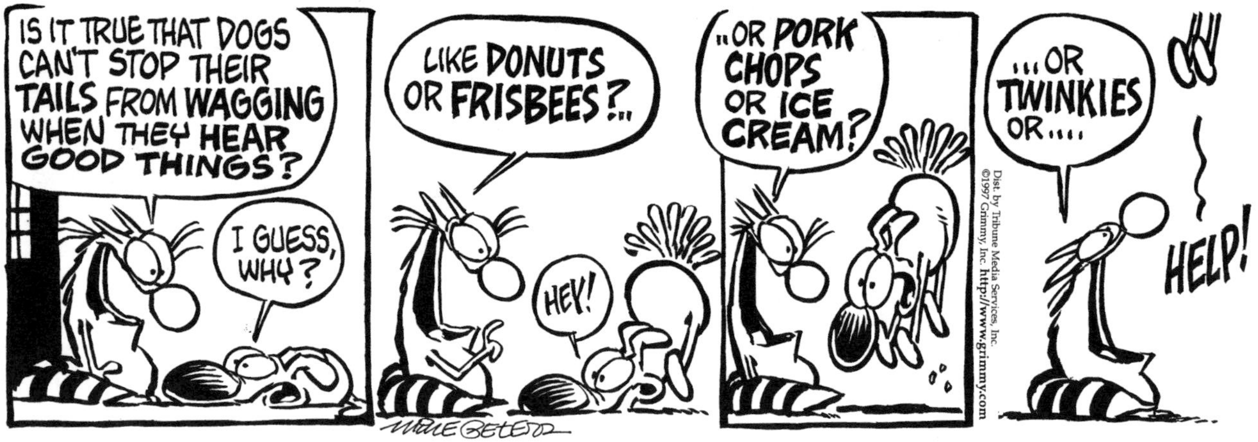
IS IT TRUE THAT DOGS CAN'T STOP THEIR TAILS FROM WAGGING WHEN THEY HEAR GOOD THINGS?
I GUESS, WHY?
LIKE DONUTS OR FRISBEES?..
HEY!
..OR PORK CHOPS OR ICE CREAM?
Dist. by Tribune Media Services, Inc. ©1997 Grimmy, Inc. http://www.grimmy.com
...OR TWINKIES OR....
HELP!

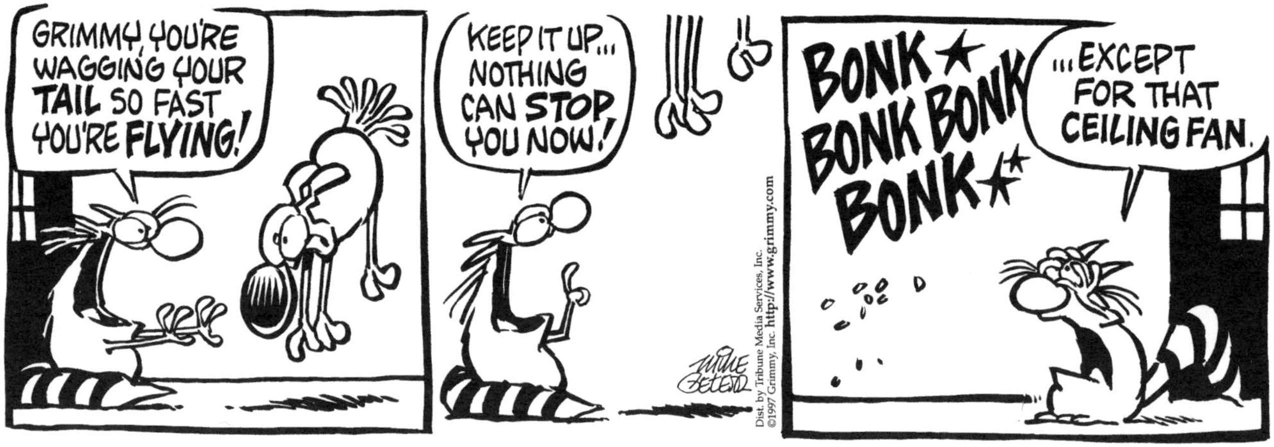
GRIMMY, YOU'RE WAGGING YOUR TAIL SO FAST YOU'RE FLYING!
KEEP IT UP... NOTHING CAN STOP YOU NOW!
Dist. by Tribune Media Services, Inc. ©1997 Grimmy, Inc. http://www.grimmy.com
BONK BONK BONK BONK
...EXCEPT FOR THAT CEILING FAN.

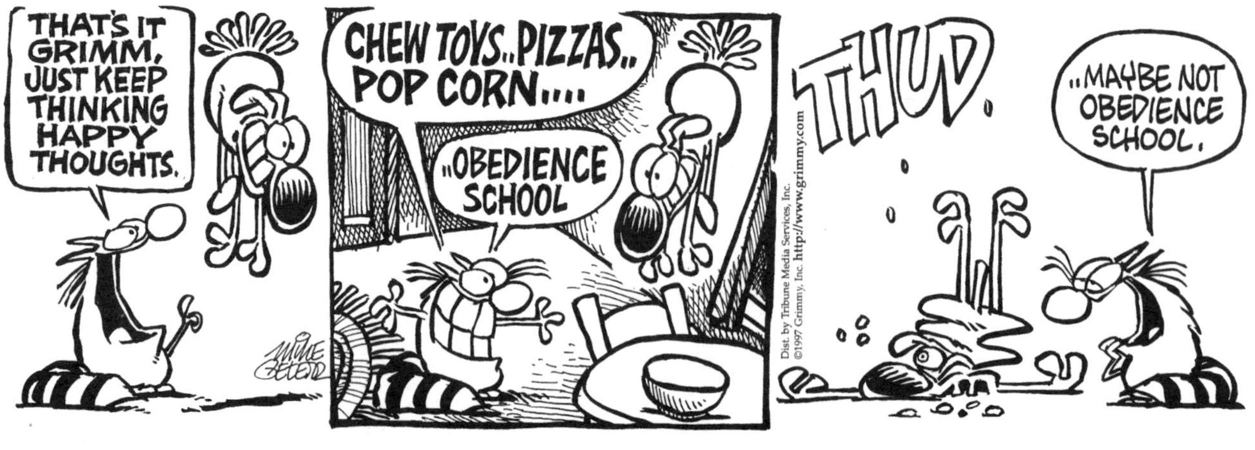
THAT'S IT GRIMM, JUST KEEP THINKING HAPPY THOUGHTS.
CHEW TOYS..PIZZAS.. POP CORN....
..OBEDIENCE SCHOOL
Dist. by Tribune Media Services, Inc. ©1997 Grimmy, Inc. http://www.grimmy.com
THUD.
..MAYBE NOT OBEDIENCE SCHOOL.

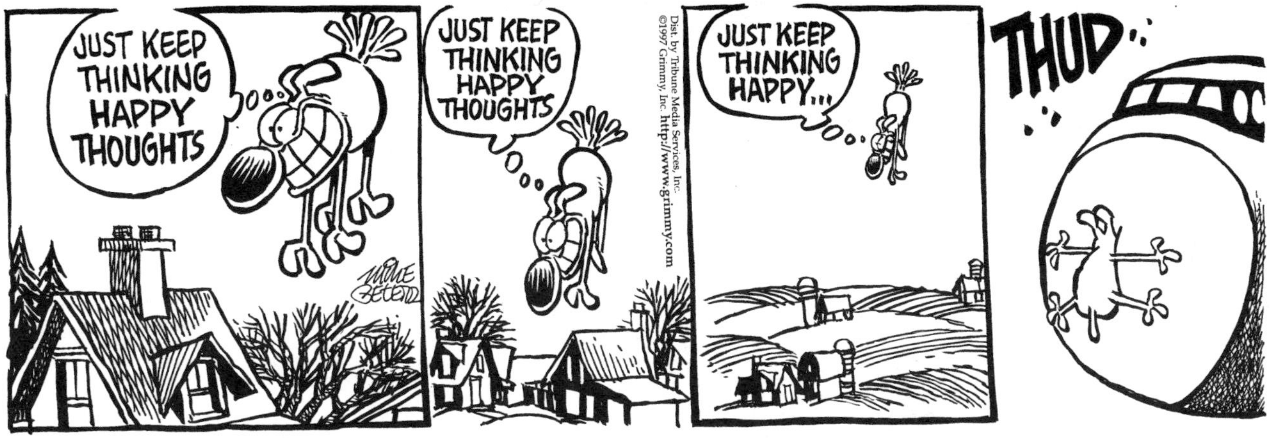
JUST KEEP THINKING HAPPY THOUGHTS
JUST KEEP THINKING HAPPY THOUGHTS
Dist. by Tribune Media Services, Inc. ©1997 Grimmy, Inc. http://www.grimmy.com
JUST KEEP THINKING HAPPY...
THUD

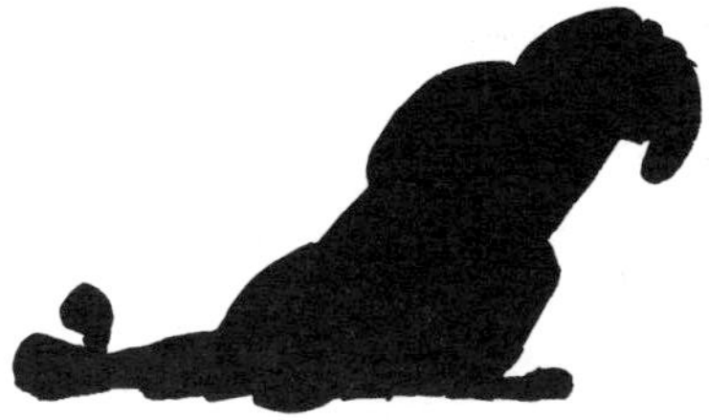

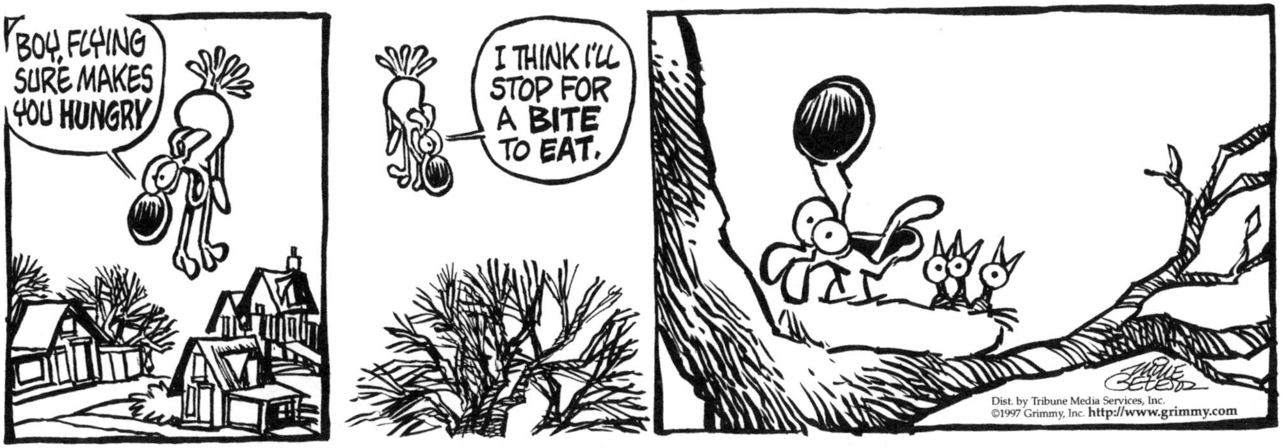
BOY, FLYING SURE MAKES YOU HUNGRY
I THINK I'LL STOP FOR A BITE TO EAT.
Dist. by Tribune Media Services, Inc. ©1997 Grimmy, Inc. http://www.grimmy.com

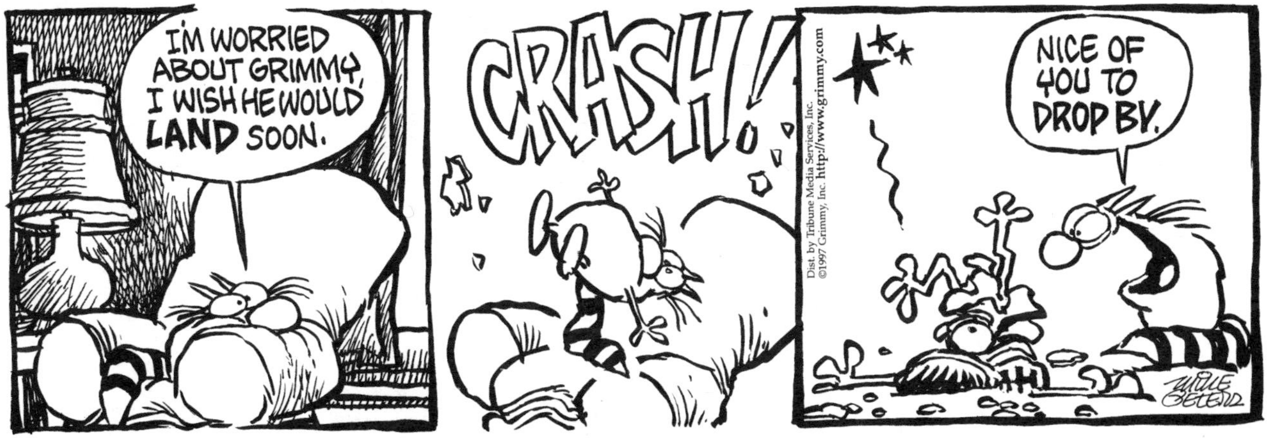
I'M WORRIED ABOUT GRIMMY, I WISH HE WOULD LAND SOON.
CRASH!
Dist. by Tribune Media Services, Inc. ©1997 Grimmy, Inc. http://www.grimmy.com
NICE OF YOU TO DROP BY.

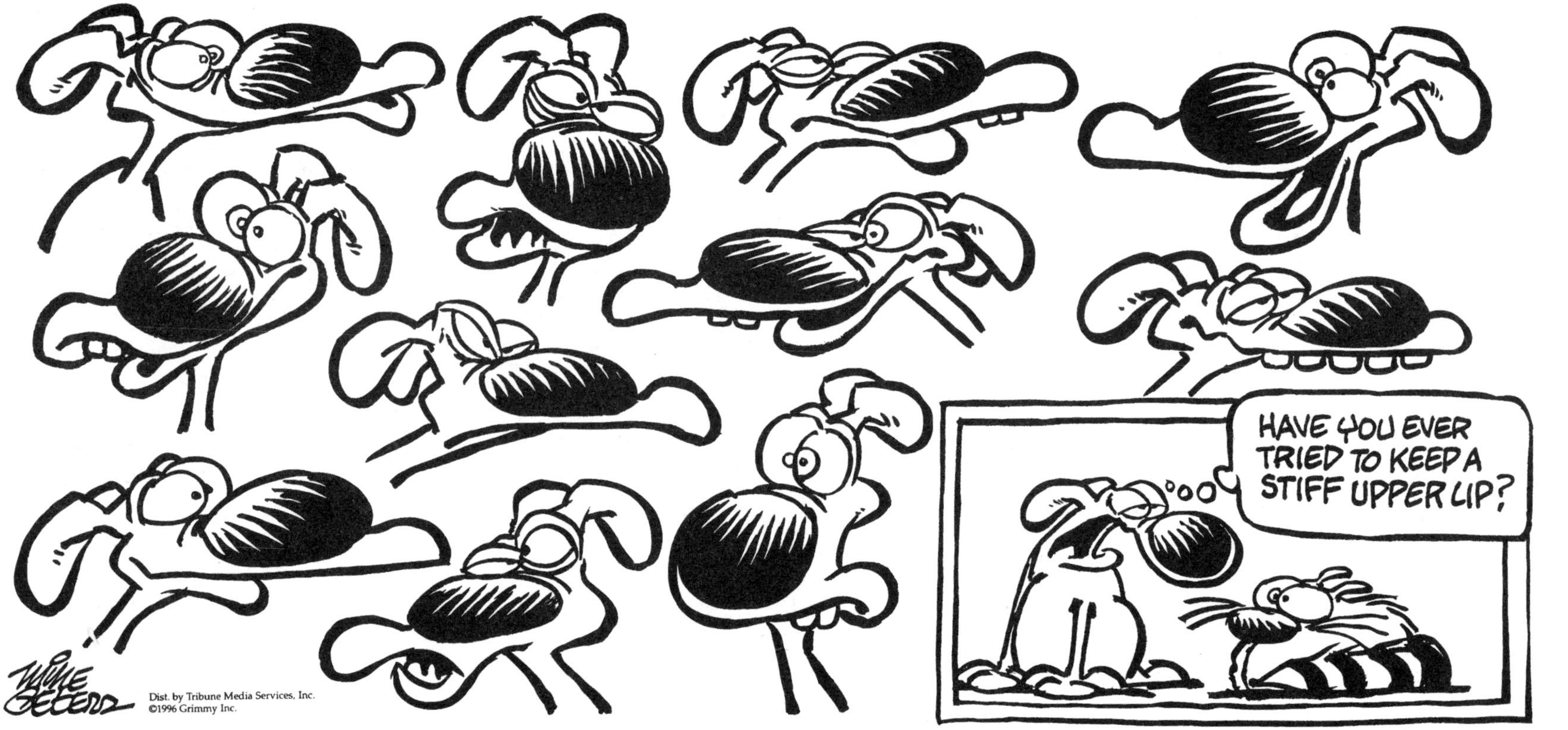
HAVE YOU EVER TRIED TO KEEP A STIFF UPPER LIP?

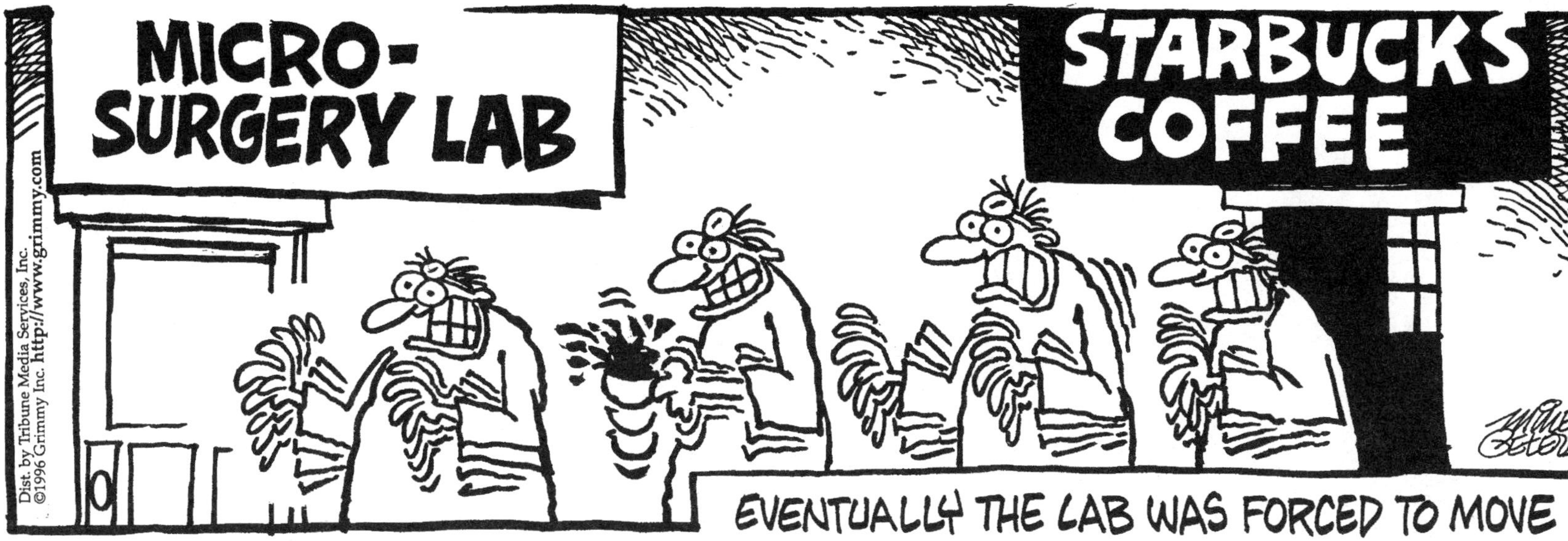
MICRO-SURGERY LAB
STARBUCKS COFFEE
EVENTUALLY THE LAB WAS FORCED TO MOVE
Dist. by Tribune Media Services, Inc.
©1996 Grimmy Inc. http://www.grimmy.com

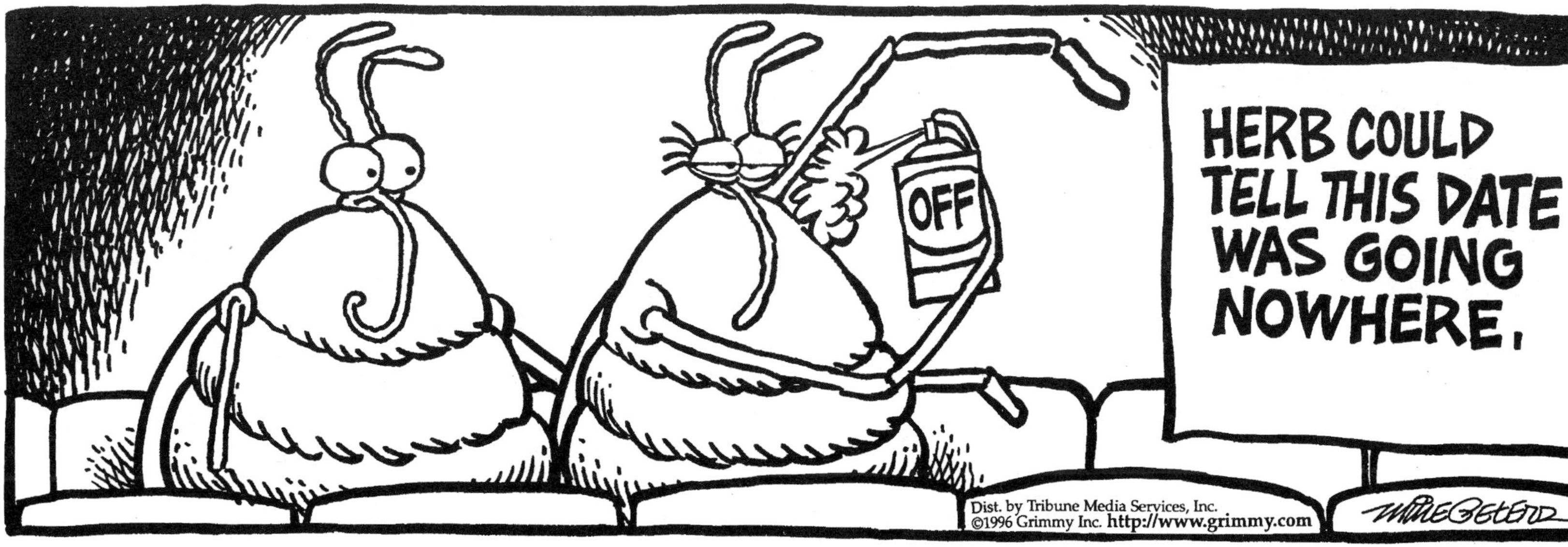
OFF
HERB COULD TELL THIS DATE WAS GOING NOWHERE.
Dist. by Tribune Media Services, Inc.
©1996 Grimmy Inc. http://www.grimmy.com

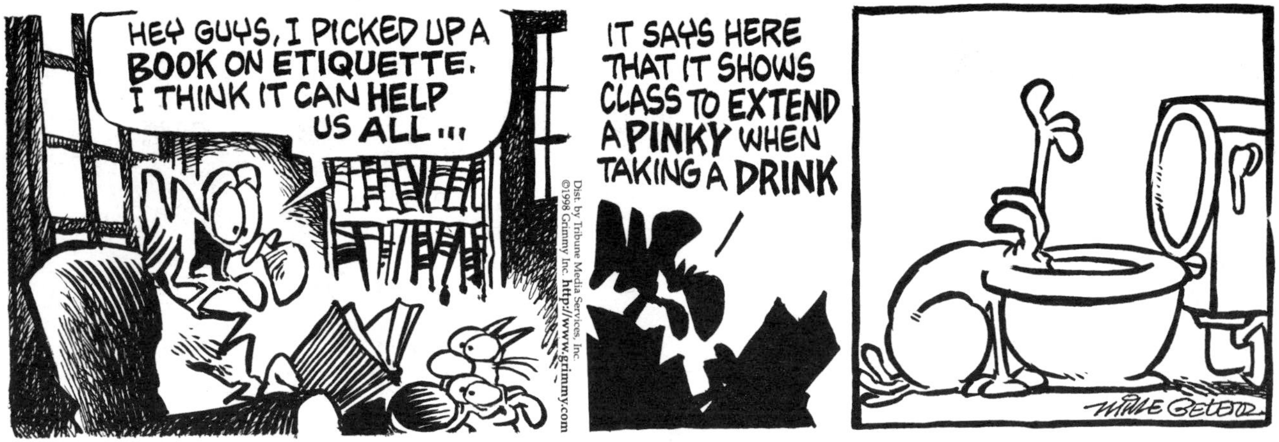
HEY GUYS, I PICKED UP A BOOK ON ETIQUETTE. I THINK IT CAN HELP US ALL...
Dist. by Tribune Media Services, Inc. ©1998 Grimmy Inc. http://www.grimmy.com
IT SAYS HERE THAT IT SHOWS CLASS TO EXTEND A PINKY WHEN TAKING A DRINK

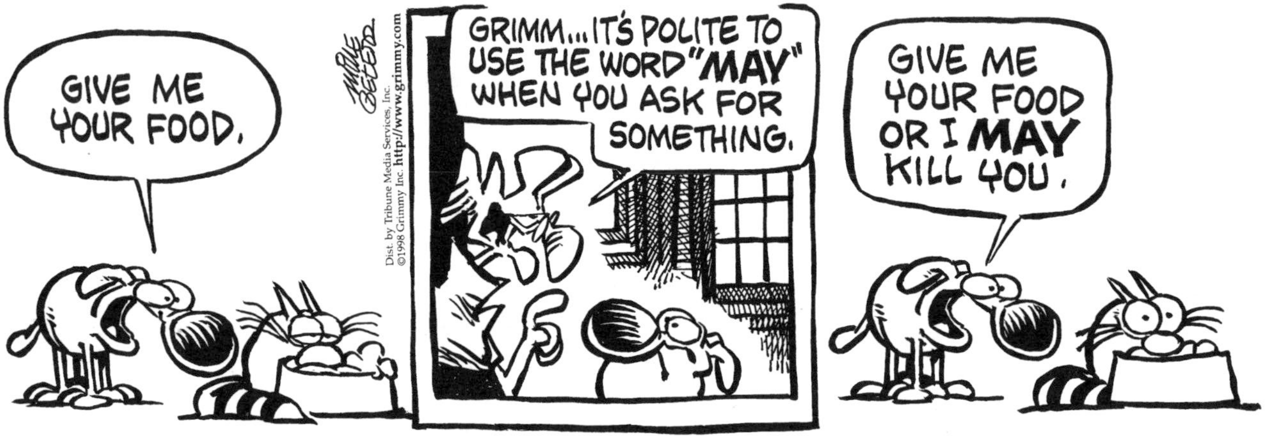
GIVE ME YOUR FOOD.
Dist. by Tribune Media Services, Inc. ©1998 Grimmy Inc. http://www.grimmy.com
GRIMM... IT'S POLITE TO USE THE WORD "MAY" WHEN YOU ASK FOR SOMETHING.
GIVE ME YOUR FOOD OR I MAY KILL YOU.

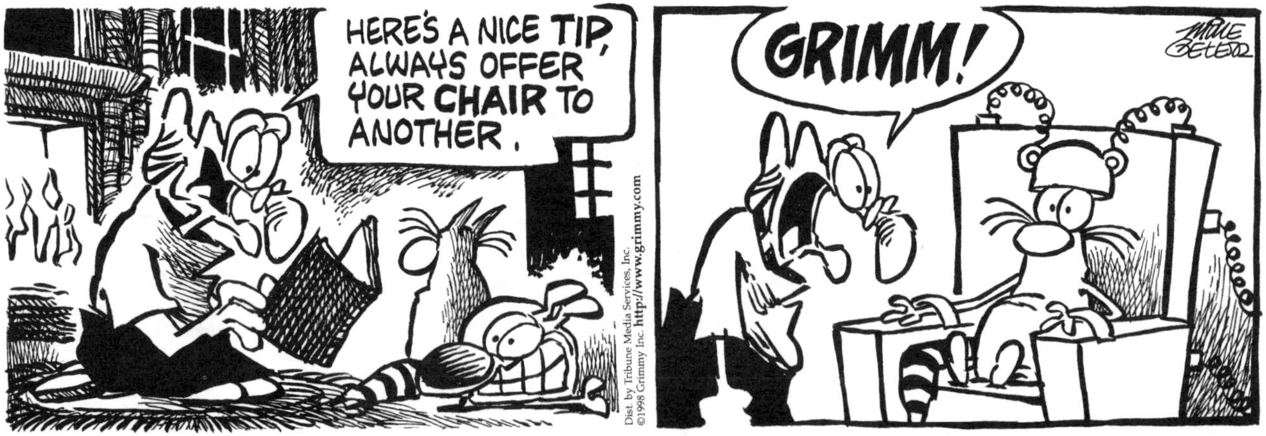
HERE'S A NICE TIP, ALWAYS OFFER YOUR CHAIR TO ANOTHER.
Dist. by Tribune Media Services, Inc. ©1998 Grimmy Inc. http://www.grimmy.com
GRIMM!

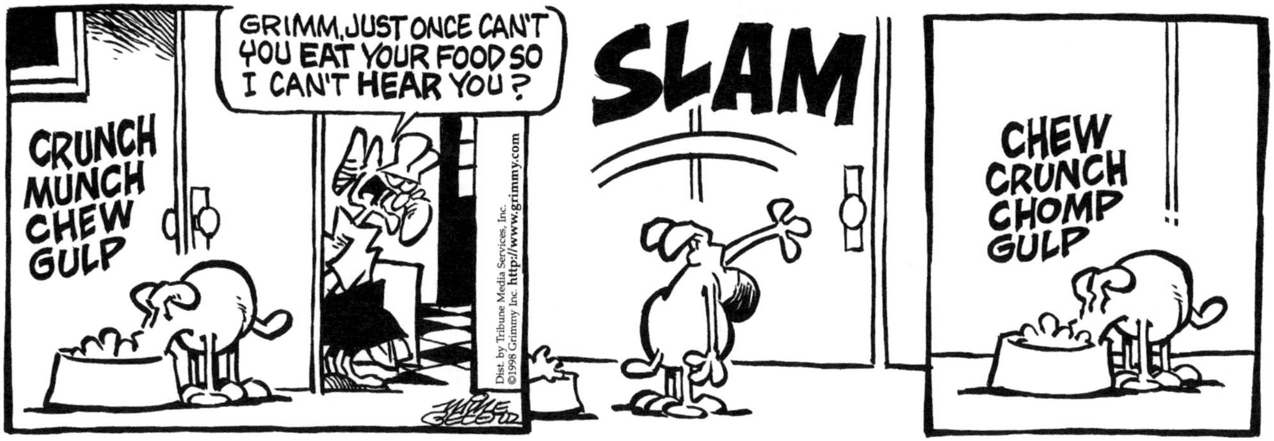
CRUNCH
MUNCH
CHEW
GULP
GRIMM, JUST ONCE CAN'T YOU EAT YOUR FOOD SO I CAN'T HEAR YOU?
Dist. by Tribune Media Services, Inc.
©1998 Grimmy Inc. http://www.grimmy.com
SLAM
CHEW
CRUNCH
CHOMP
GULP

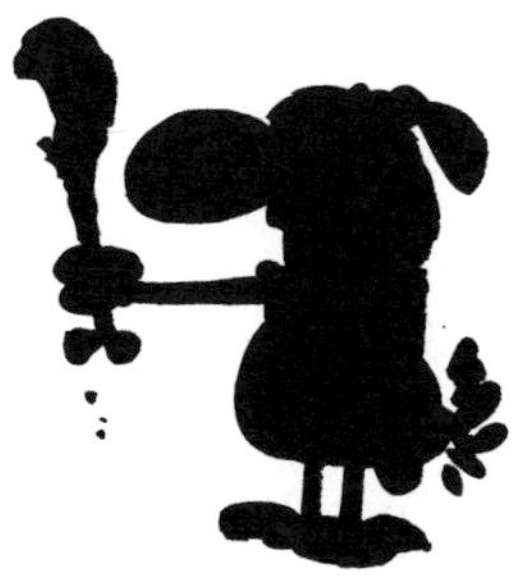

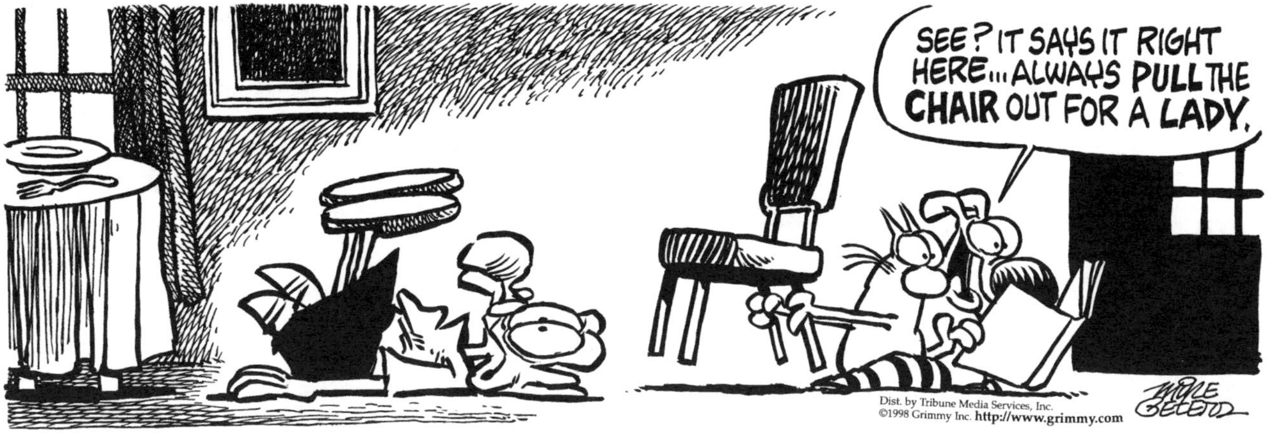
SEE? IT SAYS IT RIGHT HERE... ALWAYS PULL THE CHAIR OUT FOR A LADY.
Dist. by Tribune Media Services, Inc.
©1998 Grimmy Inc. http://www.grimmy.com

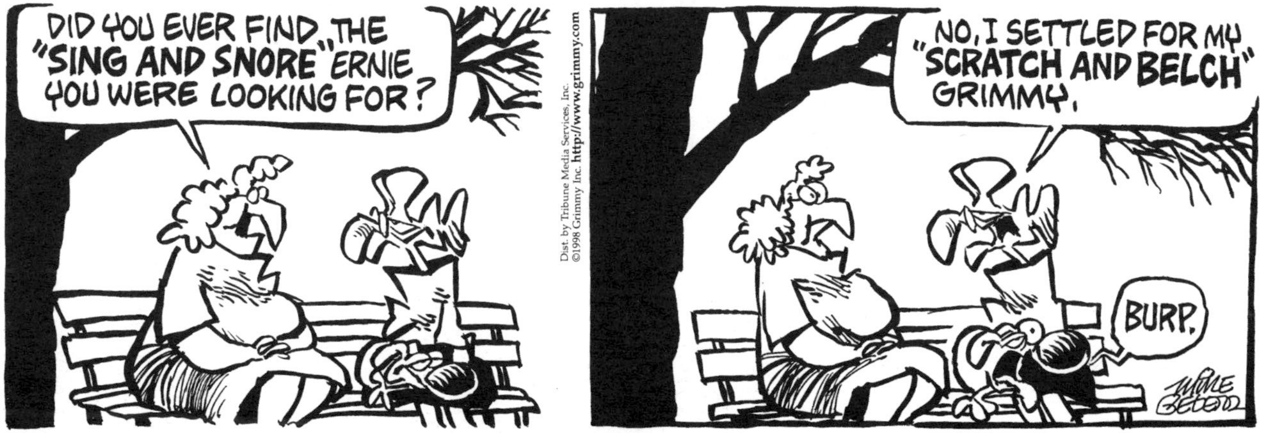
DID YOU EVER FIND THE "SING AND SNORE" ERNIE YOU WERE LOOKING FOR?
Dist. by Tribune Media Services, Inc.
©1998 Grimmy Inc. http://www.grimmy.com
...NO, I SETTLED FOR MY "SCRATCH AND BELCH" GRIMMY.
BURP.

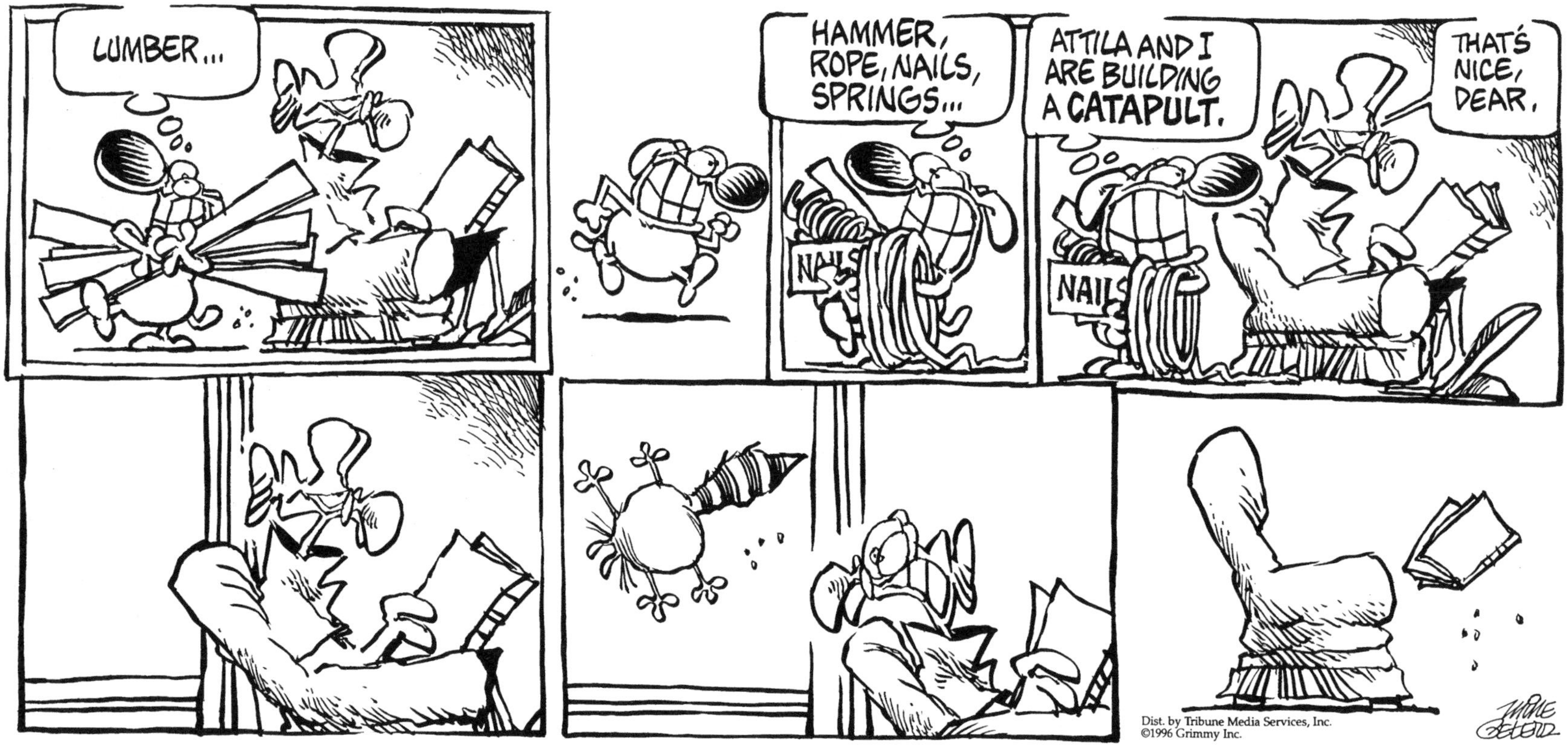
LUMBER...
HAMMER, ROPE, NAILS, SPRINGS...
NAILS
ATTILA AND I ARE BUILDING A CATAPULT.
THAT'S NICE, DEAR.
NAILS

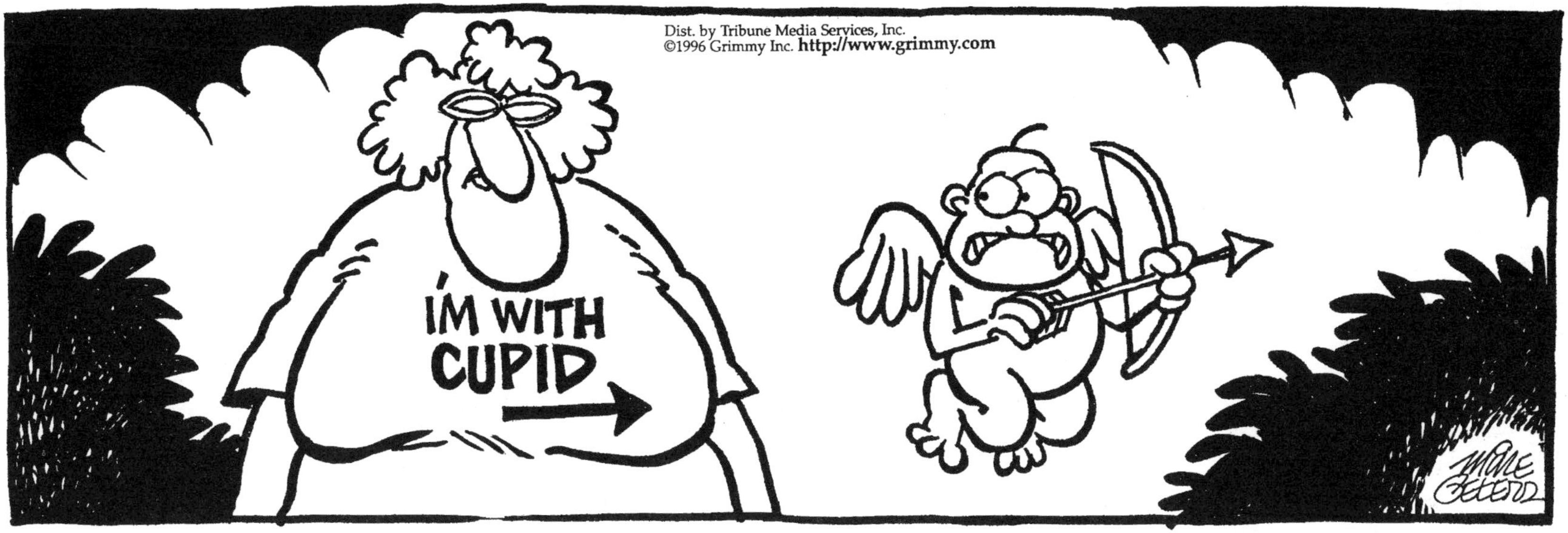
Dist. by Tribune Media Services, Inc.
©1996 Grimmy Inc. http://www.grimmy.com
I'M WITH CUPID

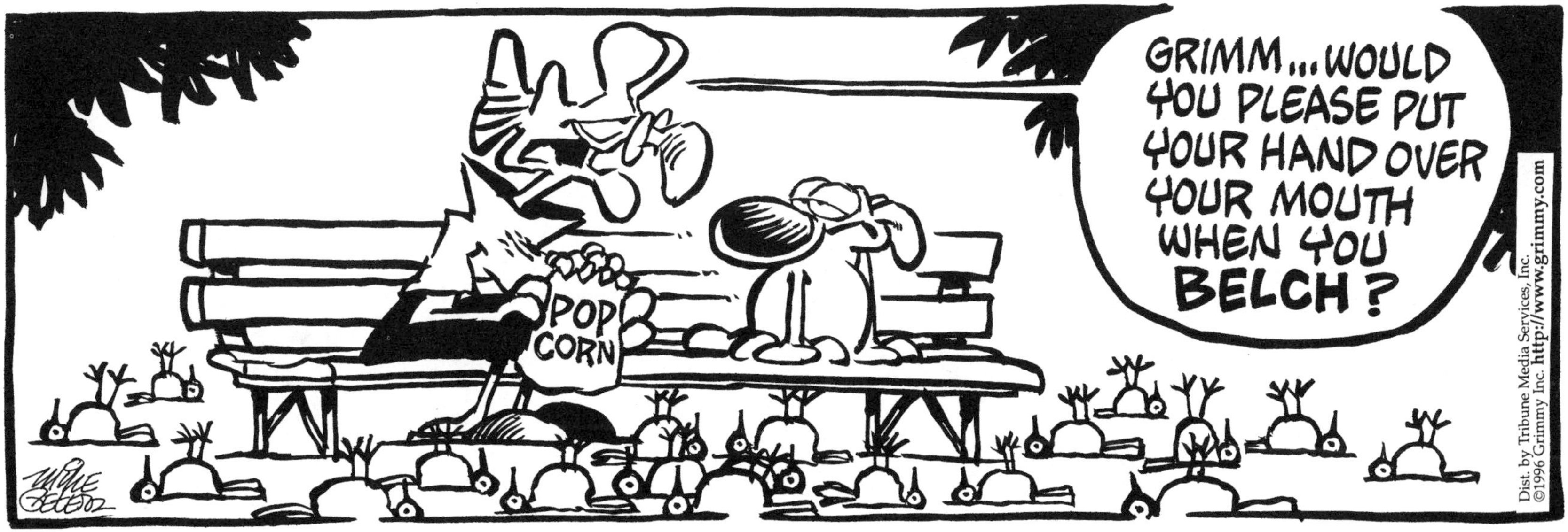
GRIMM...WOULD YOU PLEASE PUT YOUR HAND OVER YOUR MOUTH WHEN YOU BELCH?
POP CORN
Dist. by Tribune Media Services, Inc.
©1996 Grimmy Inc. http://www.grimmy.com

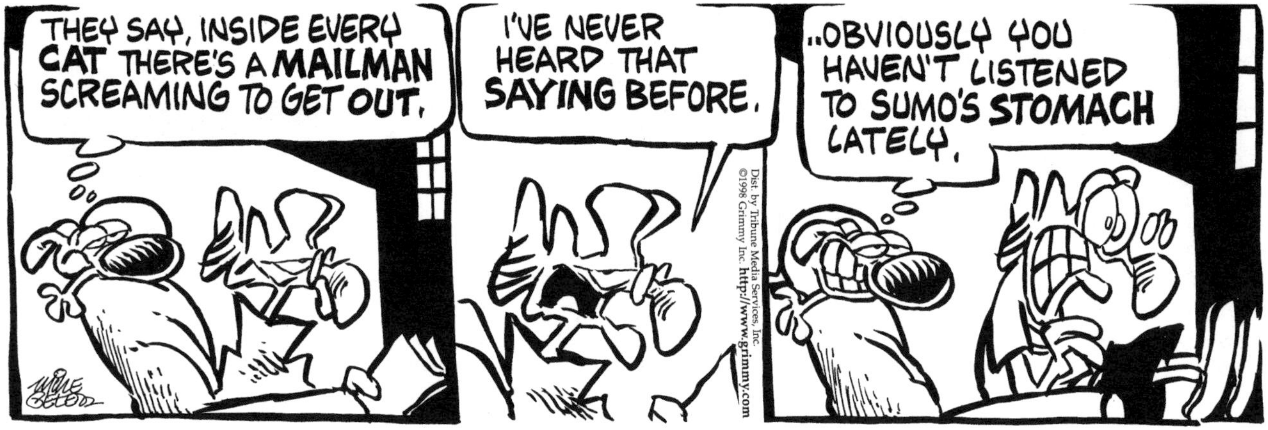
THEY SAY, INSIDE EVERY CAT THERE'S A MAILMAN SCREAMING TO GET OUT.
I'VE NEVER HEARD THAT SAYING BEFORE.
Dist. by Tribune Media Services, Inc. ©1998 Grimmy Inc. http://www.grimmy.com
..OBVIOUSLY YOU HAVEN'T LISTENED TO SUMO'S STOMACH LATELY.

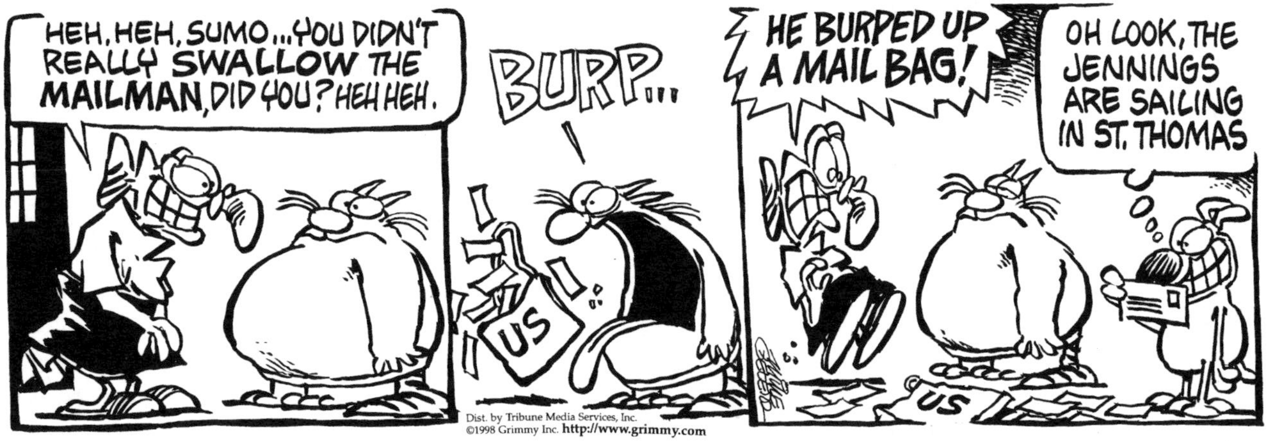
HEH, HEH, SUMO...YOU DIDN'T REALLY SWALLOW THE MAILMAN, DID YOU? HEH HEH.
BURP...
US
Dist. by Tribune Media Services, Inc. ©1998 Grimmy Inc. http://www.grimmy.com
HE BURPED UP A MAIL BAG!
OH LOOK, THE JENNINGS ARE SAILING IN ST. THOMAS
US

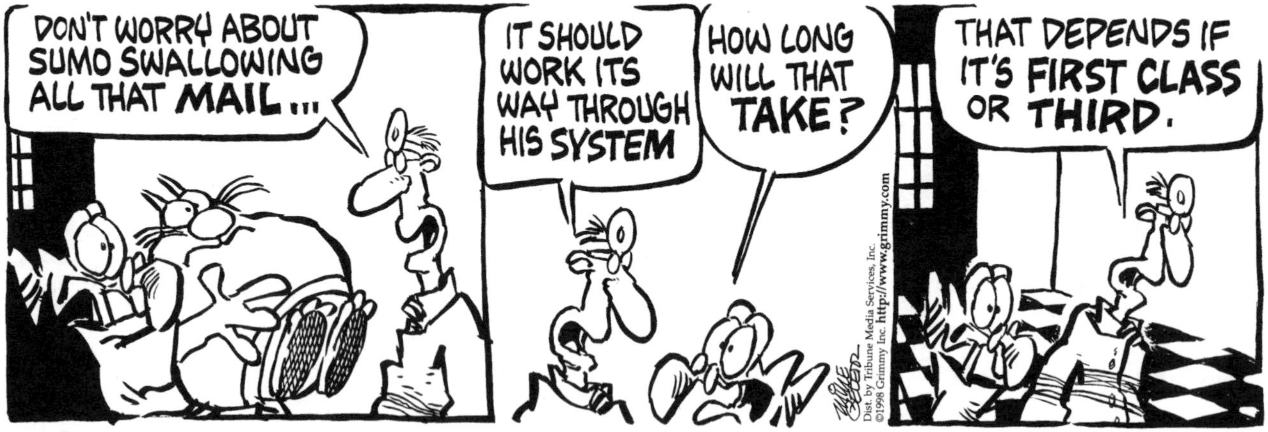
DON'T WORRY ABOUT SUMO SWALLOWING ALL THAT MAIL...
IT SHOULD WORK ITS WAY THROUGH HIS SYSTEM
HOW LONG WILL THAT TAKE?
Dist. by Tribune Media Services, Inc. ©1998 Grimmy Inc. http://www.grimmy.com
THAT DEPENDS IF IT'S FIRST CLASS OR THIRD.

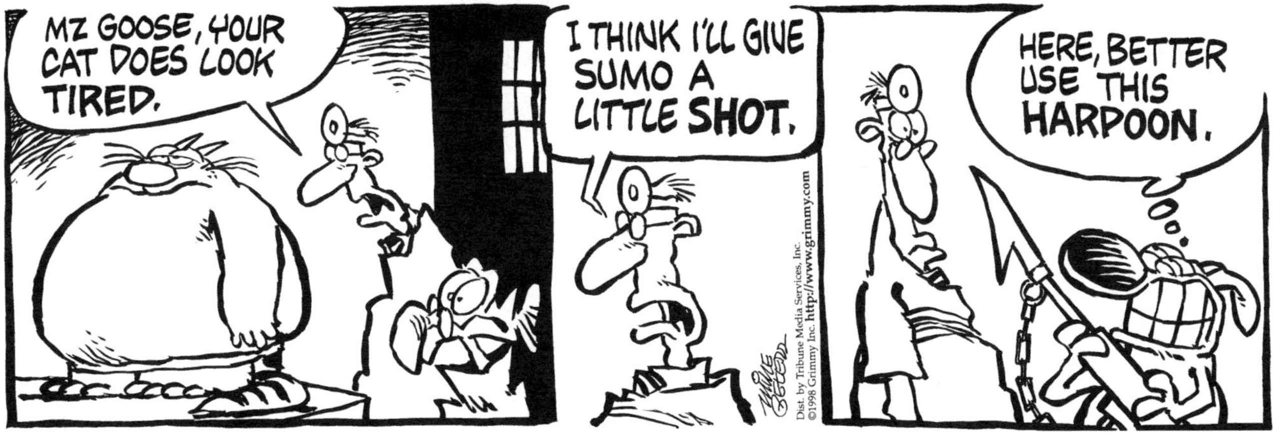
MZ GOOSE, YOUR CAT DOES LOOK TIRED.
I THINK I'LL GIVE SUMO A LITTLE SHOT.
Dist. by Tribune Media Services, Inc. ©1998 Grimmy Inc. http://www.grimmy.com
HERE, BETTER USE THIS HARPOON.

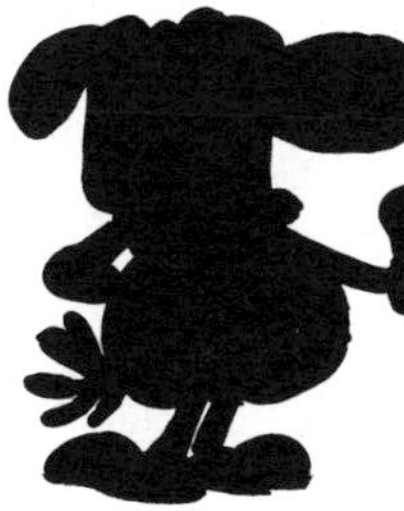

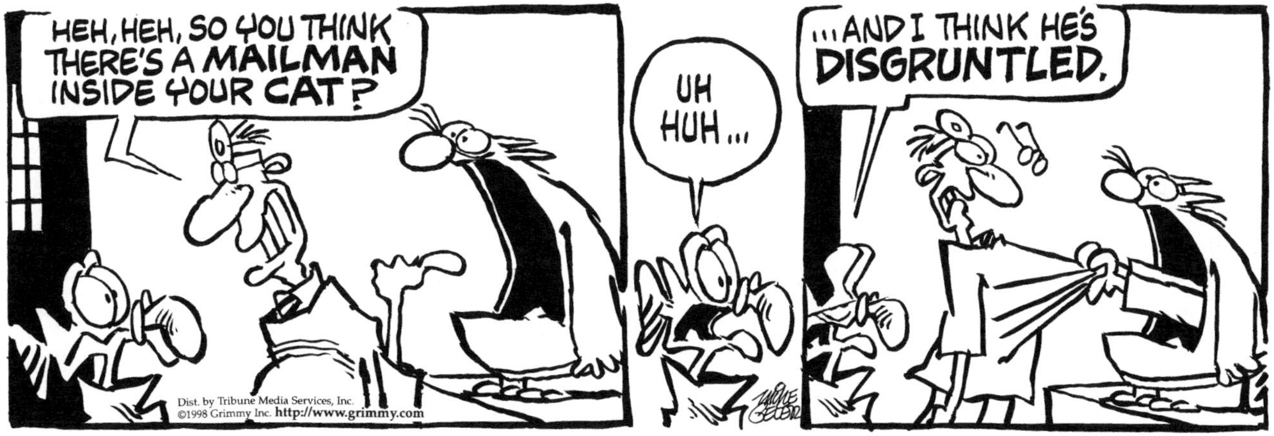
HEH, HEH, SO YOU THINK THERE'S A MAILMAN INSIDE YOUR CAT?
Dist. by Tribune Media Services, Inc. ©1998 Grimmy Inc. http://www.grimmy.com
UH HUH...
...AND I THINK HE'S DISGRUNTLED.

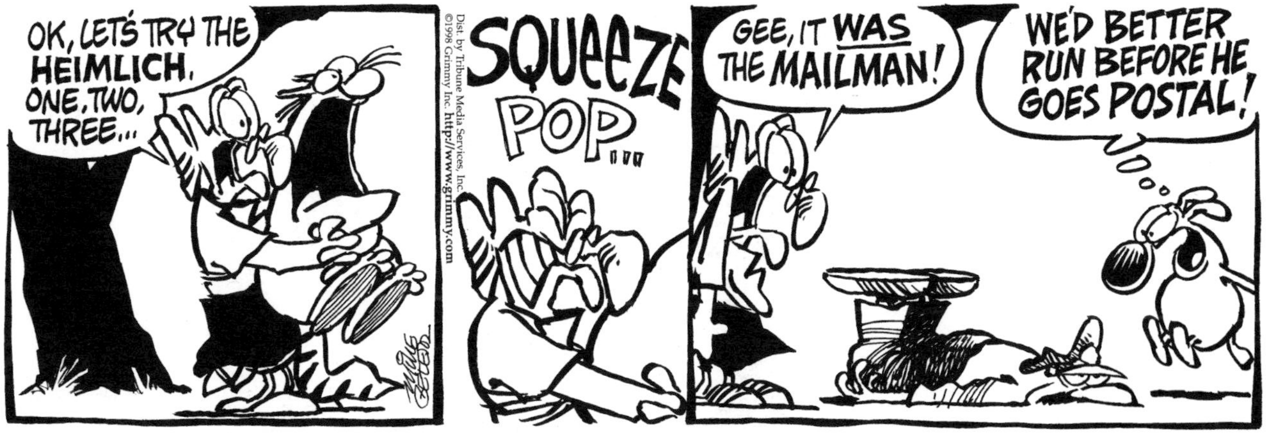
OK, LET'S TRY THE HEIMLICH. ONE, TWO, THREE...
Dist. by Tribune Media Services, Inc. ©1998 Grimmy Inc. http://www.grimmy.com
SQUEEZE
POP...
GEE, IT WAS THE MAILMAN!
WE'D BETTER RUN BEFORE HE GOES POSTAL!

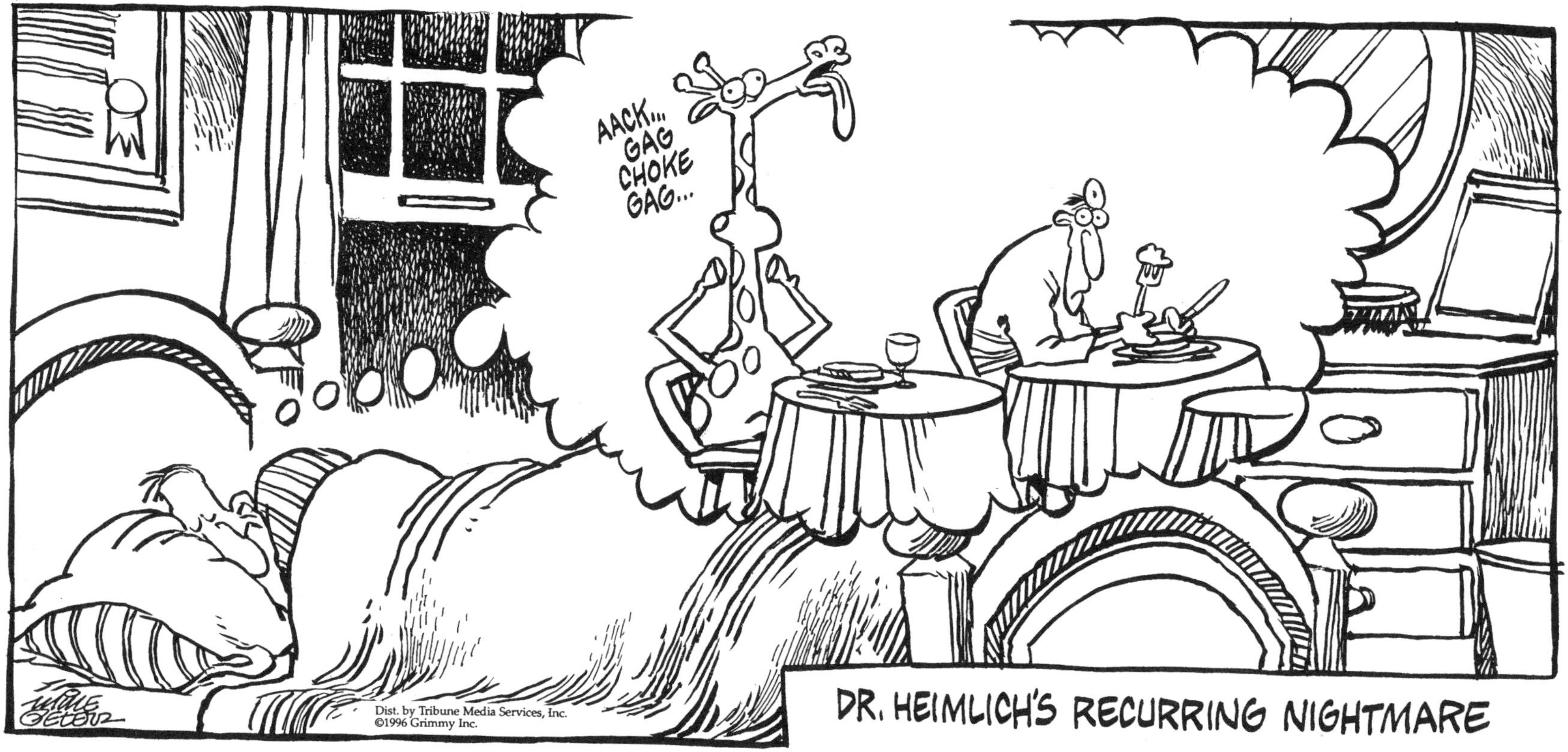
AACK... GAG CHOKE GAG...

DR. HEIMLICH'S RECURRING NIGHTMARE

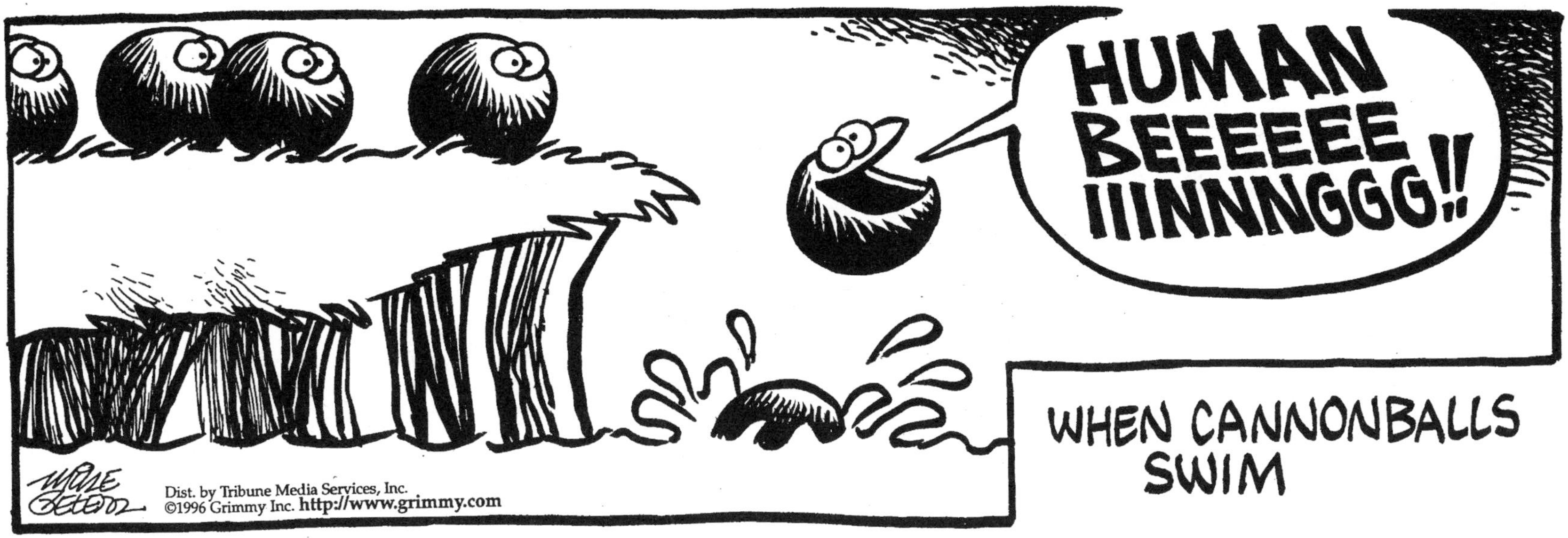
HUMAN BEEEEEE IIINNNGGG!!
WHEN CANNONBALLS SWIM
Dist. by Tribune Media Services, Inc.
©1996 Grimmy Inc. http://www.grimmy.com

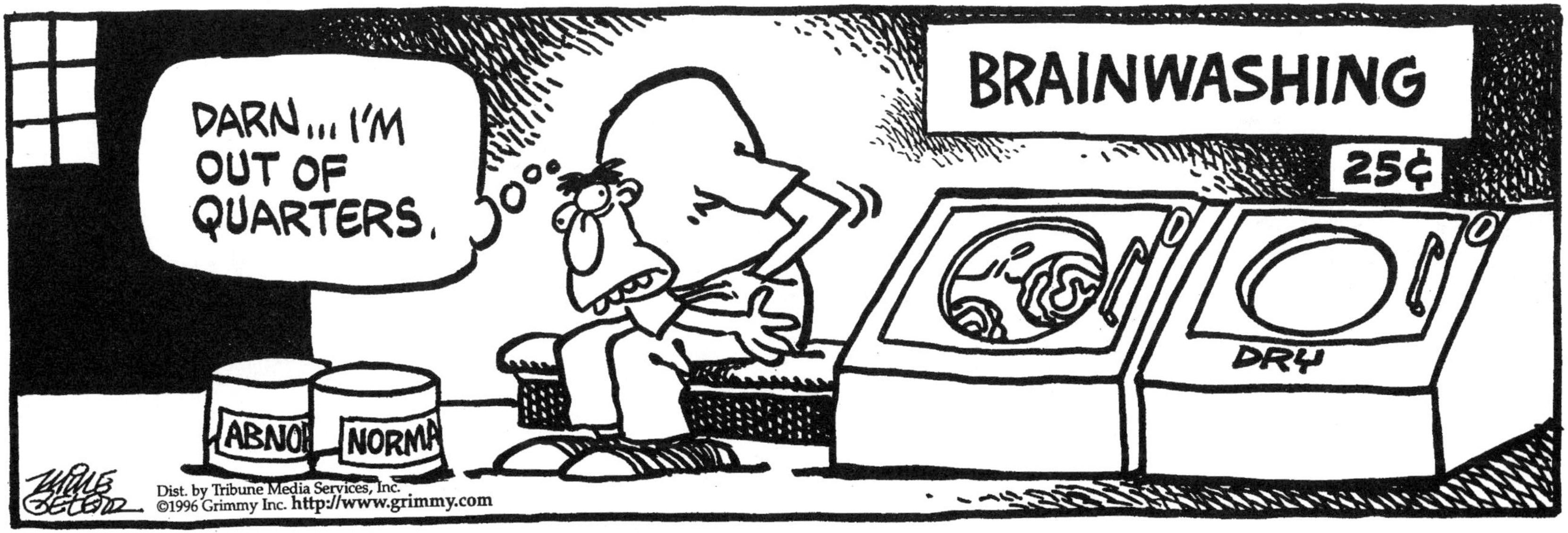
DARN... I'M OUT OF QUARTERS.
BRAINWASHING
25¢
DRY
ABNOR
NORMA
Dist. by Tribune Media Services, Inc.
©1996 Grimmy Inc. http://www.grimmy.com

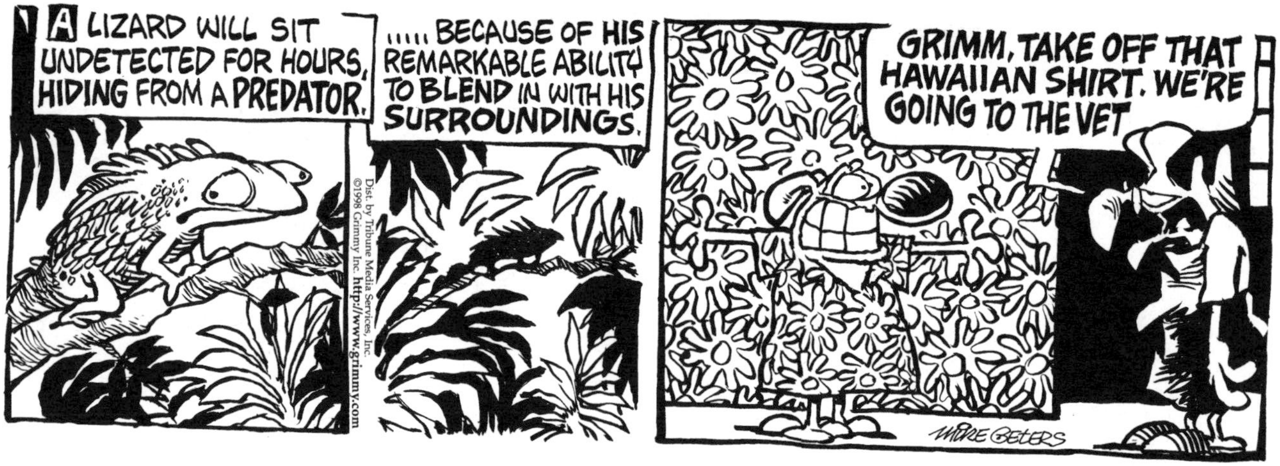
A LIZARD WILL SIT UNDETECTED FOR HOURS, HIDING FROM A PREDATOR.
.....BECAUSE OF HIS REMARKABLE ABILITY TO BLEND IN WITH HIS SURROUNDINGS.
GRIMM, TAKE OFF THAT HAWAIIAN SHIRT. WE'RE GOING TO THE VET
Dist. by Tribune Media Services, Inc. ©1998 Grimmy Inc. http://www.grimmy.com
MIKE PETERS

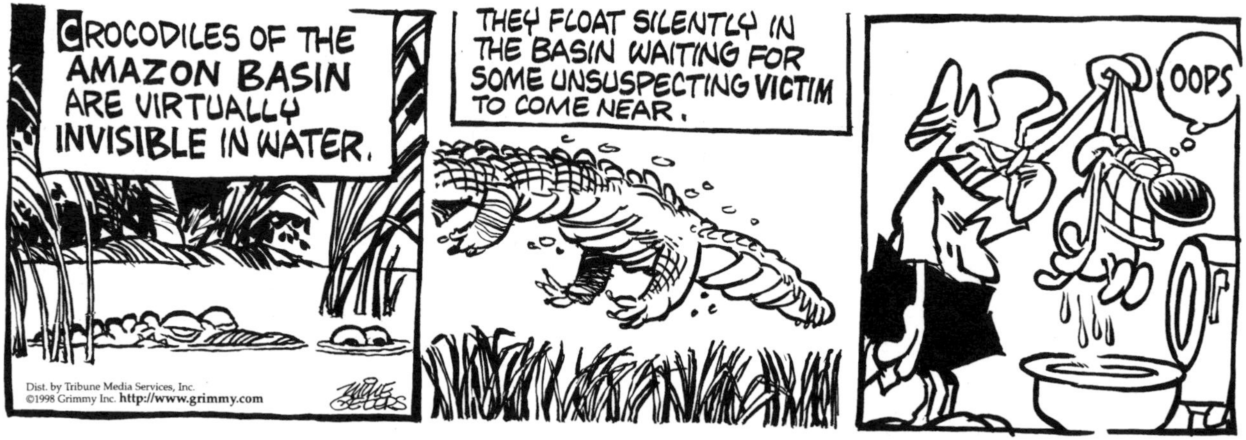
CROCODILES OF THE AMAZON BASIN ARE VIRTUALLY INVISIBLE IN WATER.
Dist. by Tribune Media Services, Inc. ©1998 Grimmy Inc. http://www.grimmy.com
MIKE PETERS
THEY FLOAT SILENTLY IN THE BASIN WAITING FOR SOME UNSUSPECTING VICTIM TO COME NEAR.
OOPS

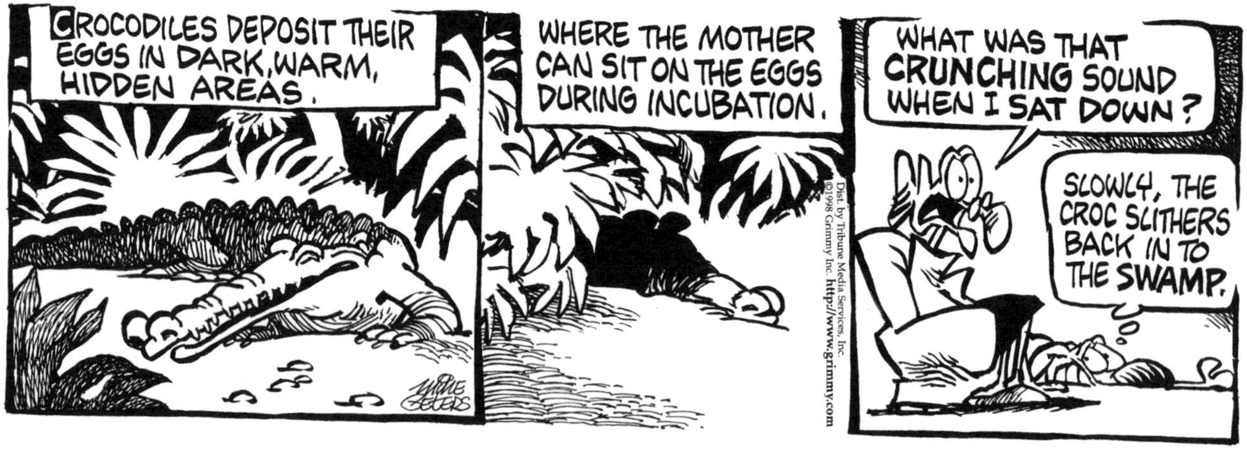
CROCODILES DEPOSIT THEIR EGGS IN DARK, WARM, HIDDEN AREAS.
MIKE PETERS
WHERE THE MOTHER CAN SIT ON THE EGGS DURING INCUBATION.
Dist. by Tribune Media Services, Inc. ©1998 Grimmy Inc. http://www.grimmy.com
WHAT WAS THAT CRUNCHING SOUND WHEN I SAT DOWN?
SLOWLY, THE CROC SLITHERS BACK IN TO THE SWAMP.

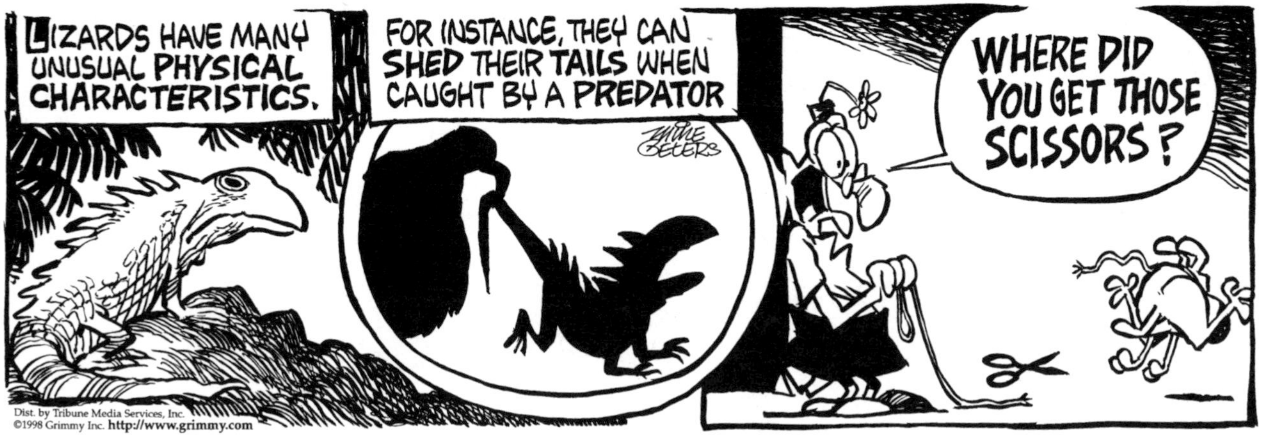
LIZARDS HAVE MANY UNUSUAL PHYSICAL CHARACTERISTICS.
FOR INSTANCE, THEY CAN SHED THEIR TAILS WHEN CAUGHT BY A PREDATOR
WHERE DID YOU GET THOSE SCISSORS?
MIKE PETERS
Dist. by Tribune Media Services, Inc.
©1998 Grimmy Inc. http://www.grimmy.com

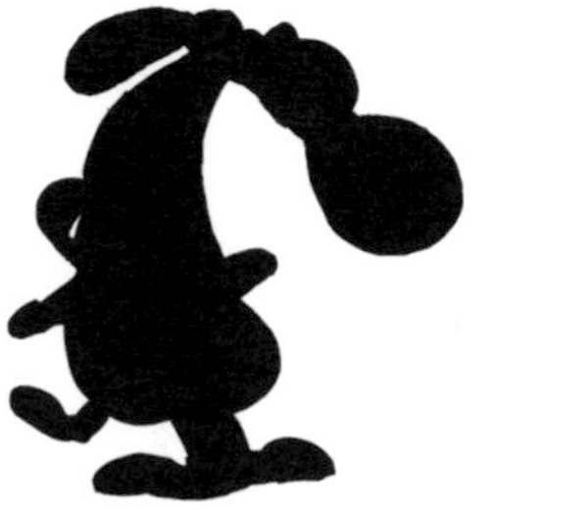

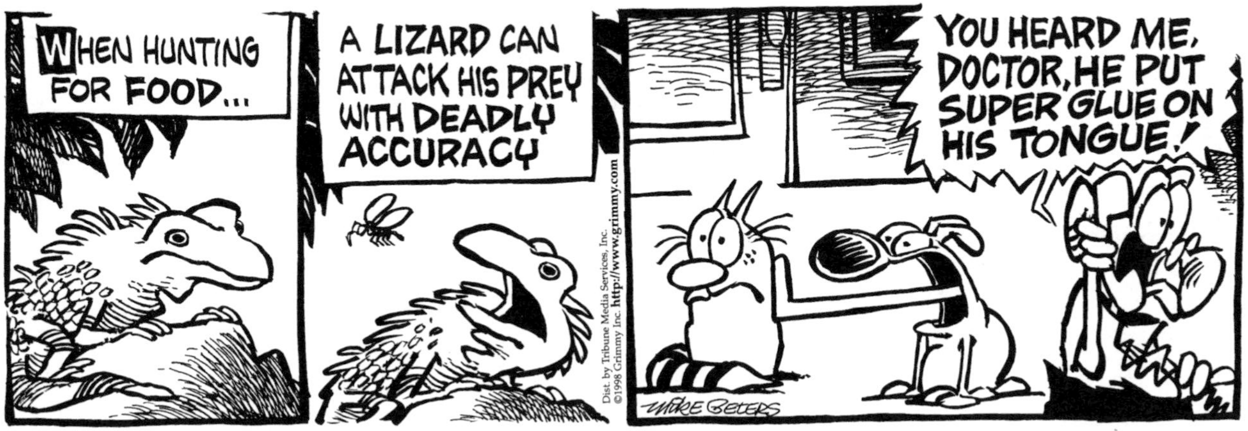
WHEN HUNTING FOR FOOD...
A LIZARD CAN ATTACK HIS PREY WITH DEADLY ACCURACY
Dist. by Tribune Media Services, Inc.
©1998 Grimmy Inc. http://www.grimmy.com
YOU HEARD ME, DOCTOR, HE PUT SUPER GLUE ON HIS TONGUE!
MIKE PETERS

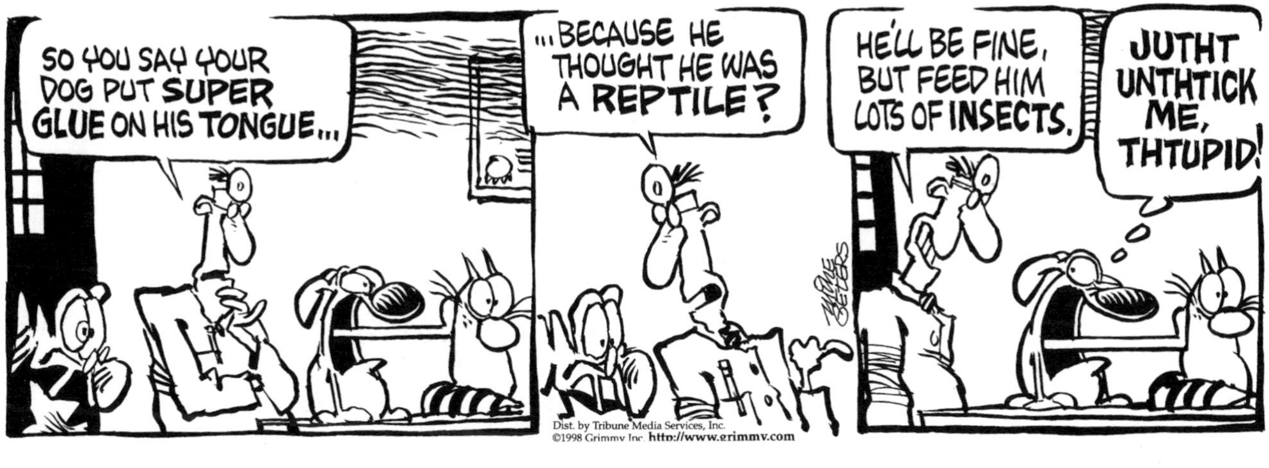
SO YOU SAY YOUR DOG PUT SUPER GLUE ON HIS TONGUE...
...BECAUSE HE THOUGHT HE WAS A REPTILE?
HE'LL BE FINE, BUT FEED HIM LOTS OF INSECTS.
JUTHT UNTHTICK ME, THTUPID!
MIKE PETERS
Dist. by Tribune Media Services, Inc.
©1998 Grimmy Inc. http://www.grimmy.com

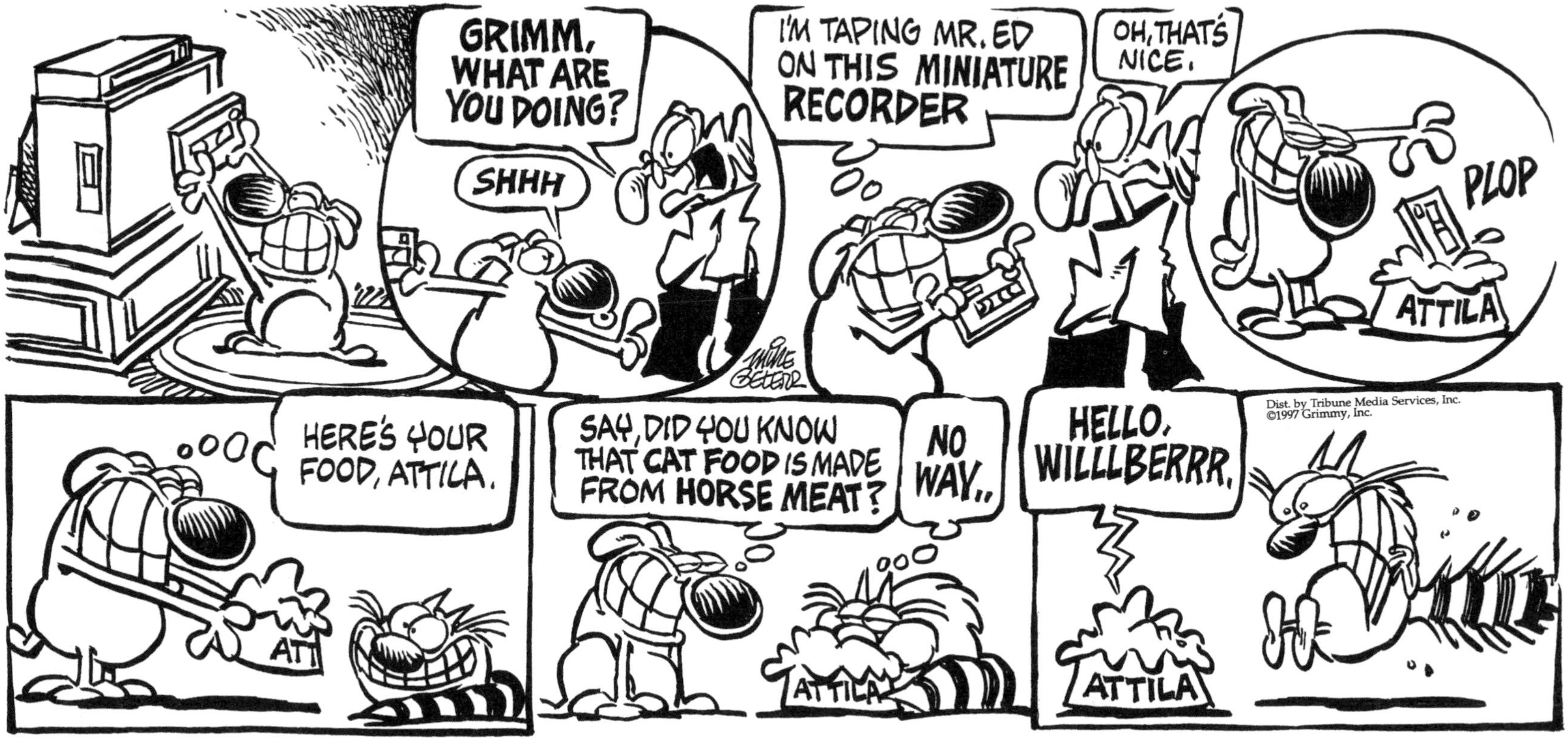
GRIMM, WHAT ARE YOU DOING?
SHHH
I'M TAPING MR. ED ON THIS MINIATURE RECORDER
OH, THAT'S NICE.
PLOP
ATTILA
HERE'S YOUR FOOD, ATTILA.
ATT
SAY, DID YOU KNOW THAT CAT FOOD IS MADE FROM HORSE MEAT?
NO WAY..
ATTILA
HELLO, WILLLBERRR.
ATTILA

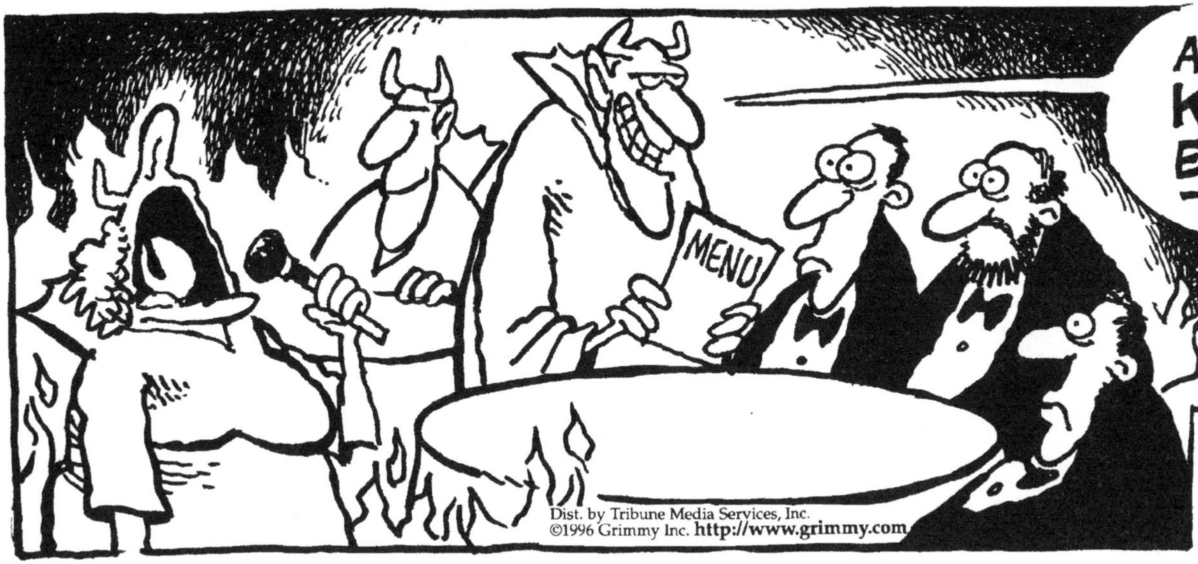
AND WE HAVE KARAOKE EVERY NIGHT.
MENU
Dist. by Tribune Media Services, Inc.
©1996 Grimmy Inc. http://www.grimmy.com

THE 3 TENORS IN HELL

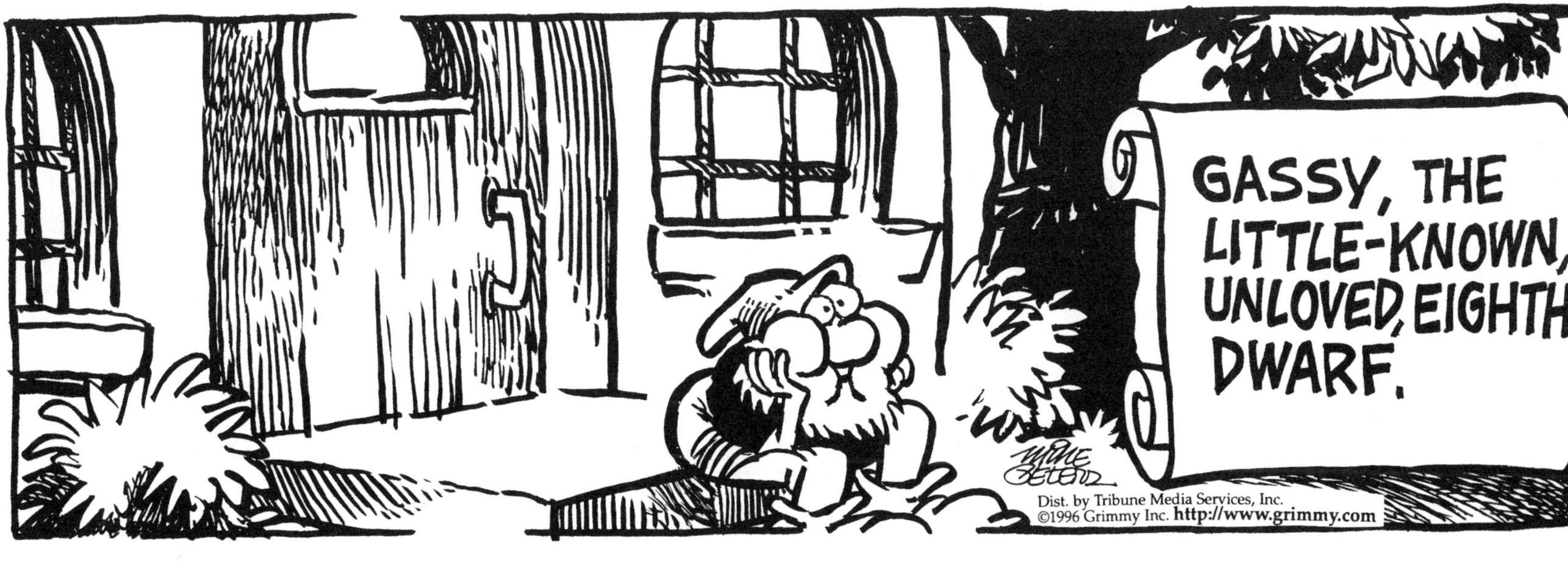
GASSY, THE LITTLE-KNOWN, UNLOVED, EIGHTH DWARF.
Dist. by Tribune Media Services, Inc.
©1996 Grimmy Inc. http://www.grimmy.com

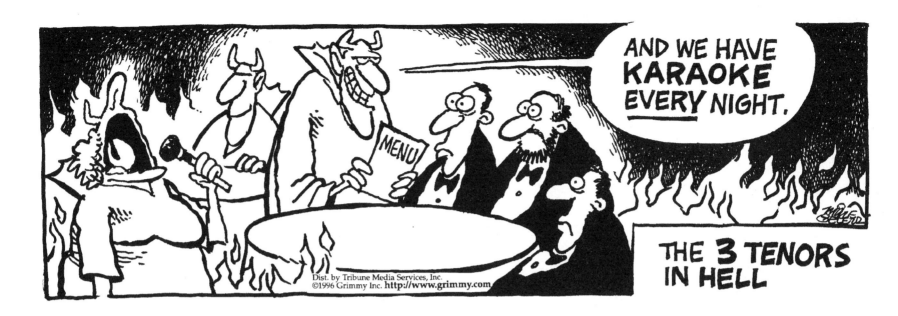

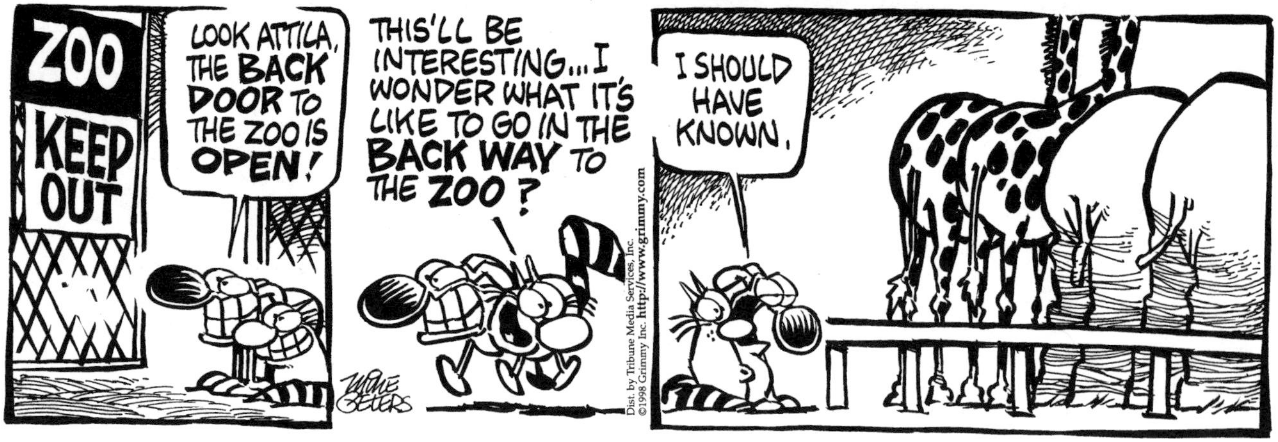
ZOO
KEEP OUT
LOOK ATTILA, THE BACK DOOR TO THE ZOO IS OPEN!
THIS'LL BE INTERESTING... I WONDER WHAT IT'S LIKE TO GO IN THE BACK WAY TO THE ZOO?
I SHOULD HAVE KNOWN.
Dist. by Tribune Media Services, Inc. ©1998 Grimmy Inc. http://www.grimmy.com
MIKE PETERS

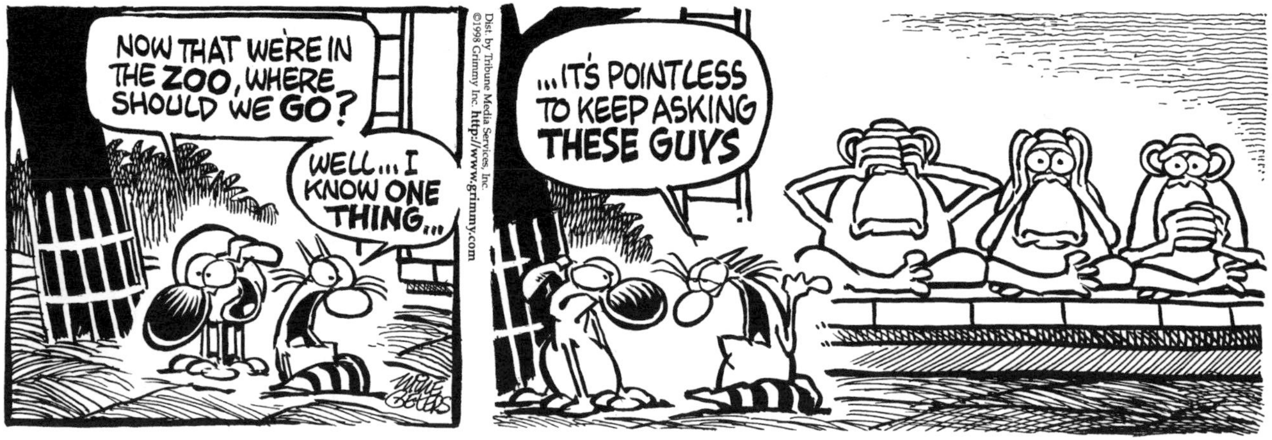
NOW THAT WE'RE IN THE ZOO, WHERE SHOULD WE GO?
WELL... I KNOW ONE THING...
...IT'S POINTLESS TO KEEP ASKING THESE GUYS
Dist. by Tribune Media Services, Inc. ©1998 Grimmy Inc. http://www.grimmy.com
MIKE PETERS

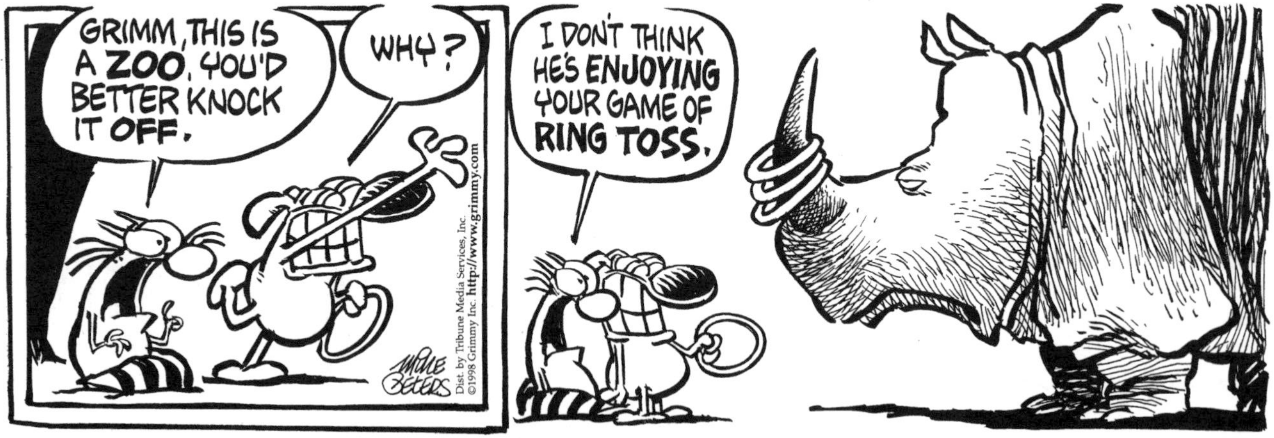
GRIMM, THIS IS A ZOO. YOU'D BETTER KNOCK IT OFF.
WHY?
I DON'T THINK HE'S ENJOYING YOUR GAME OF RING TOSS.
Dist. by Tribune Media Services, Inc. ©1998 Grimmy Inc. http://www.grimmy.com
MIKE PETERS

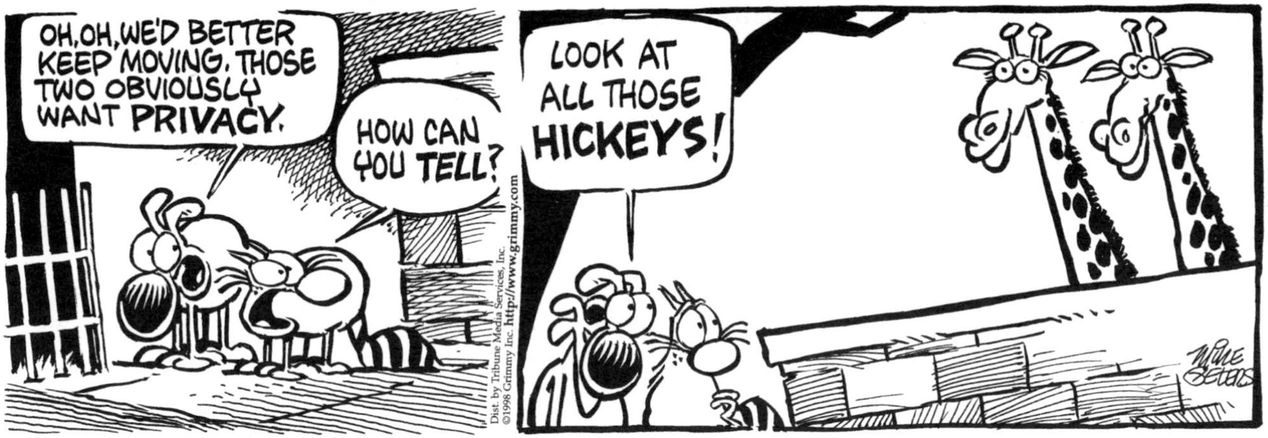
OH, OH, WE'D BETTER KEEP MOVING. THOSE TWO OBVIOUSLY WANT **PRIVACY**.
HOW CAN YOU **TELL**?
LOOK AT ALL THOSE **HICKEYS**!
MIKE PETERS

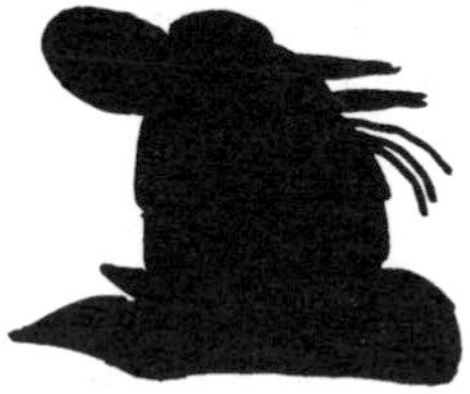

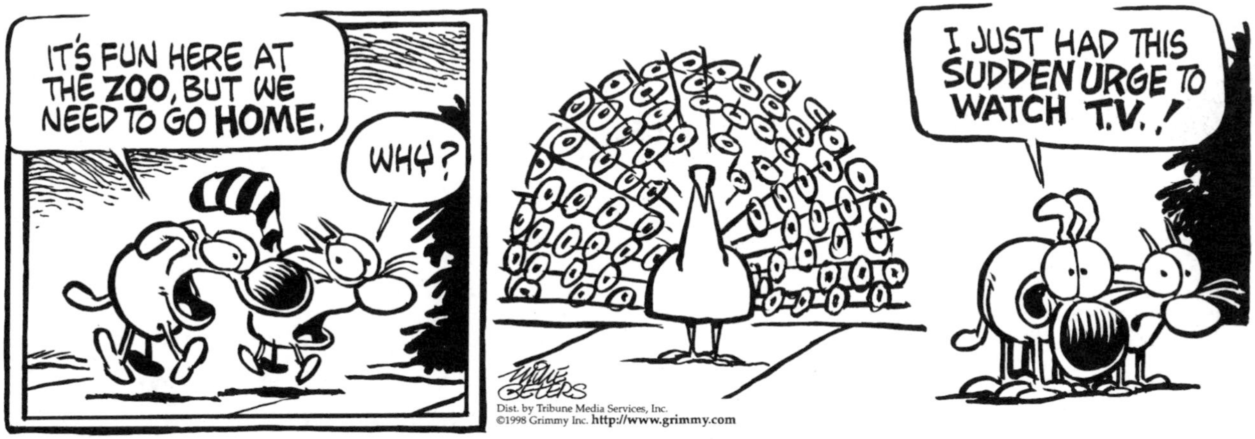
IT'S FUN HERE AT THE **ZOO**, BUT WE NEED TO GO **HOME**.
WHY?
I JUST HAD THIS **SUDDEN URGE** TO **WATCH T.V.**!
MIKE PETERS

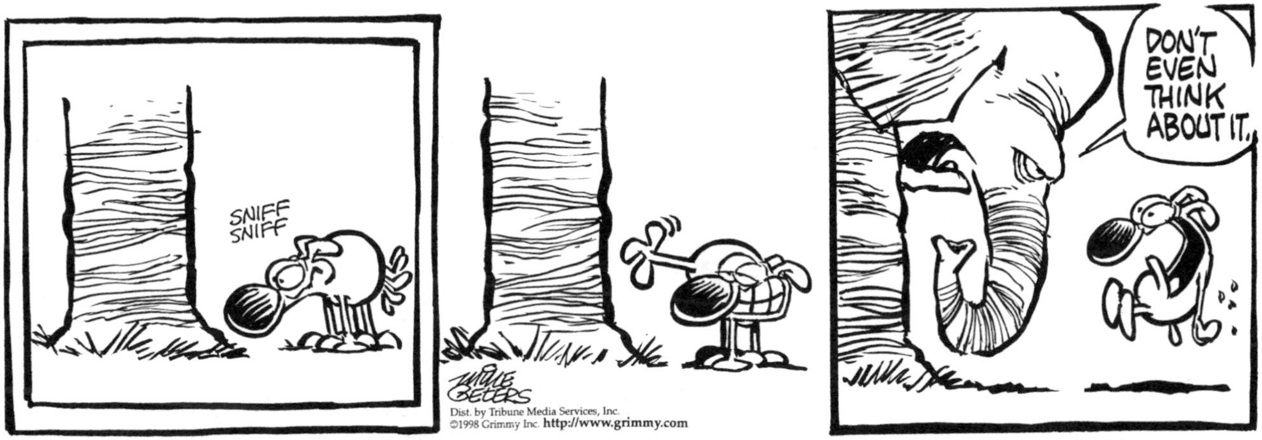
SNIFF SNIFF
DON'T EVEN THINK ABOUT IT.
MIKE PETERS

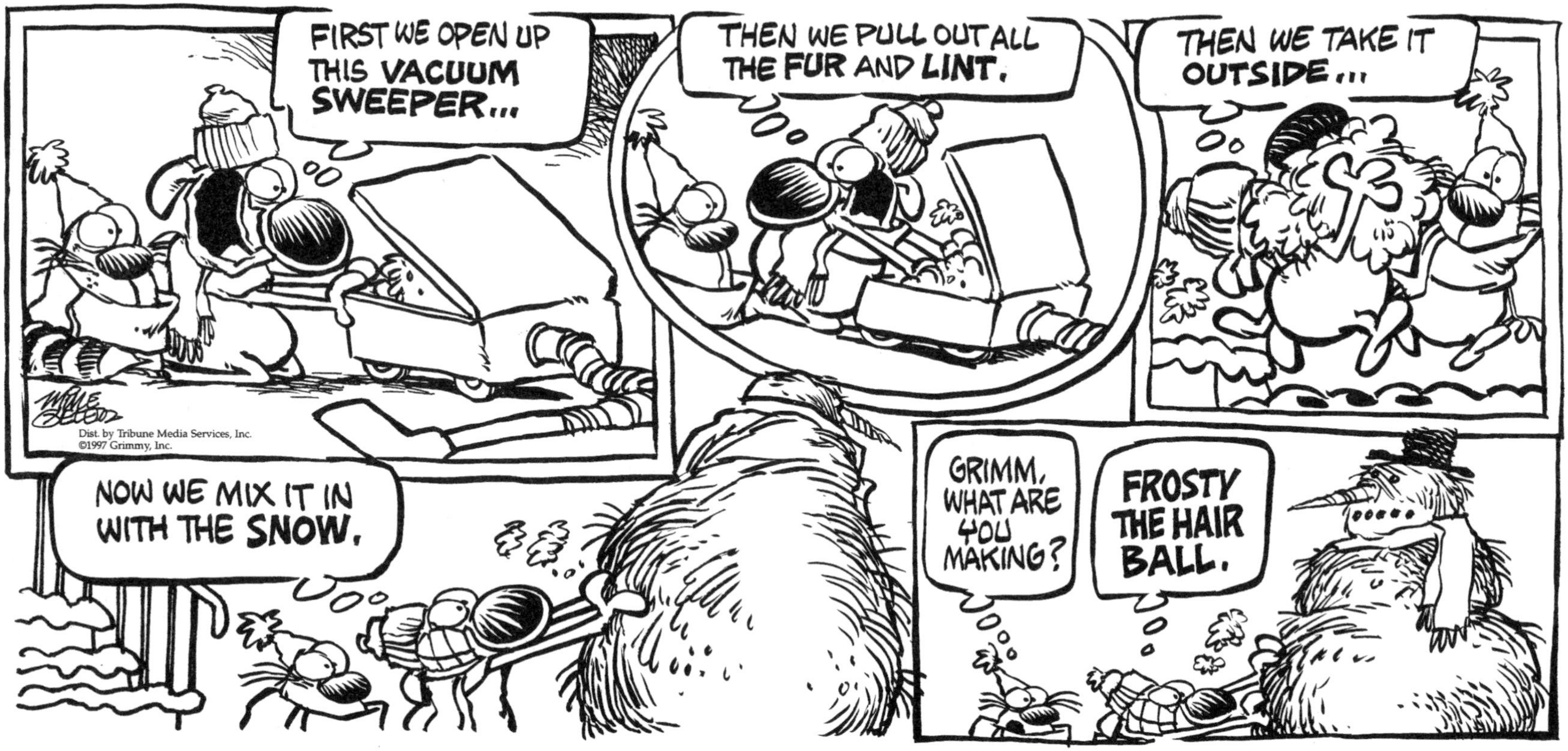
FIRST WE OPEN UP THIS VACUUM SWEEPER...
THEN WE PULL OUT ALL THE FUR AND LINT.
THEN WE TAKE IT OUTSIDE...
NOW WE MIX IT IN WITH THE SNOW.
GRIMM, WHAT ARE YOU MAKING?
FROSTY THE HAIR BALL.

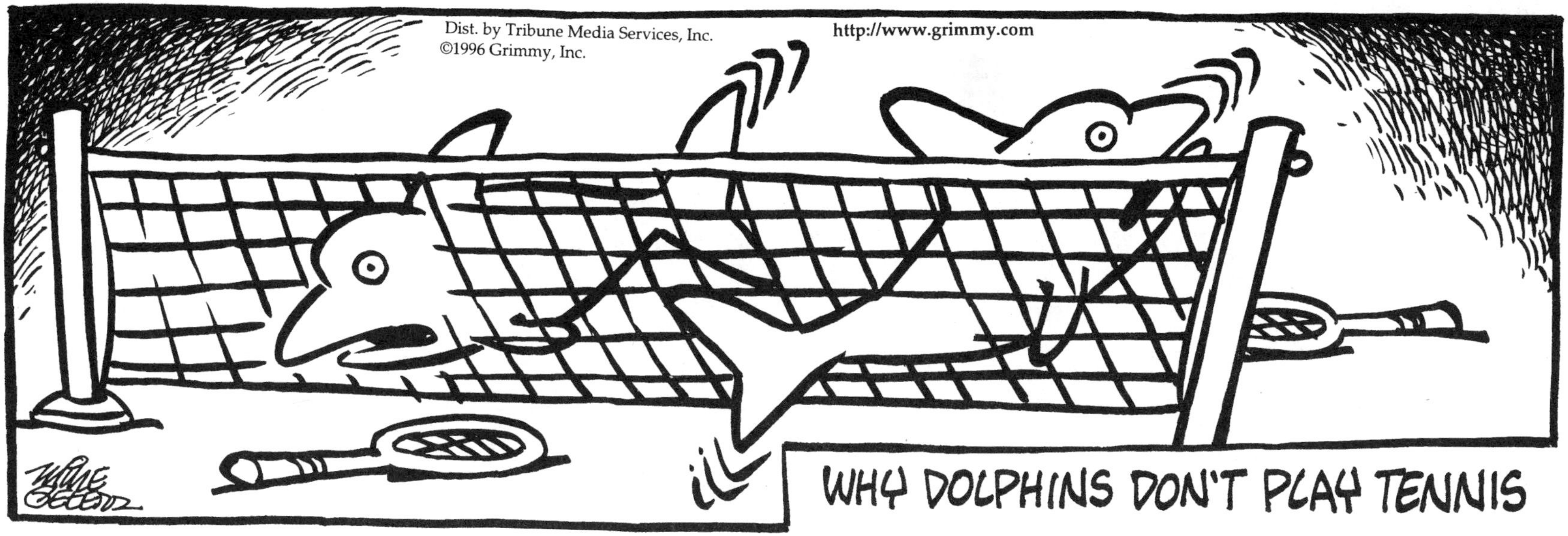
Dist. by Tribune Media Services, Inc.
©1996 Grimmy, Inc.
http://www.grimmy.com
WHY DOLPHINS DON'T PLAY TENNIS

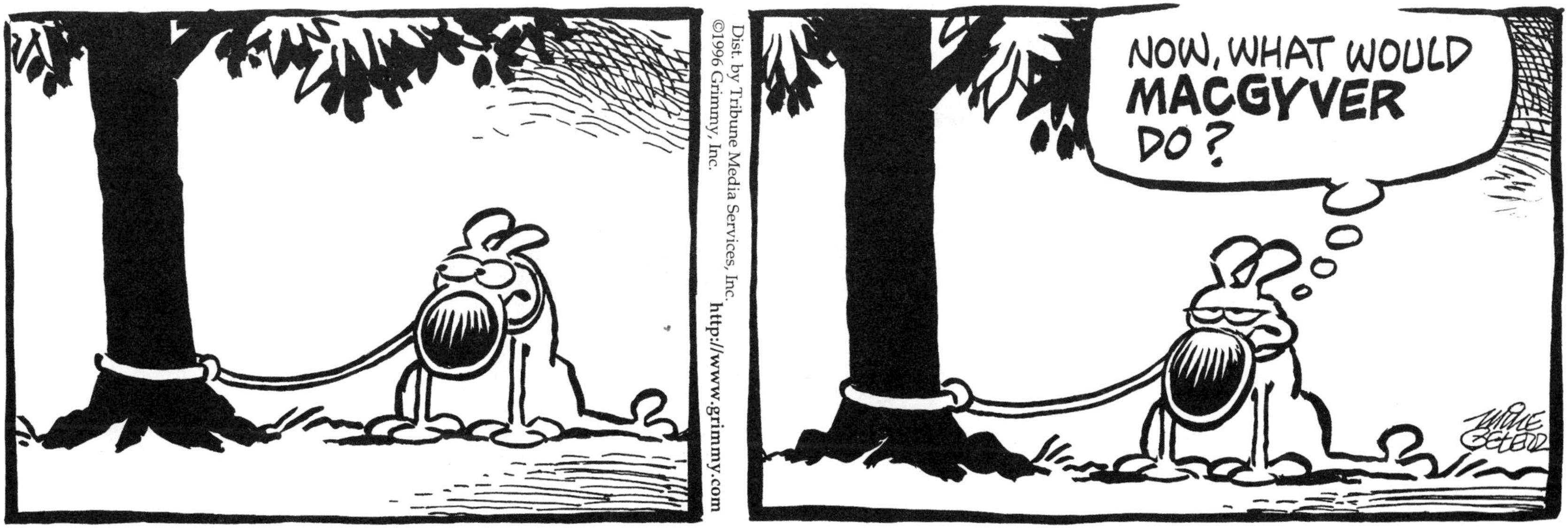
Dist. by Tribune Media Services, Inc.
©1996 Grimmy, Inc.
http://www.grimmy.com
NOW, WHAT WOULD **MACGYVER** DO?

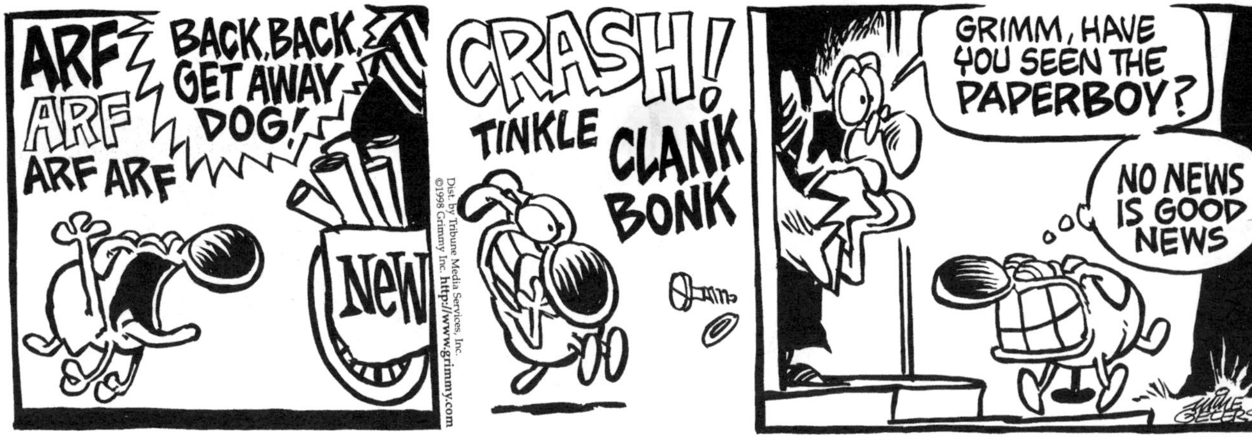
ARF
ARF
ARF ARF
BACK, BACK, GET AWAY DOG!
NEW
CRASH!
TINKLE
CLANK
BONK
Dist. by Tribune Media Services, Inc.
©1998 Grimmy Inc. http://www.grimmy.com
GRIMM, HAVE YOU SEEN THE PAPERBOY?
NO NEWS IS GOOD NEWS
MIKE PETERS

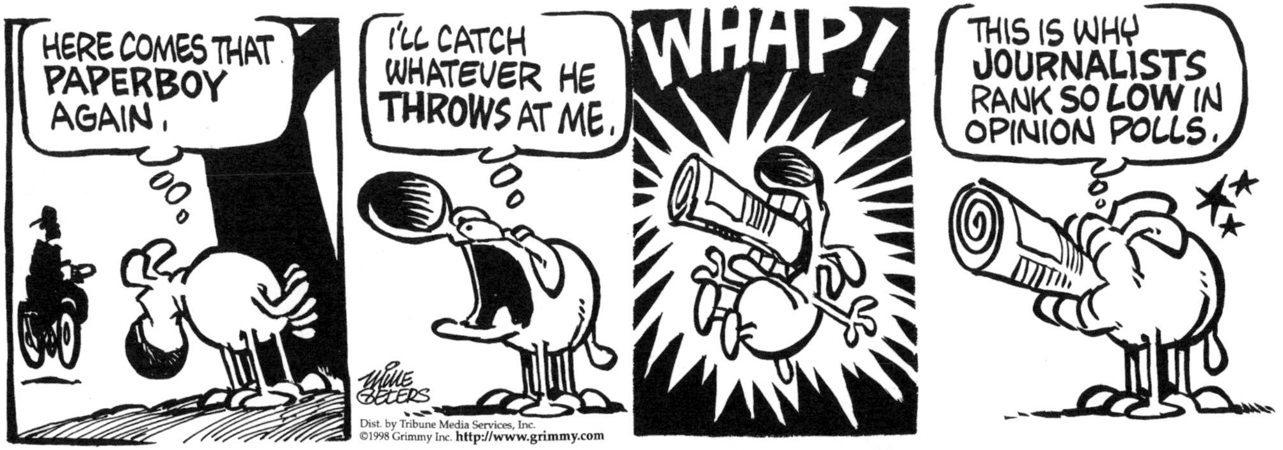
HERE COMES THAT PAPERBOY AGAIN.
I'LL CATCH WHATEVER HE THROWS AT ME.
MIKE PETERS
Dist. by Tribune Media Services, Inc.
©1998 Grimmy Inc. http://www.grimmy.com
WHAP!
THIS IS WHY JOURNALISTS RANK SO LOW IN OPINION POLLS.

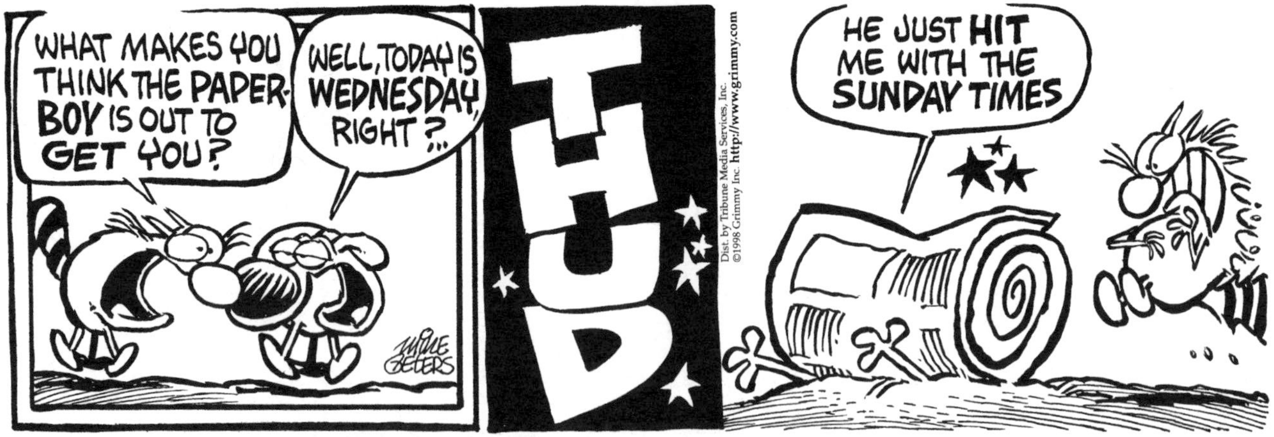
WHAT MAKES YOU THINK THE PAPER-BOY IS OUT TO GET YOU?
WELL, TODAY IS WEDNESDAY, RIGHT?..
MIKE PETERS
THUD
Dist. by Tribune Media Services, Inc.
©1998 Grimmy Inc. http://www.grimmy.com
HE JUST HIT ME WITH THE SUNDAY TIMES

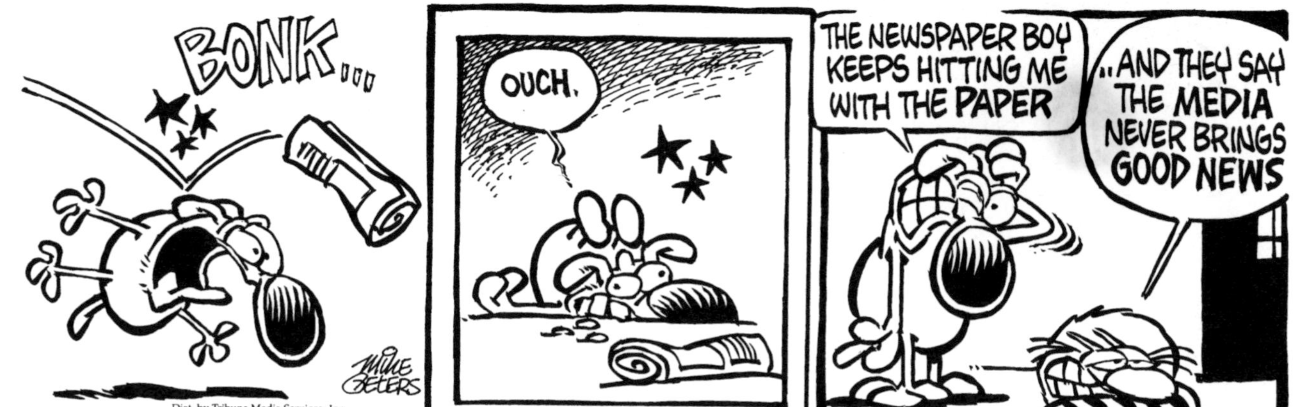
BONK...
OUCH.
THE NEWSPAPER BOY KEEPS HITTING ME WITH THE PAPER
...AND THEY SAY THE MEDIA NEVER BRINGS GOOD NEWS

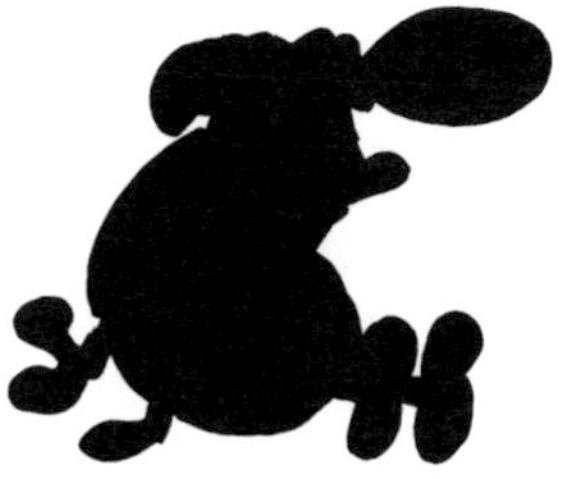

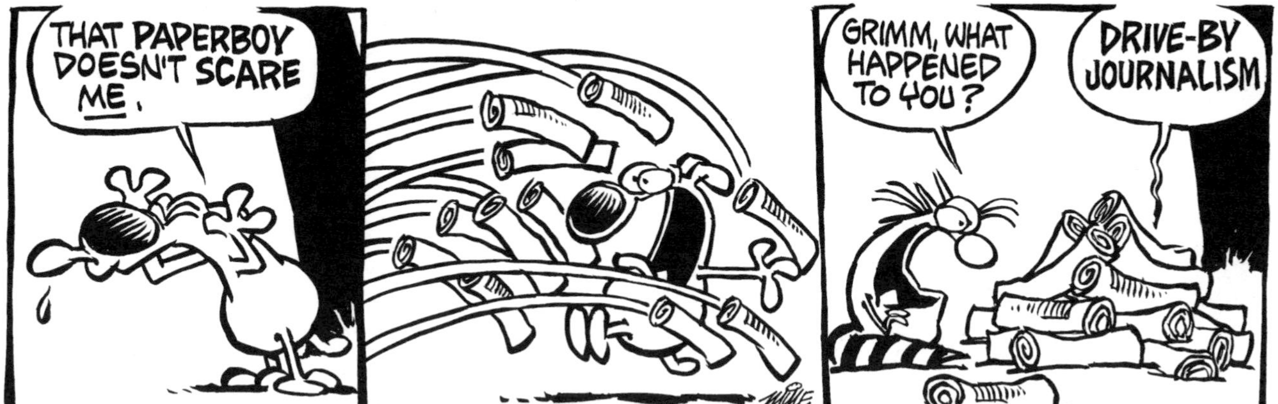
THAT PAPERBOY DOESN'T SCARE ME.
GRIMM, WHAT HAPPENED TO YOU?
DRIVE-BY JOURNALISM

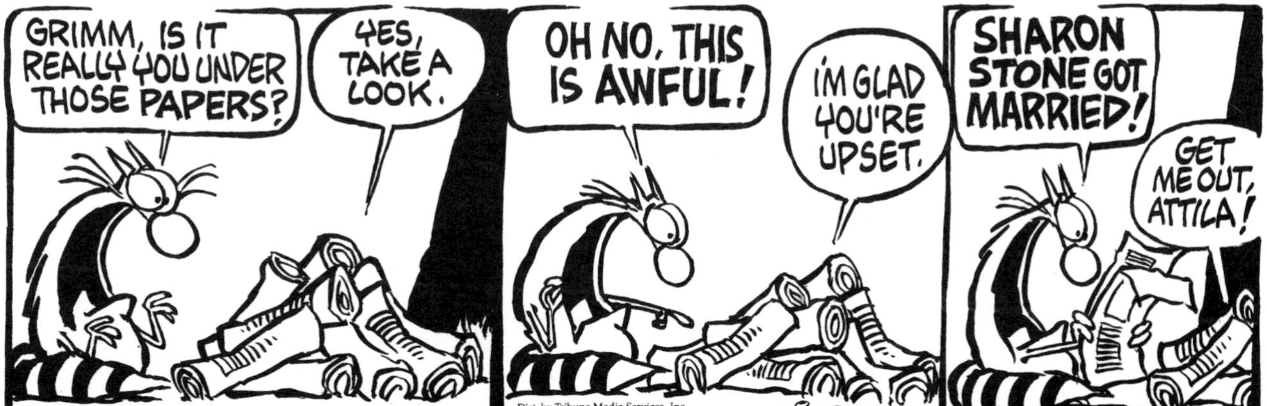
GRIMM, IS IT REALLY YOU UNDER THOSE PAPERS?
YES, TAKE A LOOK.
OH NO, THIS IS AWFUL!
I'M GLAD YOU'RE UPSET.
SHARON STONE GOT MARRIED!
GET ME OUT, ATTILA!

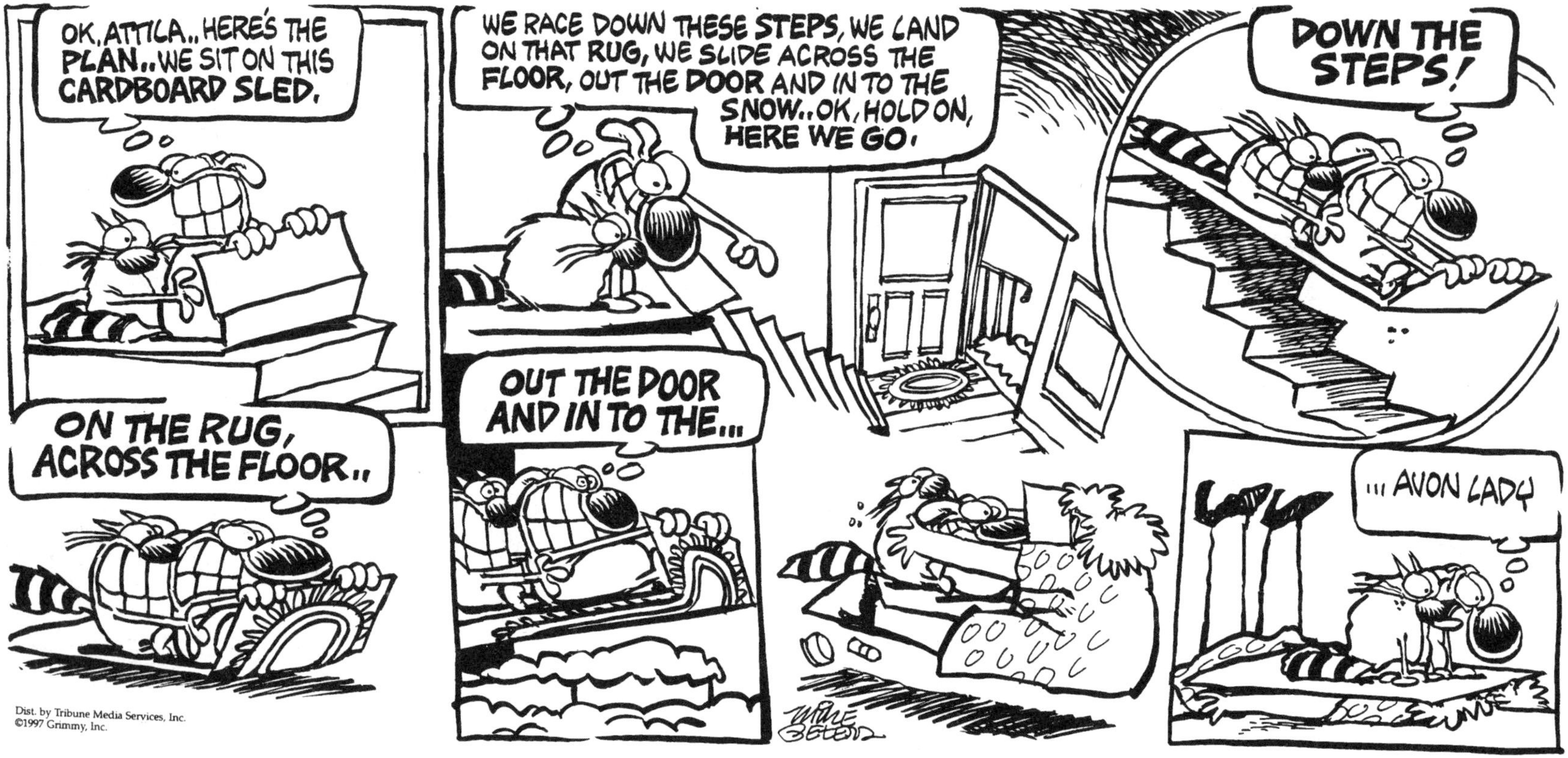
OK, ATTICA.. HERE'S THE PLAN.. WE SIT ON THIS CARDBOARD SLED.
WE RACE DOWN THESE STEPS, WE LAND ON THAT RUG, WE SLIDE ACROSS THE FLOOR, OUT THE DOOR AND IN TO THE SNOW.. OK, HOLD ON, HERE WE GO.
DOWN THE STEPS!
ON THE RUG, ACROSS THE FLOOR..
OUT THE DOOR AND IN TO THE...
... AVON LADY

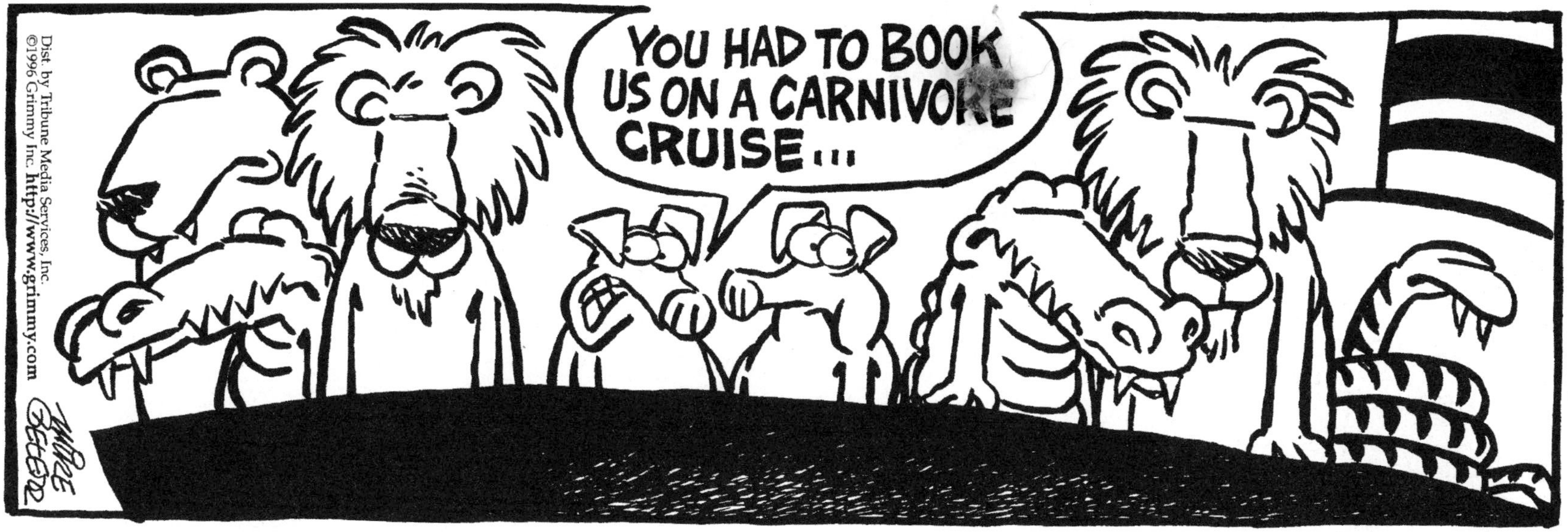
YOU HAD TO BOOK US ON A CARNIVORE CRUISE...
Dist. by Tribune Media Services, Inc.
©1996 Grimmy Inc. http://www.grimmy.com
MIKE PETERS

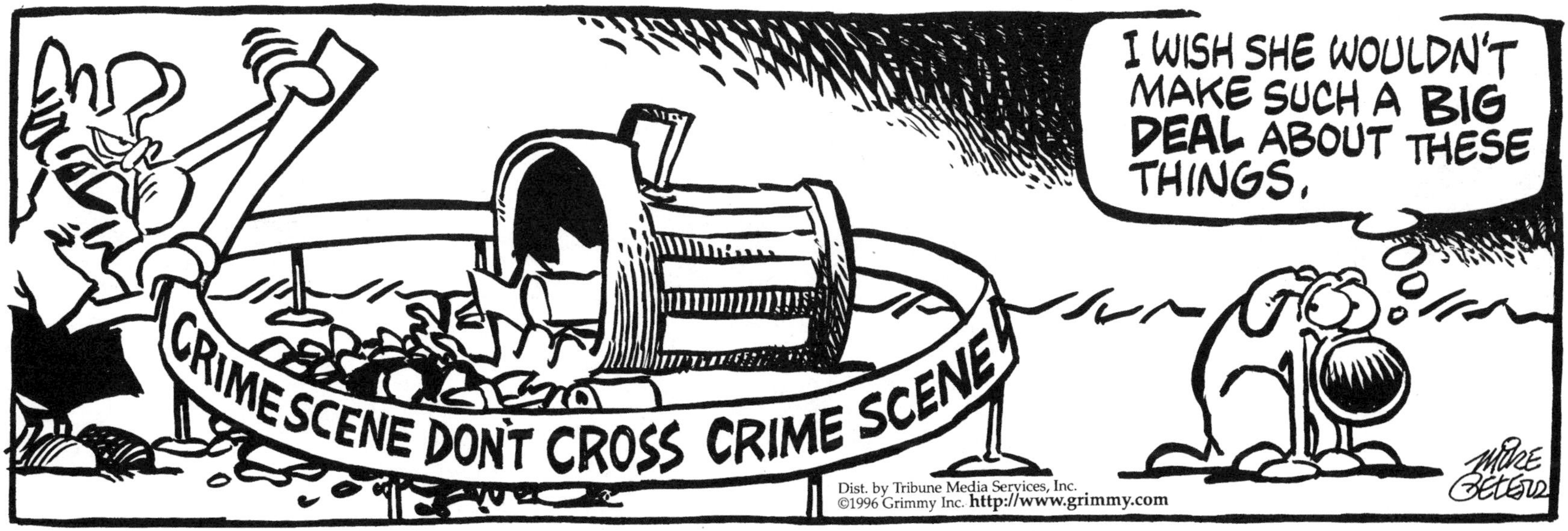
CRIME SCENE DON'T CROSS CRIME SCENE
I WISH SHE WOULDN'T MAKE SUCH A BIG DEAL ABOUT THESE THINGS.
Dist. by Tribune Media Services, Inc.
©1996 Grimmy Inc. http://www.grimmy.com
MIKE PETERS

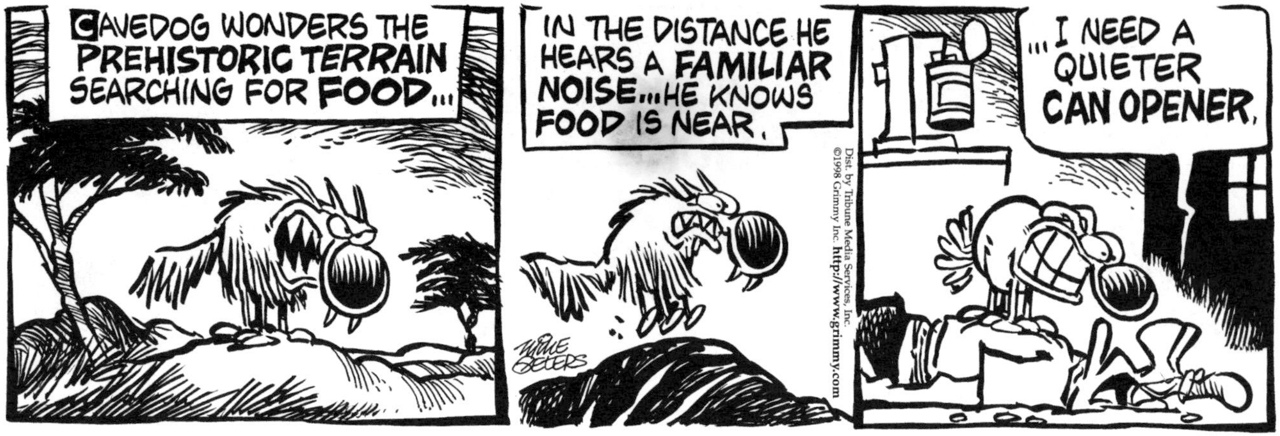
CAVEDOG WONDERS THE PREHISTORIC TERRAIN SEARCHING FOR FOOD...
IN THE DISTANCE HE HEARS A FAMILIAR NOISE...HE KNOWS FOOD IS NEAR.
...I NEED A QUIETER CAN OPENER.
Dist. by Tribune Media Services, Inc. ©1998 Grimmy Inc. http://www.grimmy.com
MIKE PETERS

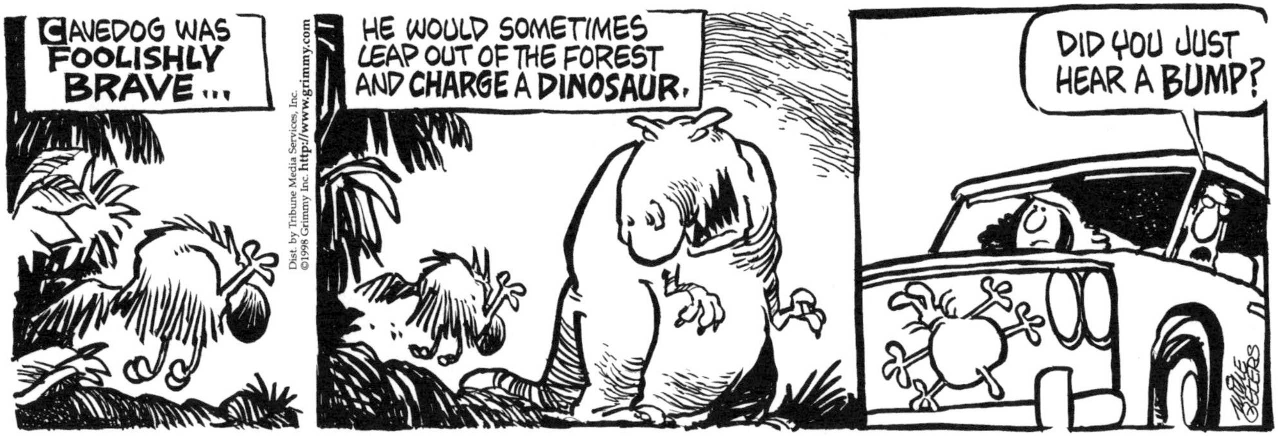
CAVEDOG WAS FOOLISHLY BRAVE...
HE WOULD SOMETIMES LEAP OUT OF THE FOREST AND CHARGE A DINOSAUR.
DID YOU JUST HEAR A BUMP?
Dist. by Tribune Media Services, Inc. ©1998 Grimmy Inc. http://www.grimmy.com
MIKE PETERS

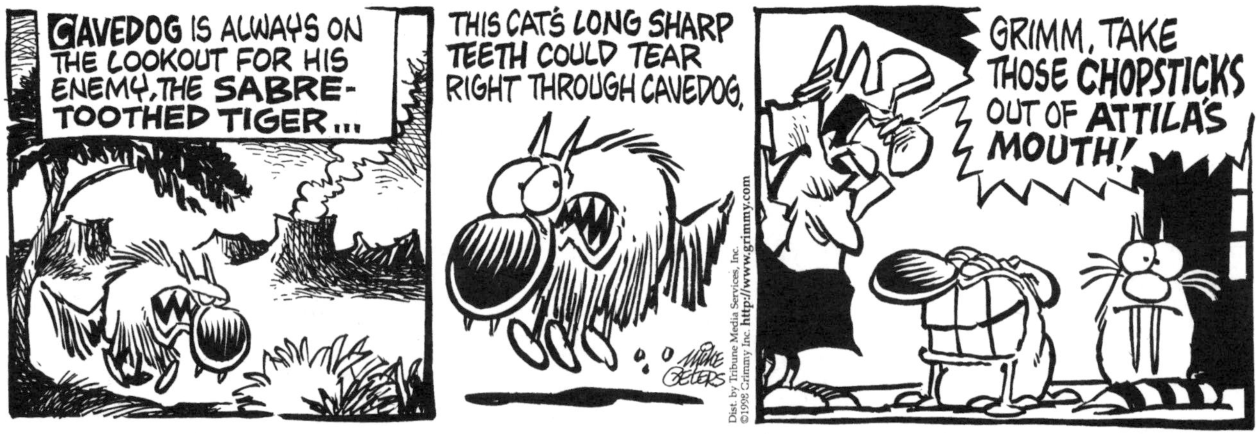
CAVEDOG IS ALWAYS ON THE LOOKOUT FOR HIS ENEMY, THE SABRE-TOOTHED TIGER...
THIS CAT'S LONG SHARP TEETH COULD TEAR RIGHT THROUGH CAVEDOG.
GRIMM, TAKE THOSE CHOPSTICKS OUT OF ATTILA'S MOUTH!
Dist. by Tribune Media Services, Inc. ©1998 Grimmy Inc. http://www.grimmy.com
MIKE PETERS

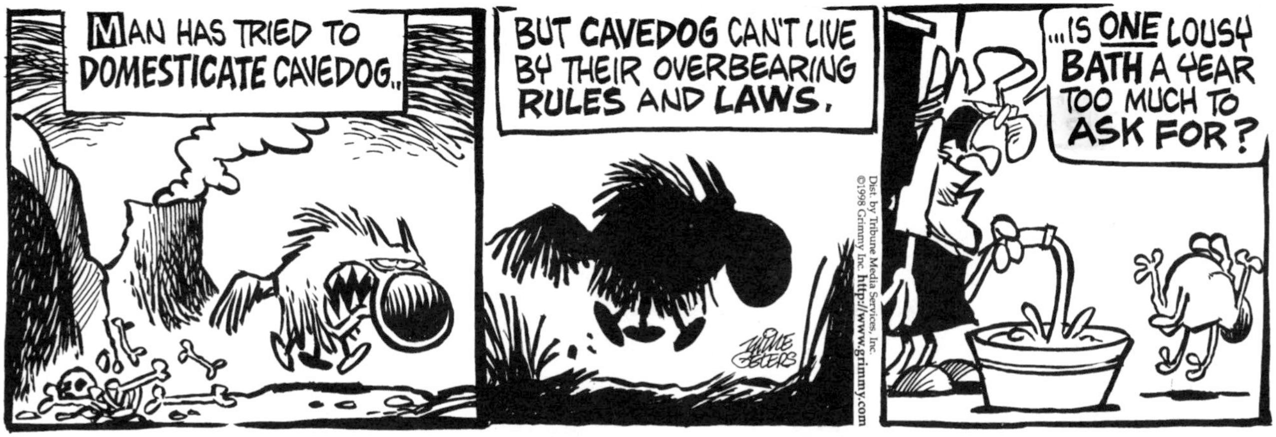
MAN HAS TRIED TO DOMESTICATE CAVEDOG..
BUT CAVEDOG CAN'T LIVE BY THEIR OVERBEARING RULES AND LAWS.
Dist. by Tribune Media Services, Inc. ©1998 Grimmy Inc. http://www.grimmy.com
MIKE PETERS
...IS ONE LOUSY BATH A YEAR TOO MUCH TO ASK FOR?

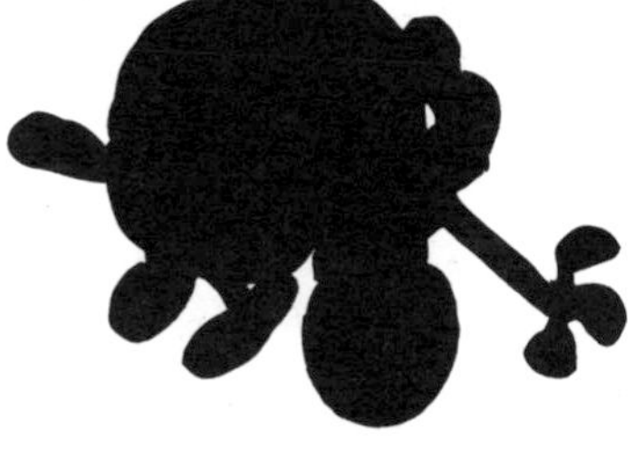

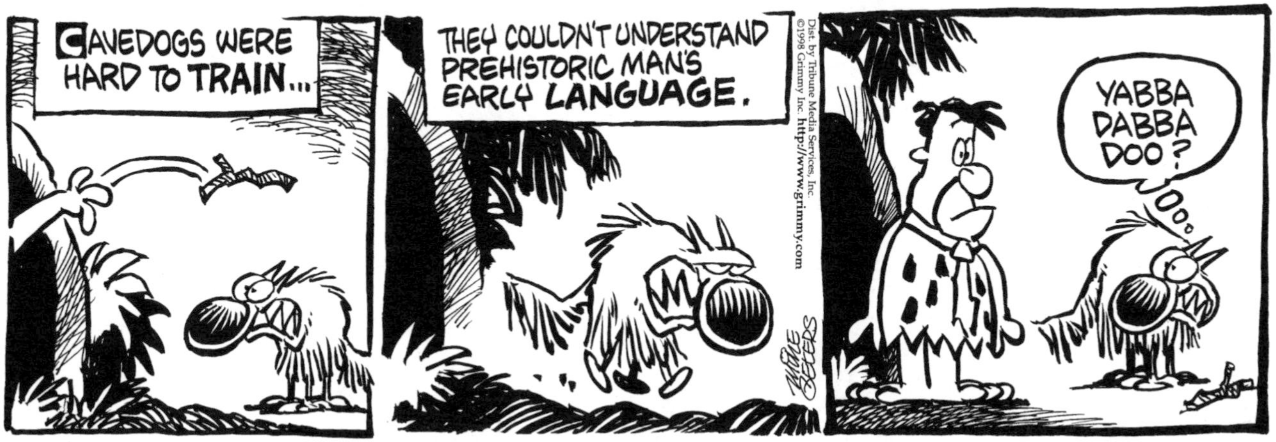
CAVEDOGS WERE HARD TO TRAIN...
THEY COULDN'T UNDERSTAND PREHISTORIC MAN'S EARLY LANGUAGE.
Dist. by Tribune Media Services, Inc. ©1998 Grimmy Inc. http://www.grimmy.com
MIKE PETERS
YABBA DABBA DOO?

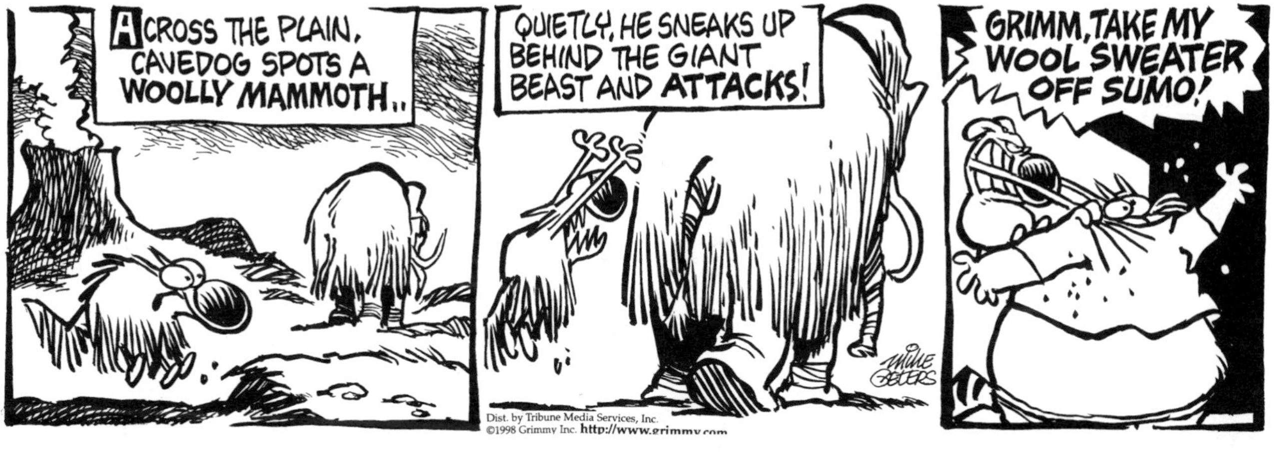
ACROSS THE PLAIN, CAVEDOG SPOTS A WOOLLY MAMMOTH..
QUIETLY, HE SNEAKS UP BEHIND THE GIANT BEAST AND ATTACKS!
MIKE PETERS
Dist. by Tribune Media Services, Inc. ©1998 Grimmy Inc. http://www.grimmy.com
GRIMM, TAKE MY WOOL SWEATER OFF SUMO!

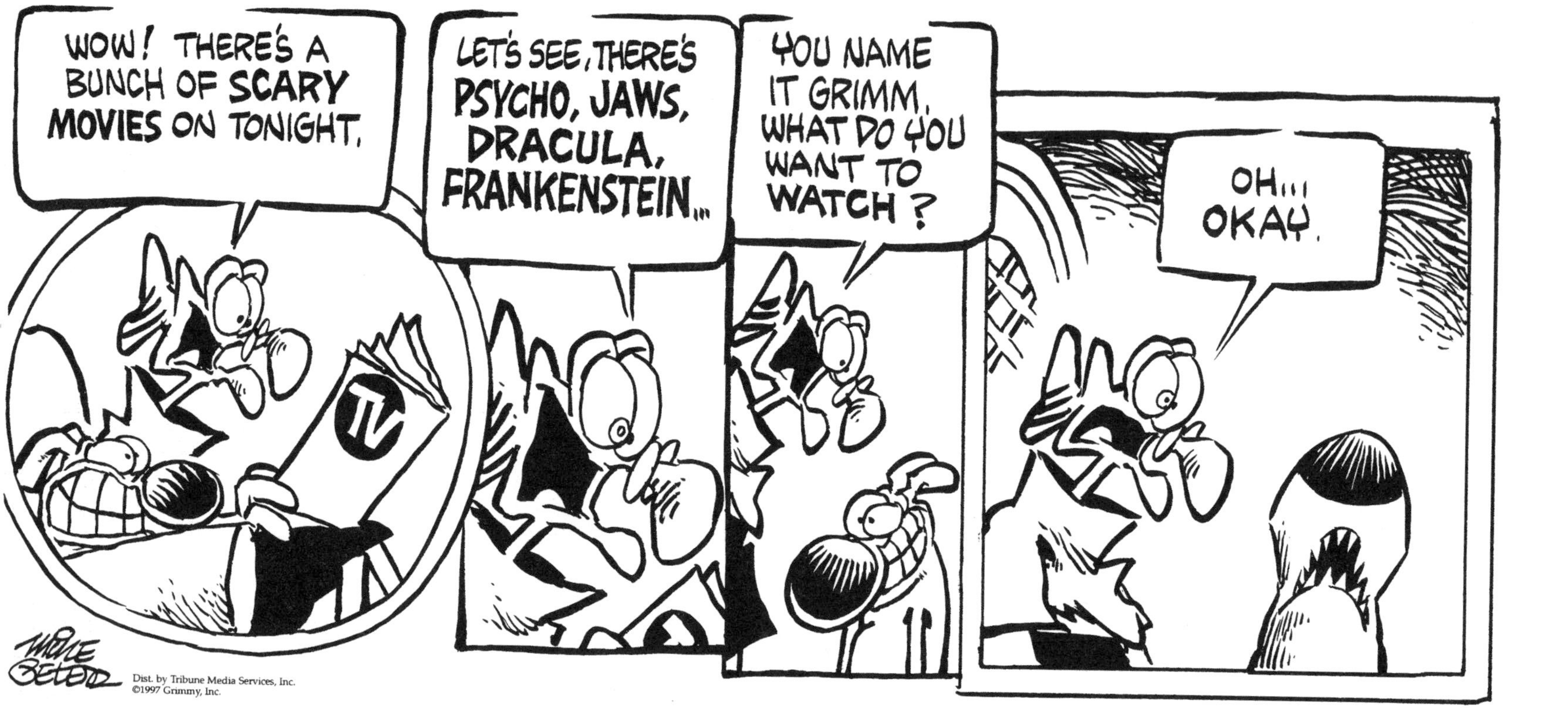

WOW! THERE'S A BUNCH OF SCARY MOVIES ON TONIGHT.
TV
LET'S SEE, THERE'S PSYCHO, JAWS, DRACULA, FRANKENSTEIN...
YOU NAME IT GRIMM, WHAT DO YOU WANT TO WATCH?
OH... OKAY.
MIKE PETERS

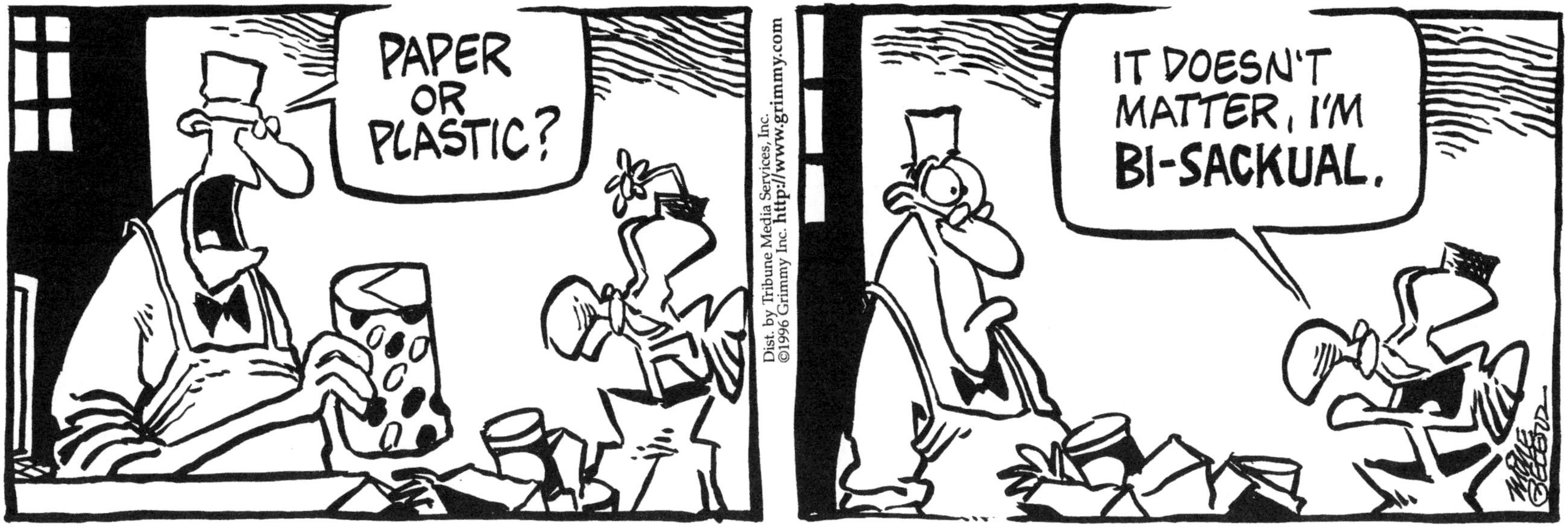
PAPER OR PLASTIC?
IT DOESN'T MATTER, I'M BI-SACKUAL.
Dist. by Tribune Media Services, Inc.
©1996 Grimmy Inc. http://www.grimmy.com

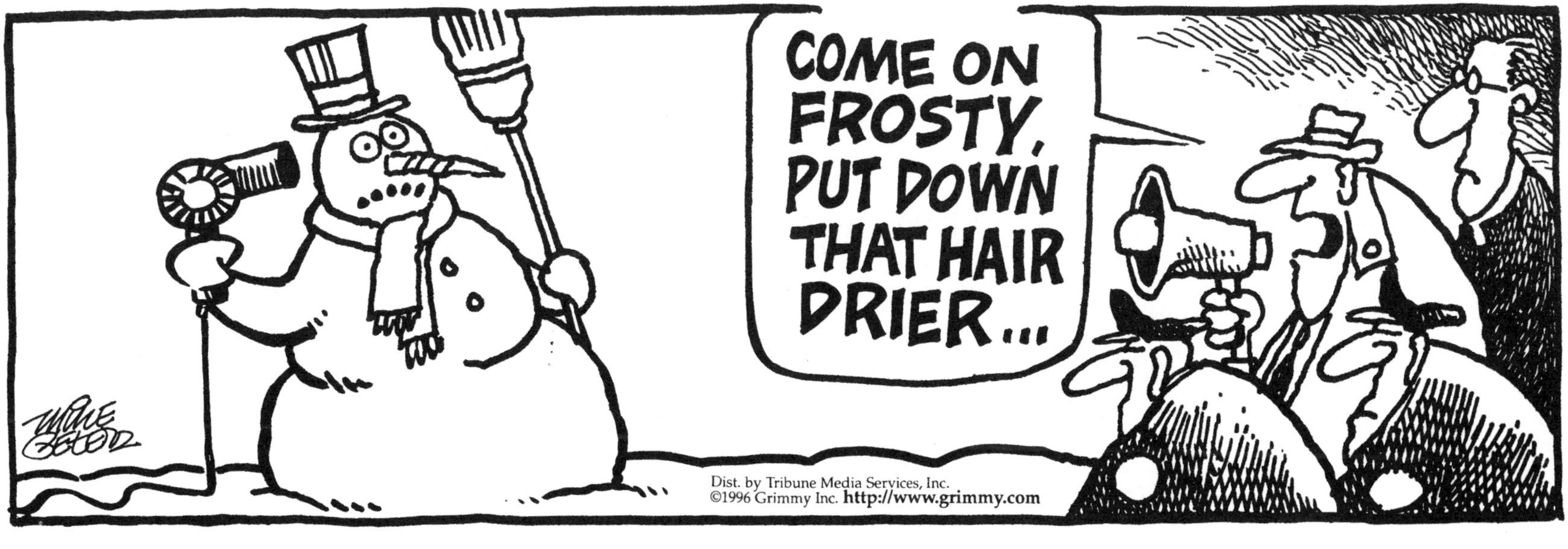
COME ON FROSTY, PUT DOWN THAT HAIR DRIER...
Dist. by Tribune Media Services, Inc.
©1996 Grimmy Inc. http://www.grimmy.com

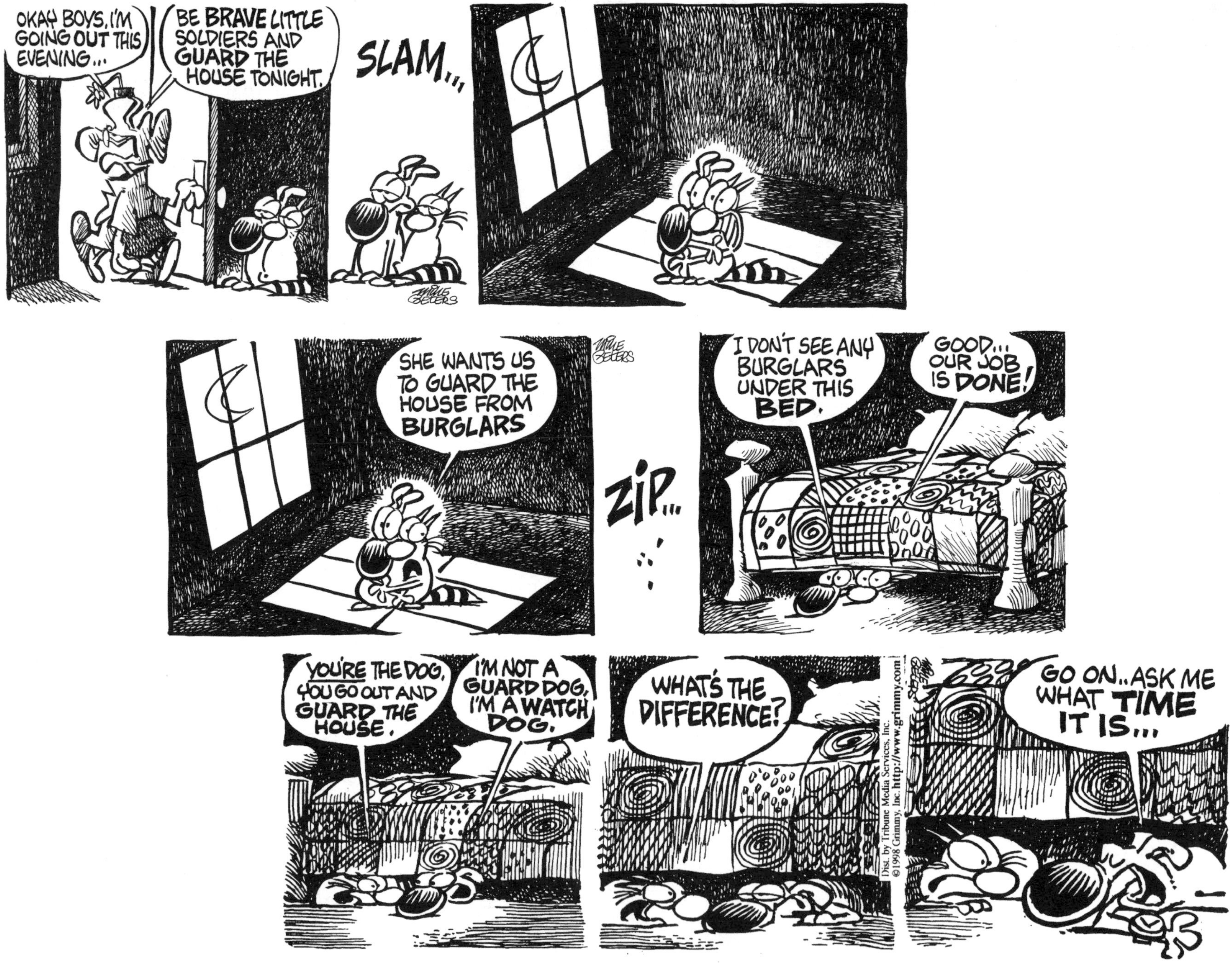

OKAY BOYS, I'M GOING OUT THIS EVENING...
BE BRAVE LITTLE SOLDIERS AND GUARD THE HOUSE TONIGHT.
SLAM...
SHE WANTS US TO GUARD THE HOUSE FROM BURGLARS
ZIP...
I DON'T SEE ANY BURGLARS UNDER THIS BED.
GOOD... OUR JOB IS DONE!
YOU'RE THE DOG, YOU GO OUT AND GUARD THE HOUSE.
I'M NOT A GUARD DOG, I'M A WATCH DOG.
WHAT'S THE DIFFERENCE?
GO ON.. ASK ME WHAT TIME IT IS...
Dist. by Tribune Media Services, Inc.
©1998 Grimmy, Inc. http://www.grimmy.com

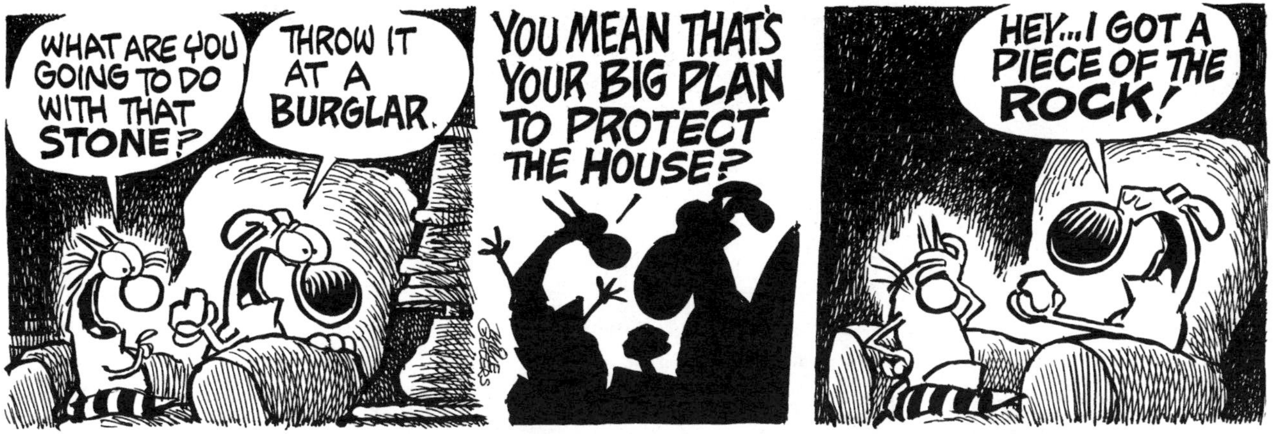
WHAT ARE YOU GOING TO DO WITH THAT STONE?
THROW IT AT A BURGLAR.
YOU MEAN THAT'S YOUR BIG PLAN TO PROTECT THE HOUSE?
HEY... I GOT A PIECE OF THE ROCK!

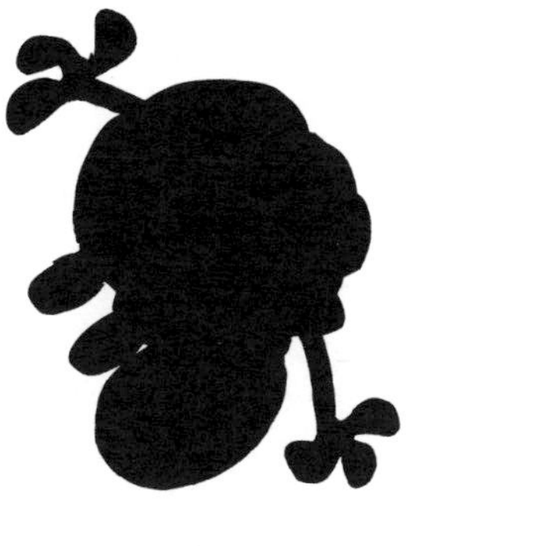

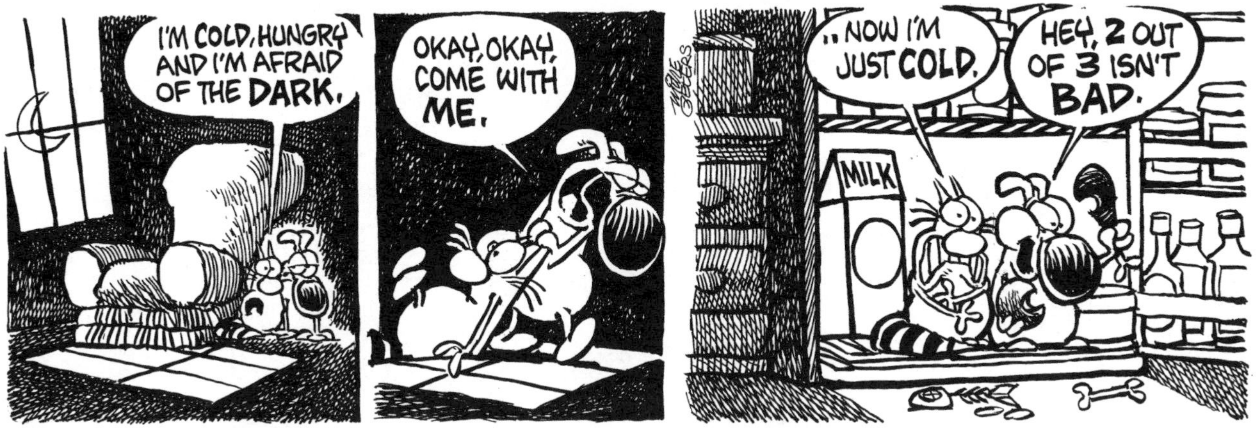
I'M COLD, HUNGRY AND I'M AFRAID OF THE DARK.
OKAY, OKAY, COME WITH ME.
.. NOW I'M JUST COLD.
HEY, 2 OUT OF 3 ISN'T BAD.
MILK

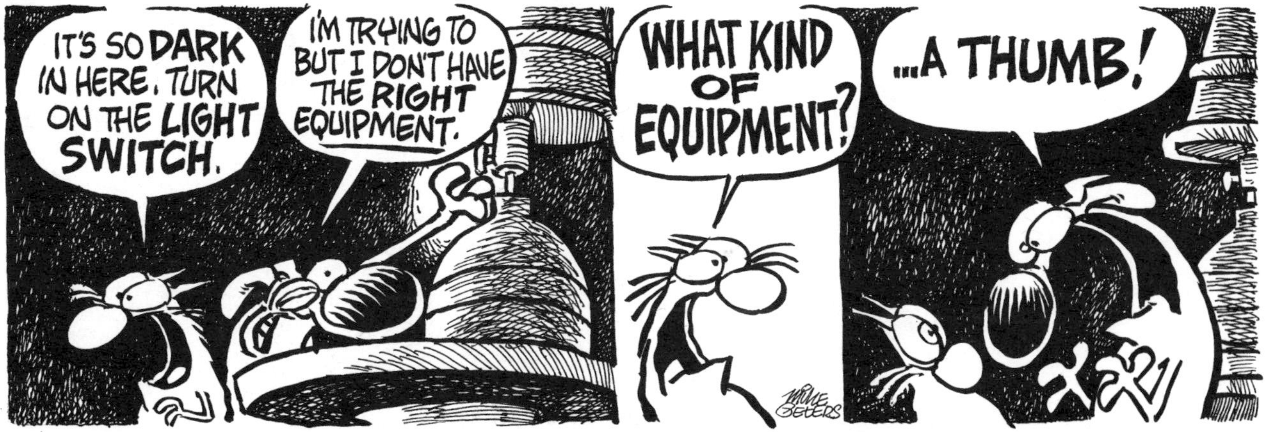
IT'S SO DARK IN HERE. TURN ON THE LIGHT SWITCH.
I'M TRYING TO BUT I DON'T HAVE THE RIGHT EQUIPMENT.
WHAT KIND OF EQUIPMENT?
...A THUMB!

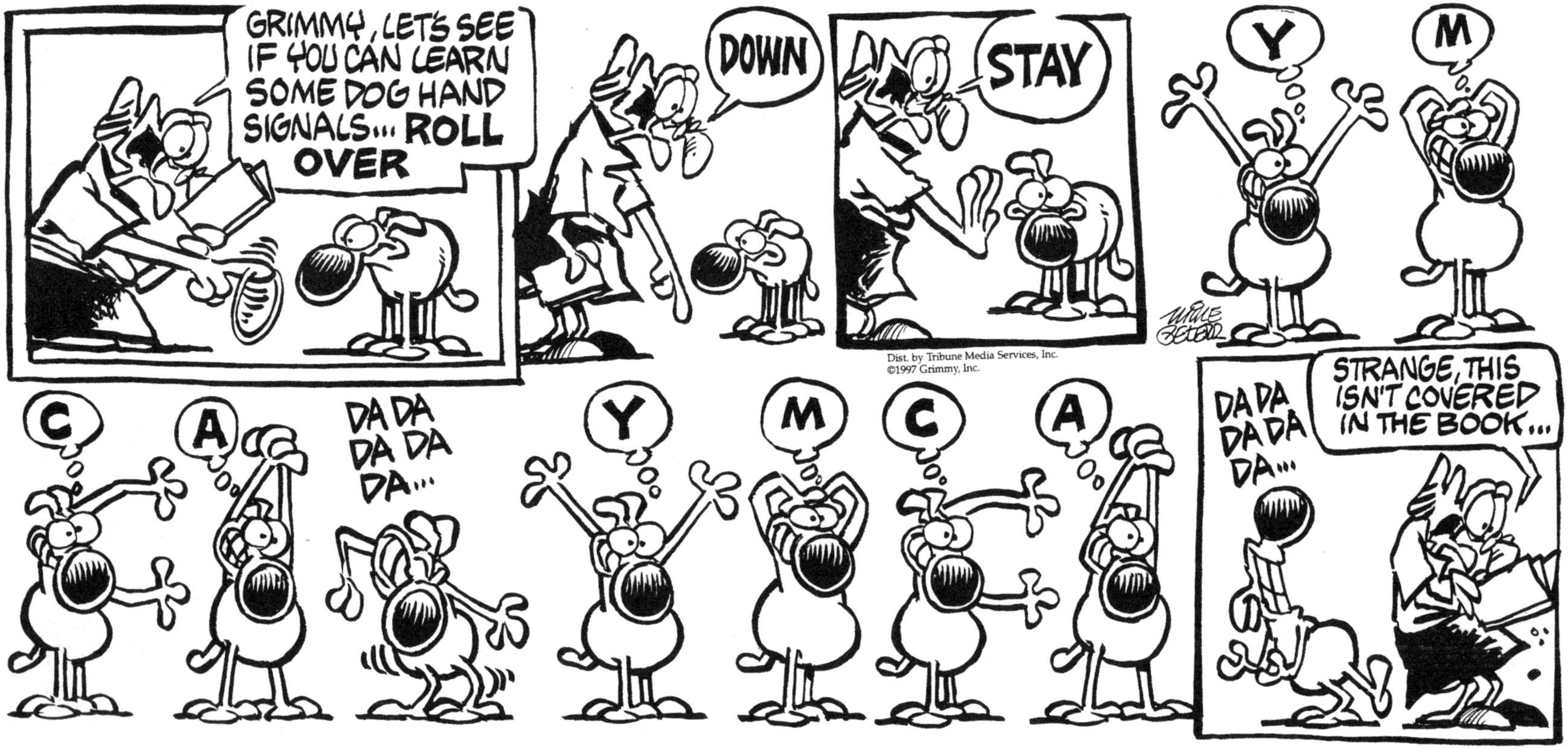
GRIMMY, LET'S SEE IF YOU CAN LEARN SOME DOG HAND SIGNALS... ROLL OVER
DOWN
STAY
Y
M
Dist. by Tribune Media Services, Inc.
©1997 Grimmy, Inc.
C
A
DA DA DA DA DA...
Y
M
C
A
DA DA DA DA DA...
STRANGE, THIS ISN'T COVERED IN THE BOOK...

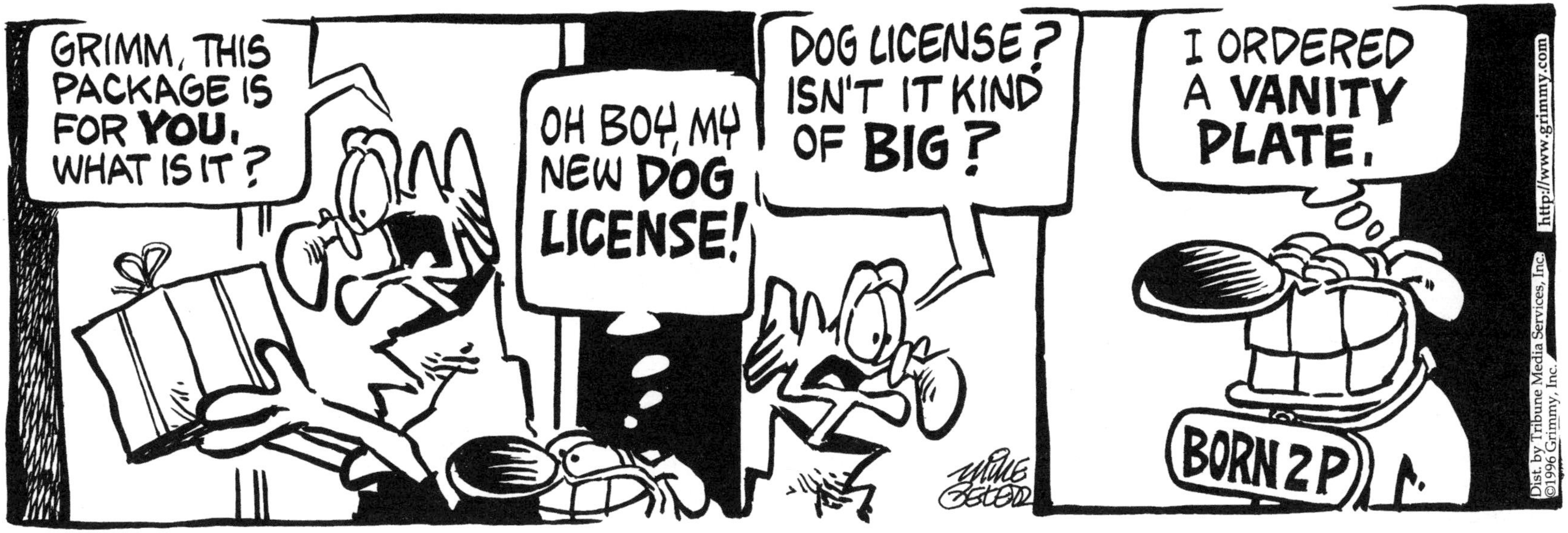
GRIMM, THIS PACKAGE IS FOR **YOU.** WHAT IS IT?
OH BOY, MY NEW **DOG LICENSE!**
DOG LICENSE? ISN'T IT KIND OF **BIG?**
I ORDERED A **VANITY PLATE.**
BORN 2 P
Dist. by Tribune Media Services, Inc. ©1996 Grimmy, Inc. http://www.grimmy.com

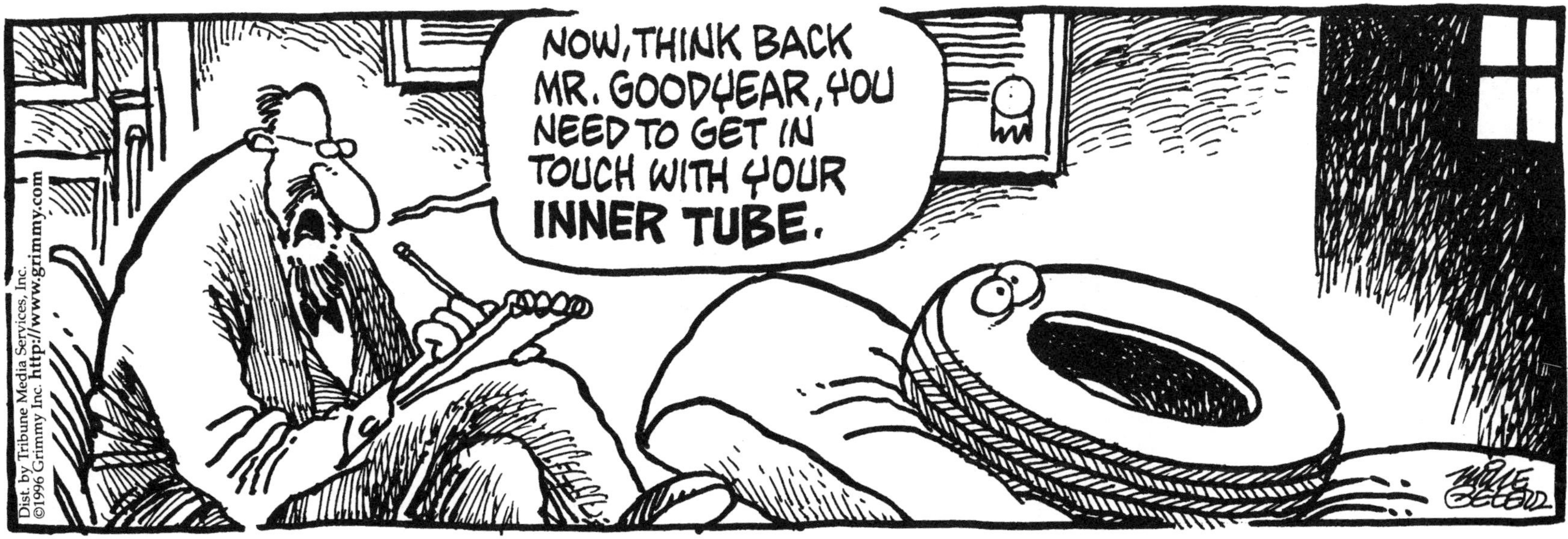
NOW, THINK BACK MR. GOODYEAR, YOU NEED TO GET IN TOUCH WITH YOUR **INNER TUBE.**
Dist. by Tribune Media Services, Inc. ©1996 Grimmy Inc. http://www.grimmy.com

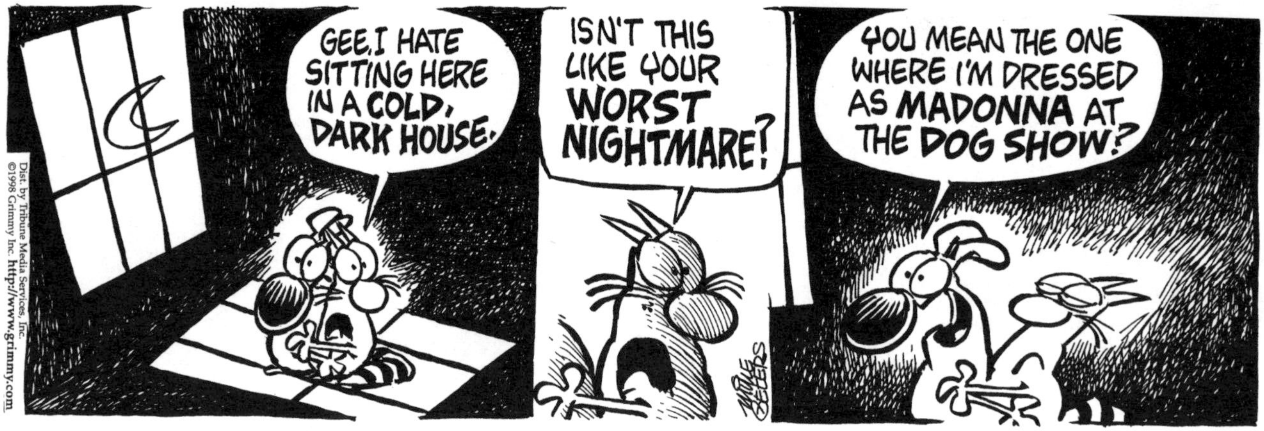
GEE, I HATE SITTING HERE IN A COLD, DARK HOUSE.
ISN'T THIS LIKE YOUR WORST NIGHTMARE?
YOU MEAN THE ONE WHERE I'M DRESSED AS MADONNA AT THE DOG SHOW?
Dist. by Tribune Media Services, Inc. ©1998 Grimmy Inc. http://www.grimmy.com

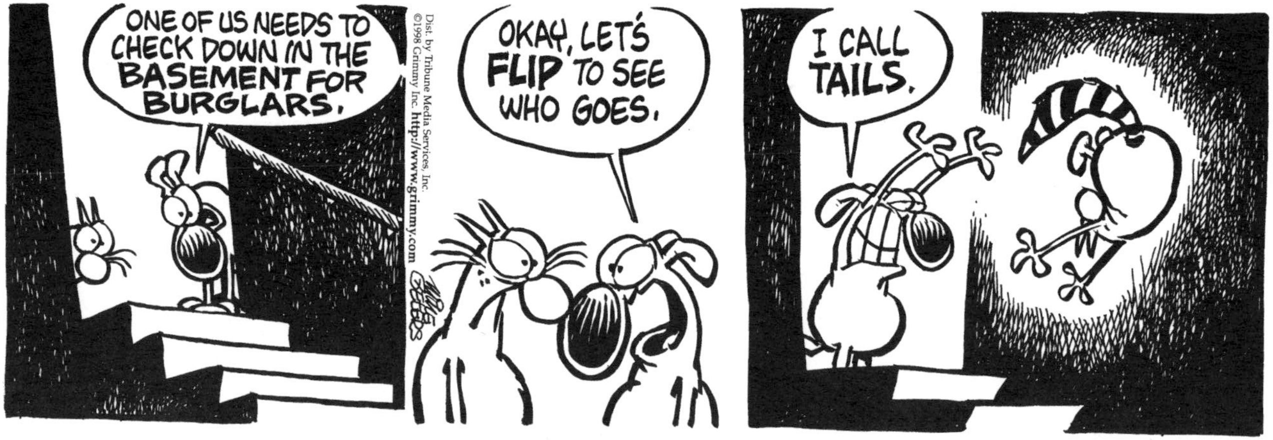
ONE OF US NEEDS TO CHECK DOWN IN THE BASEMENT FOR BURGLARS.
OKAY, LET'S FLIP TO SEE WHO GOES.
I CALL TAILS.
Dist. by Tribune Media Services, Inc. ©1998 Grimmy Inc. http://www.grimmy.com

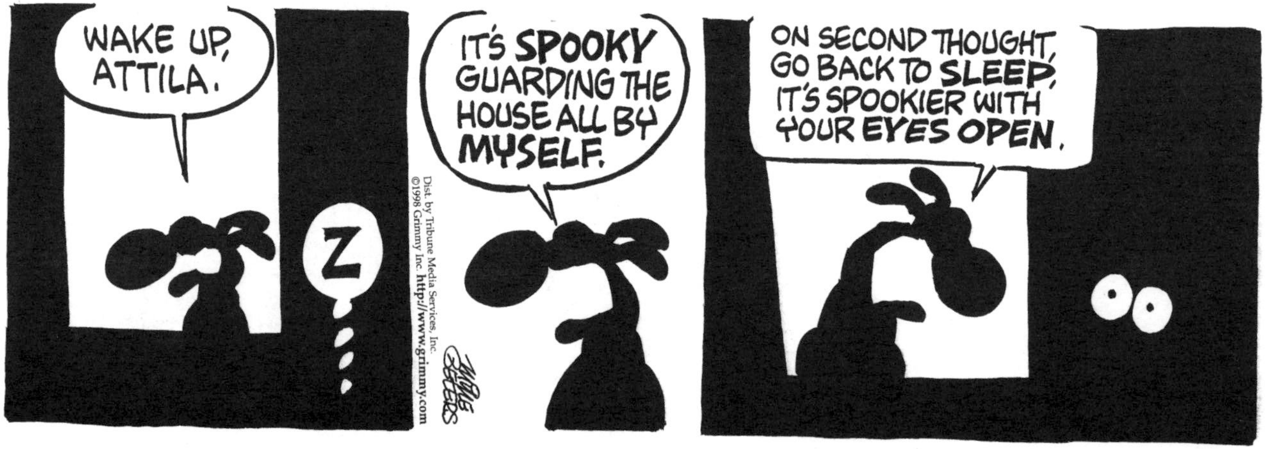
WAKE UP, ATTILA.
Z
IT'S SPOOKY GUARDING THE HOUSE ALL BY MYSELF.
ON SECOND THOUGHT, GO BACK TO SLEEP, IT'S SPOOKIER WITH YOUR EYES OPEN.
Dist. by Tribune Media Services, Inc. ©1998 Grimmy Inc. http://www.grimmy.com

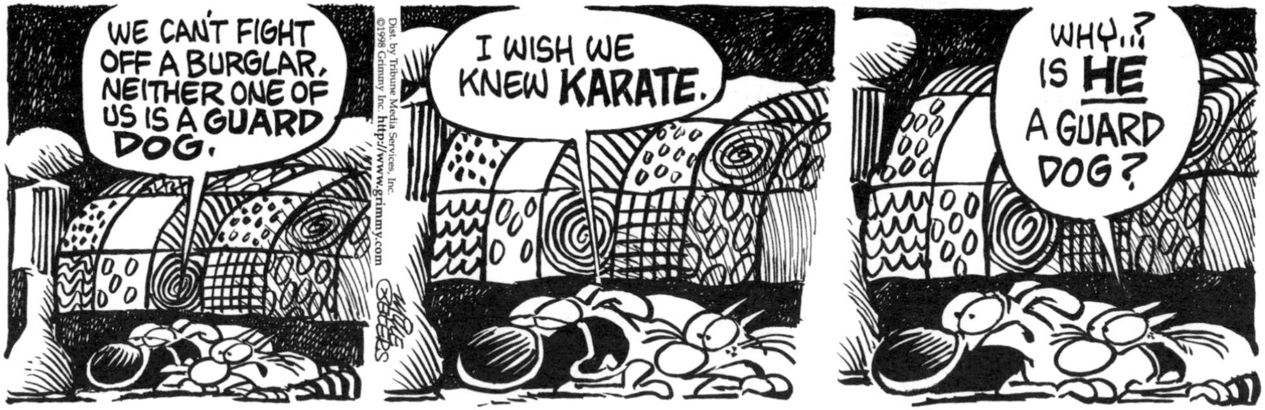
WE CAN'T FIGHT OFF A BURGLAR, NEITHER ONE OF US IS A GUARD DOG.
Dist. by Tribune Media Services, Inc. ©1998 Grimmy Inc. http://www.grimmy.com
I WISH WE KNEW KARATE.
WHY...? IS HE A GUARD DOG?

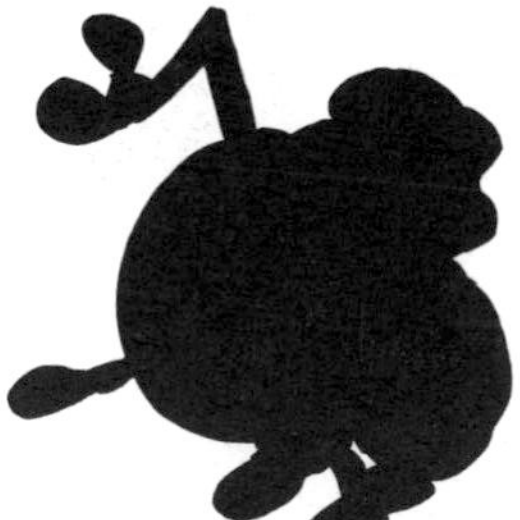

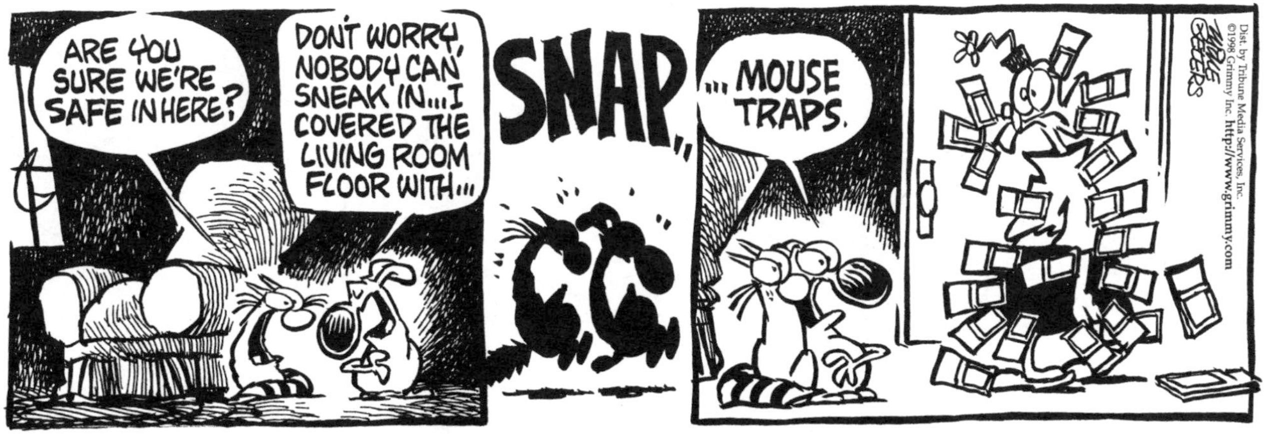
ARE YOU SURE WE'RE SAFE IN HERE?
DON'T WORRY, NOBODY CAN SNEAK IN...I COVERED THE LIVING ROOM FLOOR WITH...
SNAP,,
...MOUSE TRAPS.
Dist. by Tribune Media Services, Inc. ©1998 Grimmy Inc. http://www.grimmy.com

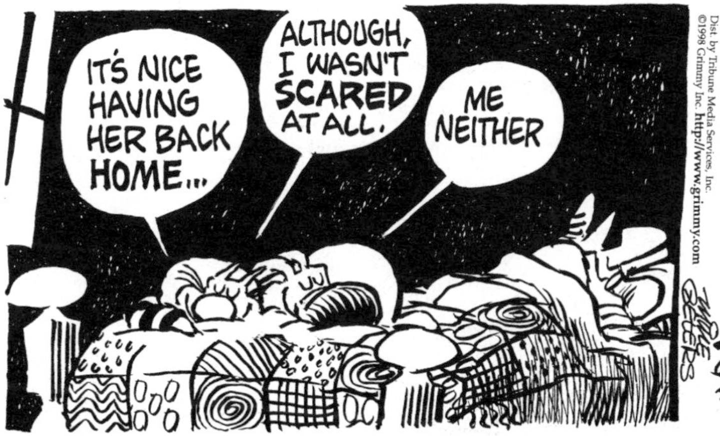
IT'S NICE HAVING HER BACK HOME...
ALTHOUGH, I WASN'T SCARED AT ALL.
ME NEITHER
Dist. by Tribune Media Services, Inc. ©1998 Grimmy Inc. http://www.grimmy.com

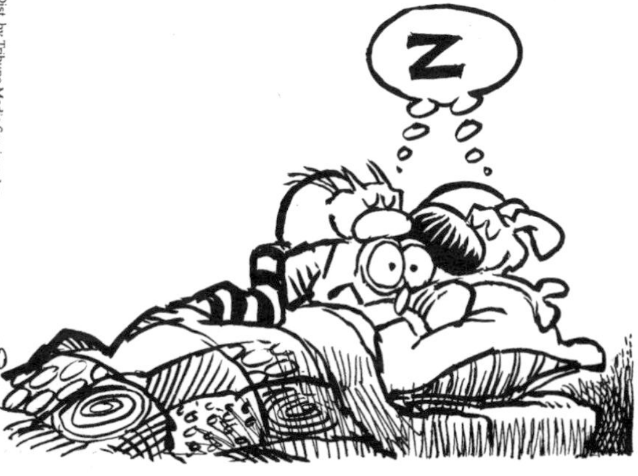
Z

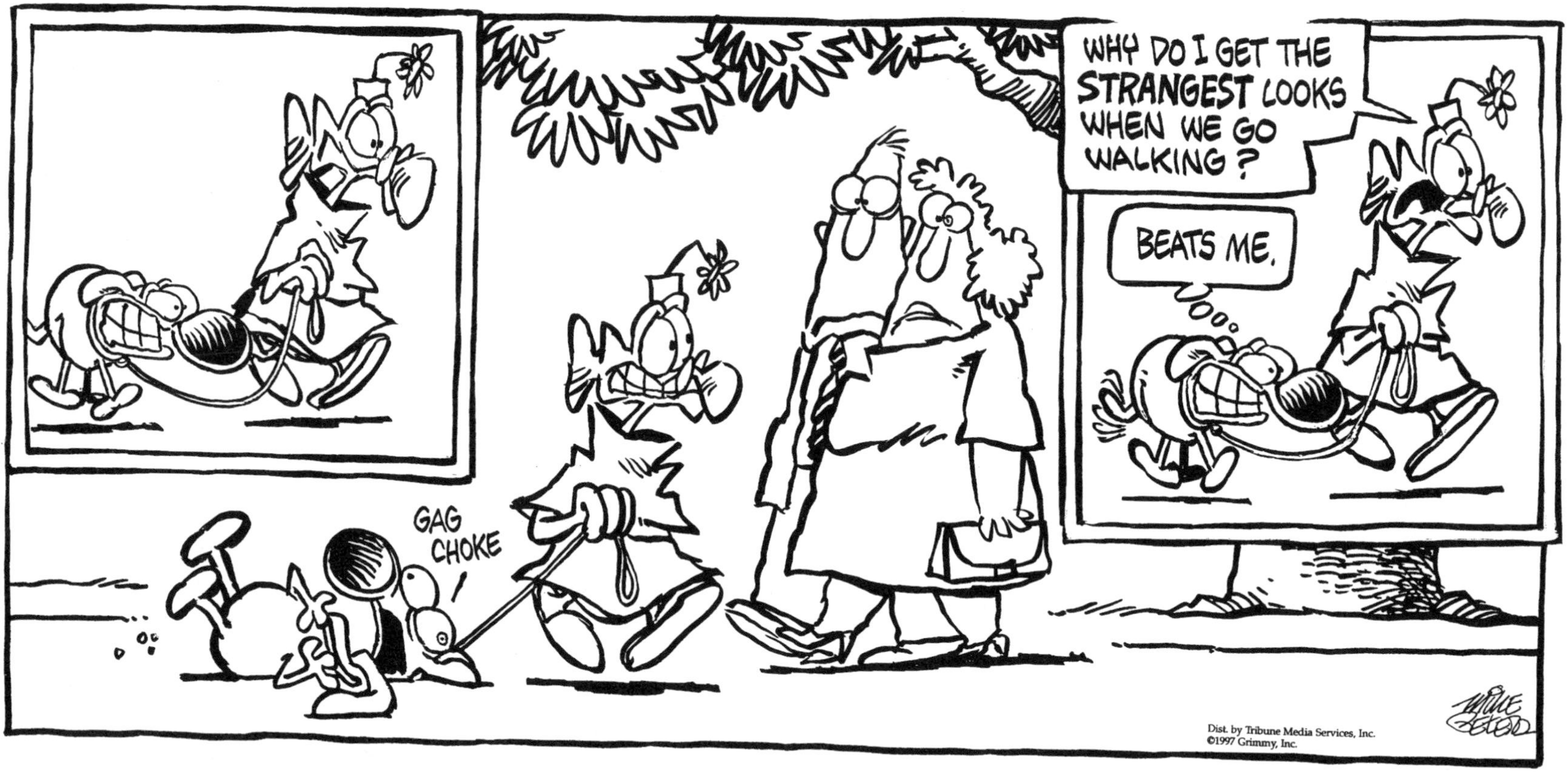
GAG
CHOKE
WHY DO I GET THE STRANGEST LOOKS WHEN WE GO WALKING?
BEATS ME.

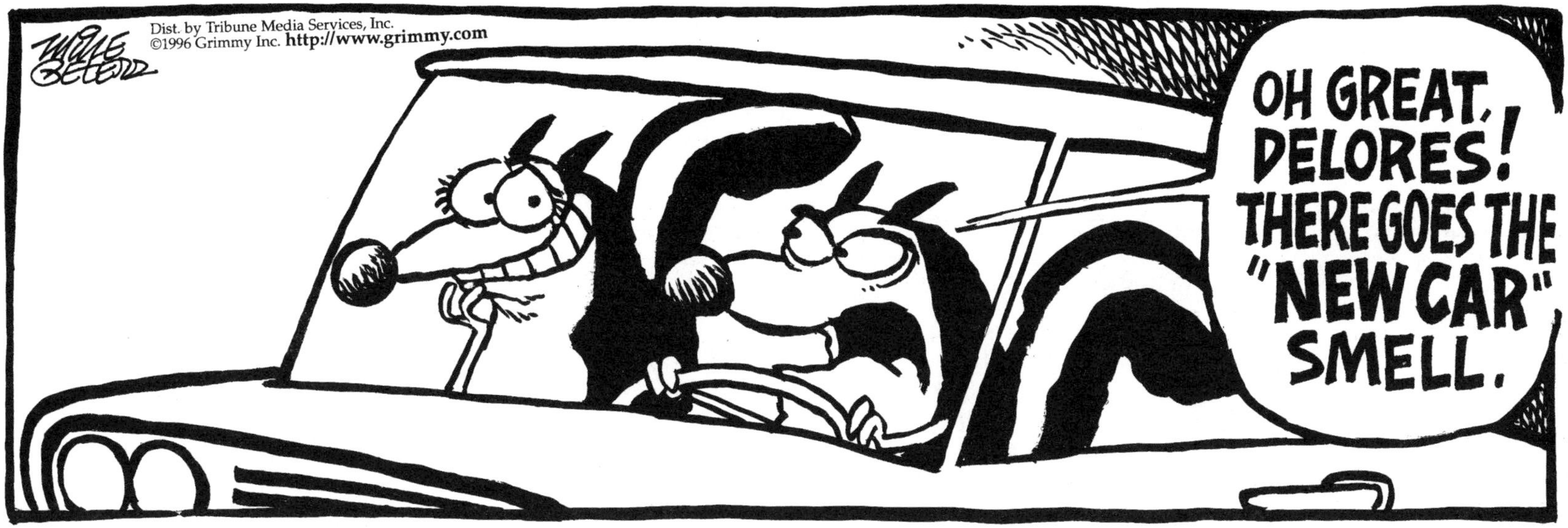
Dist. by Tribune Media Services, Inc.
©1996 Grimmy Inc. http://www.grimmy.com
OH GREAT, DELORES! THERE GOES THE "NEW CAR" SMELL.

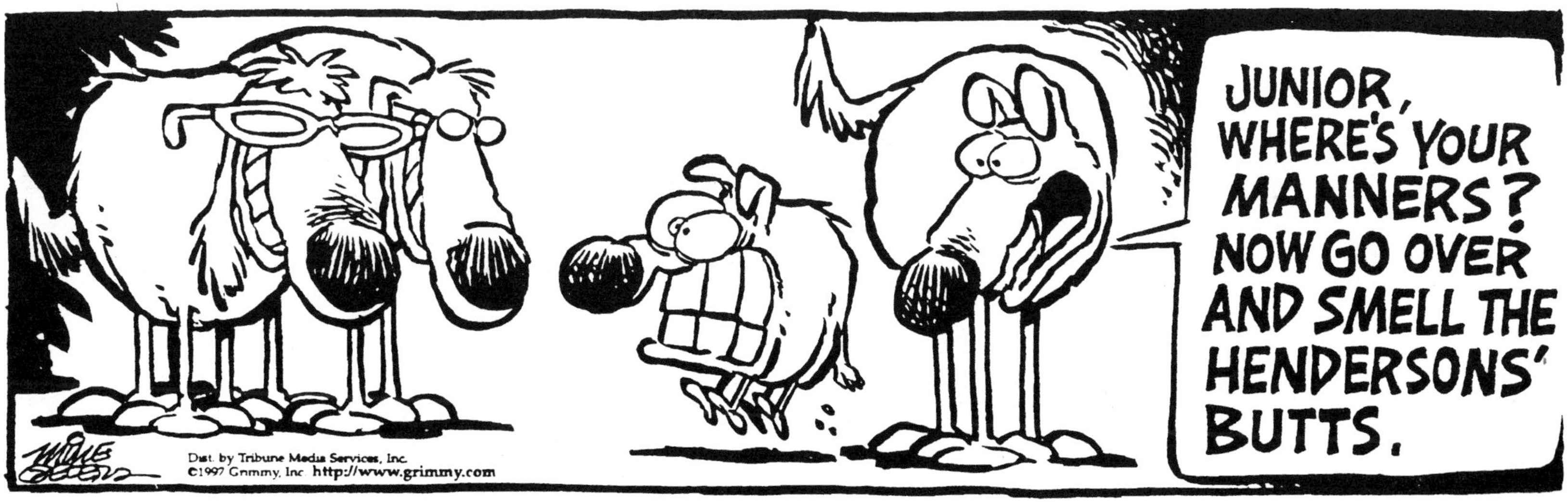
JUNIOR, WHERE'S YOUR MANNERS? NOW GO OVER AND SMELL THE HENDERSONS' BUTTS.
Dist. by Tribune Media Services, Inc.
©1997 Grimmy, Inc http://www.grimmy.com

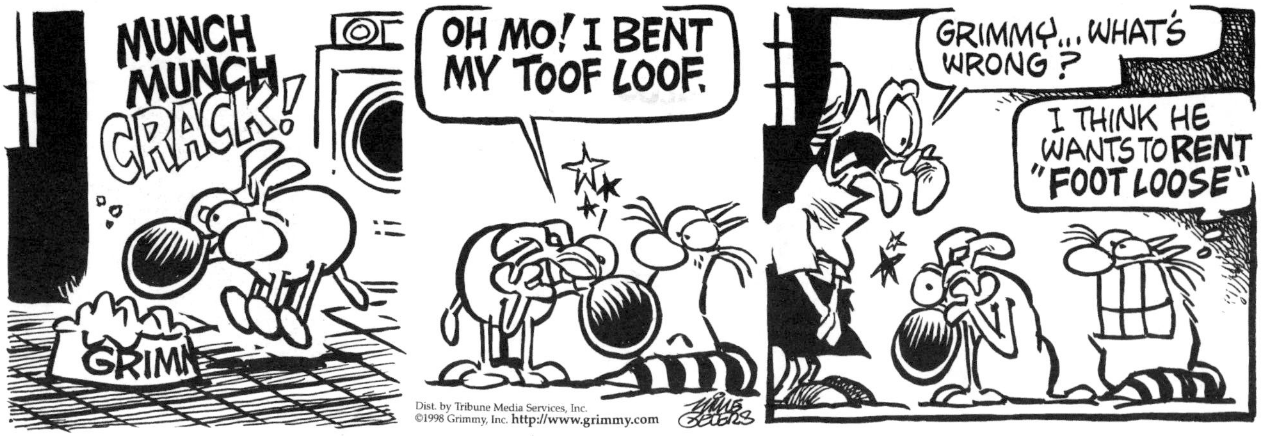
MUNCH MUNCH CRACK!
GRIMM
OH MO! I BENT MY TOOF LOOF.
Dist. by Tribune Media Services, Inc. ©1998 Grimmy, Inc. http://www.grimmy.com
GRIMMY... WHAT'S WRONG?
I THINK HE WANTS TO RENT "FOOT LOOSE"

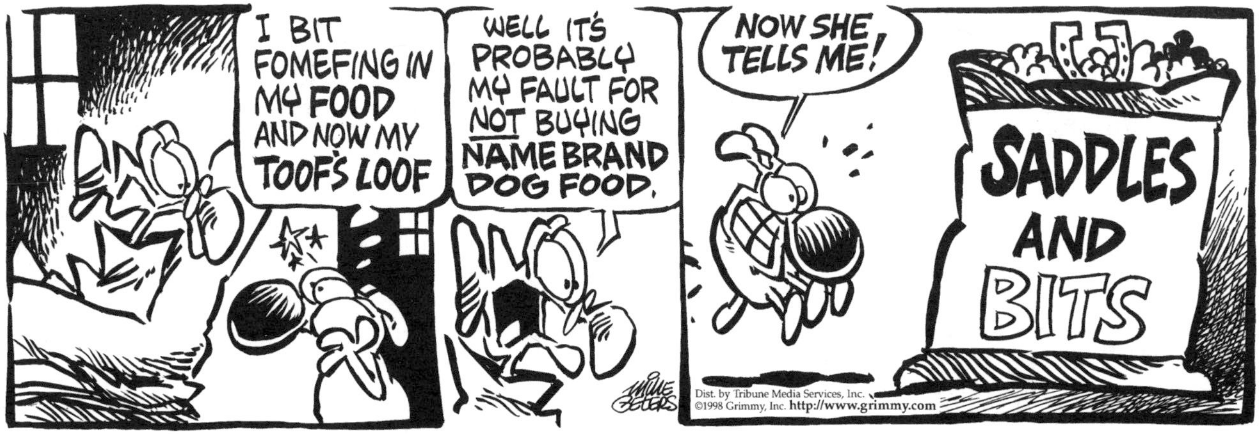
I BIT FOMEFING IN MY FOOD AND NOW MY TOOF'S LOOF
WELL IT'S PROBABLY MY FAULT FOR NOT BUYING NAME BRAND DOG FOOD.
NOW SHE TELLS ME!
SADDLES AND BITS
Dist. by Tribune Media Services, Inc. ©1998 Grimmy, Inc. http://www.grimmy.com

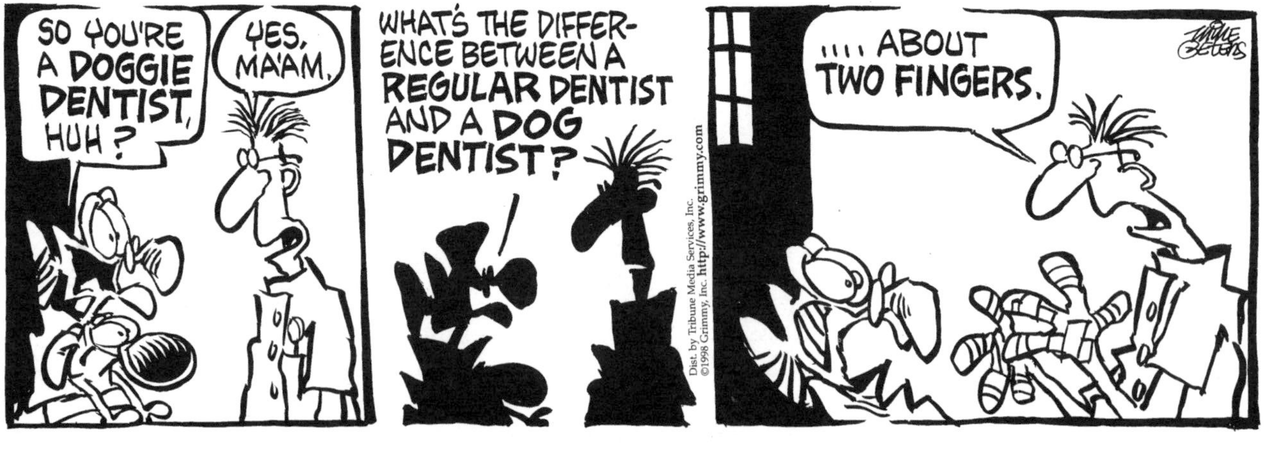
SO YOU'RE A DOGGIE DENTIST, HUH?
YES, MA'AM.
WHAT'S THE DIFFERENCE BETWEEN A REGULAR DENTIST AND A DOG DENTIST?
Dist. by Tribune Media Services, Inc. ©1998 Grimmy, Inc. http://www.grimmy.com
.... ABOUT TWO FINGERS.

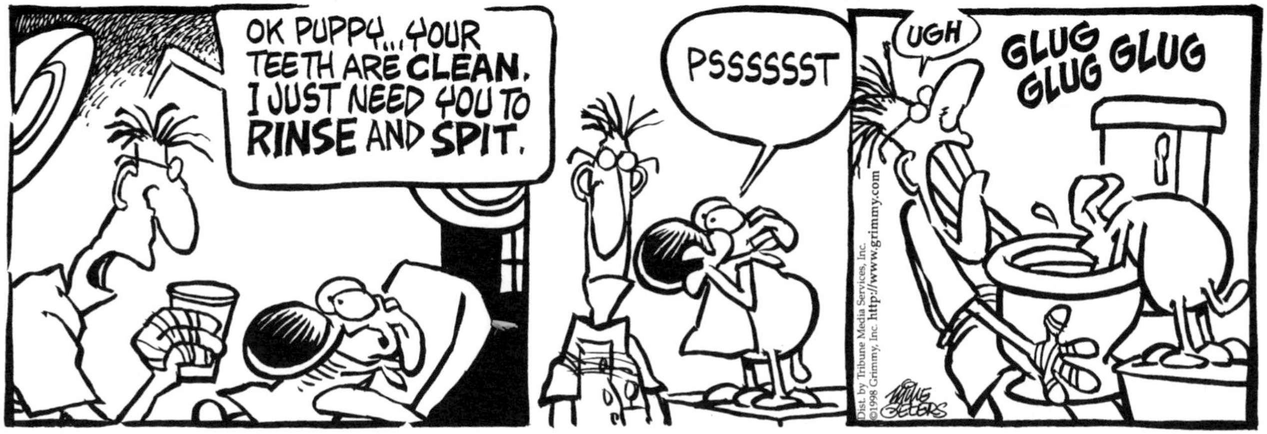
OK PUPPY... YOUR TEETH ARE CLEAN. I JUST NEED YOU TO RINSE AND SPIT.
PSSSSSST
UGH
GLUG GLUG GLUG
Dist. by Tribune Media Services, Inc. ©1998 Grimmy, Inc. http://www.grimmy.com

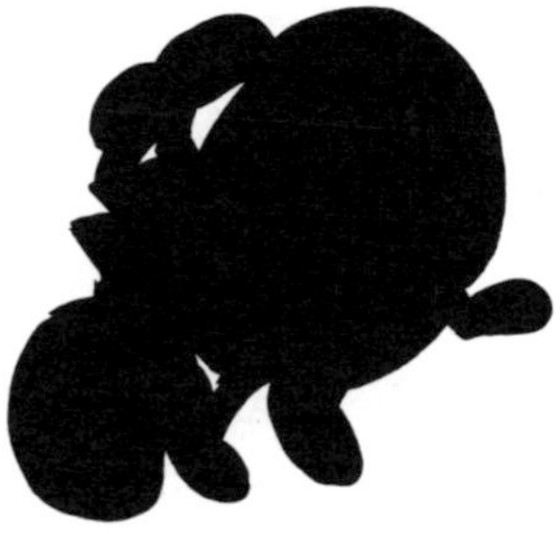

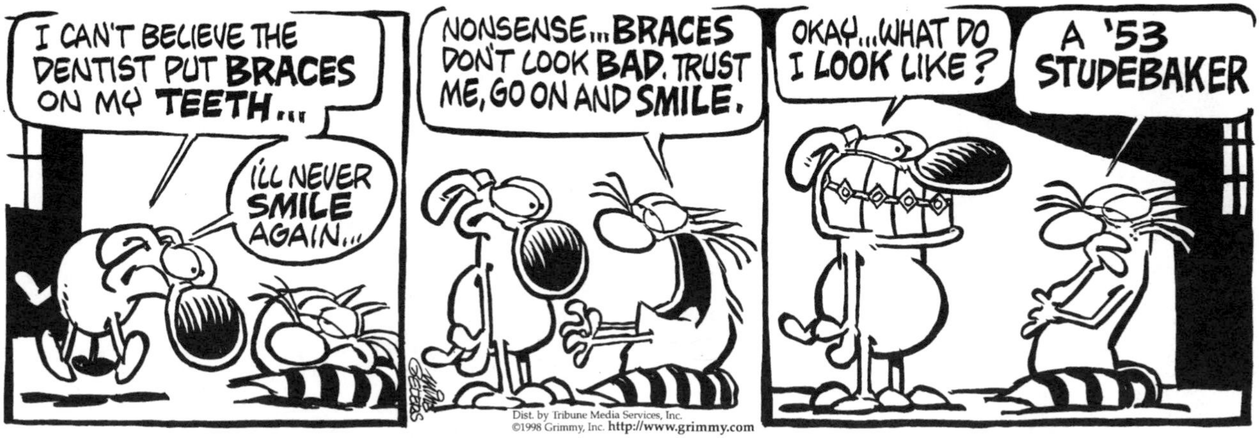
I CAN'T BELIEVE THE DENTIST PUT BRACES ON MY TEETH...
I'LL NEVER SMILE AGAIN...
NONSENSE... BRACES DON'T LOOK BAD. TRUST ME, GO ON AND SMILE.
OKAY... WHAT DO I LOOK LIKE?
A '53 STUDEBAKER
Dist. by Tribune Media Services, Inc. ©1998 Grimmy, Inc. http://www.grimmy.com

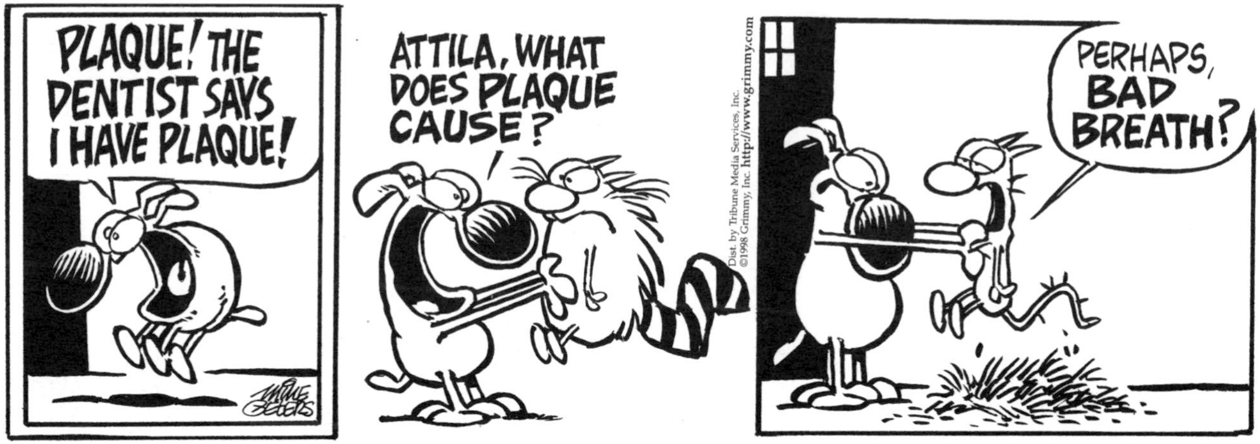
PLAQUE! THE DENTIST SAYS I HAVE PLAQUE!
ATTILA, WHAT DOES PLAQUE CAUSE?
PERHAPS, BAD BREATH?
Dist. by Tribune Media Services, Inc. ©1998 Grimmy, Inc. http://www.grimmy.com

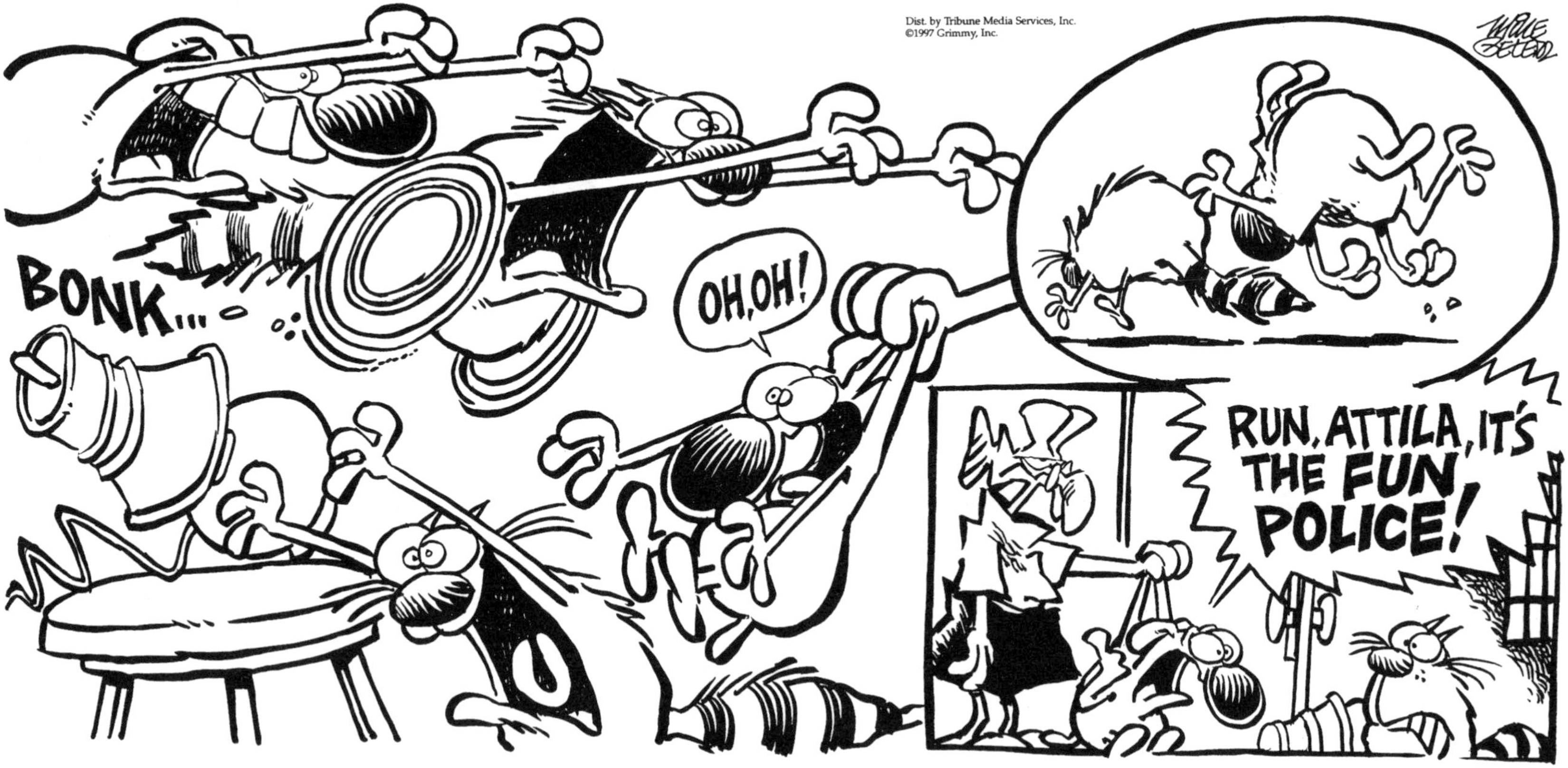
BONK...
OH,OH!
RUN, ATTILA, IT'S THE FUN POLICE!
Dist. by Tribune Media Services, Inc.
©1997 Grimmy, Inc.

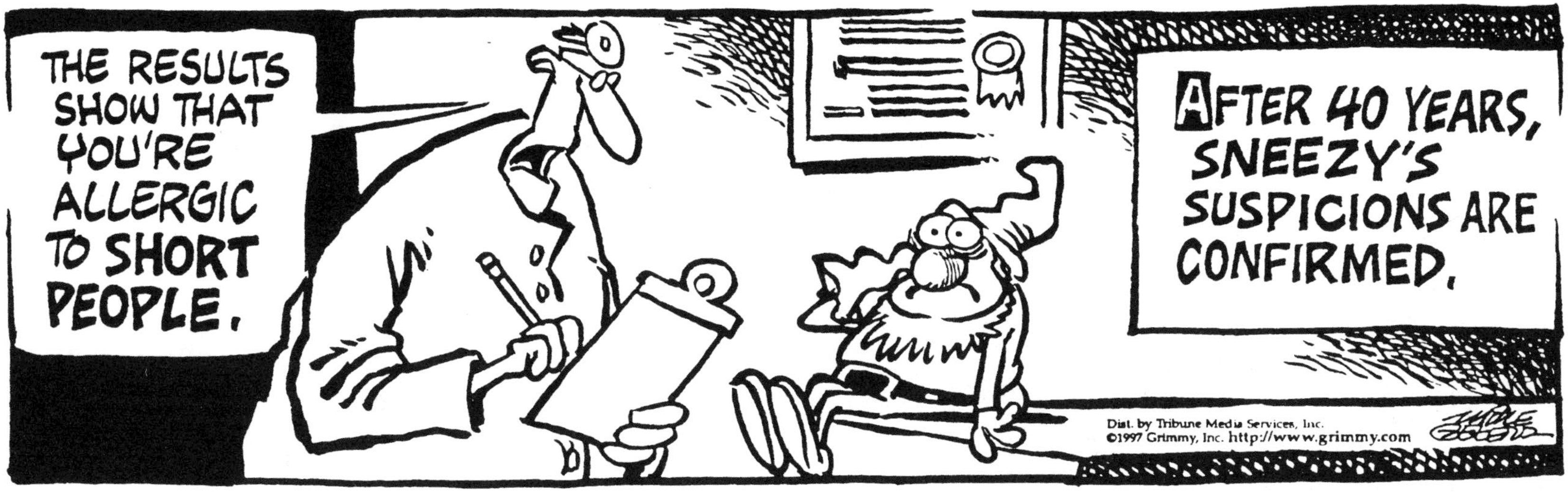

THE RESULTS SHOW THAT YOU'RE ALLERGIC TO SHORT PEOPLE.
AFTER 40 YEARS, SNEEZY'S SUSPICIONS ARE CONFIRMED.
Dist. by Tribune Media Services, Inc.
©1997 Grimmy, Inc. http://www.grimmy.com

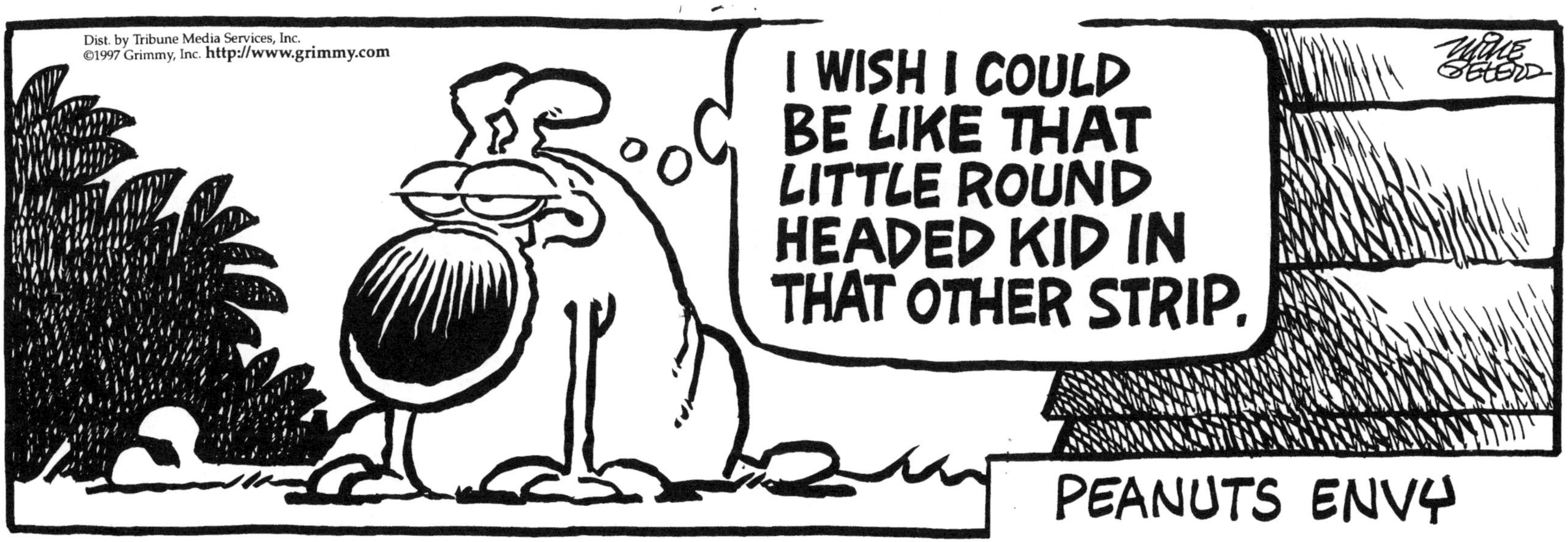

Dist. by Tribune Media Services, Inc.
©1997 Grimmy, Inc. http://www.grimmy.com
I WISH I COULD BE LIKE THAT LITTLE ROUND HEADED KID IN THAT OTHER STRIP.
PEANUTS ENVY

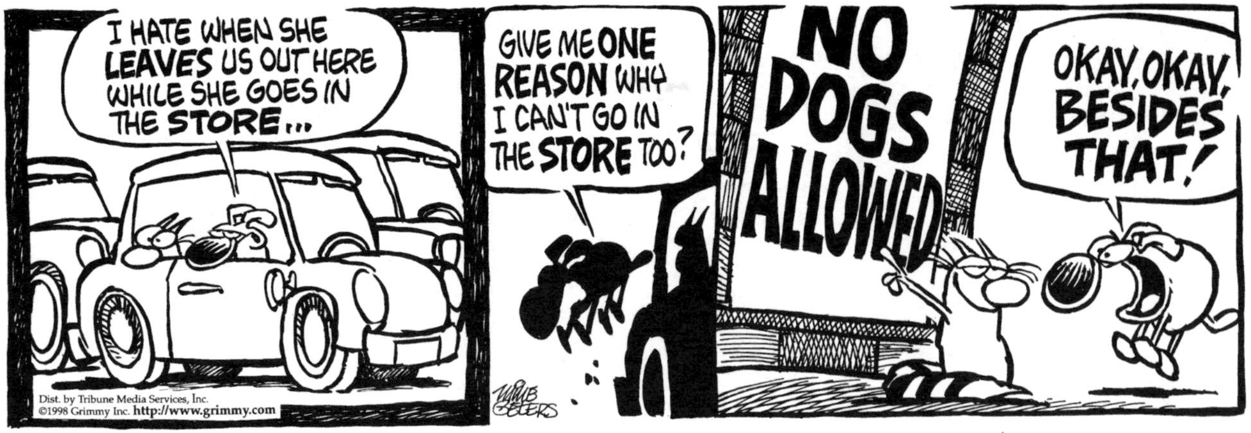
I HATE WHEN SHE LEAVES US OUT HERE WHILE SHE GOES IN THE STORE...
Dist. by Tribune Media Services, Inc. ©1998 Grimmy Inc. http://www.grimmy.com
GIVE ME ONE REASON WHY I CAN'T GO IN THE STORE TOO?
NO DOGS ALLOWED
OKAY, OKAY, BESIDES THAT!

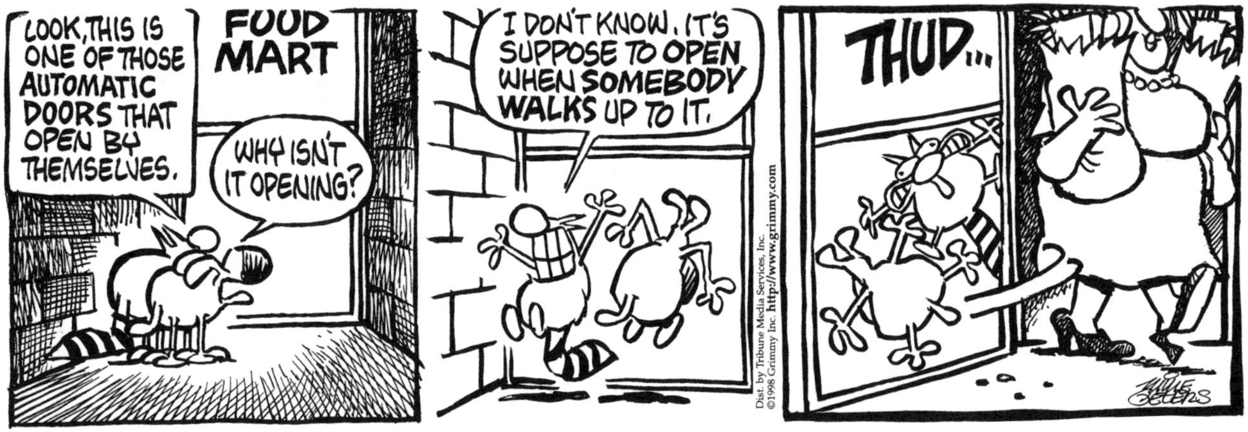
LOOK, THIS IS ONE OF THOSE AUTOMATIC DOORS THAT OPEN BY THEMSELVES.
FOOD MART
WHY ISN'T IT OPENING?
I DON'T KNOW. IT'S SUPPOSE TO OPEN WHEN SOMEBODY WALKS UP TO IT.
Dist. by Tribune Media Services, Inc. ©1998 Grimmy Inc. http://www.grimmy.com
THUD...

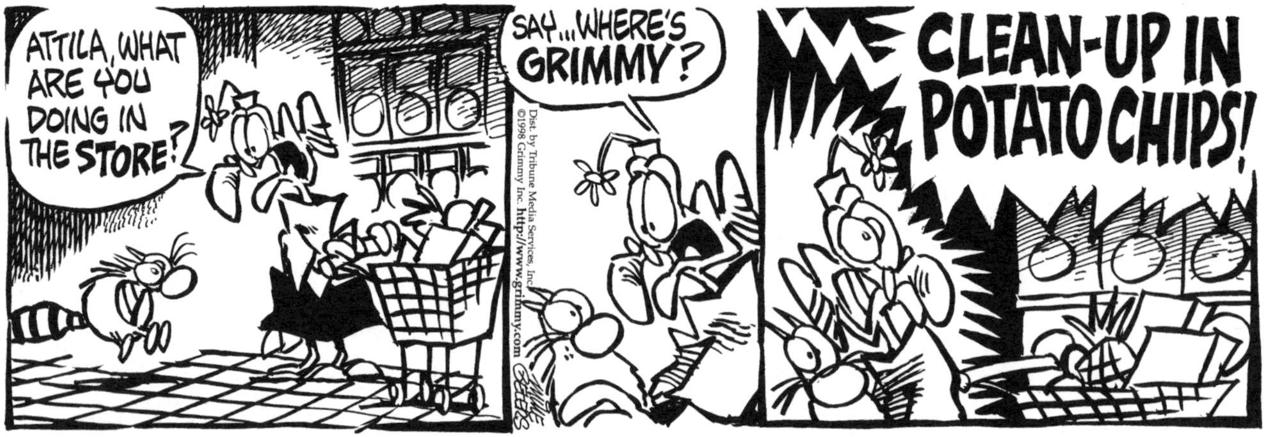
ATTILA, WHAT ARE YOU DOING IN THE STORE?
SAY... WHERE'S GRIMMY?
Dist. by Tribune Media Services, Inc. ©1998 Grimmy Inc. http://www.grimmy.com
CLEAN-UP IN POTATO CHIPS!

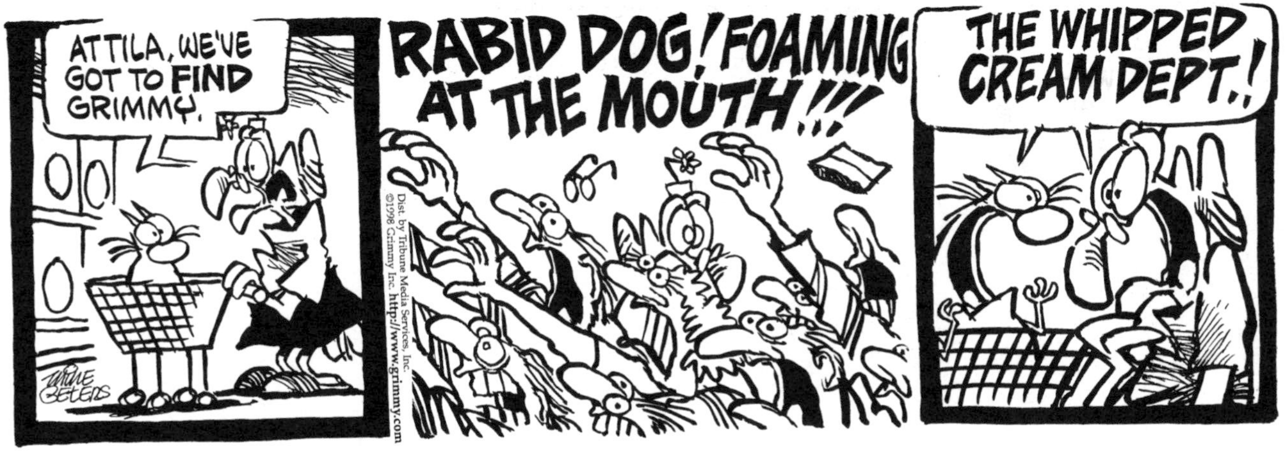
ATTILA, WE'VE GOT TO FIND GRIMMY.
RABID DOG! FOAMING AT THE MOUTH!!!
THE WHIPPED CREAM DEPT.!
Dist. by Tribune Media Services, Inc.
©1998 Grimmy Inc. http://www.grimmy.com

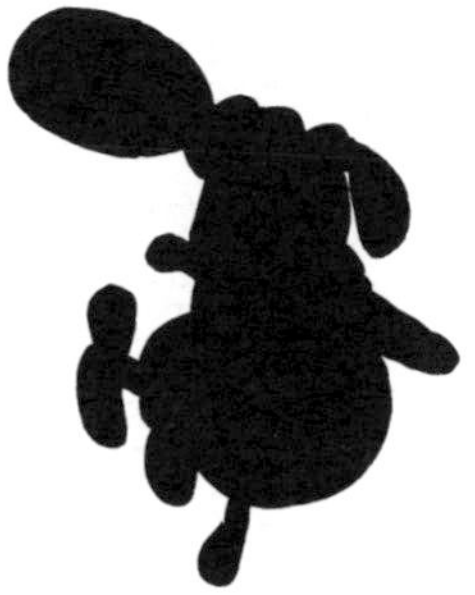

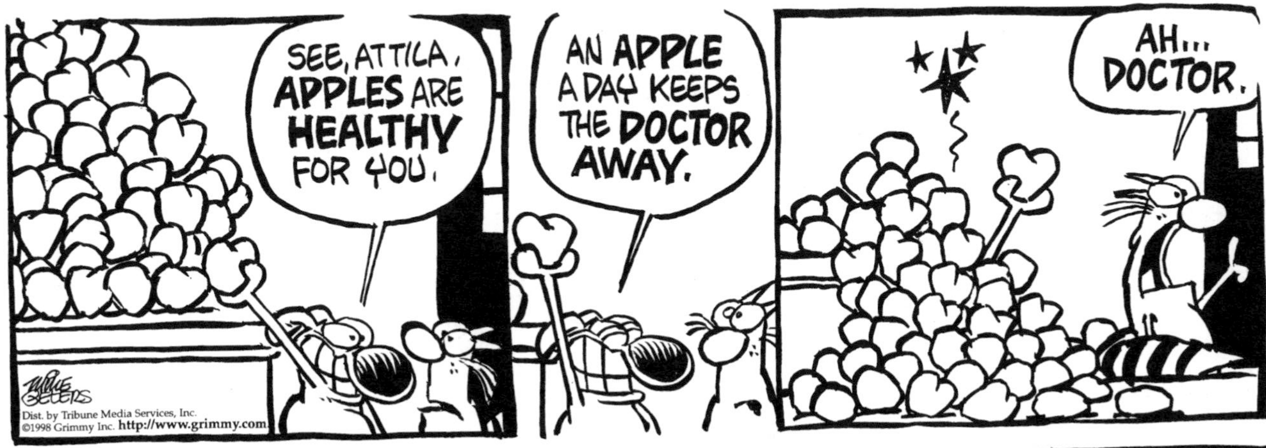
SEE, ATTILA, APPLES ARE HEALTHY FOR YOU.
AN APPLE A DAY KEEPS THE DOCTOR AWAY.
AH... DOCTOR.
Dist. by Tribune Media Services, Inc.
©1998 Grimmy Inc. http://www.grimmy.com

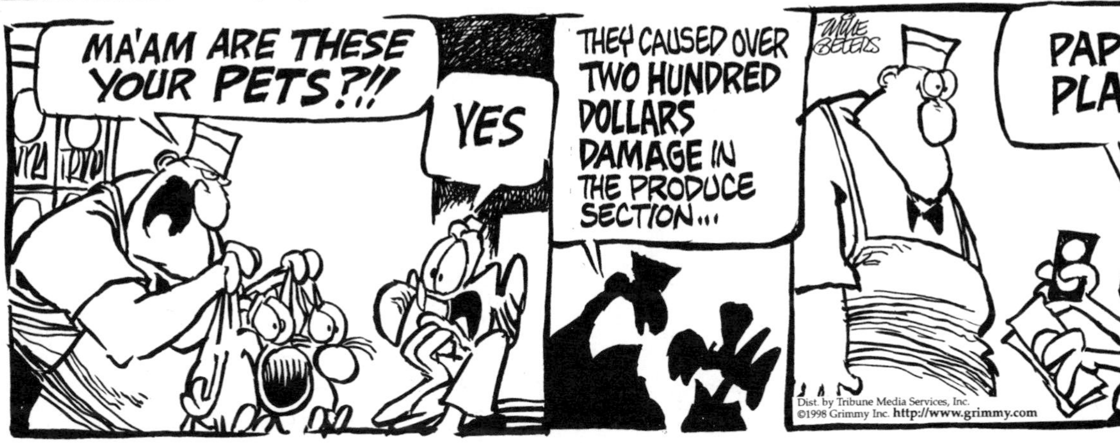
MA'AM ARE THESE YOUR PETS?!!
YES
THEY CAUSED OVER TWO HUNDRED DOLLARS DAMAGE IN THE PRODUCE SECTION...
PAPER OR PLASTIC?
Dist. by Tribune Media Services, Inc.
©1998 Grimmy Inc. http://www.grimmy.com

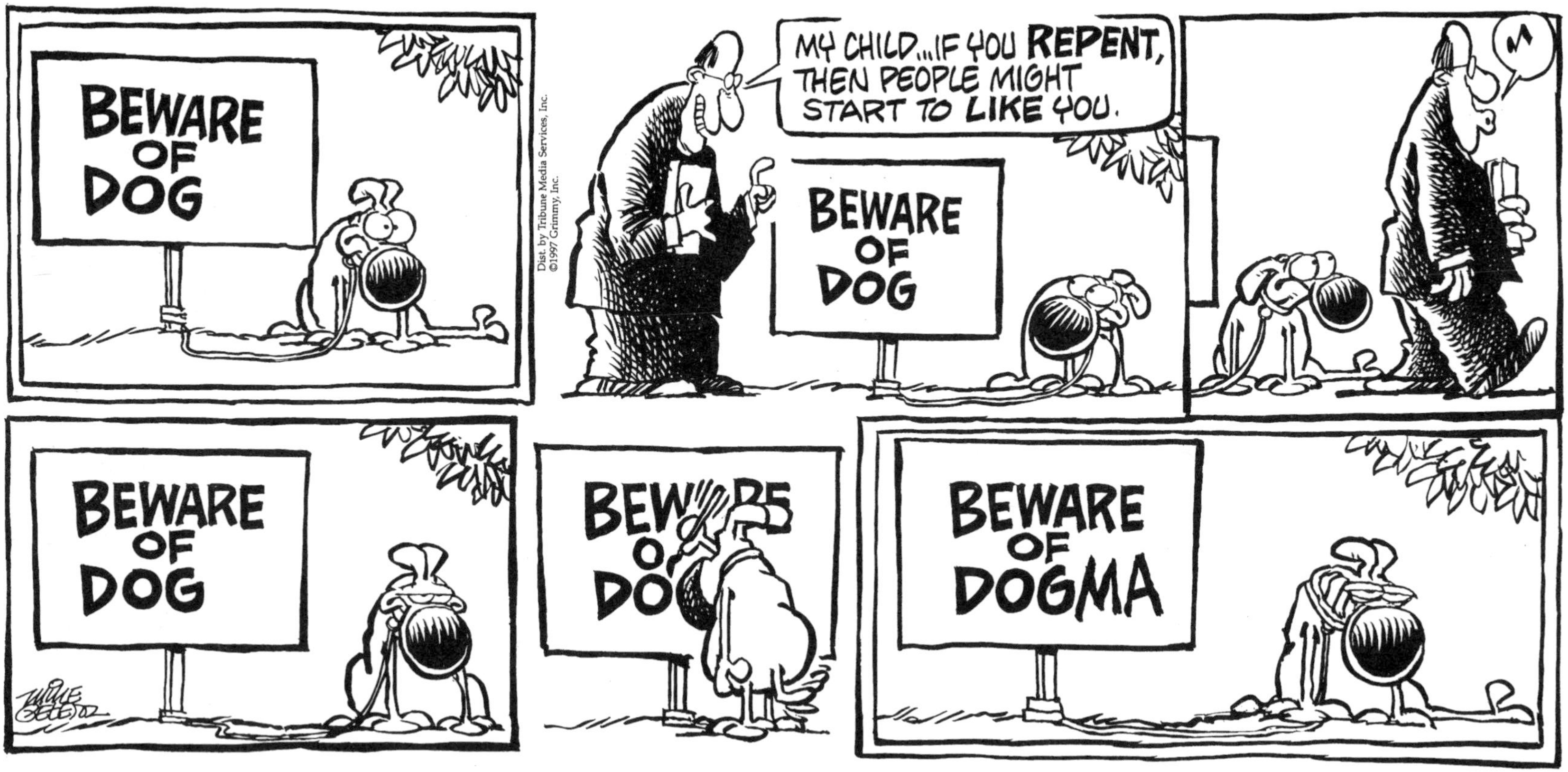
BEWARE OF DOG
Dist. by Tribune Media Services, Inc. ©1997 Grimmy, Inc.
MY CHILD... IF YOU REPENT, THEN PEOPLE MIGHT START TO LIKE YOU.
BEWARE OF DOG
BEWARE OF DOG
BEWARE OF DOGMA

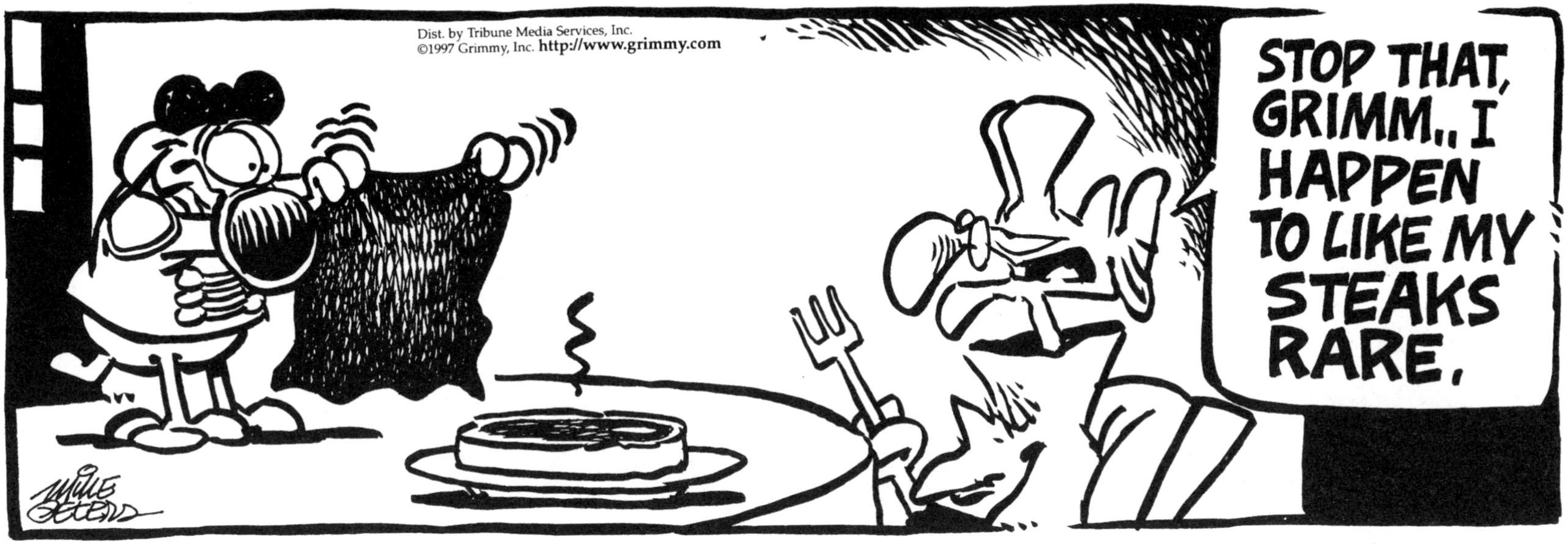
Dist. by Tribune Media Services, Inc.
©1997 Grimmy, Inc. http://www.grimmy.com
STOP THAT, GRIMM.. I HAPPEN TO LIKE MY STEAKS RARE.

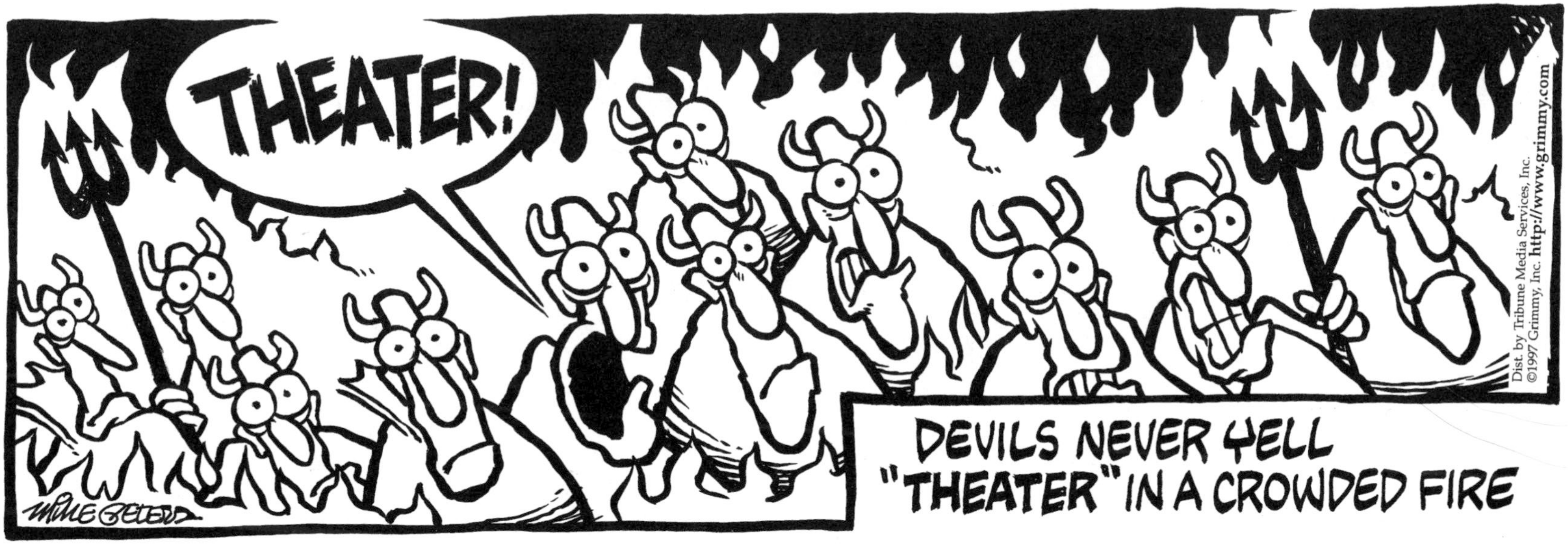
THEATER!
Dist. by Tribune Media Services, Inc.
©1997 Grimmy, Inc. http://www.grimmy.com
DEVILS NEVER YELL "THEATER" IN A CROWDED FIRE

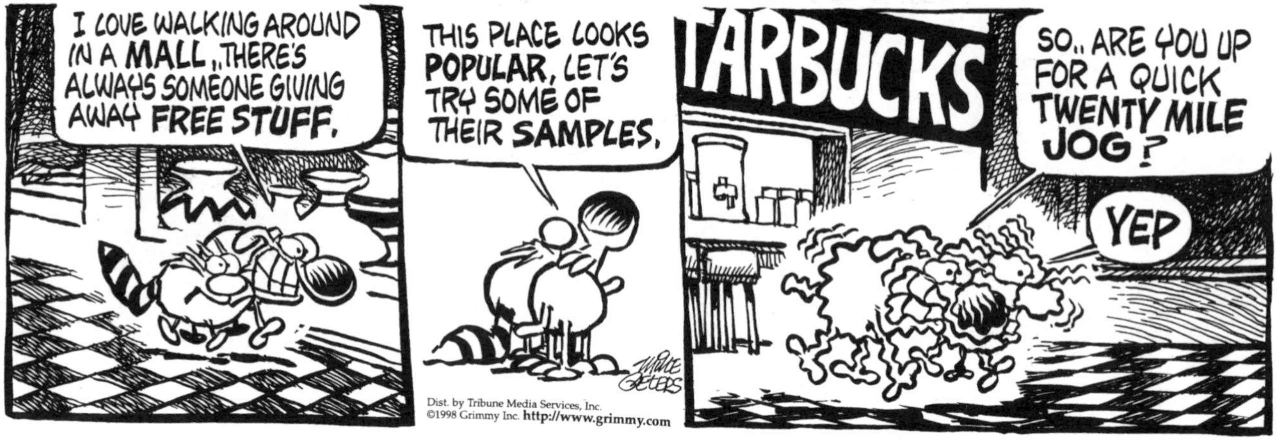

I LOVE WALKING AROUND IN A MALL.. THERE'S ALWAYS SOMEONE GIVING AWAY FREE STUFF.
THIS PLACE LOOKS POPULAR, LET'S TRY SOME OF THEIR SAMPLES.
TARBUCKS
SO.. ARE YOU UP FOR A QUICK TWENTY MILE JOG?
YEP
Dist. by Tribune Media Services, Inc.
©1998 Grimmy Inc. http://www.grimmy.com

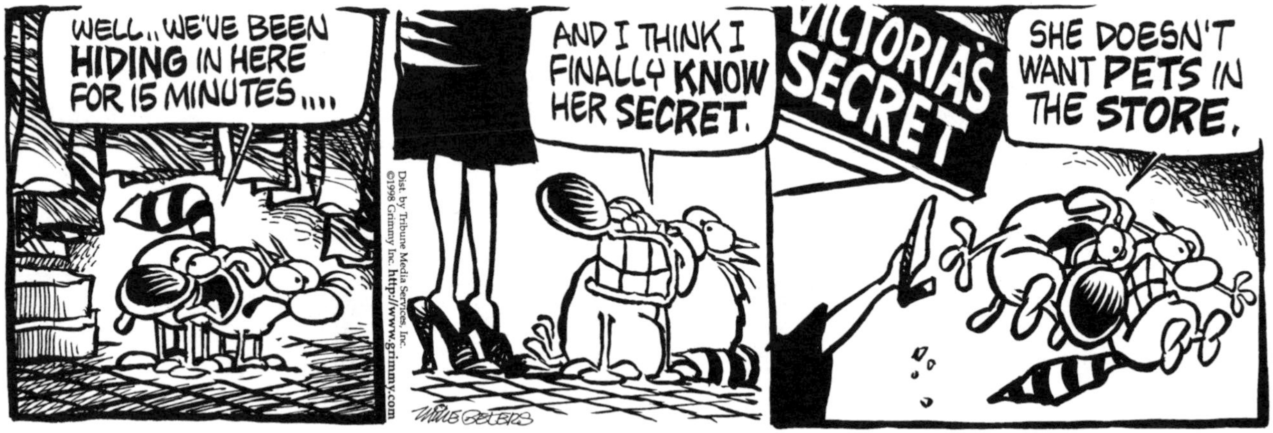

WELL.. WE'VE BEEN HIDING IN HERE FOR 15 MINUTES....
AND I THINK I FINALLY KNOW HER SECRET.
VICTORIA'S SECRET
SHE DOESN'T WANT PETS IN THE STORE.
Dist. by Tribune Media Services, Inc.
©1998 Grimmy Inc. http://www.grimmy.com

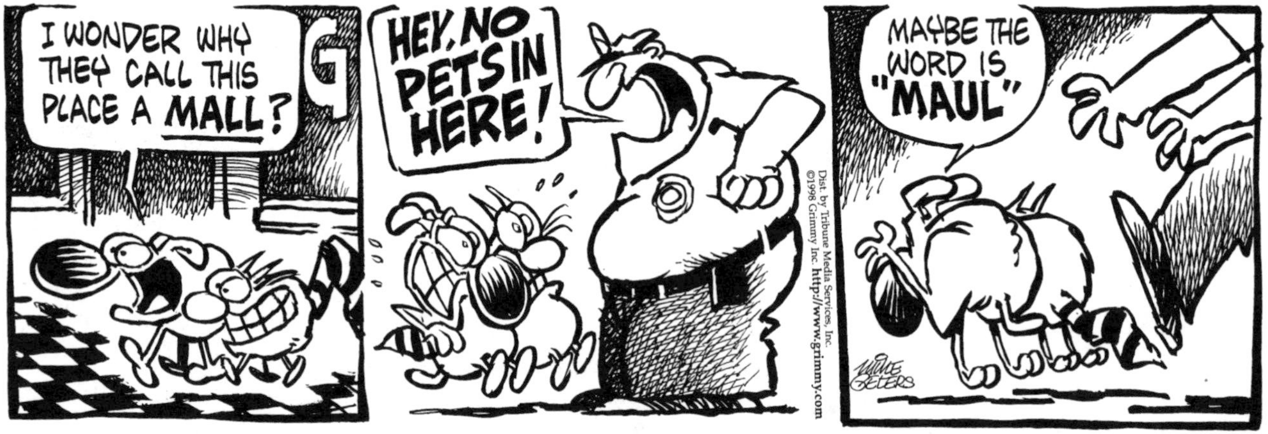

I WONDER WHY THEY CALL THIS PLACE A MALL?
HEY, NO PETS IN HERE!
MAYBE THE WORD IS "MAUL"
Dist. by Tribune Media Services, Inc.
©1998 Grimmy Inc. http://www.grimmy.com

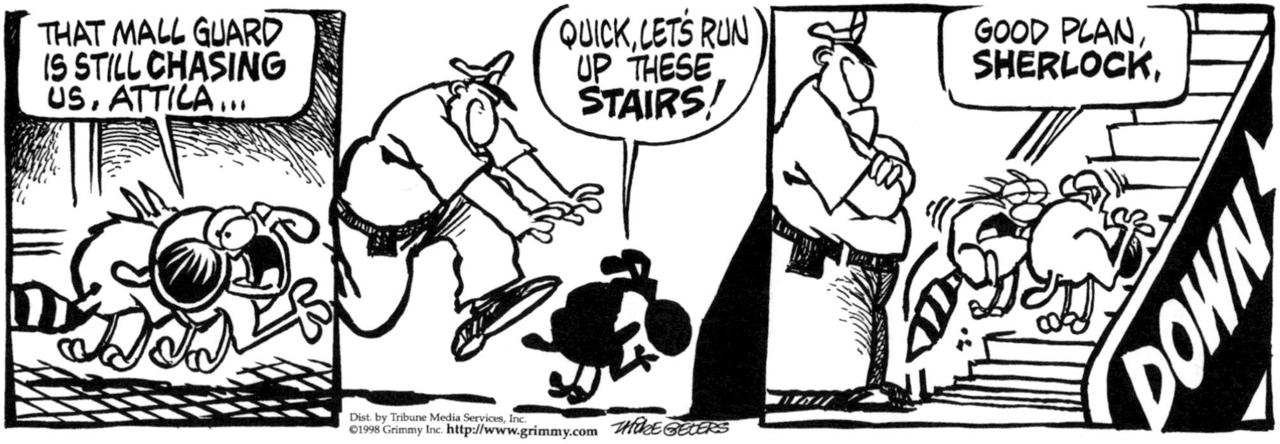
THAT MALL GUARD IS STILL CHASING US, ATTILA...
QUICK, LET'S RUN UP THESE STAIRS!
GOOD PLAN, SHERLOCK.
DOWN
Dist. by Tribune Media Services, Inc.
©1998 Grimmy Inc. http://www.grimmy.com
MIKE PETERS

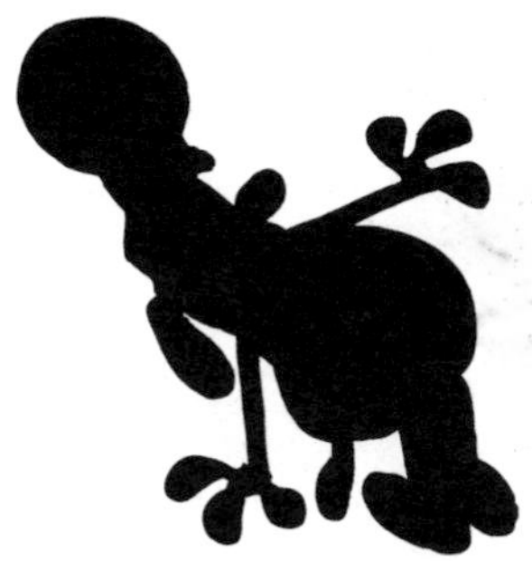

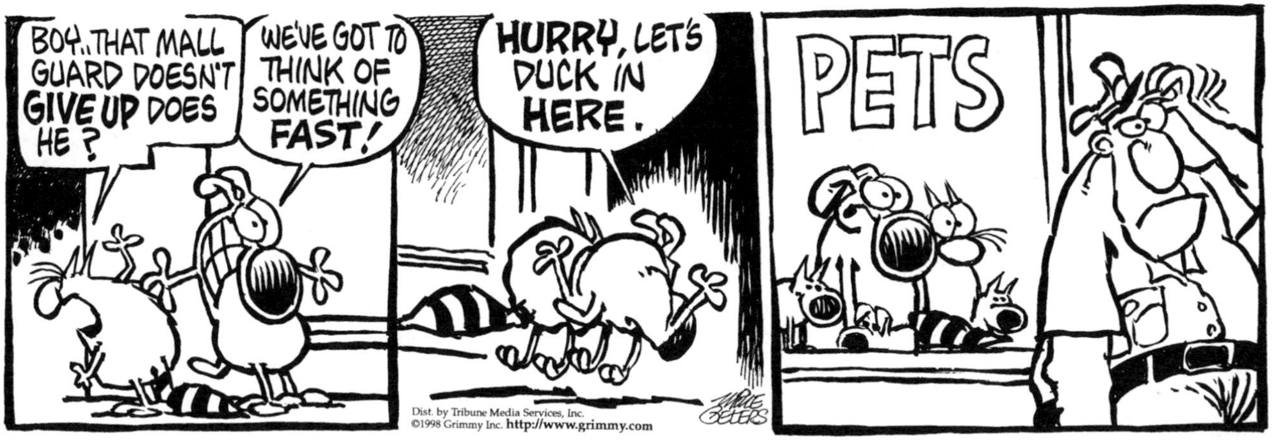
BOY.. THAT MALL GUARD DOESN'T GIVE UP DOES HE?
WE'VE GOT TO THINK OF SOMETHING FAST!
HURRY, LET'S DUCK IN HERE.
Dist. by Tribune Media Services, Inc.
©1998 Grimmy Inc. http://www.grimmy.com
MIKE PETERS
PETS

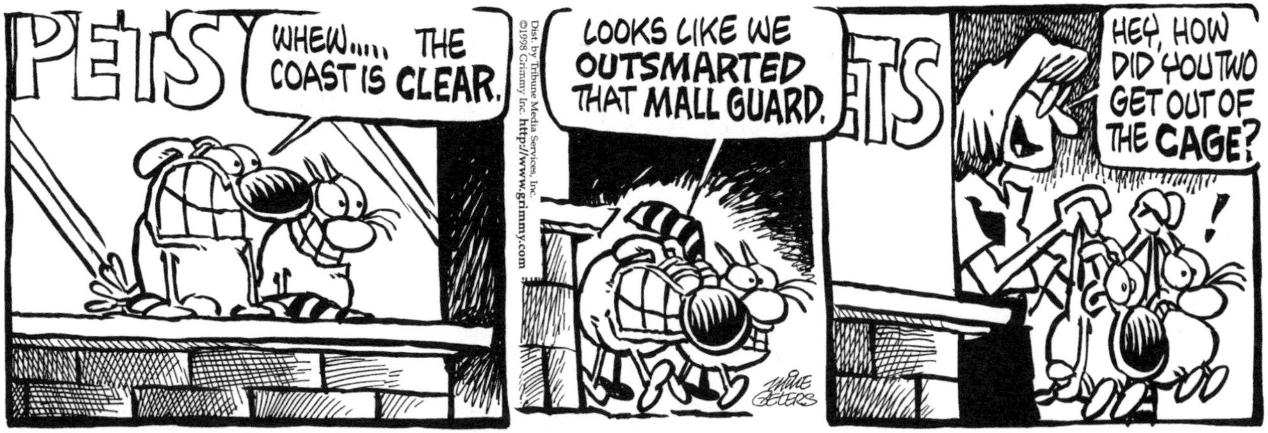
PETS
WHEW..... THE COAST IS CLEAR.
Dist. by Tribune Media Services, Inc.
©1998 Grimmy Inc. http://www.grimmy.com
LOOKS LIKE WE OUTSMARTED THAT MALL GUARD.
MIKE PETERS
ETS
HEY, HOW DID YOU TWO GET OUT OF THE CAGE?
!

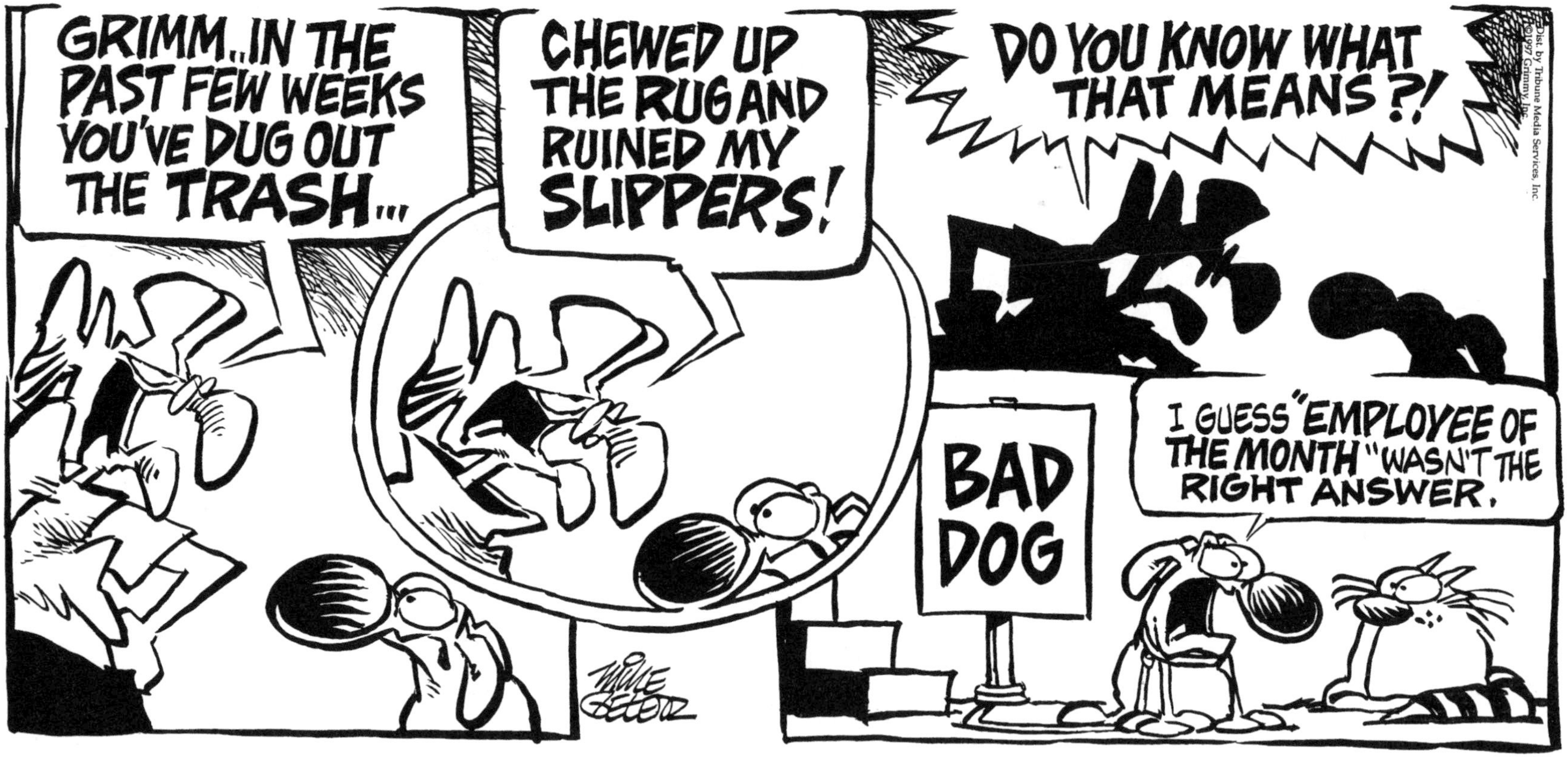
GRIMM..IN THE PAST FEW WEEKS YOU'VE DUG OUT THE TRASH...
CHEWED UP THE RUG AND RUINED MY SLIPPERS!
DO YOU KNOW WHAT THAT MEANS ?!
BAD DOG
I GUESS "EMPLOYEE OF THE MONTH" WASN'T THE RIGHT ANSWER.
MIKE PETERS
Dist. by Tribune Media Services, Inc.
©1997 Grimmy, Inc.

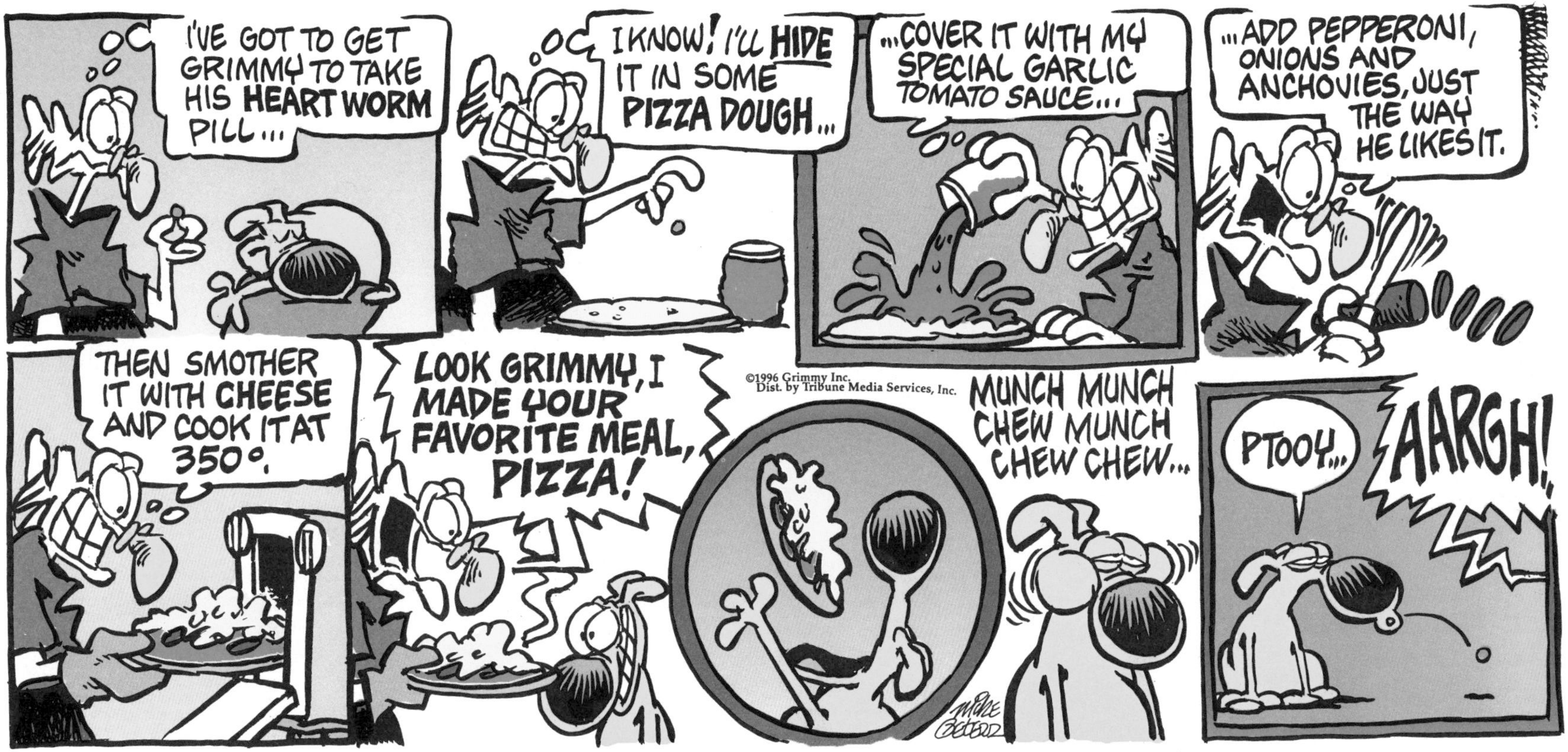
I'VE GOT TO GET GRIMMY TO TAKE HIS HEARTWORM PILL...
I KNOW! I'LL HIDE IT IN SOME PIZZA DOUGH...
...COVER IT WITH MY SPECIAL GARLIC TOMATO SAUCE...
...ADD PEPPERONI, ONIONS AND ANCHOVIES, JUST THE WAY HE LIKES IT.
THEN SMOTHER IT WITH CHEESE AND COOK IT AT 350°.
LOOK GRIMMY, I MADE YOUR FAVORITE MEAL, PIZZA!
©1996 Grimmy Inc.
Dist. by Tribune Media Services, Inc.
MUNCH MUNCH CHEW MUNCH CHEW CHEW...
PTOOY...
AARGH!

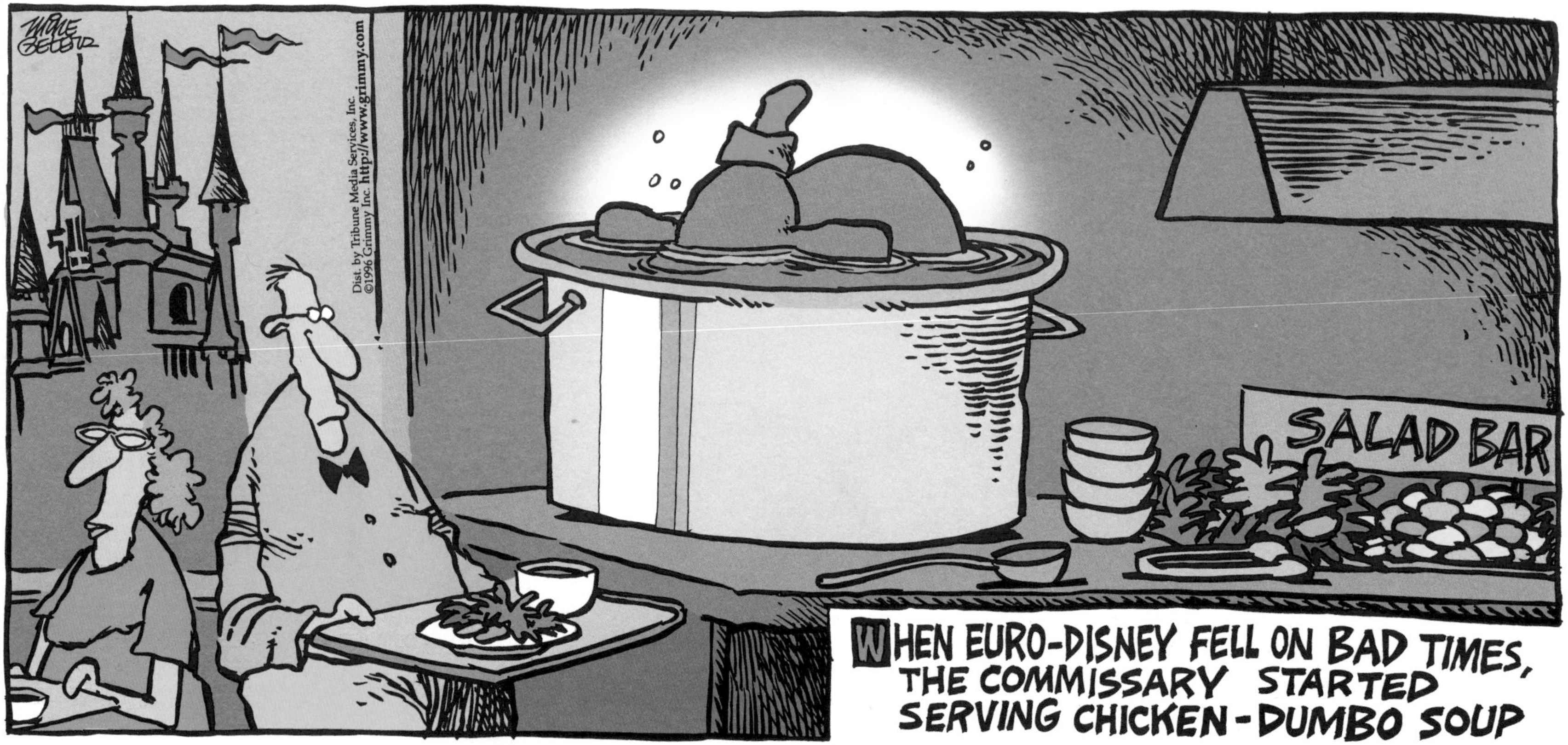
Dist. by Tribune Media Services, Inc.
©1996 Grimmy Inc. http://www.grimmy.com
SALAD BAR
WHEN EURO-DISNEY FELL ON BAD TIMES, THE COMMISSARY STARTED SERVING CHICKEN-DUMBO SOUP

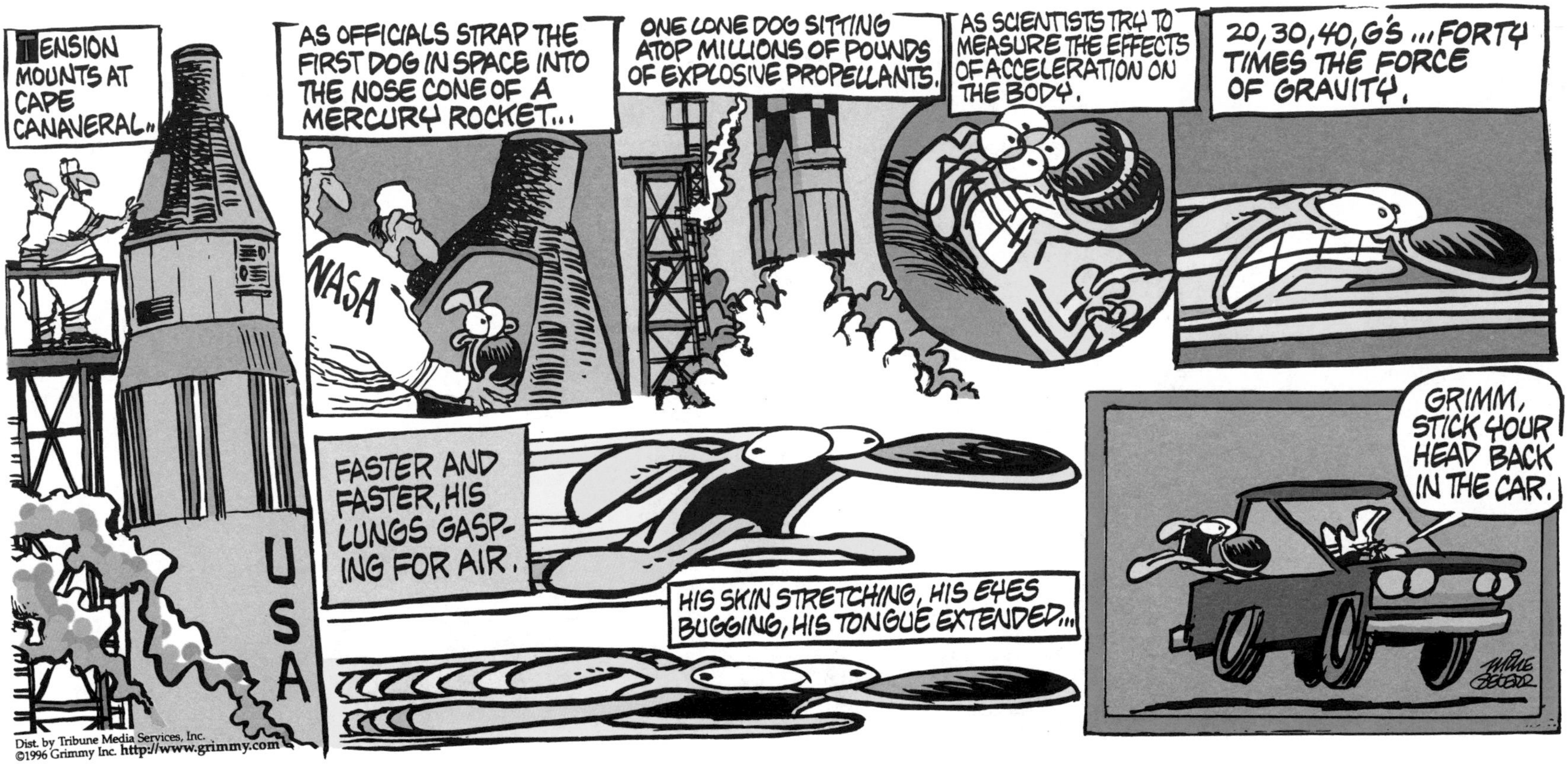
TENSION MOUNTS AT CAPE CANAVERAL..
USA
AS OFFICIALS STRAP THE FIRST DOG IN SPACE INTO THE NOSE CONE OF A MERCURY ROCKET...
NASA
ONE LONE DOG SITTING ATOP MILLIONS OF POUNDS OF EXPLOSIVE PROPELLANTS.
AS SCIENTISTS TRY TO MEASURE THE EFFECTS OF ACCELERATION ON THE BODY.
20, 30, 40, G'S ... FORTY TIMES THE FORCE OF GRAVITY.
FASTER AND FASTER, HIS LUNGS GASPING FOR AIR.
HIS SKIN STRETCHING, HIS EYES BUGGING, HIS TONGUE EXTENDED...
GRIMM, STICK YOUR HEAD BACK IN THE CAR.
Dist. by Tribune Media Services, Inc.
©1996 Grimmy Inc. http://www.grimmy.com

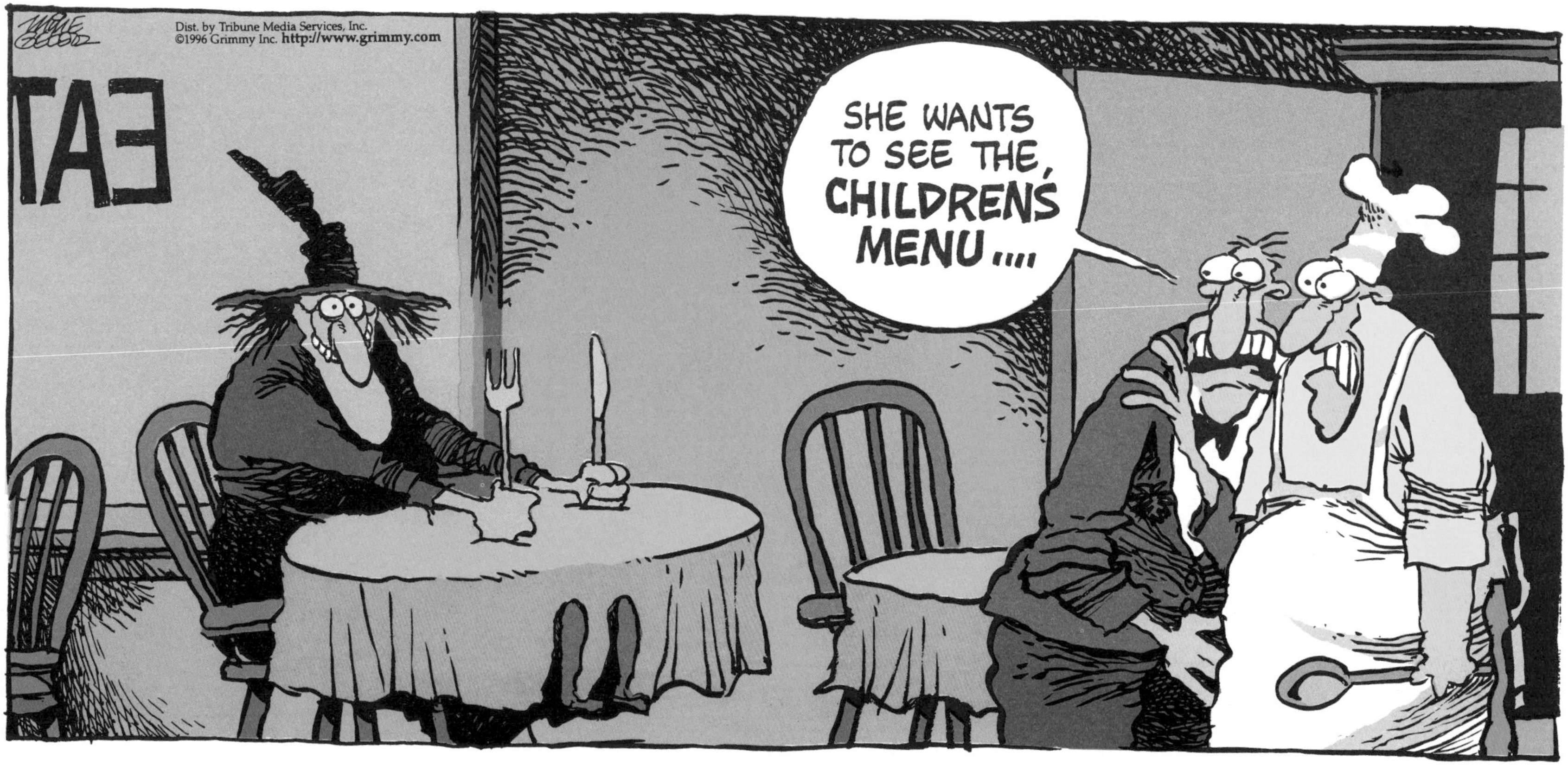

Dist. by Tribune Media Services, Inc.
©1996 Grimmy Inc. http://www.grimmy.com
EAT
SHE WANTS TO SEE THE, CHILDREN'S MENU....

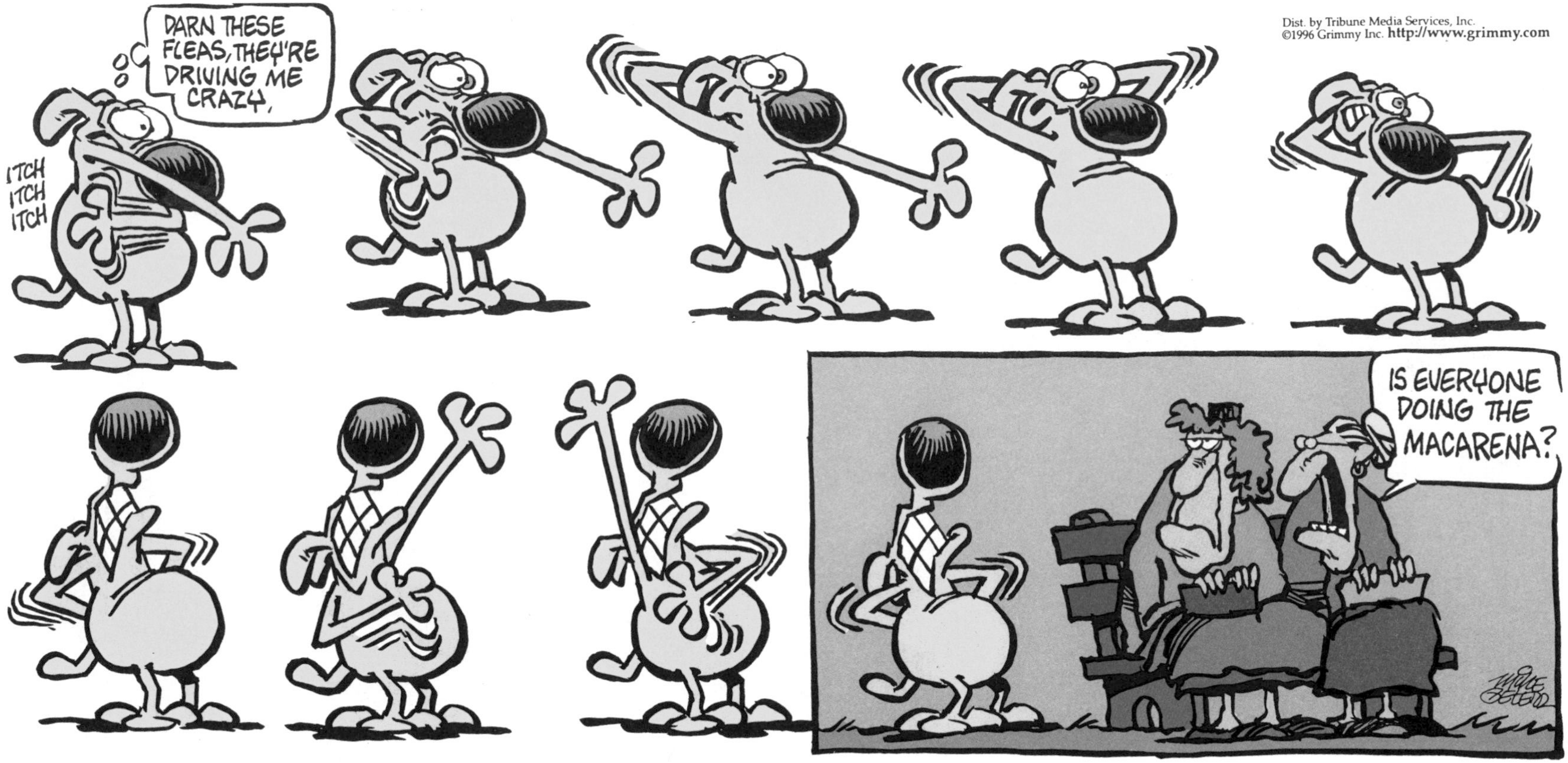
DARN THESE FLEAS, THEY'RE DRIVING ME CRAZY,
ITCH ITCH ITCH
Dist. by Tribune Media Services, Inc.
©1996 Grimmy Inc. http://www.grimmy.com
IS EVERYONE DOING THE MACARENA?

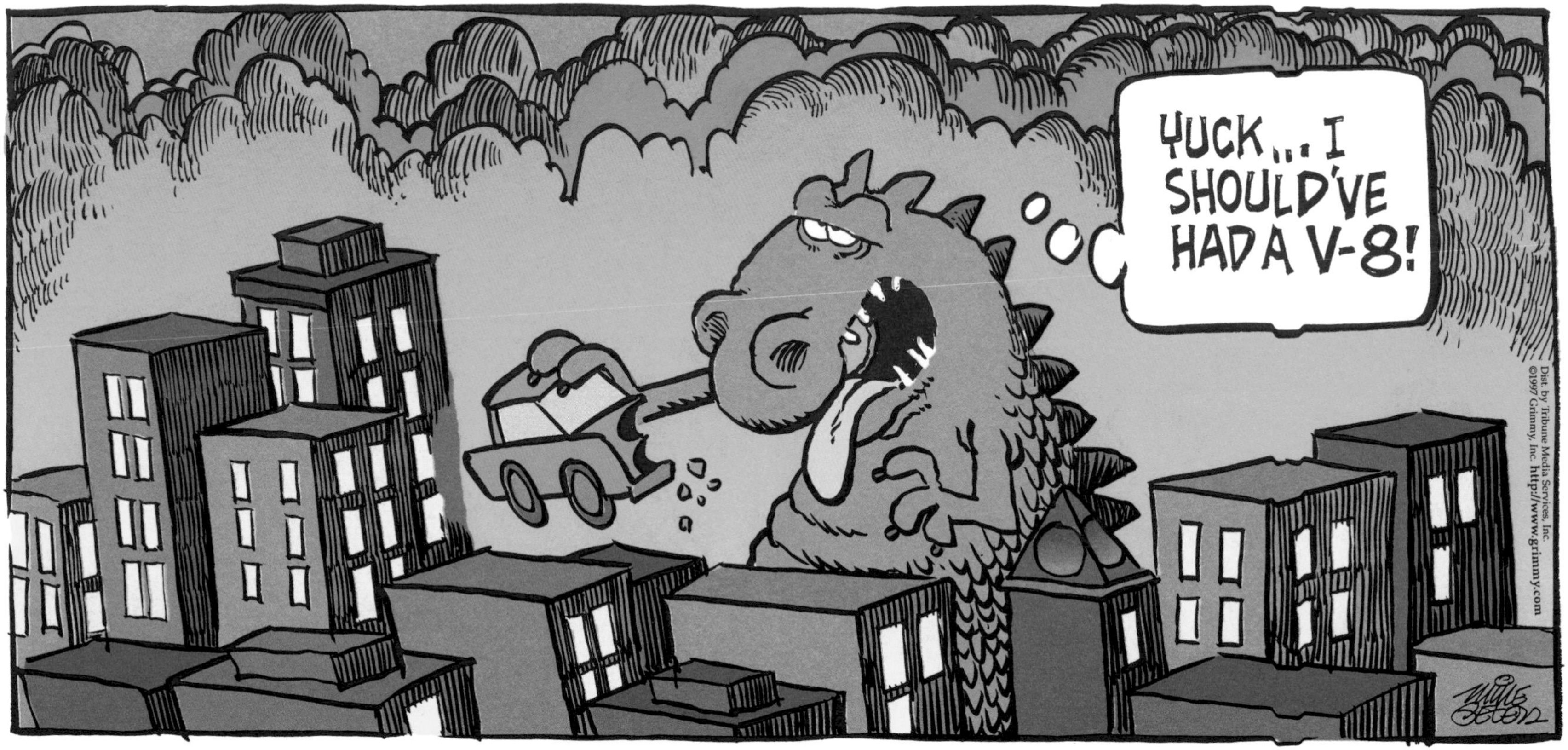
YUCK... I SHOULD'VE HAD A V-8!
Dist. by Tribune Media Services, Inc. ©1997 Grimmy, Inc. http://www.grimmy.com

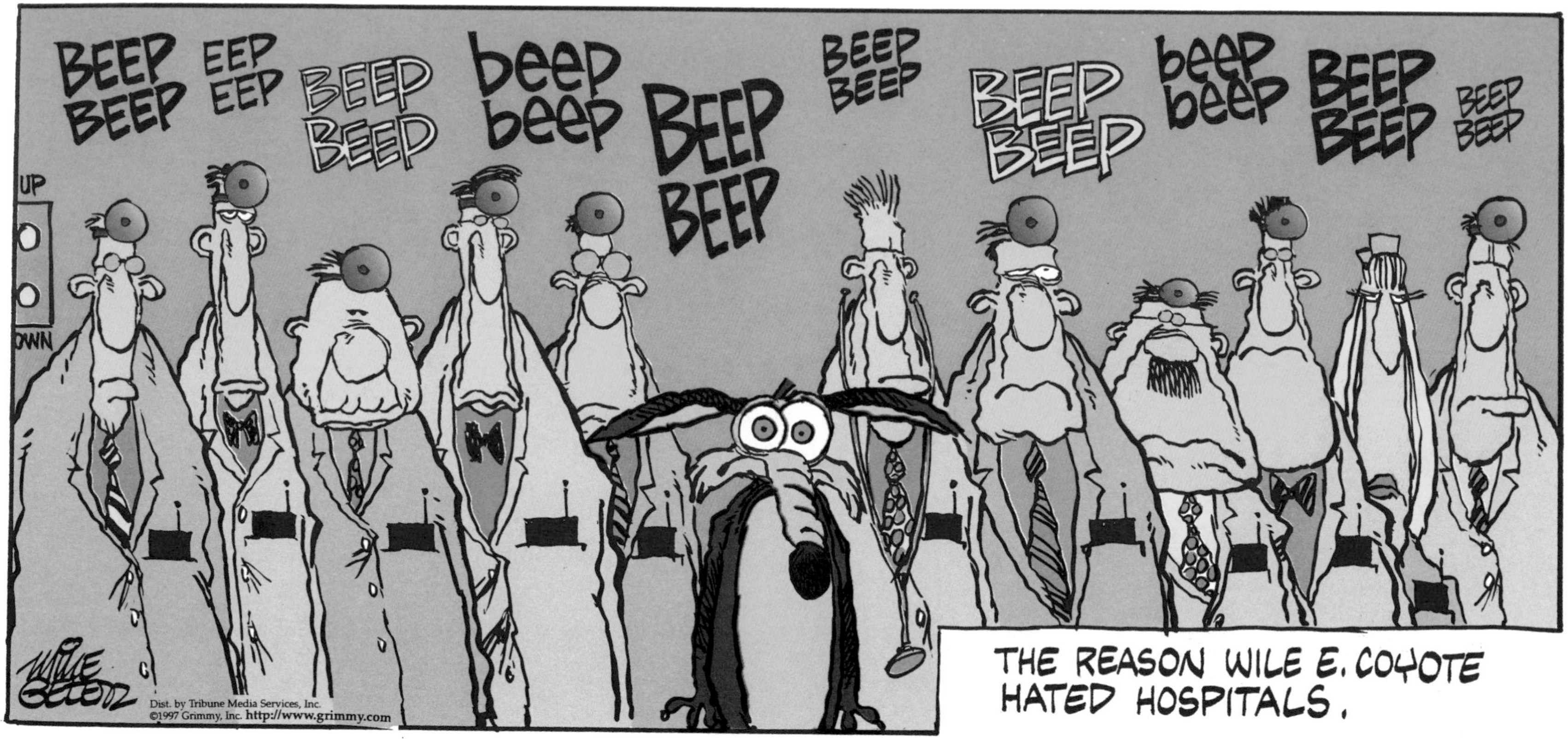
BEEP BEEP
EEP EEP
BEEP BEEP
beep beep
BEEP BEEP
BEEP BEEP
BEEP BEEP
beep beep
BEEP BEEP
BEEP BEEP
UP
DOWN
WILEY GELETZ
Dist. by Tribune Media Services, Inc.
©1997 Grimmy, Inc. http://www.grimmy.com

THE REASON WILE E. COYOTE HATED HOSPITALS.

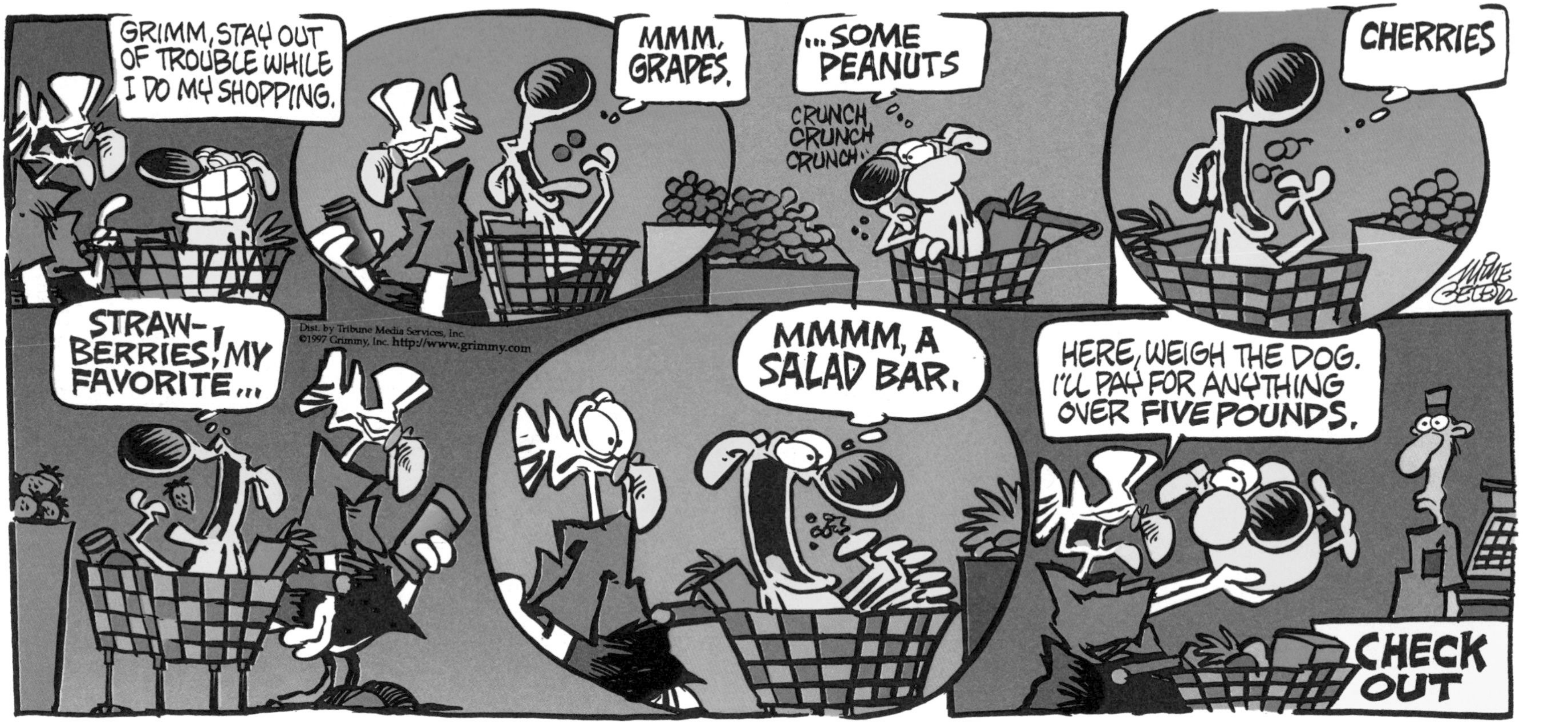
GRIMM, STAY OUT OF TROUBLE WHILE I DO MY SHOPPING.
MMM, GRAPES.
...SOME PEANUTS
CRUNCH CRUNCH CRUNCH
CHERRIES
STRAW-BERRIES! MY FAVORITE...
Dist. by Tribune Media Services, Inc. ©1997 Grimmy, Inc. http://www.grimmy.com
MMMM, A SALAD BAR.
HERE, WEIGH THE DOG. I'LL PAY FOR ANYTHING OVER FIVE POUNDS.
CHECK OUT

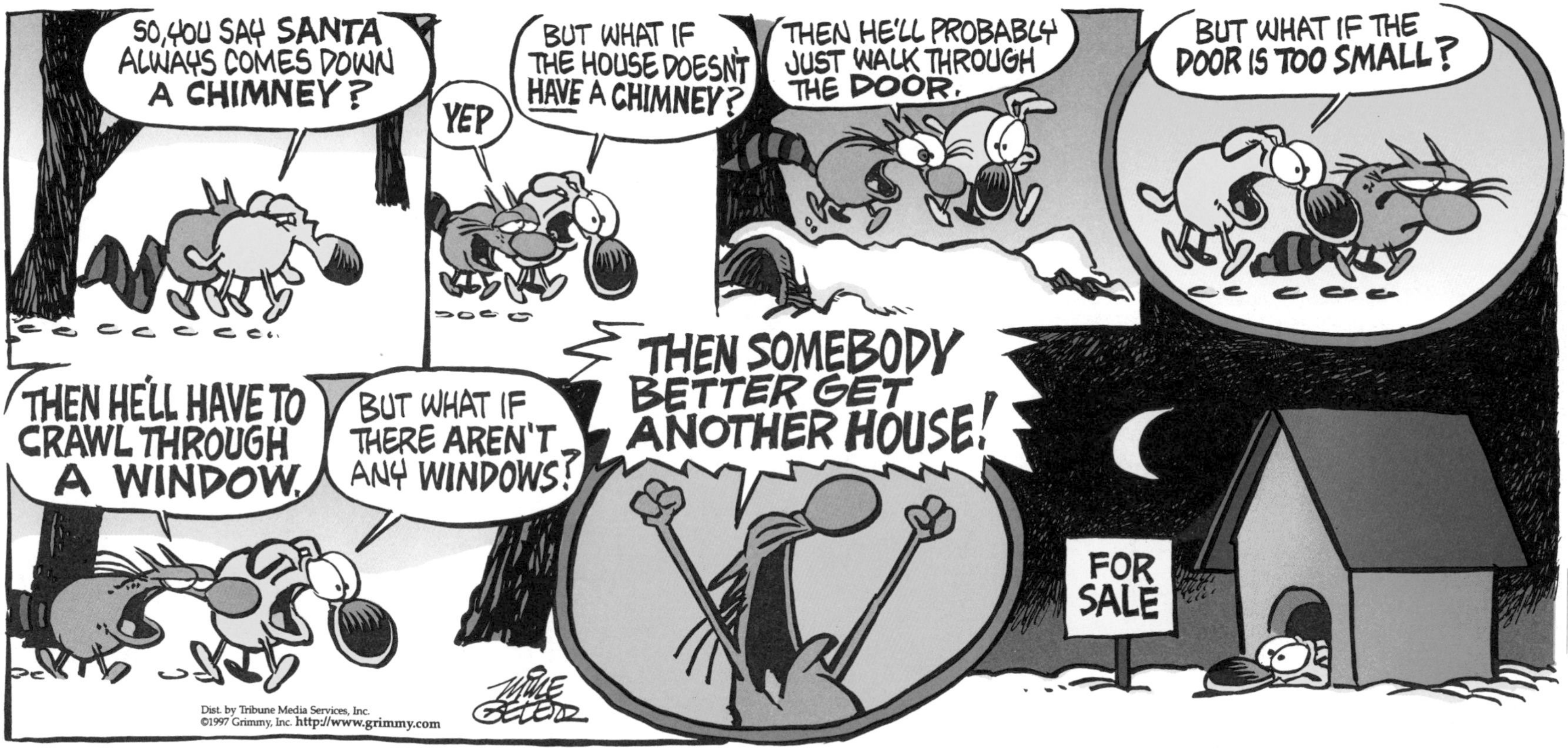
SO, YOU SAY SANTA ALWAYS COMES DOWN A CHIMNEY?
YEP
BUT WHAT IF THE HOUSE DOESN'T HAVE A CHIMNEY?
THEN HE'LL PROBABLY JUST WALK THROUGH THE DOOR.
BUT WHAT IF THE DOOR IS TOO SMALL?
THEN HE'LL HAVE TO CRAWL THROUGH A WINDOW.
BUT WHAT IF THERE AREN'T ANY WINDOWS?
THEN SOMEBODY BETTER GET ANOTHER HOUSE!
FOR SALE
MIKE PETERS
Dist. by Tribune Media Services, Inc.
©1997 Grimmy, Inc. http://www.grimmy.com

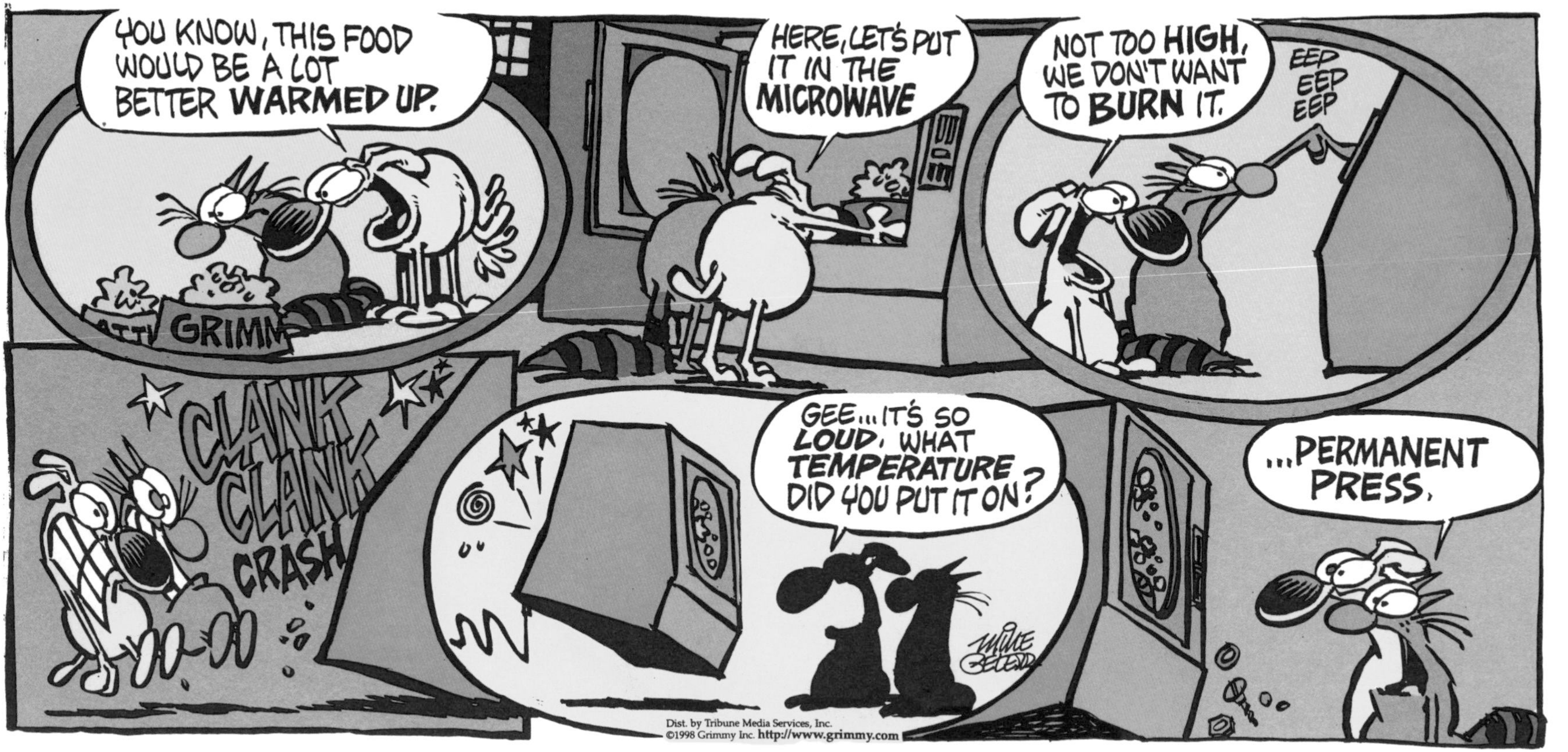

YOU KNOW, THIS FOOD WOULD BE A LOT BETTER **WARMED UP**.
HERE, LET'S PUT IT IN THE **MICROWAVE**
NOT TOO **HIGH**, WE DON'T WANT TO **BURN** IT.
EEP EEP EEP
CLANK CLANK CRASH
GEE... IT'S SO **LOUD**, WHAT **TEMPERATURE** DID YOU PUT IT ON?
...PERMANENT PRESS.

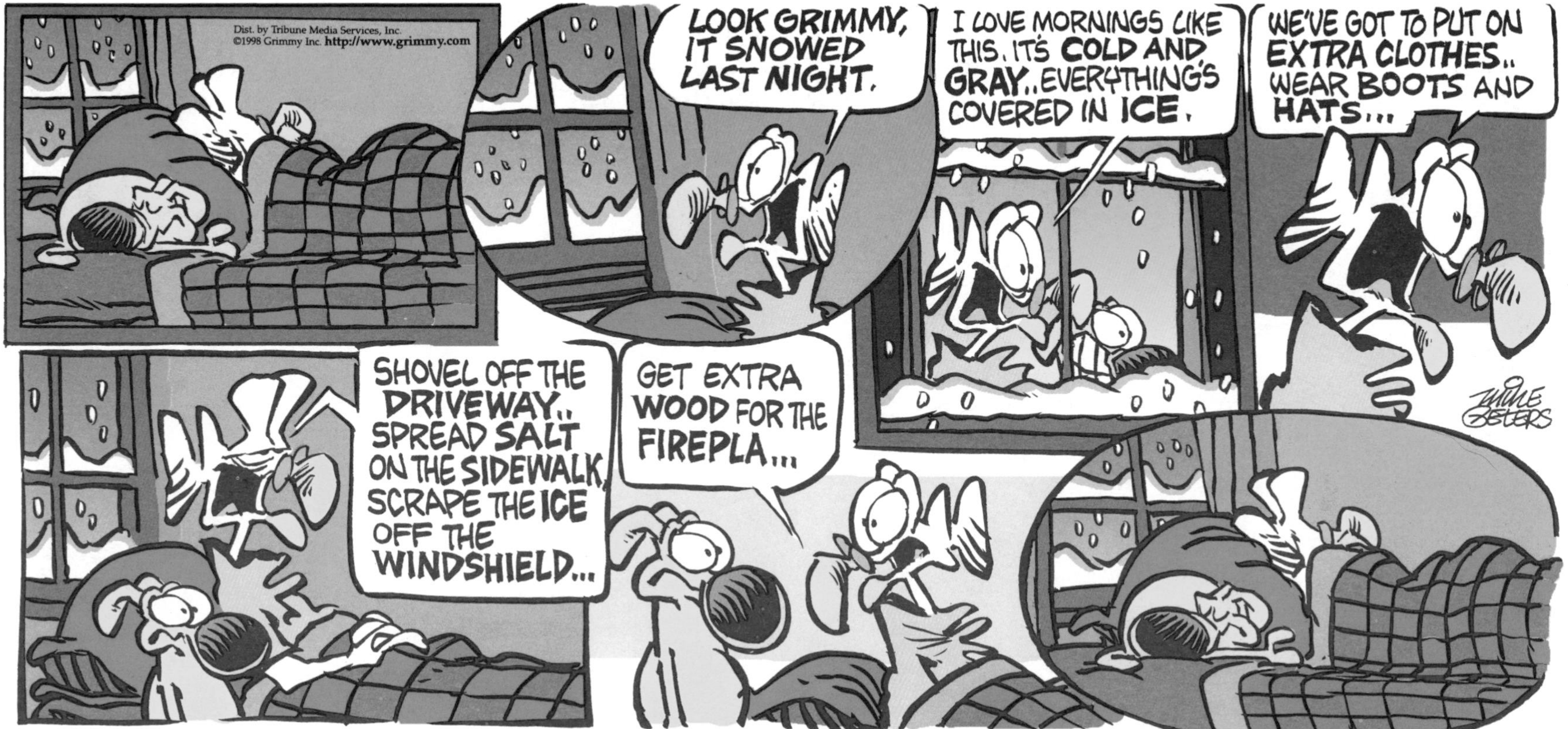
Dist. by Tribune Media Services, Inc.
©1998 Grimmy Inc. http://www.grimmy.com
LOOK GRIMMY, IT SNOWED LAST NIGHT.
I LOVE MORNINGS LIKE THIS. IT'S COLD AND GRAY.. EVERYTHING'S COVERED IN ICE.
WE'VE GOT TO PUT ON EXTRA CLOTHES.. WEAR BOOTS AND HATS...
SHOVEL OFF THE DRIVEWAY.. SPREAD SALT ON THE SIDEWALK, SCRAPE THE ICE OFF THE WINDSHIELD...
GET EXTRA WOOD FOR THE FIREPLA...
MIKE PETERS

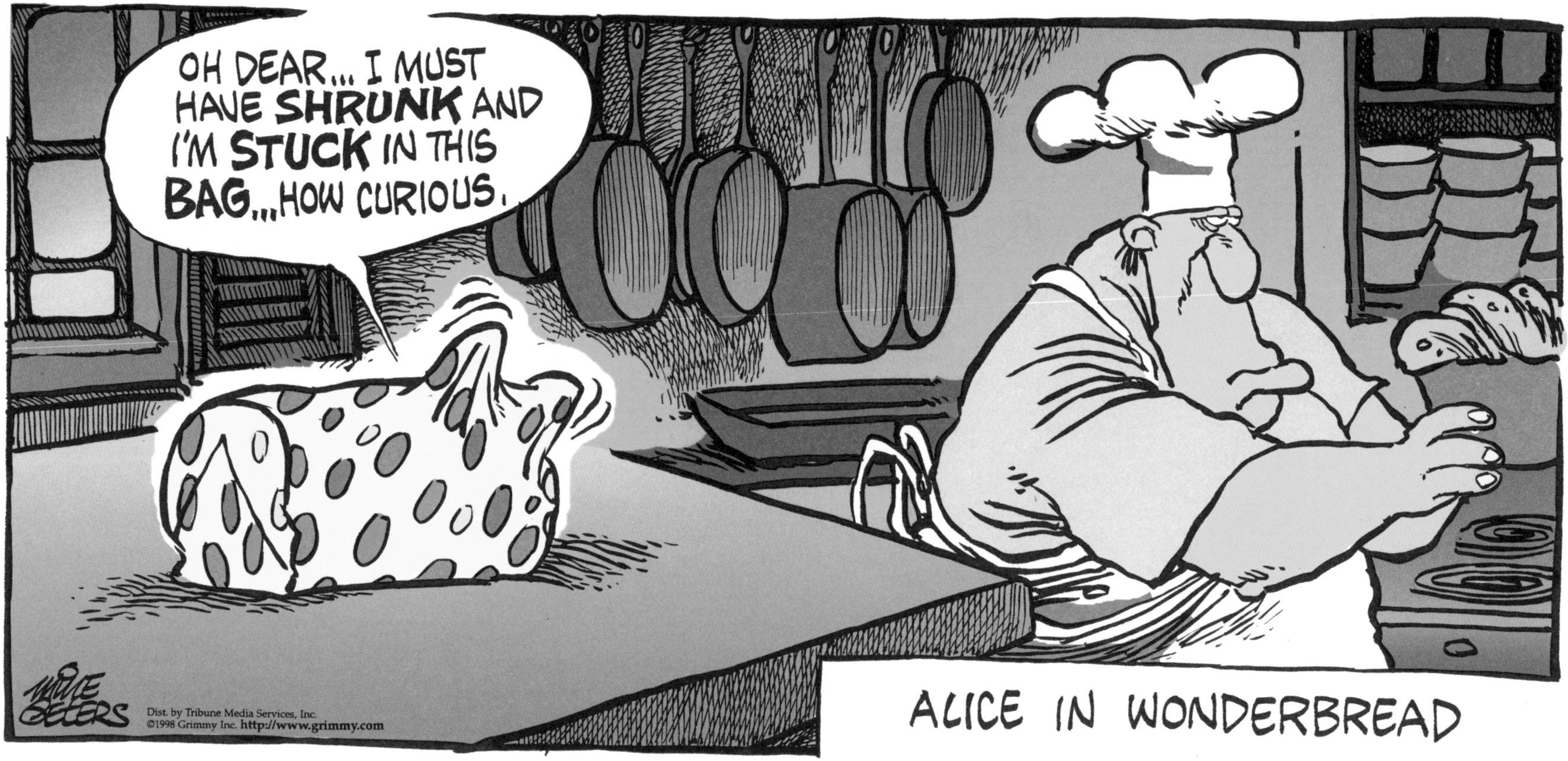
OH DEAR... I MUST HAVE **SHRUNK** AND I'M **STUCK** IN THIS **BAG**... HOW CURIOUS.
MIKE PETERS
Dist. by Tribune Media Services, Inc.
©1998 Grimmy Inc. http://www.grimmy.com

ALICE IN WONDERBREAD

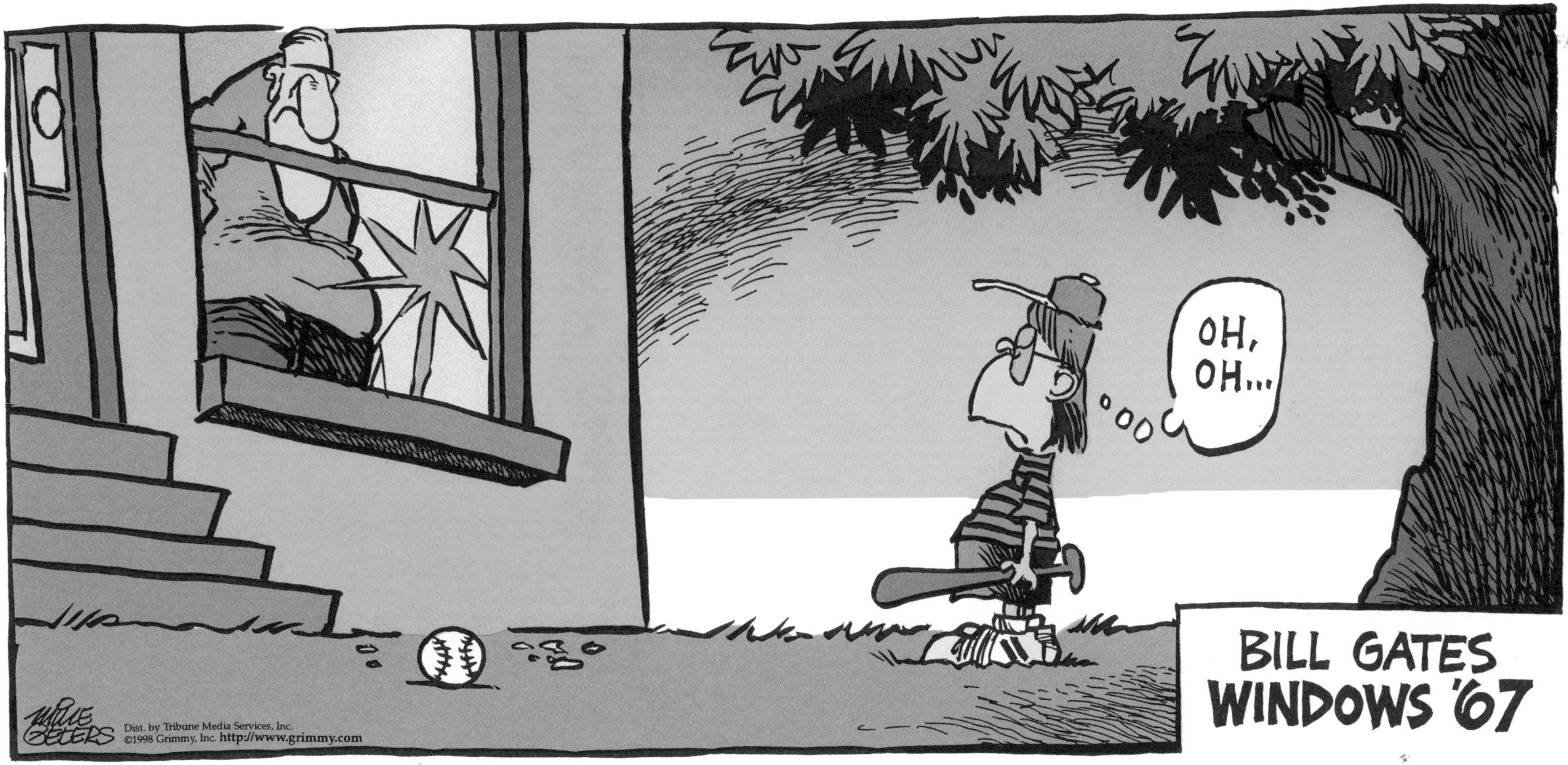
OH, OH...
BILL GATES WINDOWS '67
Dist. by Tribune Media Services, Inc.
©1998 Grimmy, Inc. http://www.grimmy.com

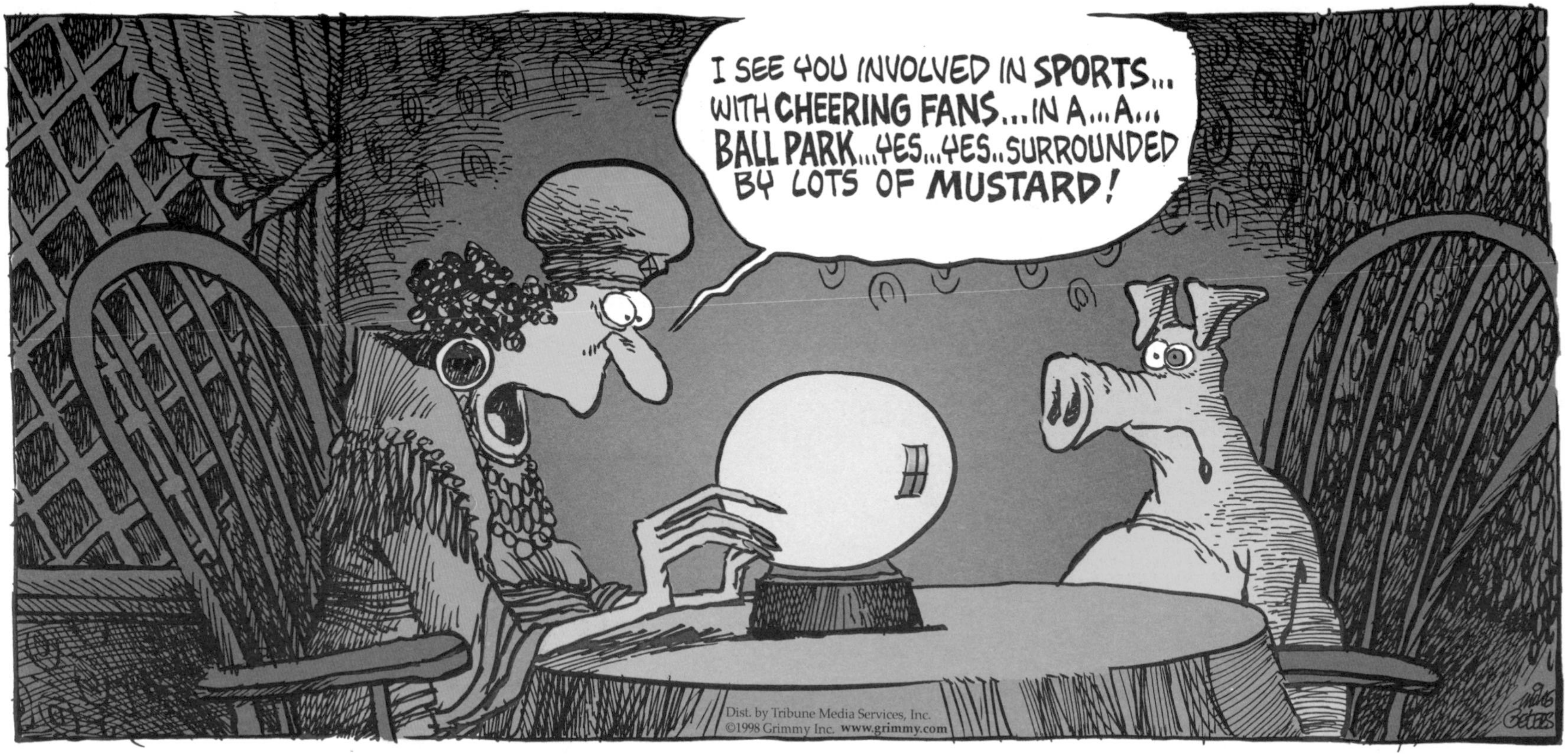
I SEE YOU INVOLVED IN SPORTS... WITH CHEERING FANS... IN A...A... BALL PARK...YES...YES..SURROUNDED BY LOTS OF MUSTARD!
Dist. by Tribune Media Services, Inc. ©1998 Grimmy Inc. www.grimmy.com

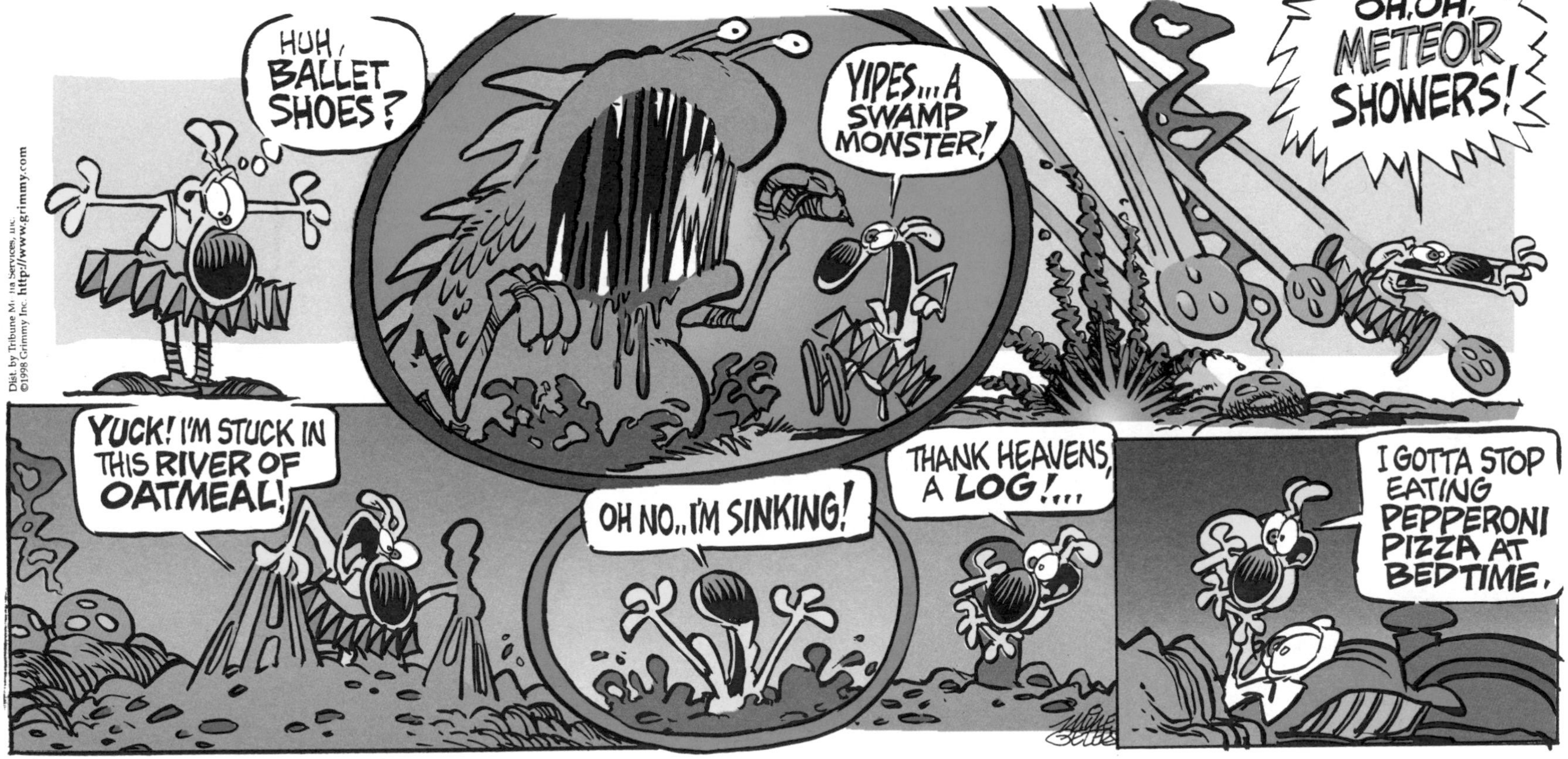
HUH, BALLET SHOES?
YIPES... A SWAMP MONSTER!
OH, OH, METEOR SHOWERS!
YUCK! I'M STUCK IN THIS RIVER OF OATMEAL!
OH NO.. I'M SINKING!
THANK HEAVENS, A LOG!...
I GOTTA STOP EATING PEPPERONI PIZZA AT BEDTIME.

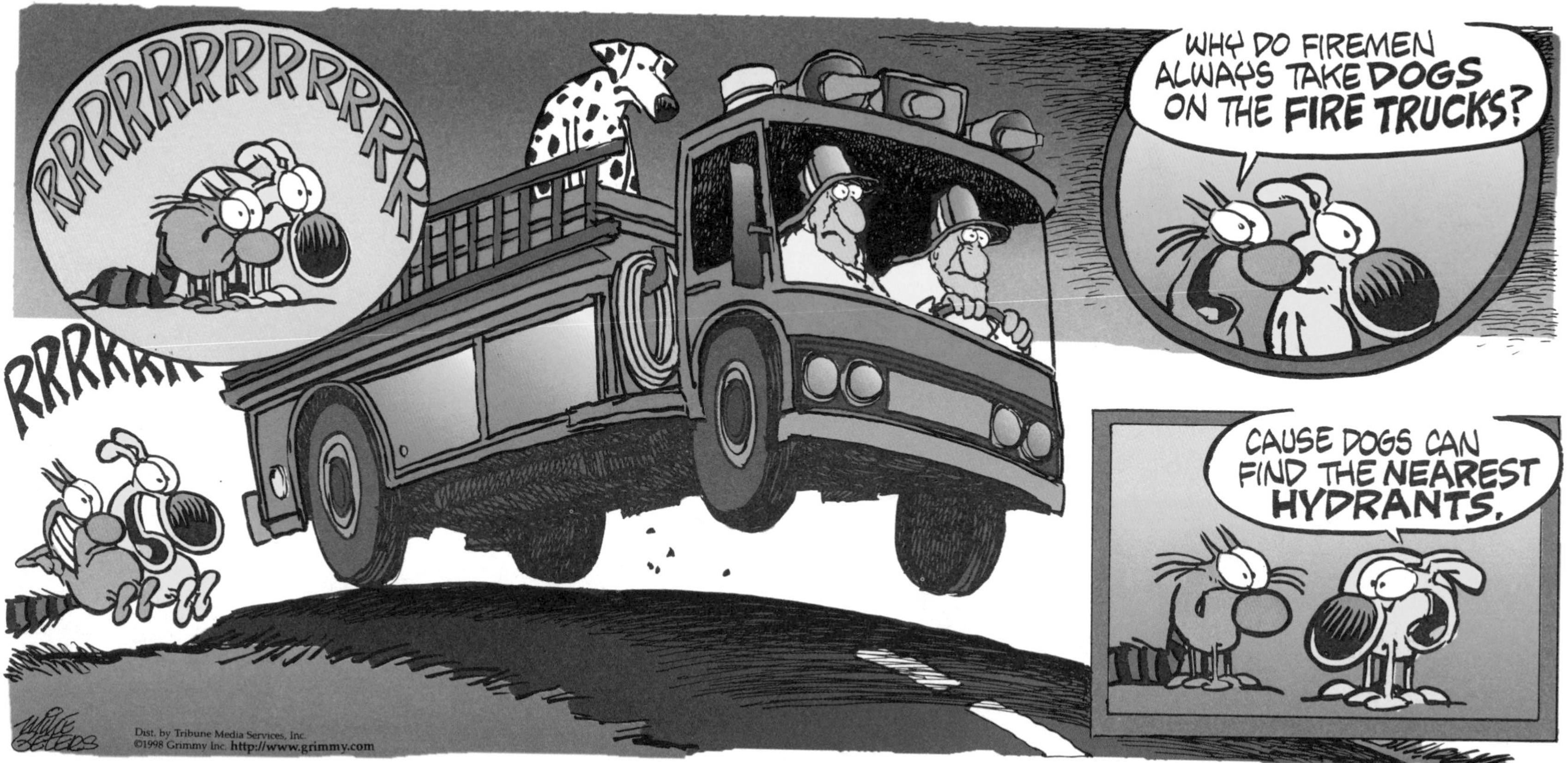
RRRRRRRRRRRRRRRRR
RRRRRR
WHY DO FIREMEN ALWAYS TAKE DOGS ON THE FIRE TRUCKS?
CAUSE DOGS CAN FIND THE NEAREST HYDRANTS.
Dist. by Tribune Media Services, Inc.
©1998 Grimmy Inc. http://www.grimmy.com

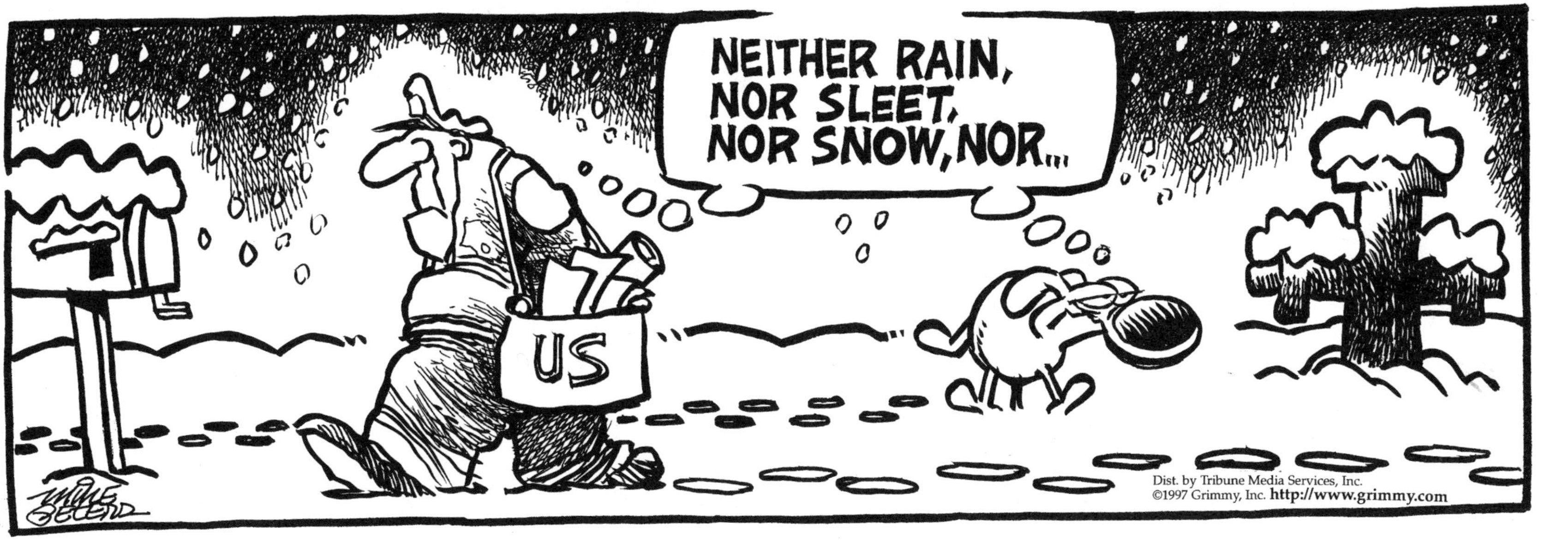
NEITHER RAIN, NOR SLEET, NOR SNOW, NOR...
US
Dist. by Tribune Media Services, Inc.
©1997 Grimmy, Inc. http://www.grimmy.com

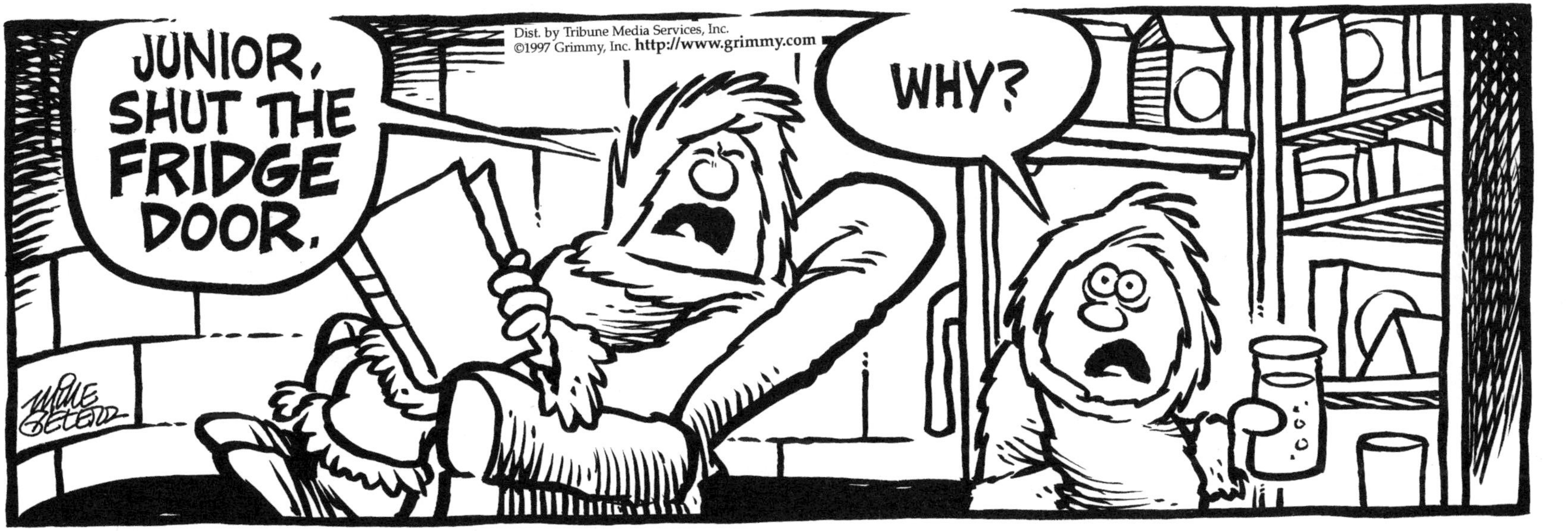
JUNIOR, SHUT THE FRIDGE DOOR.
WHY?
Dist. by Tribune Media Services, Inc.
©1997 Grimmy, Inc. http://www.grimmy.com

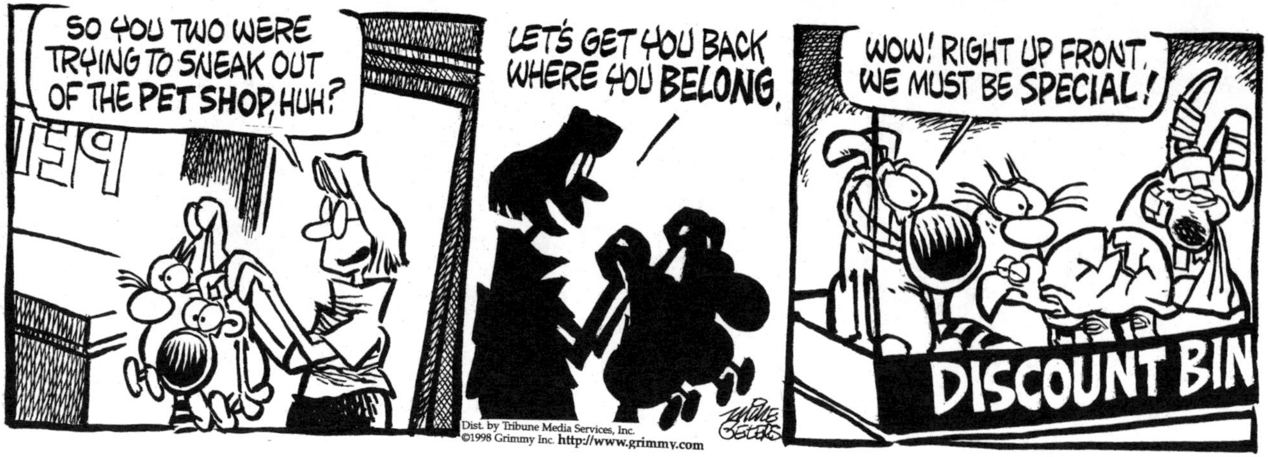
SO YOU TWO WERE TRYING TO SNEAK OUT OF THE PET SHOP, HUH?
LET'S GET YOU BACK WHERE YOU BELONG.
WOW! RIGHT UP FRONT, WE MUST BE SPECIAL!
DISCOUNT BIN
Dist. by Tribune Media Services, Inc.
©1998 Grimmy Inc. http://www.grimmy.com
MIKE PETERS

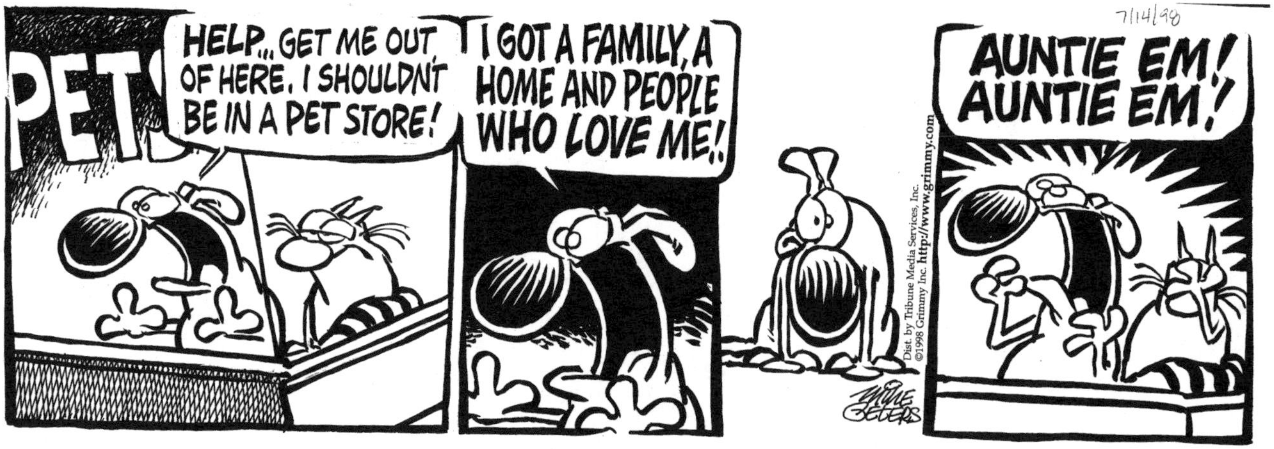
7/14/98
PETS
HELP... GET ME OUT OF HERE. I SHOULDN'T BE IN A PET STORE!
I GOT A FAMILY, A HOME AND PEOPLE WHO LOVE ME!
AUNTIE EM! AUNTIE EM!
Dist. by Tribune Media Services, Inc.
©1998 Grimmy Inc. http://www.grimmy.com
MIKE PETERS

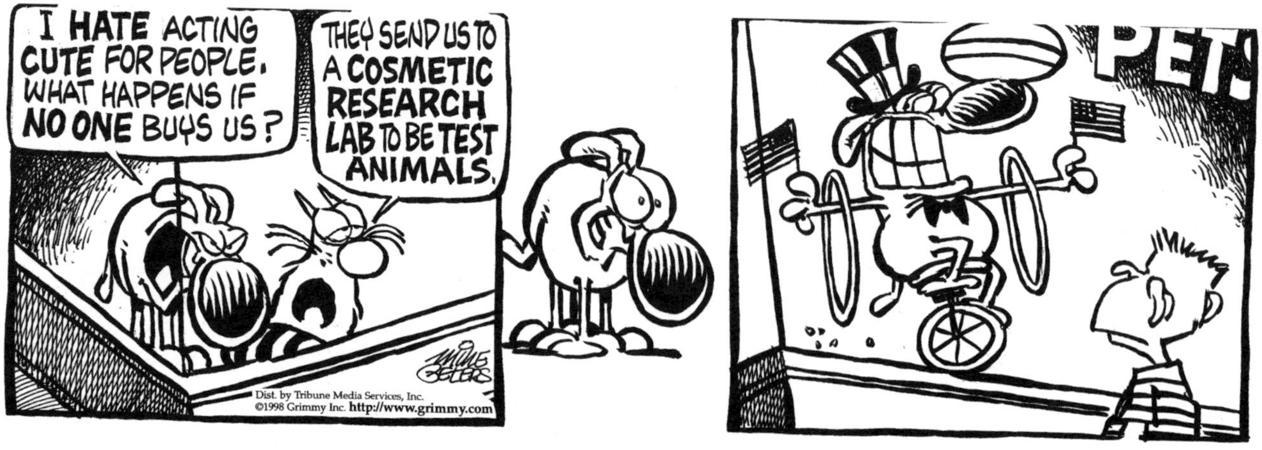
I HATE ACTING CUTE FOR PEOPLE. WHAT HAPPENS IF NO ONE BUYS US?
THEY SEND US TO A COSMETIC RESEARCH LAB TO BE TEST ANIMALS.
MIKE PETERS
Dist. by Tribune Media Services, Inc.
©1998 Grimmy Inc. http://www.grimmy.com
PETS

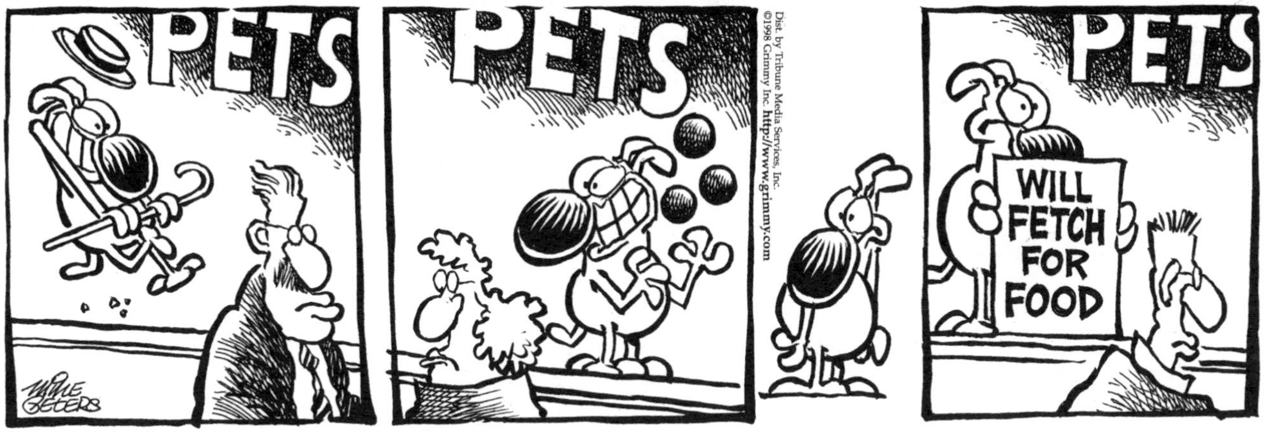
PETS
PETS
Dist. by Tribune Media Services, Inc. ©1998 Grimmy Inc. http://www.grimmy.com
PETS
WILL FETCH FOR FOOD

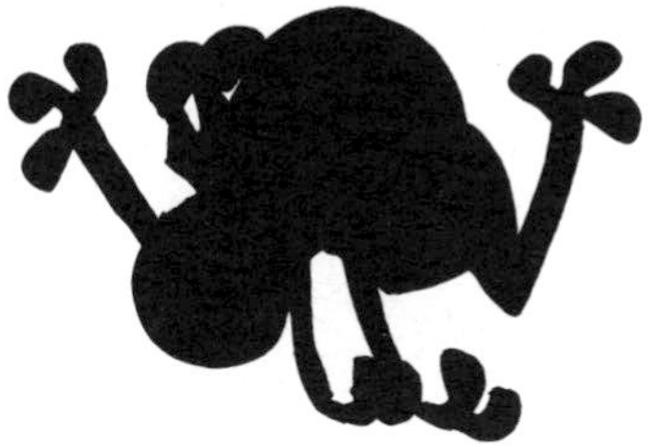

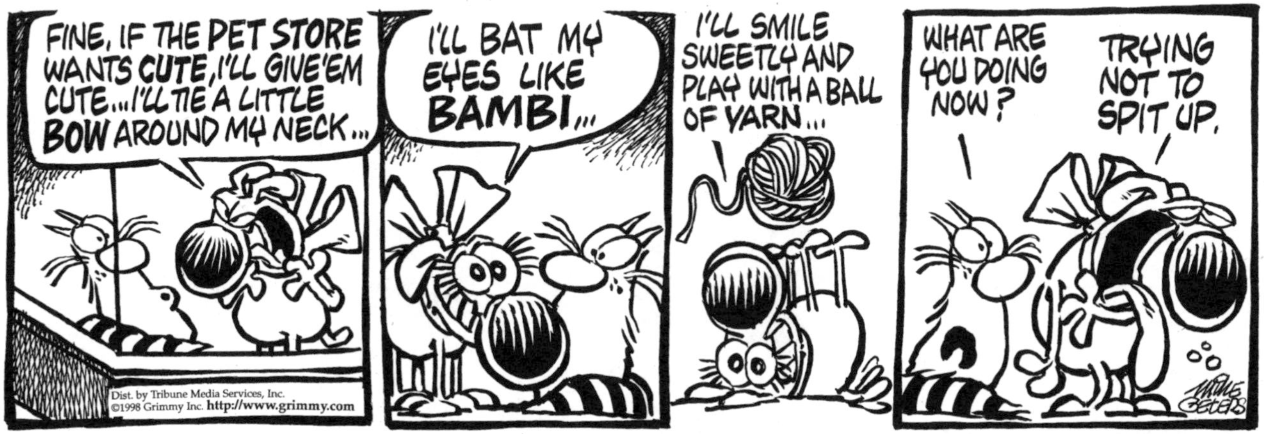
FINE, IF THE PET STORE WANTS CUTE, I'LL GIVE'EM CUTE... I'LL TIE A LITTLE BOW AROUND MY NECK...
Dist. by Tribune Media Services, Inc. ©1998 Grimmy Inc. http://www.grimmy.com
I'LL BAT MY EYES LIKE BAMBI...
I'LL SMILE SWEETLY AND PLAY WITH A BALL OF YARN...
WHAT ARE YOU DOING NOW?
TRYING NOT TO SPIT UP.

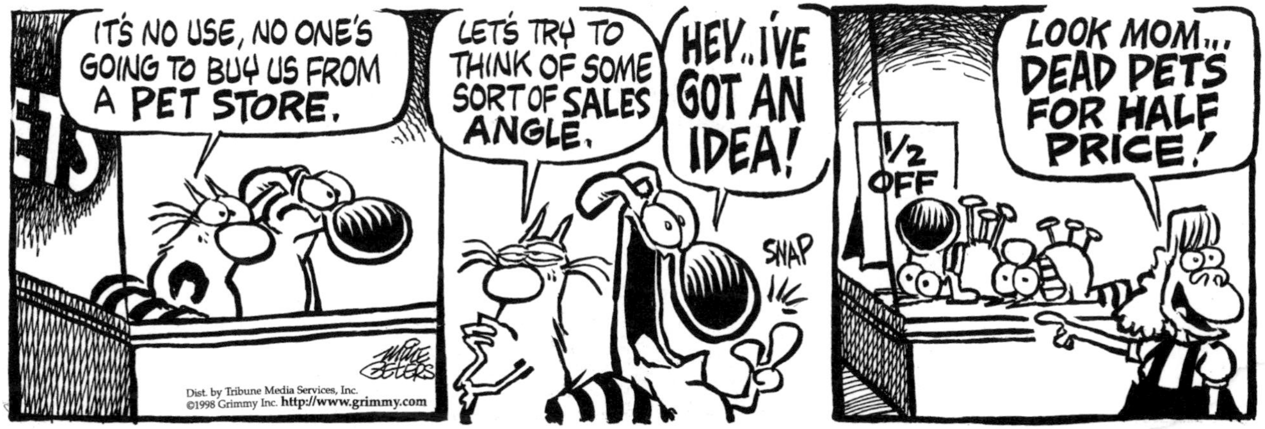
IT'S NO USE, NO ONE'S GOING TO BUY US FROM A PET STORE.
Dist. by Tribune Media Services, Inc. ©1998 Grimmy Inc. http://www.grimmy.com
LET'S TRY TO THINK OF SOME SORT OF SALES ANGLE.
HEY.. I'VE GOT AN IDEA!
SNAP
1/2 OFF
LOOK MOM... DEAD PETS FOR HALF PRICE!

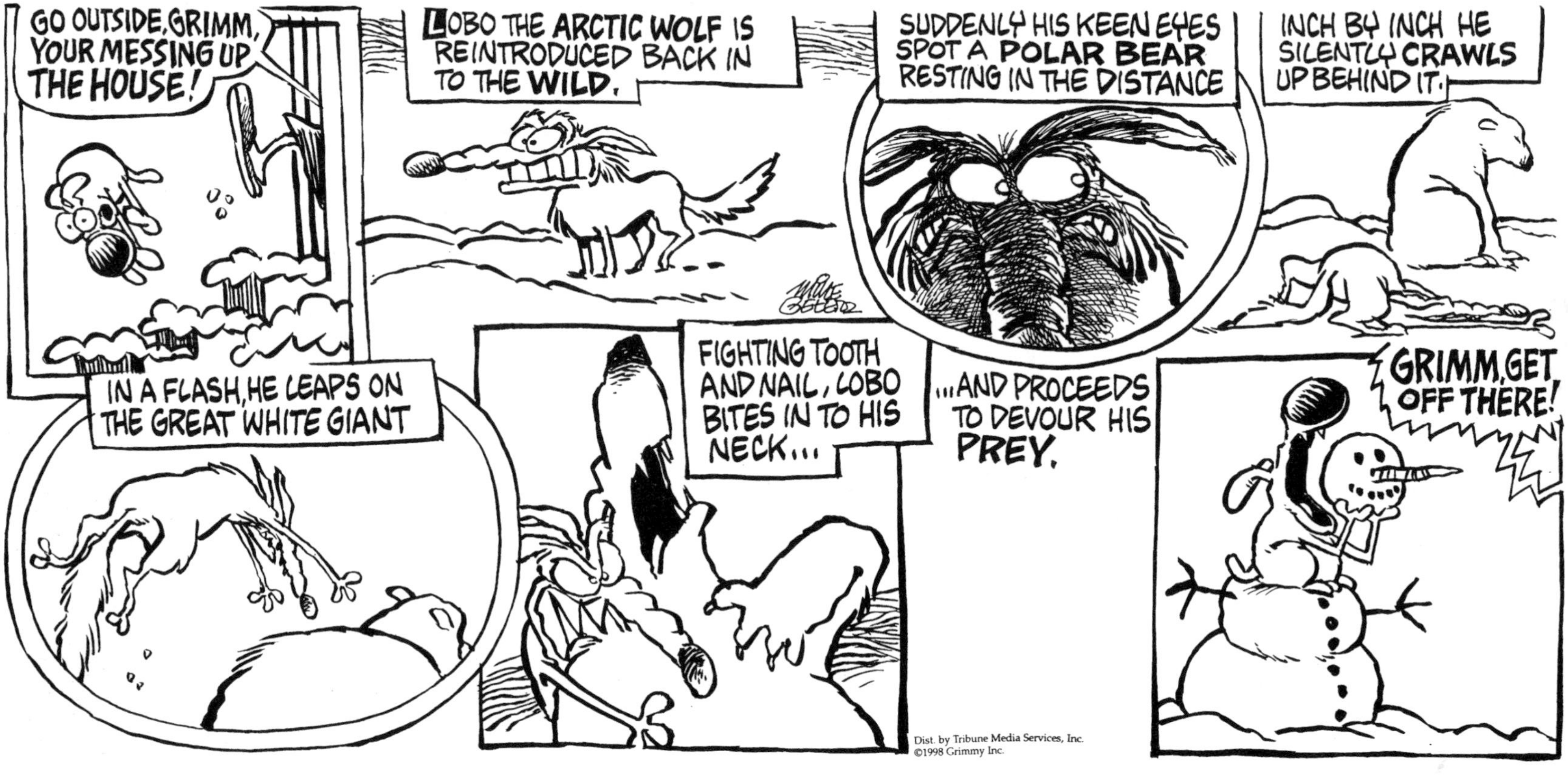
GO OUTSIDE, GRIMM, YOUR MESSING UP THE HOUSE!
LOBO THE ARCTIC WOLF IS REINTRODUCED BACK IN TO THE WILD.
SUDDENLY HIS KEEN EYES SPOT A POLAR BEAR RESTING IN THE DISTANCE
INCH BY INCH HE SILENTLY CRAWLS UP BEHIND IT.
IN A FLASH, HE LEAPS ON THE GREAT WHITE GIANT
FIGHTING TOOTH AND NAIL, LOBO BITES IN TO HIS NECK...
...AND PROCEEDS TO DEVOUR HIS PREY.
GRIMM, GET OFF THERE!
Dist. by Tribune Media Services, Inc.
©1998 Grimmy Inc.

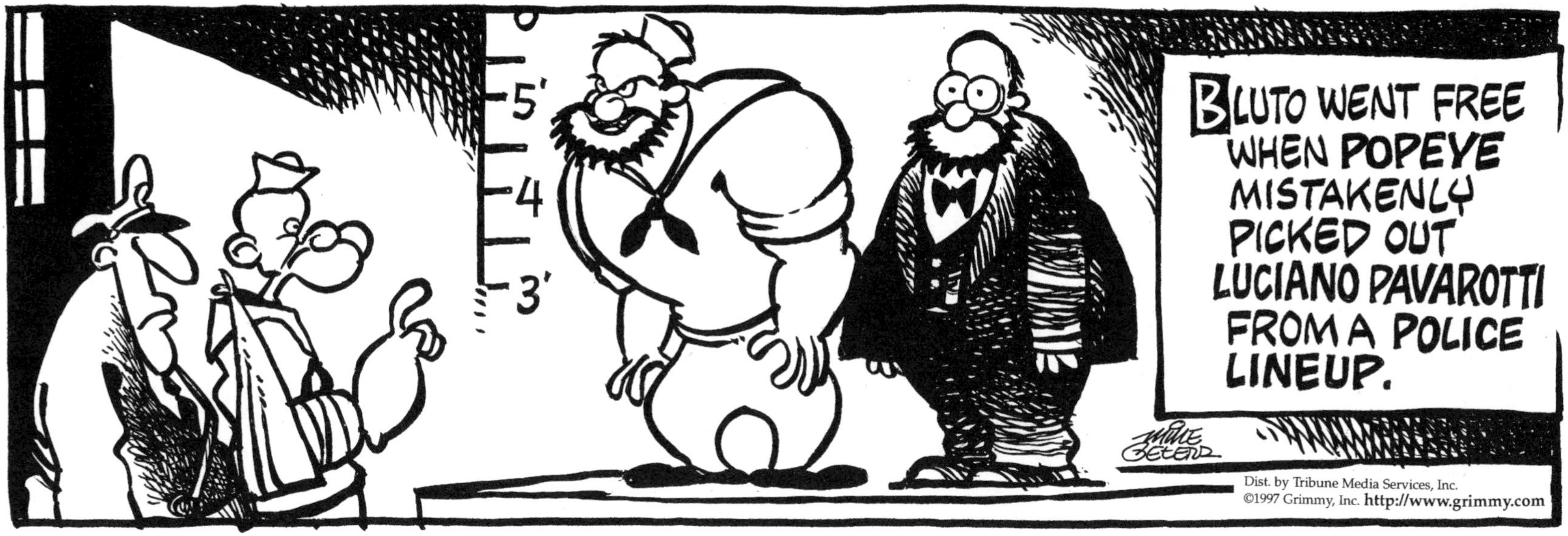
5'
4
3'
BLUTO WENT FREE WHEN POPEYE MISTAKENLY PICKED OUT LUCIANO PAVAROTTI FROM A POLICE LINEUP.
Dist. by Tribune Media Services, Inc.
©1997 Grimmy, Inc. http://www.grimmy.com

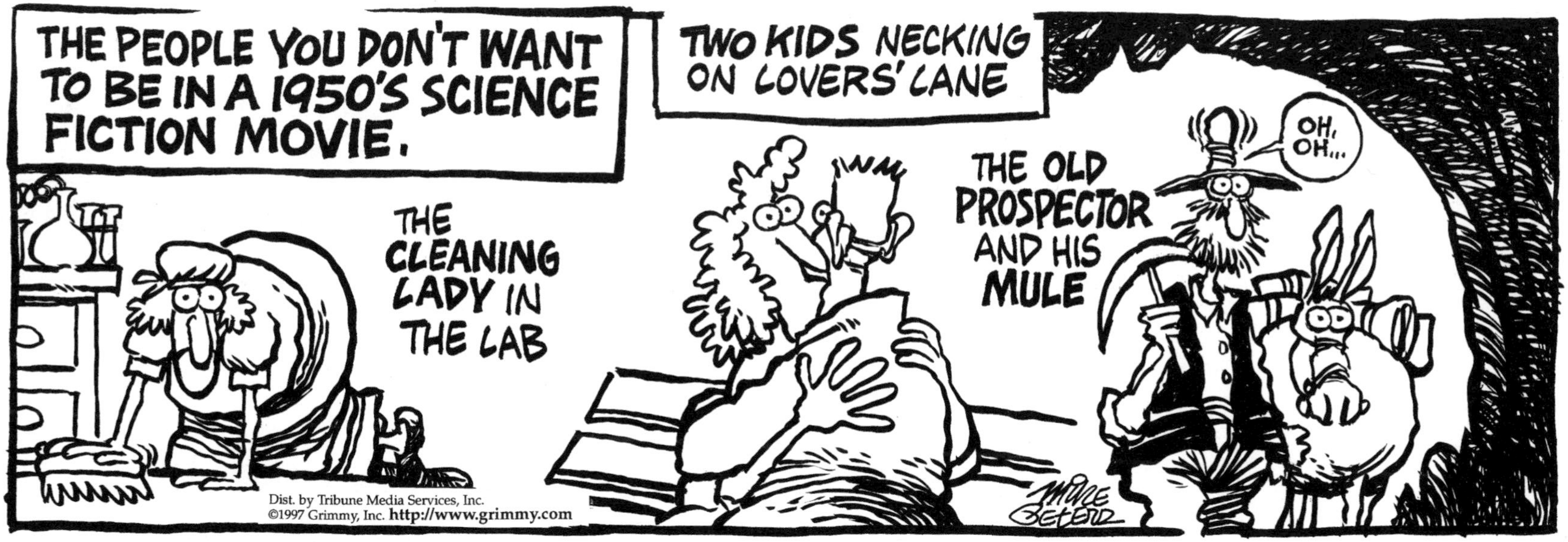
THE PEOPLE YOU DON'T WANT TO BE IN A 1950'S SCIENCE FICTION MOVIE.
THE CLEANING LADY IN THE LAB
TWO KIDS NECKING ON LOVERS' LANE
THE OLD PROSPECTOR AND HIS MULE
OH, OH...
Dist. by Tribune Media Services, Inc.
©1997 Grimmy, Inc. http://www.grimmy.com

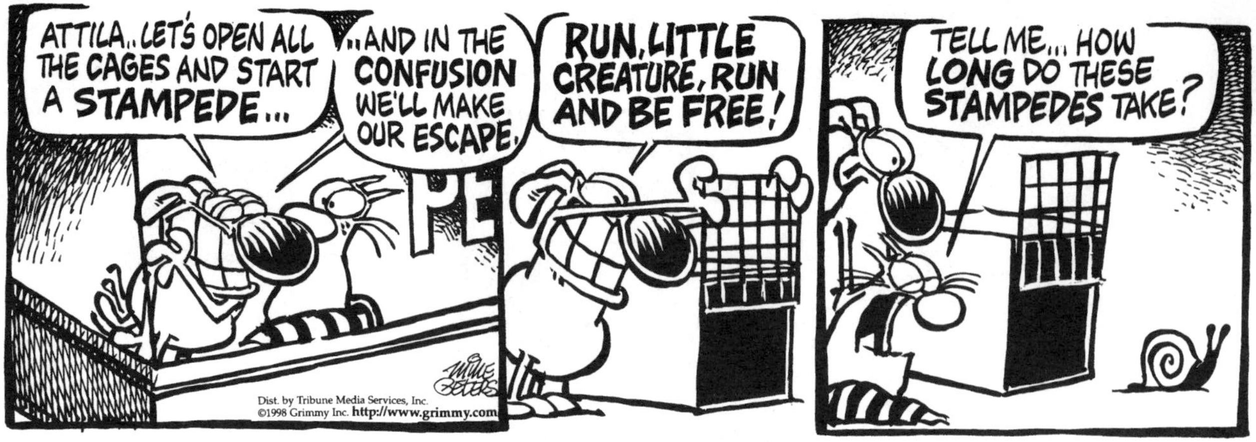
ATTILA.. LET'S OPEN ALL THE CAGES AND START A STAMPEDE...
..AND IN THE CONFUSION WE'LL MAKE OUR ESCAPE.
RUN, LITTLE CREATURE, RUN AND BE FREE!
TELL ME... HOW LONG DO THESE STAMPEDES TAKE?
Dist. by Tribune Media Services, Inc. ©1998 Grimmy Inc. http://www.grimmy.com

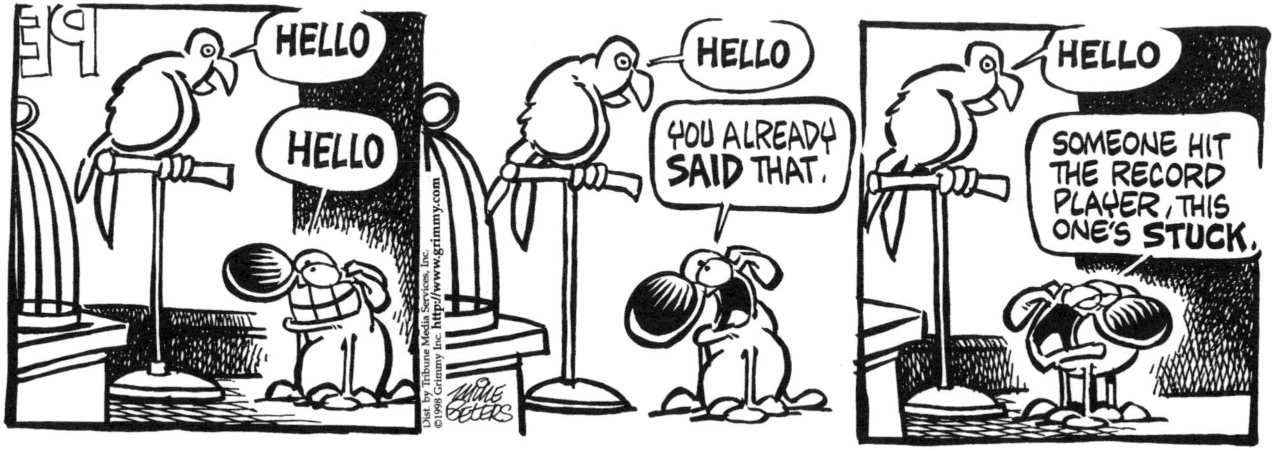
HELLO
HELLO
HELLO
YOU ALREADY SAID THAT.
HELLO
SOMEONE HIT THE RECORD PLAYER, THIS ONE'S STUCK.
Dist. by Tribune Media Services, Inc. ©1998 Grimmy Inc. http://www.grimmy.com

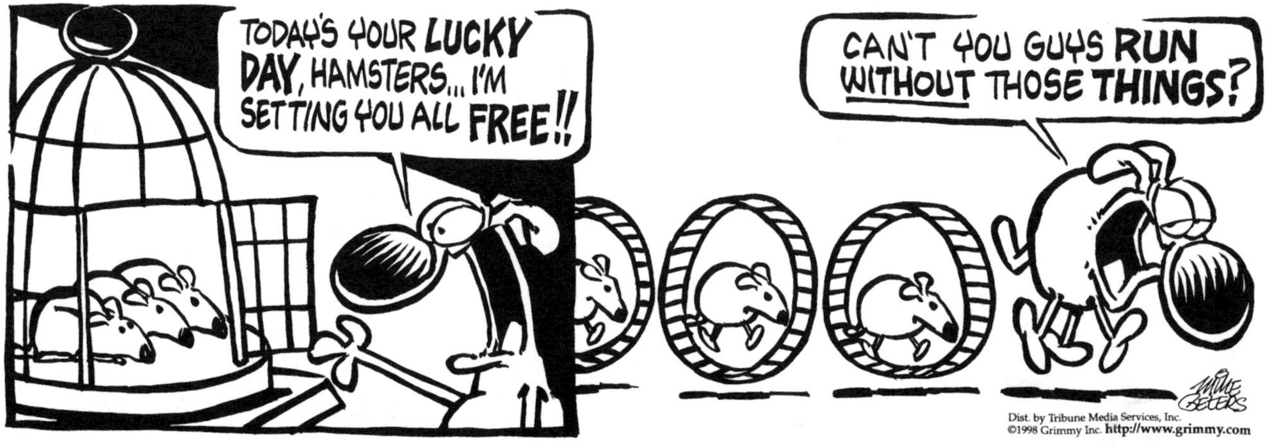
TODAY'S YOUR LUCKY DAY, HAMSTERS... I'M SETTING YOU ALL FREE!!
CAN'T YOU GUYS RUN WITHOUT THOSE THINGS?
Dist. by Tribune Media Services, Inc. ©1998 Grimmy Inc. http://www.grimmy.com

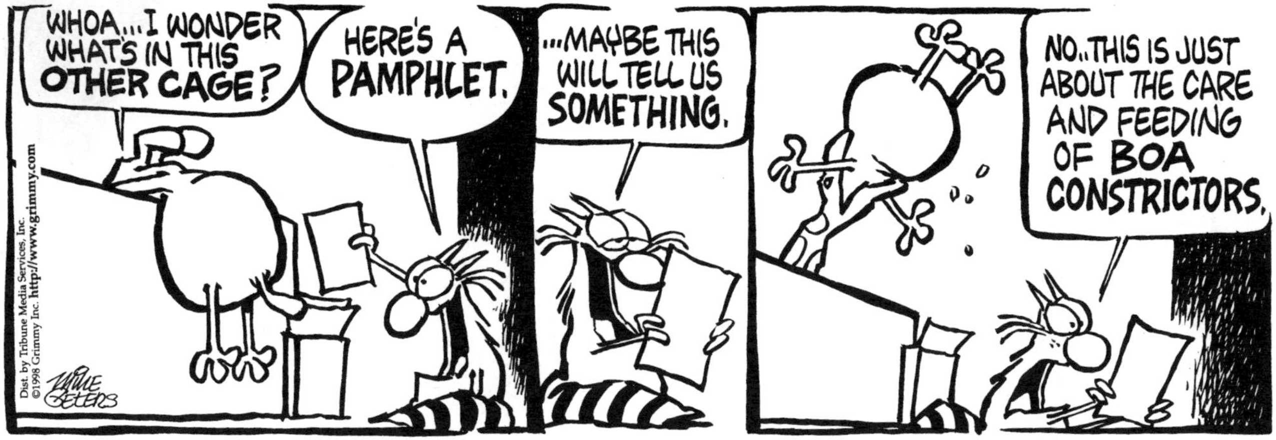
WHOA... I WONDER WHAT'S IN THIS OTHER CAGE?
HERE'S A PAMPHLET.
...MAYBE THIS WILL TELL US SOMETHING.
NO.. THIS IS JUST ABOUT THE CARE AND FEEDING OF BOA CONSTRICTORS.
Dist. by Tribune Media Services, Inc. ©1998 Grimmy Inc. http://www.grimmy.com
MIKE PETERS

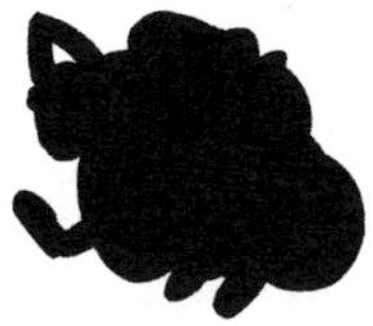

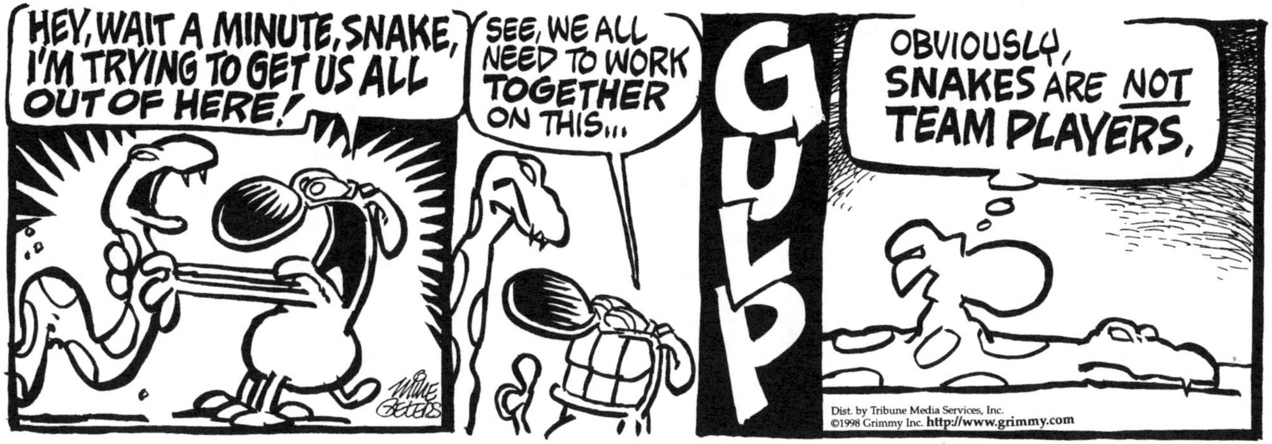
HEY, WAIT A MINUTE, SNAKE, I'M TRYING TO GET US ALL OUT OF HERE!
SEE, WE ALL NEED TO WORK TOGETHER ON THIS...
GULP
OBVIOUSLY, SNAKES ARE NOT TEAM PLAYERS.
MIKE PETERS
Dist. by Tribune Media Services, Inc. ©1998 Grimmy Inc. http://www.grimmy.com

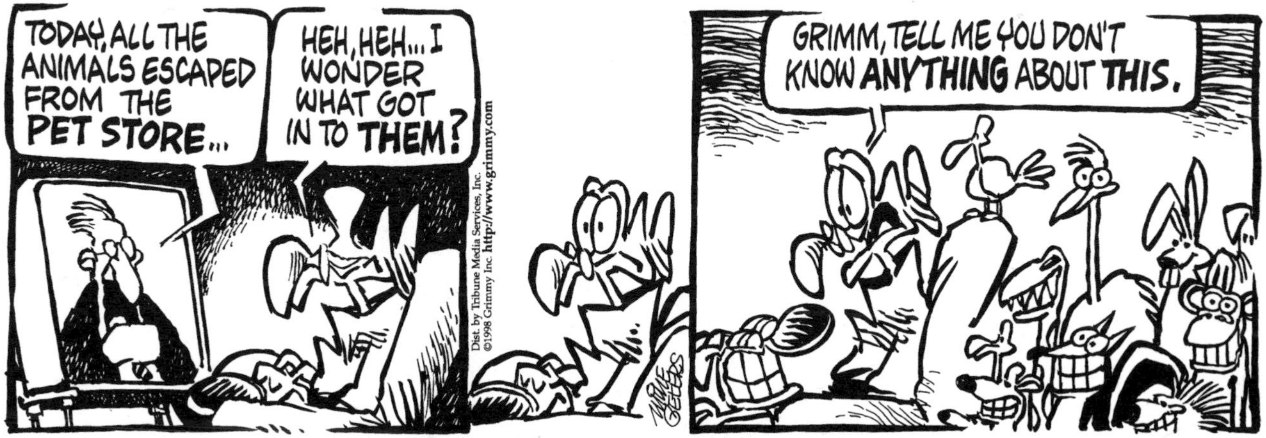
TODAY, ALL THE ANIMALS ESCAPED FROM THE PET STORE...
HEH, HEH... I WONDER WHAT GOT IN TO THEM?
Dist. by Tribune Media Services, Inc. ©1998 Grimmy Inc. http://www.grimmy.com
GRIMM, TELL ME YOU DON'T KNOW ANYTHING ABOUT THIS.
MIKE PETERS

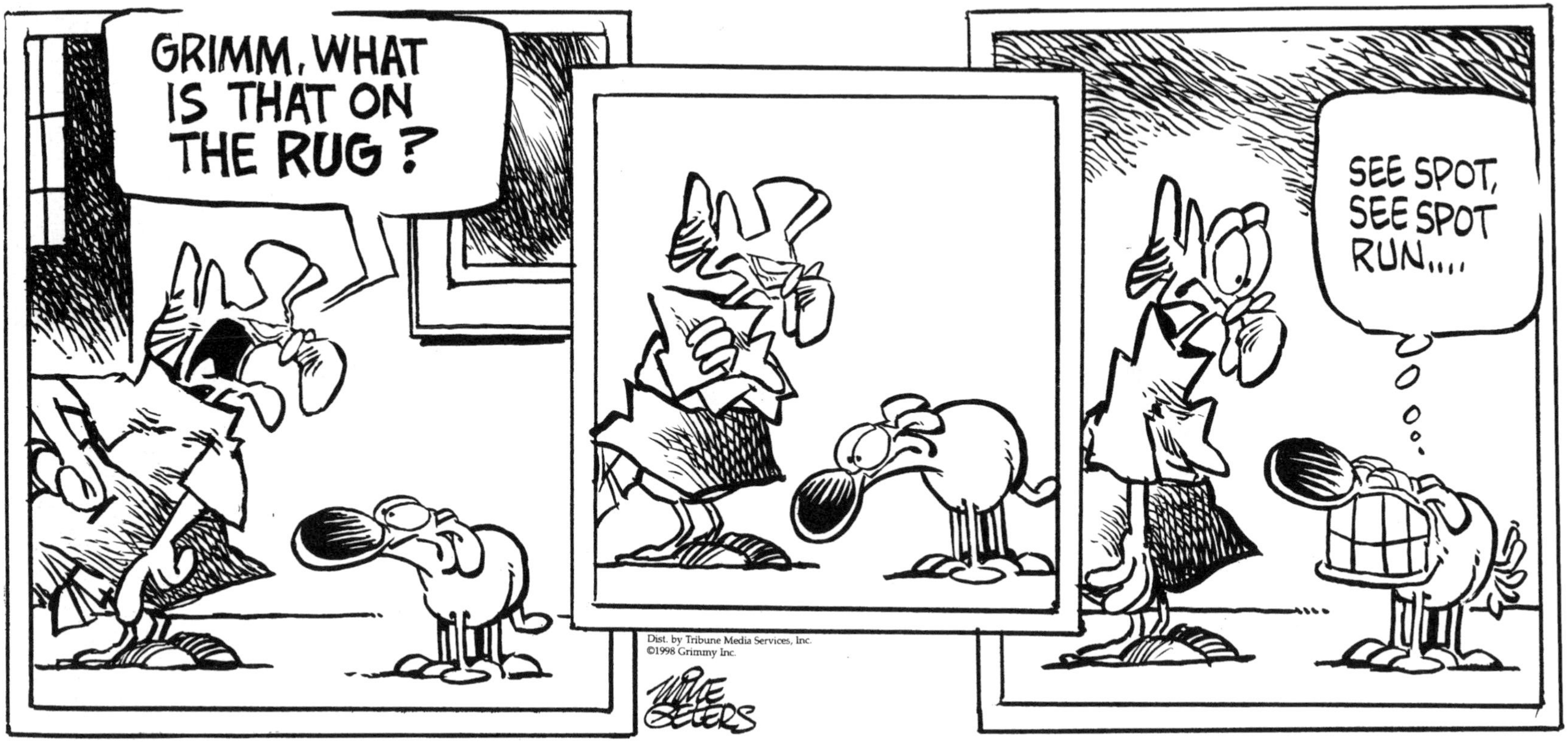
GRIMM, WHAT IS THAT ON THE RUG?
SEE SPOT, SEE SPOT RUN....
Dist. by Tribune Media Services, Inc.
©1998 Grimmy Inc.
MIKE PETERS

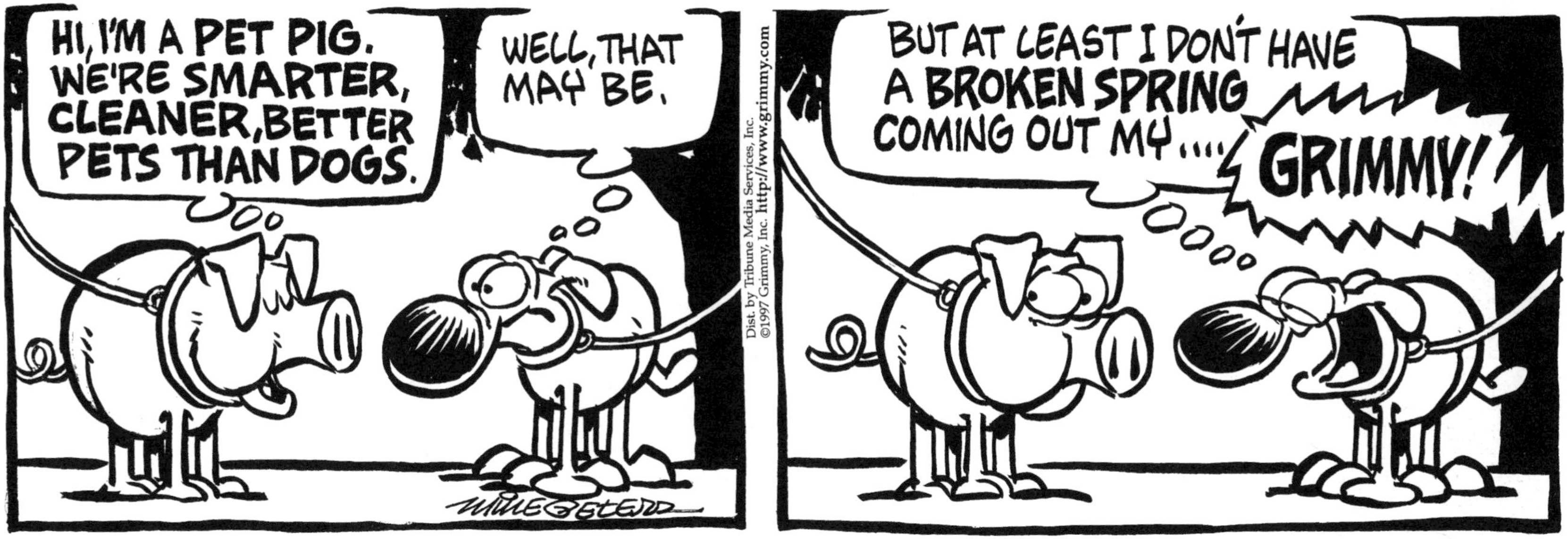
HI, I'M A PET PIG. WE'RE SMARTER, CLEANER, BETTER PETS THAN DOGS.
WELL, THAT MAY BE.
Dist. by Tribune Media Services, Inc.
©1997 Grimmy, Inc. http://www.grimmy.com
BUT AT LEAST I DON'T HAVE A BROKEN SPRING COMING OUT MY.....
GRIMMY!

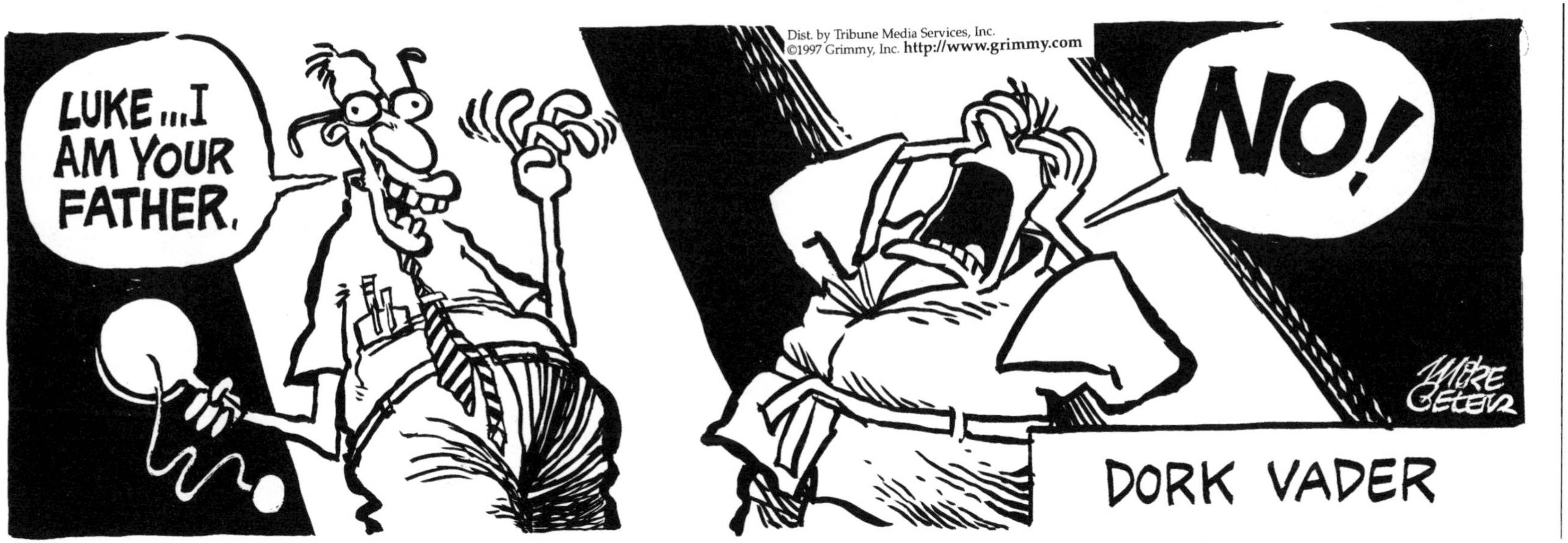
LUKE...I AM YOUR FATHER.
Dist. by Tribune Media Services, Inc.
©1997 Grimmy, Inc. http://www.grimmy.com
NO!
DORK VADER

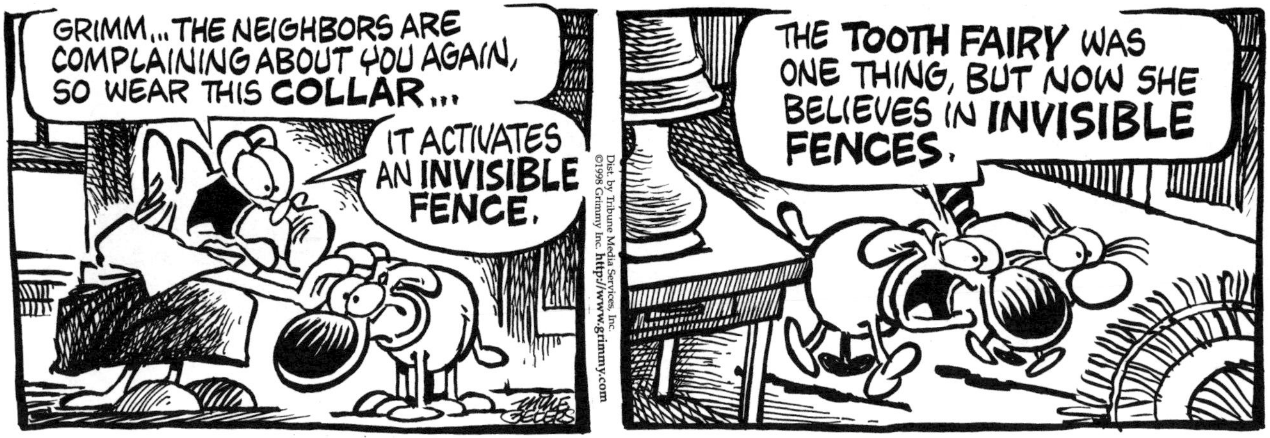
GRIMM... THE NEIGHBORS ARE COMPLAINING ABOUT YOU AGAIN, SO WEAR THIS COLLAR...
IT ACTIVATES AN INVISIBLE FENCE.
Dist. by Tribune Media Services, Inc. ©1998 Grimmy Inc. http://www.grimmy.com
THE TOOTH FAIRY WAS ONE THING, BUT NOW SHE BELIEVES IN INVISIBLE FENCES.

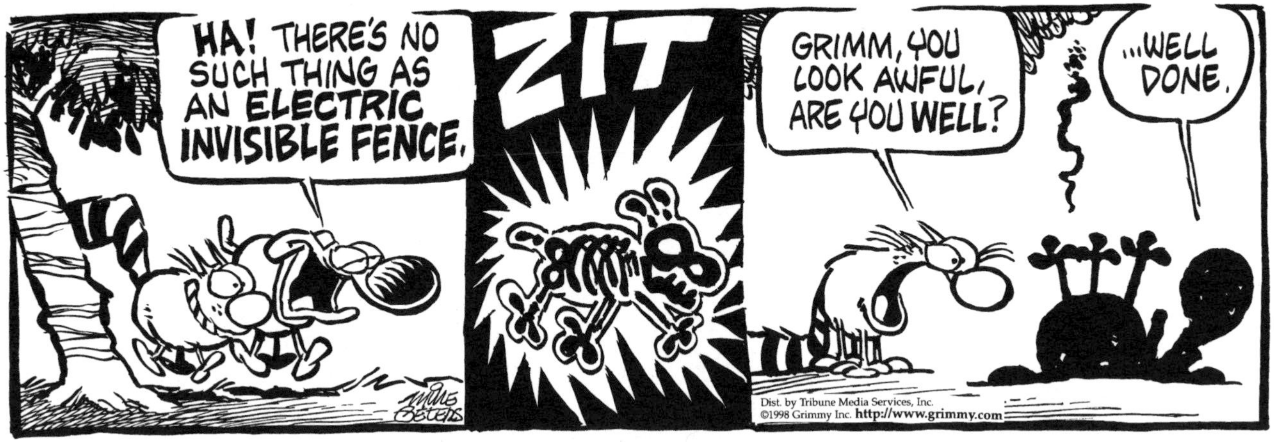
HA! THERE'S NO SUCH THING AS AN ELECTRIC INVISIBLE FENCE.
ZIT
GRIMM, YOU LOOK AWFUL, ARE YOU WELL?
...WELL DONE.
Dist. by Tribune Media Services, Inc. ©1998 Grimmy Inc. http://www.grimmy.com

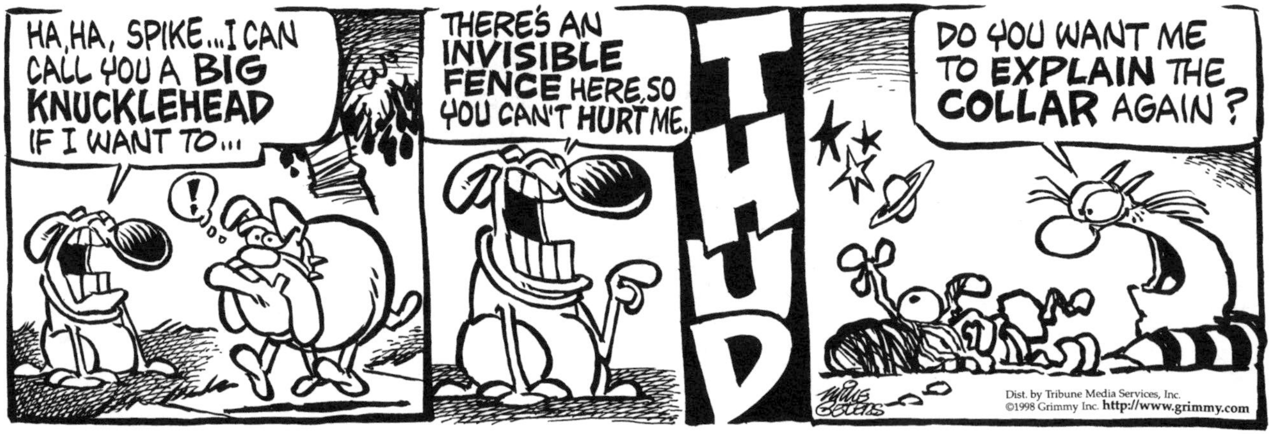
HA, HA, SPIKE... I CAN CALL YOU A BIG KNUCKLEHEAD IF I WANT TO...
!
THERE'S AN INVISIBLE FENCE HERE, SO YOU CAN'T HURT ME.
THUD
DO YOU WANT ME TO EXPLAIN THE COLLAR AGAIN?
Dist. by Tribune Media Services, Inc. ©1998 Grimmy Inc. http://www.grimmy.com

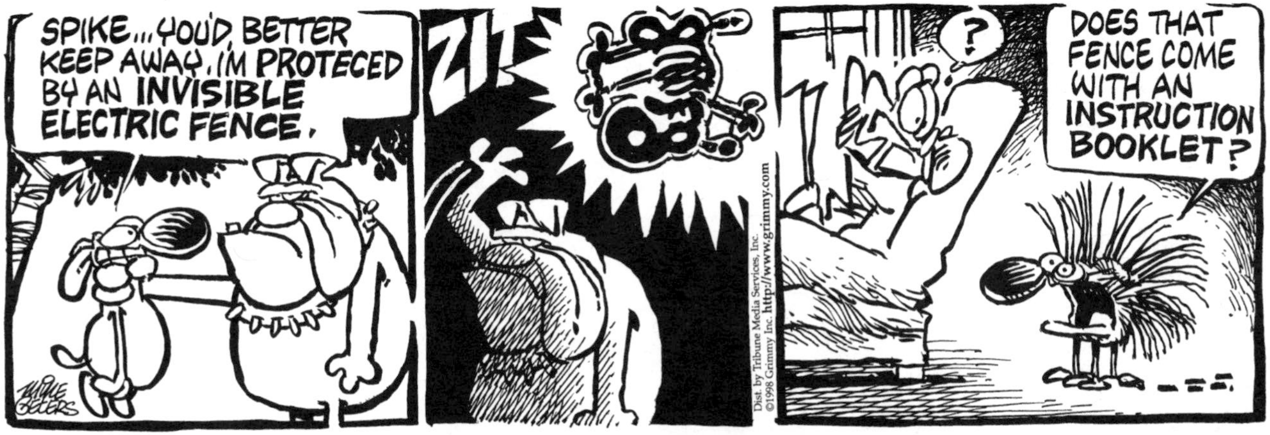
SPIKE... YOU'D BETTER KEEP AWAY. I'M PROTECED BY AN INVISIBLE ELECTRIC FENCE.
ZIT
?
DOES THAT FENCE COME WITH AN INSTRUCTION BOOKLET?
Dist. by Tribune Media Services, Inc. ©1998 Grimmy Inc. http://www.grimmy.com

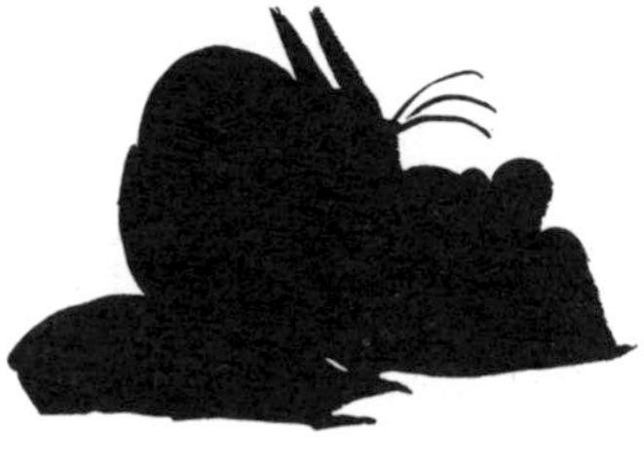

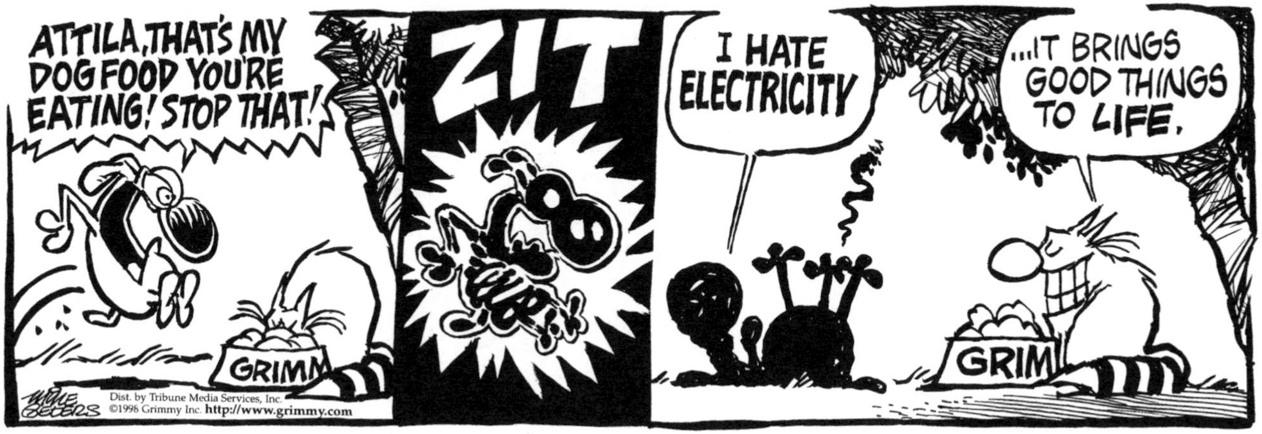
ATTILA, THAT'S MY DOG FOOD YOU'RE EATING! STOP THAT!
GRIMM
Dist. by Tribune Media Services, Inc. ©1998 Grimmy Inc. http://www.grimmy.com
ZIT
I HATE ELECTRICITY
...IT BRINGS GOOD THINGS TO LIFE.
GRIM

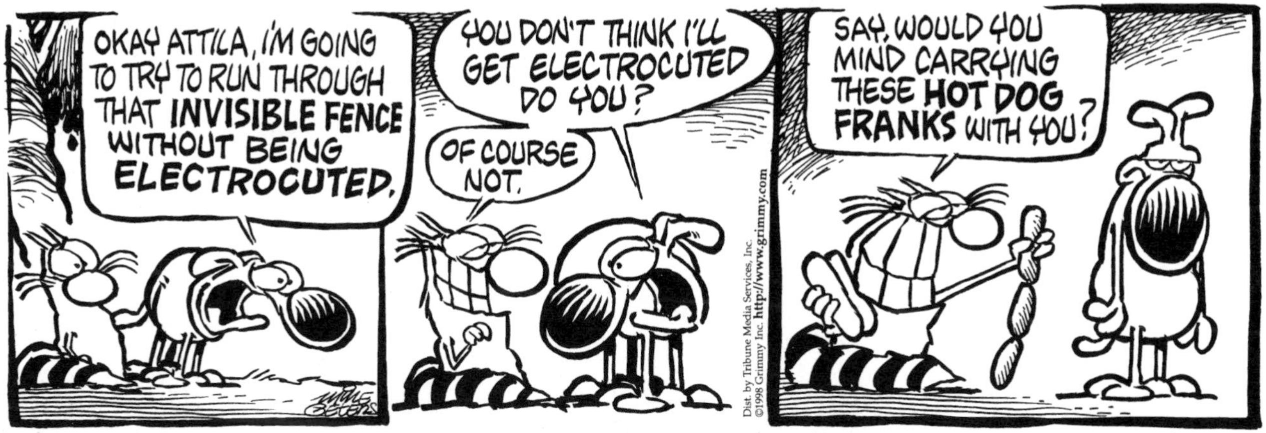
OKAY ATTILA, I'M GOING TO TRY TO RUN THROUGH THAT INVISIBLE FENCE WITHOUT BEING ELECTROCUTED.
YOU DON'T THINK I'LL GET ELECTROCUTED DO YOU?
OF COURSE NOT.
Dist. by Tribune Media Services, Inc. ©1998 Grimmy Inc. http://www.grimmy.com
SAY, WOULD YOU MIND CARRYING THESE HOT DOG FRANKS WITH YOU?

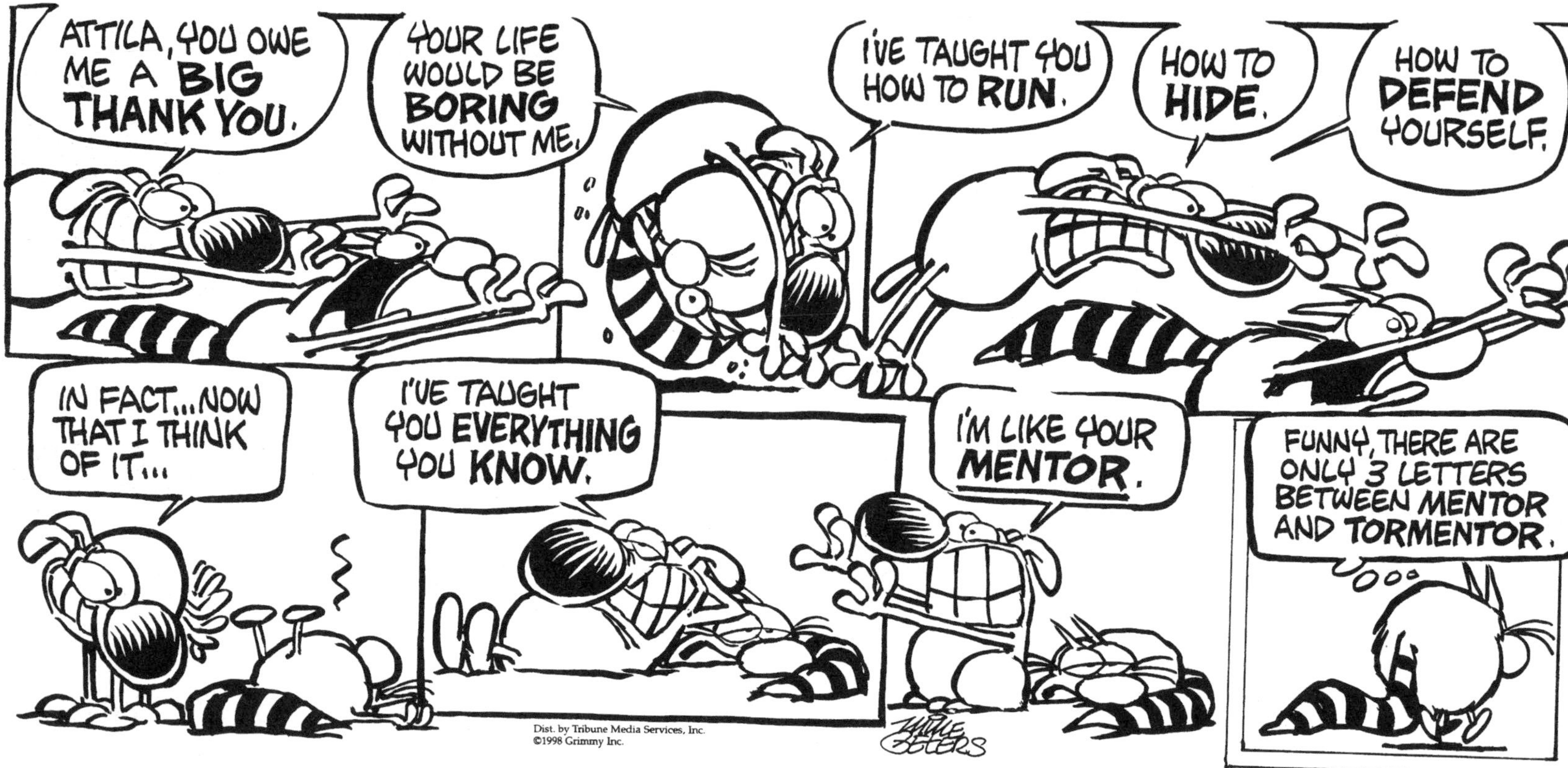
ATTILA, YOU OWE ME A **BIG THANK YOU**.
YOUR LIFE WOULD BE **BORING** WITHOUT ME.
I'VE TAUGHT YOU HOW TO **RUN**.
HOW TO **HIDE**.
HOW TO **DEFEND** YOURSELF.
IN FACT...NOW THAT I THINK OF IT...
I'VE TAUGHT YOU **EVERYTHING** YOU **KNOW**.
I'M LIKE YOUR **MENTOR**.
FUNNY, THERE ARE ONLY 3 LETTERS BETWEEN **MENTOR** AND **TORMENTOR**.
Dist. by Tribune Media Services, Inc.
©1998 Grimmy Inc.
MIKE PETERS

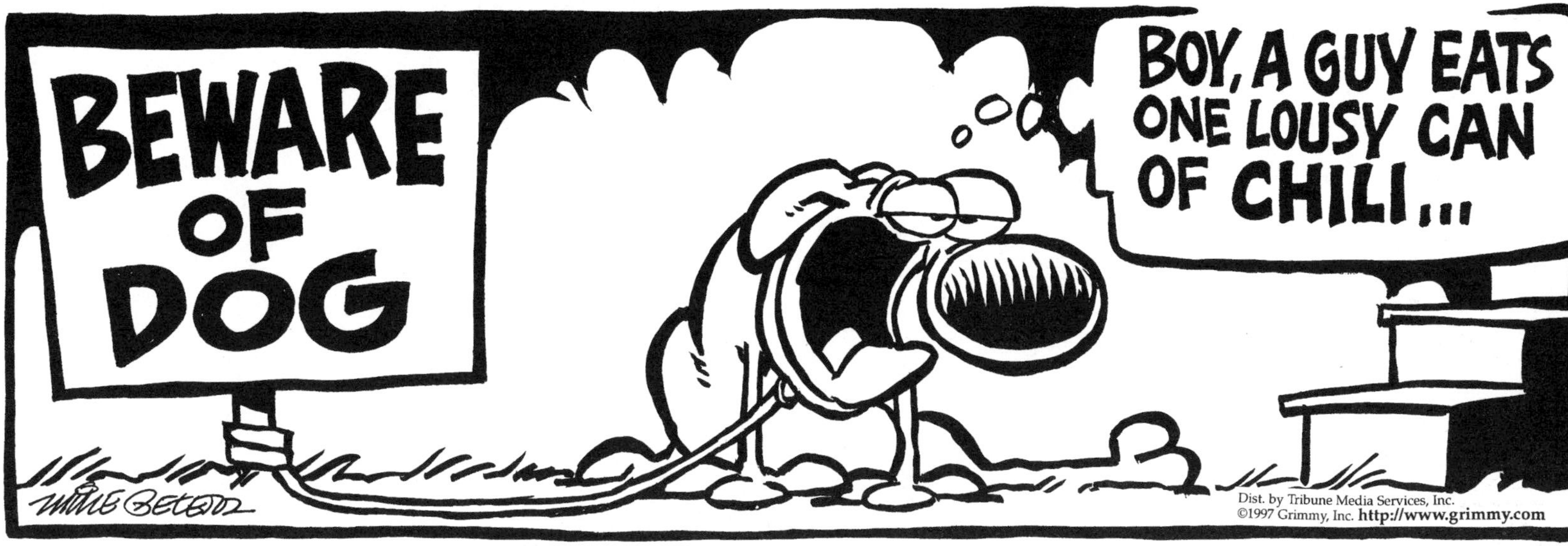
BEWARE OF DOG
BOY, A GUY EATS ONE LOUSY CAN OF CHILI...
Dist. by Tribune Media Services, Inc.
©1997 Grimmy, Inc. http://www.grimmy.com

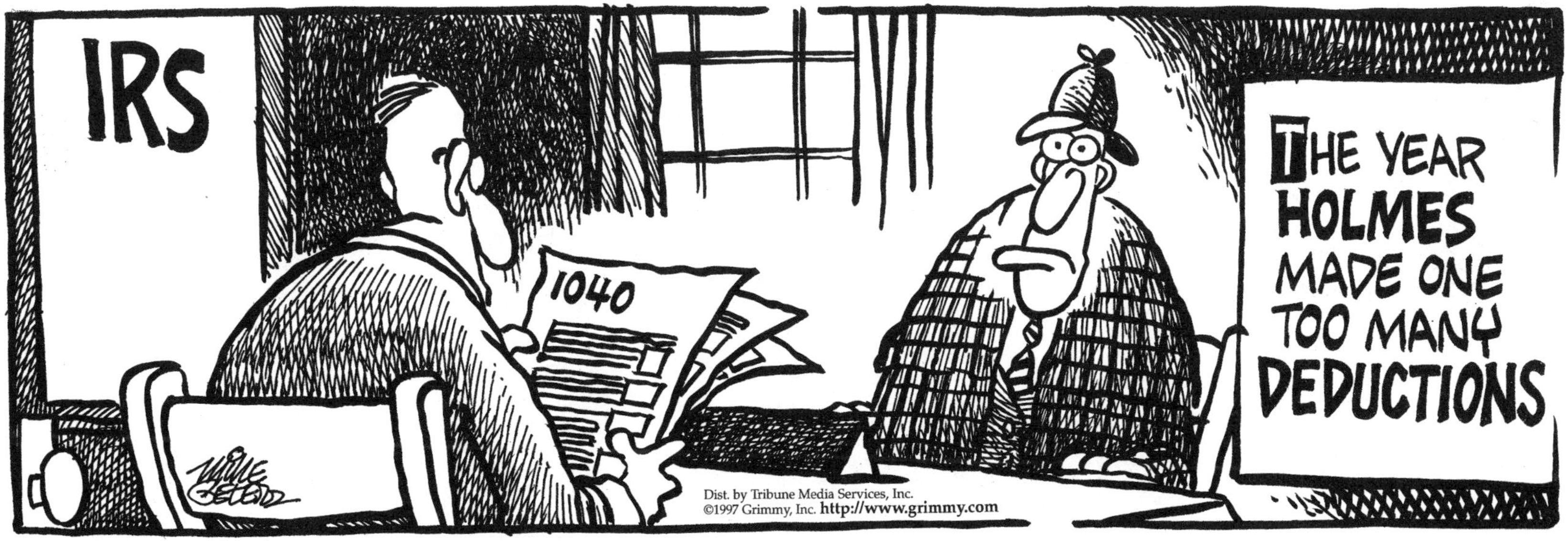
IRS
1040
THE YEAR HOLMES MADE ONE TOO MANY DEDUCTIONS
Dist. by Tribune Media Services, Inc.
©1997 Grimmy, Inc. http://www.grimmy.com

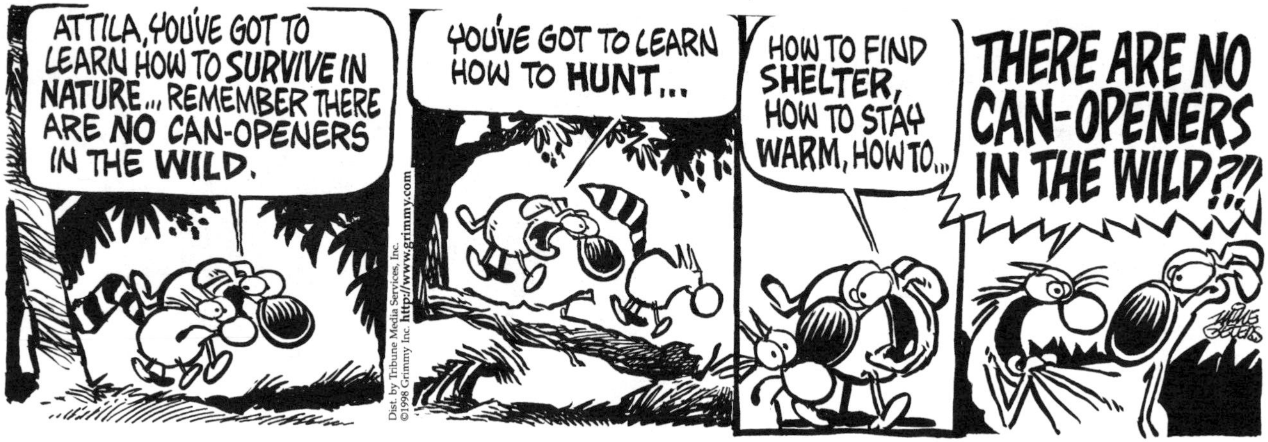
ATTILA, YOU'VE GOT TO LEARN HOW TO SURVIVE IN NATURE... REMEMBER THERE ARE NO CAN-OPENERS IN THE WILD.
YOU'VE GOT TO LEARN HOW TO HUNT...
HOW TO FIND SHELTER, HOW TO STAY WARM, HOW TO...
THERE ARE NO CAN-OPENERS IN THE WILD?!!
Dist. by Tribune Media Services, Inc. ©1998 Grimmy Inc. http://www.grimmy.com

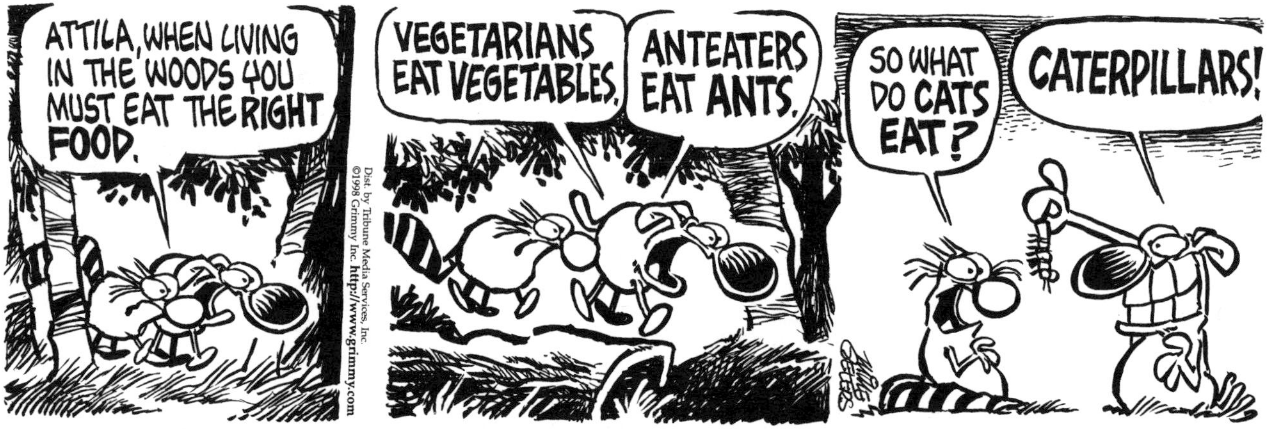
ATTILA, WHEN LIVING IN THE WOODS YOU MUST EAT THE RIGHT FOOD.
VEGETARIANS EAT VEGETABLES.
ANTEATERS EAT ANTS.
SO WHAT DO CATS EAT?
CATERPILLARS!
Dist. by Tribune Media Services, Inc. ©1998 Grimmy Inc. http://www.grimmy.com

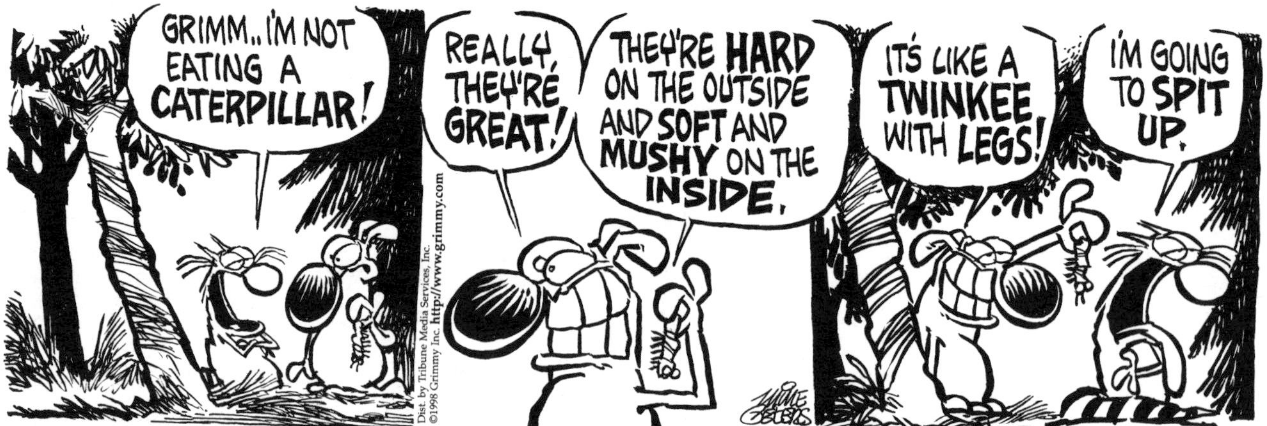
GRIMM.. I'M NOT EATING A CATERPILLAR!
REALLY, THEY'RE GREAT!
THEY'RE HARD ON THE OUTSIDE AND SOFT AND MUSHY ON THE INSIDE.
IT'S LIKE A TWINKEE WITH LEGS!
I'M GOING TO SPIT UP.
Dist. by Tribune Media Services, Inc. ©1998 Grimmy Inc. http://www.grimmy.com

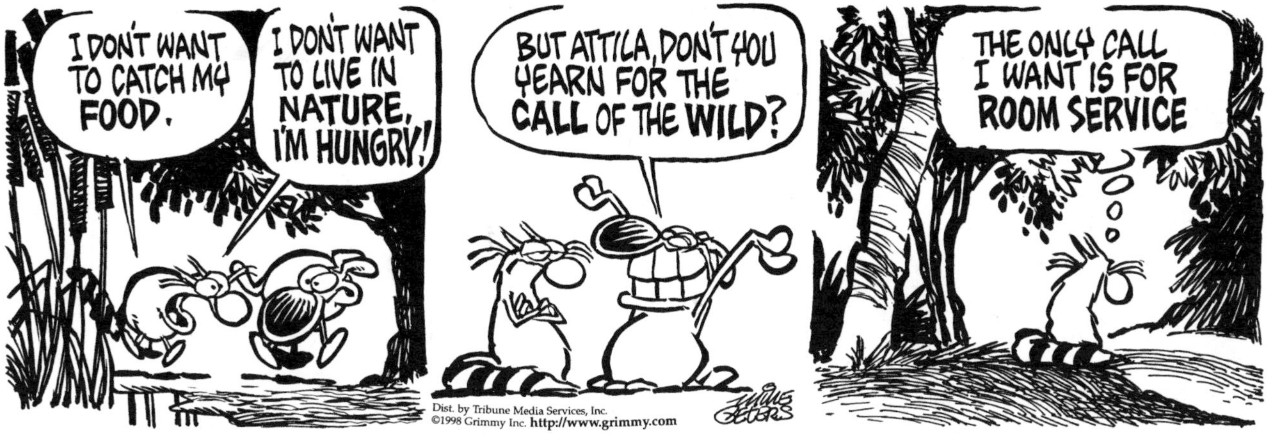

I DON'T WANT TO CATCH MY FOOD.
I DON'T WANT TO LIVE IN NATURE, I'M HUNGRY!
BUT ATTILA, DON'T YOU YEARN FOR THE CALL OF THE WILD?
THE ONLY CALL I WANT IS FOR ROOM SERVICE
Dist. by Tribune Media Services, Inc.
©1998 Grimmy Inc. http://www.grimmy.com
MIKE PETERS

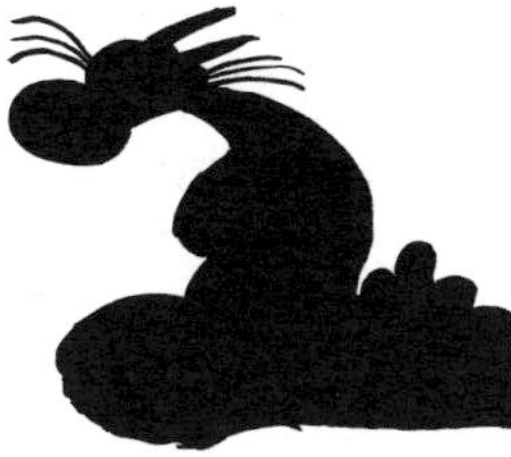

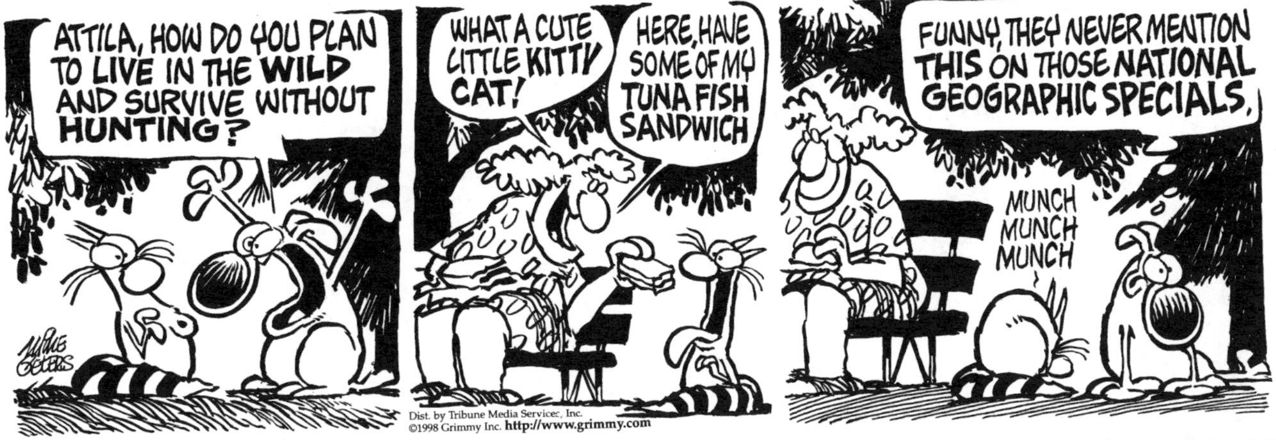

ATTILA, HOW DO YOU PLAN TO LIVE IN THE WILD AND SURVIVE WITHOUT HUNTING?
MIKE PETERS
WHAT A CUTE LITTLE KITTY CAT!
HERE, HAVE SOME OF MY TUNA FISH SANDWICH
Dist. by Tribune Media Services, Inc.
©1998 Grimmy Inc. http://www.grimmy.com
FUNNY, THEY NEVER MENTION THIS ON THOSE NATIONAL GEOGRAPHIC SPECIALS.
MUNCH MUNCH MUNCH

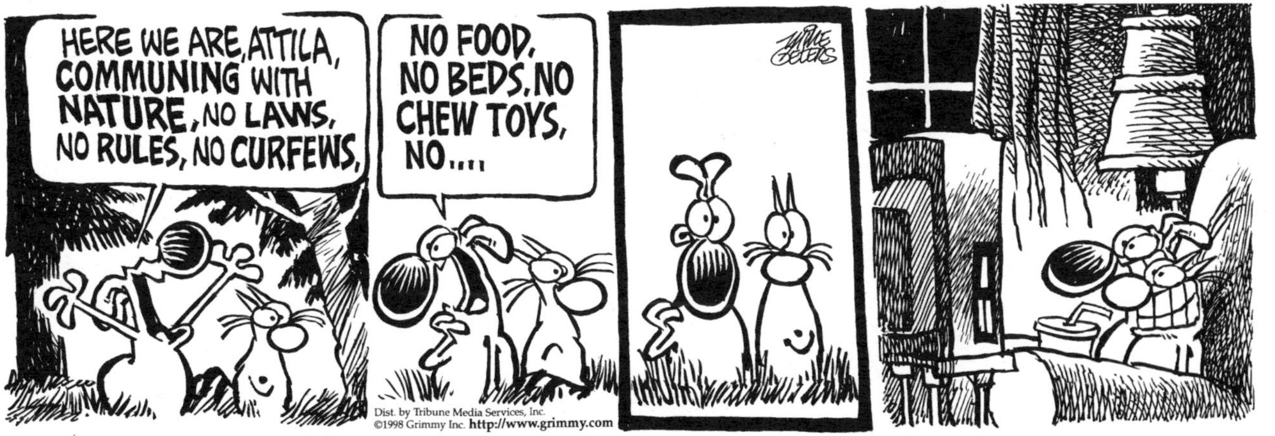

HERE WE ARE, ATTILA, COMMUNING WITH NATURE, NO LAWS, NO RULES, NO CURFEWS,
NO FOOD, NO BEDS, NO CHEW TOYS, NO....
MIKE PETERS
Dist. by Tribune Media Services, Inc.
©1998 Grimmy Inc. http://www.grimmy.com

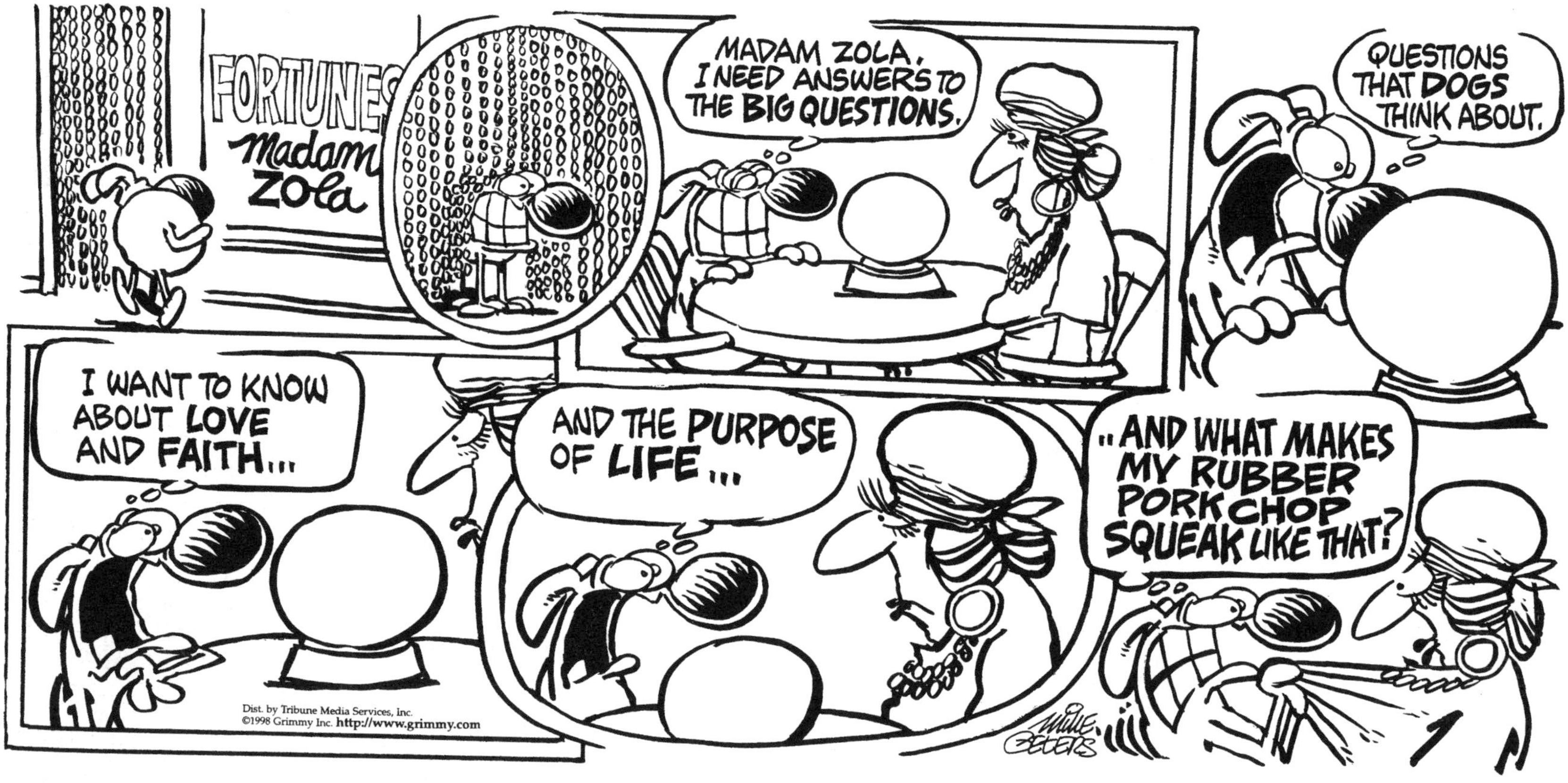

FORTUNES
Madam Zola
MADAM ZOLA, I NEED ANSWERS TO THE BIG QUESTIONS.
QUESTIONS THAT DOGS THINK ABOUT.
I WANT TO KNOW ABOUT LOVE AND FAITH...
AND THE PURPOSE OF LIFE...
..AND WHAT MAKES MY RUBBER PORKCHOP SQUEAK LIKE THAT?
Dist. by Tribune Media Services, Inc.
©1998 Grimmy Inc. http://www.grimmy.com

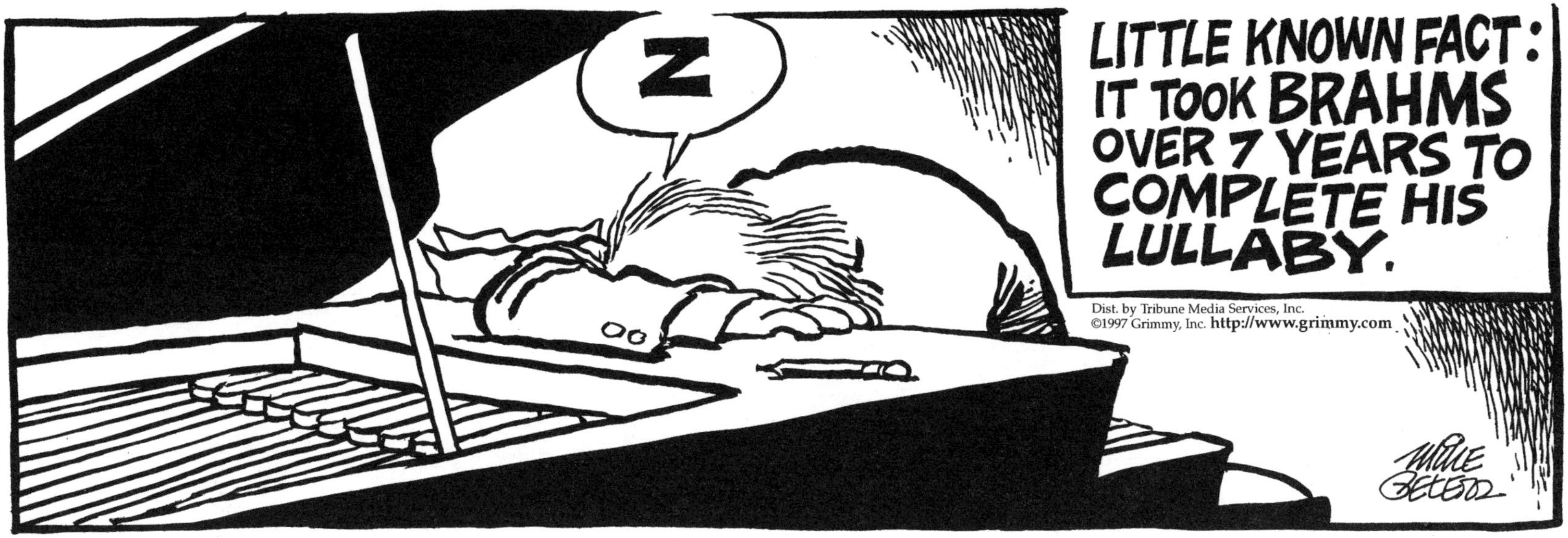
Z
LITTLE KNOWN FACT: IT TOOK BRAHMS OVER 7 YEARS TO COMPLETE HIS LULLABY.
Dist. by Tribune Media Services, Inc.
©1997 Grimmy, Inc. http://www.grimmy.com

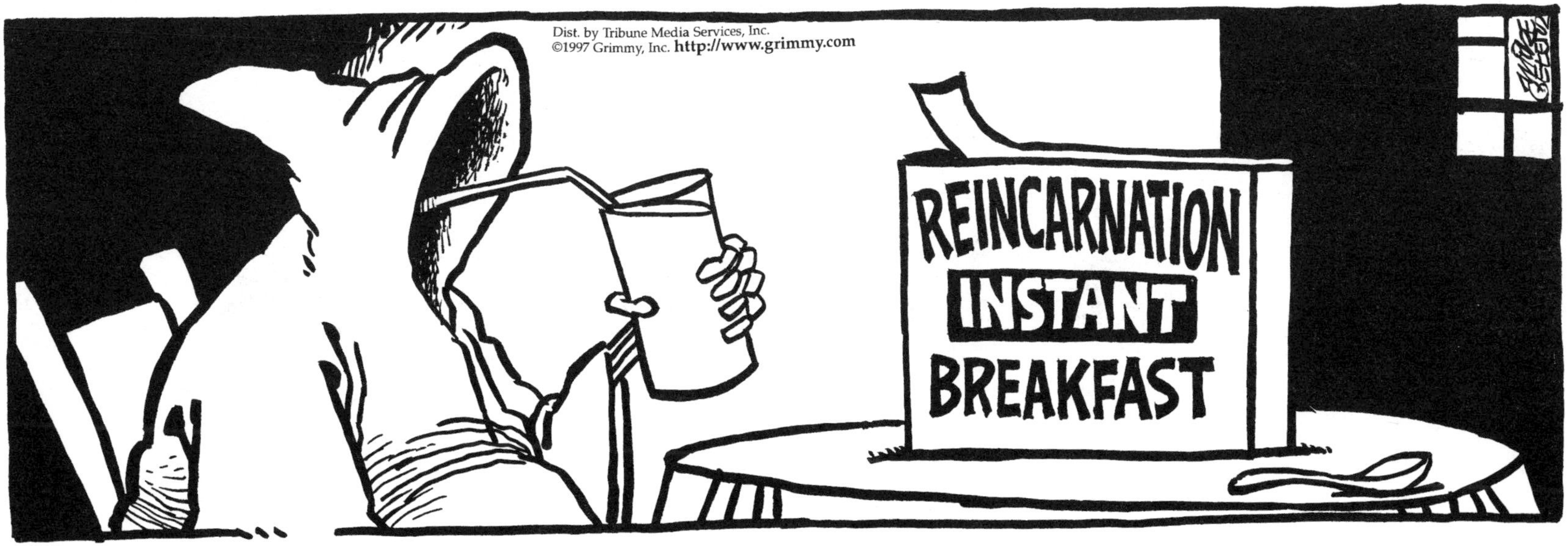
Dist. by Tribune Media Services, Inc.
©1997 Grimmy, Inc. http://www.grimmy.com
REINCARNATION
INSTANT
BREAKFAST

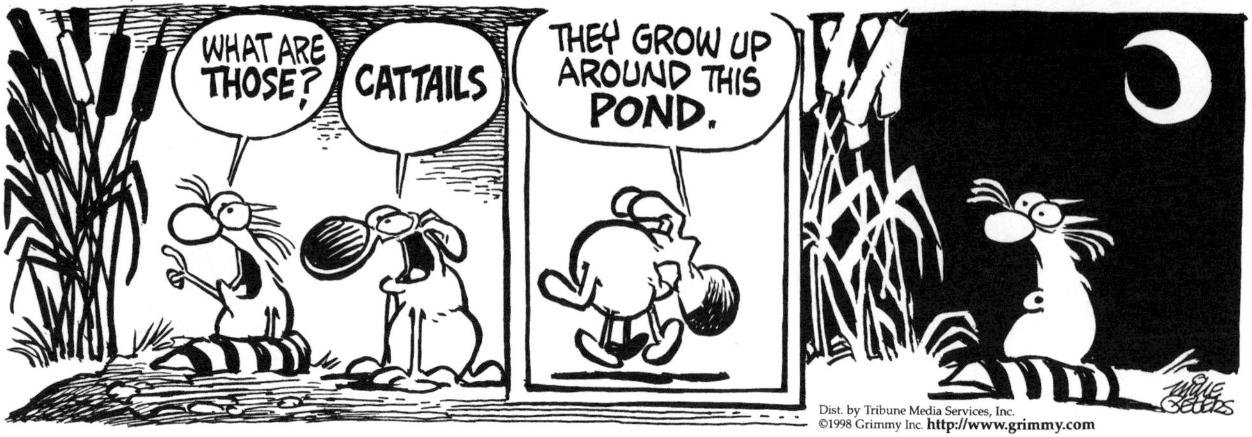
WHAT ARE THOSE?
CATTAILS
THEY GROW UP AROUND THIS POND.
Dist. by Tribune Media Services, Inc.
©1998 Grimmy Inc. http://www.grimmy.com

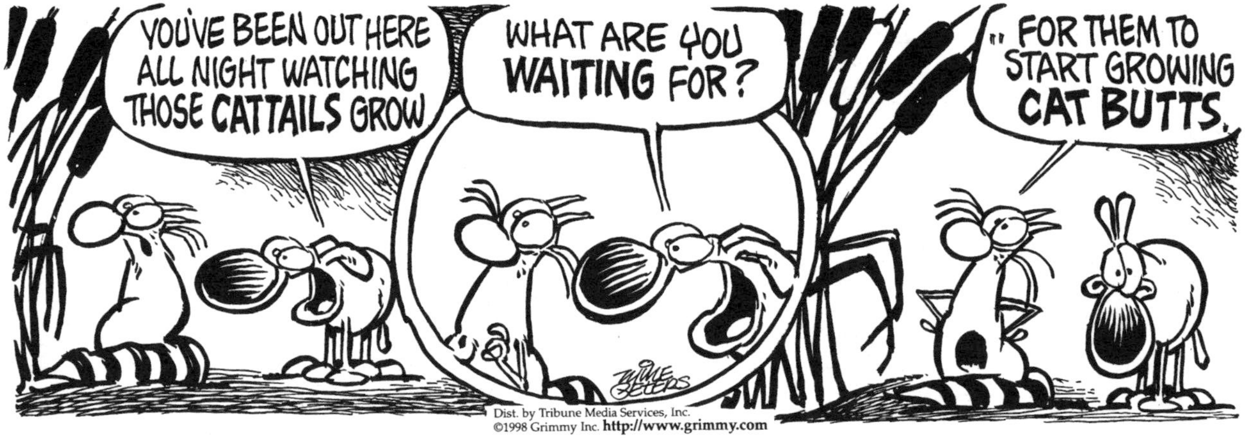
YOU'VE BEEN OUT HERE ALL NIGHT WATCHING THOSE CATTAILS GROW
WHAT ARE YOU WAITING FOR?
".. FOR THEM TO START GROWING CAT BUTTS."
Dist. by Tribune Media Services, Inc.
©1998 Grimmy Inc. http://www.grimmy.com

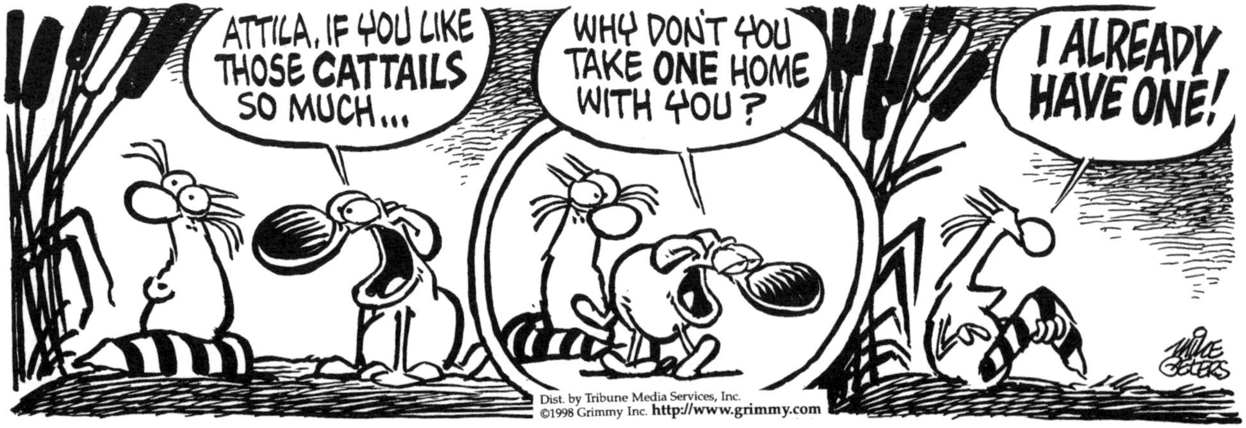
ATTILA, IF YOU LIKE THOSE CATTAILS SO MUCH...
WHY DON'T YOU TAKE ONE HOME WITH YOU?
I ALREADY HAVE ONE!
Dist. by Tribune Media Services, Inc.
©1998 Grimmy Inc. http://www.grimmy.com

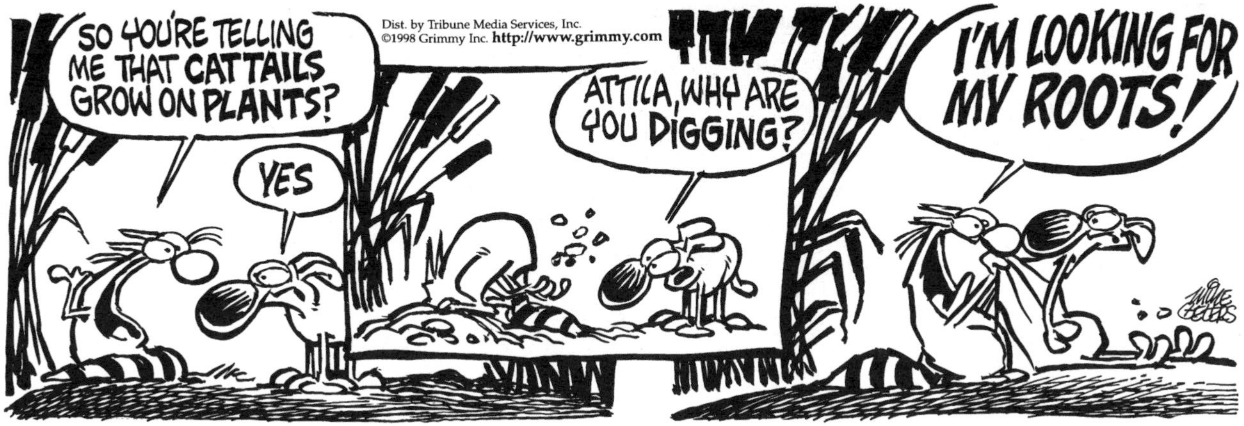
SO YOU'RE TELLING ME THAT CATTAILS GROW ON PLANTS?
YES
Dist. by Tribune Media Services, Inc. ©1998 Grimmy Inc. http://www.grimmy.com
ATTILA, WHY ARE YOU DIGGING?
I'M LOOKING FOR MY ROOTS!

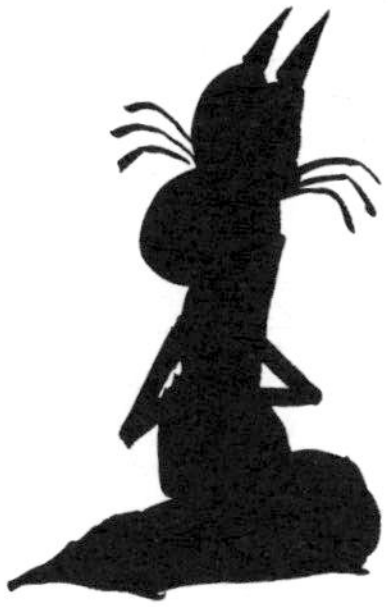

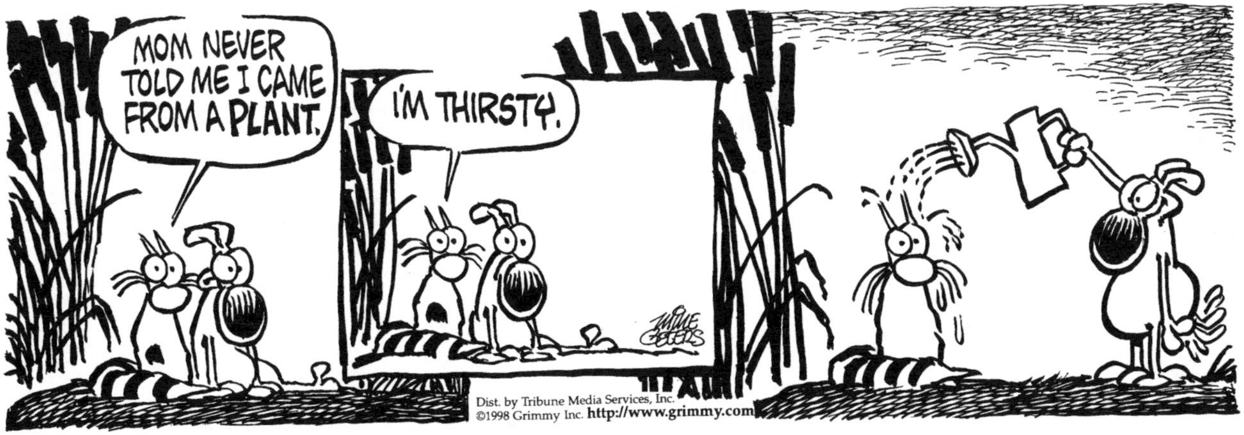
MOM NEVER TOLD ME I CAME FROM A PLANT.
I'M THIRSTY.
Dist. by Tribune Media Services, Inc. ©1998 Grimmy Inc. http://www.grimmy.com

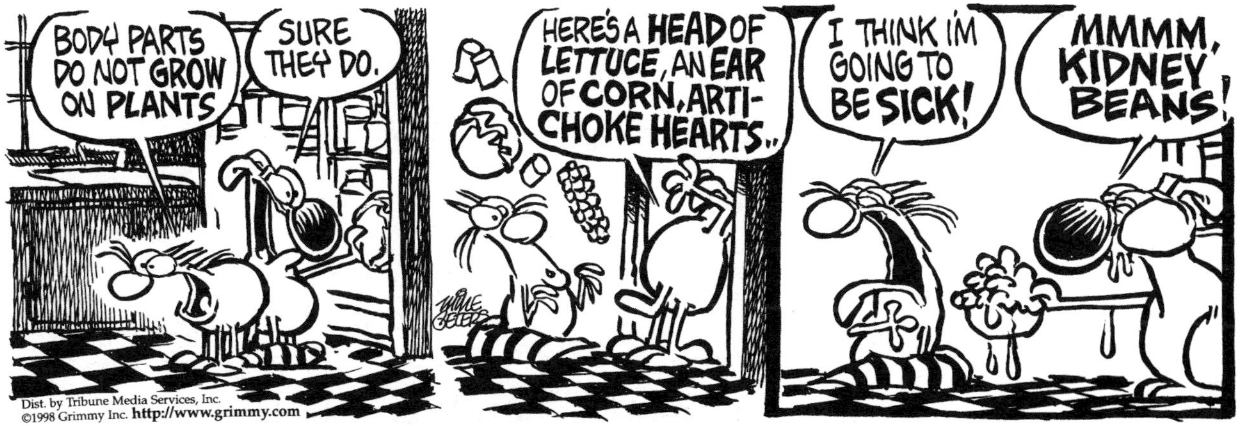
BODY PARTS DO NOT GROW ON PLANTS
SURE THEY DO.
HERE'S A HEAD OF LETTUCE, AN EAR OF CORN, ARTI-CHOKE HEARTS..
I THINK I'M GOING TO BE SICK!
MMMM, KIDNEY BEANS!
Dist. by Tribune Media Services, Inc. ©1998 Grimmy Inc. http://www.grimmy.com

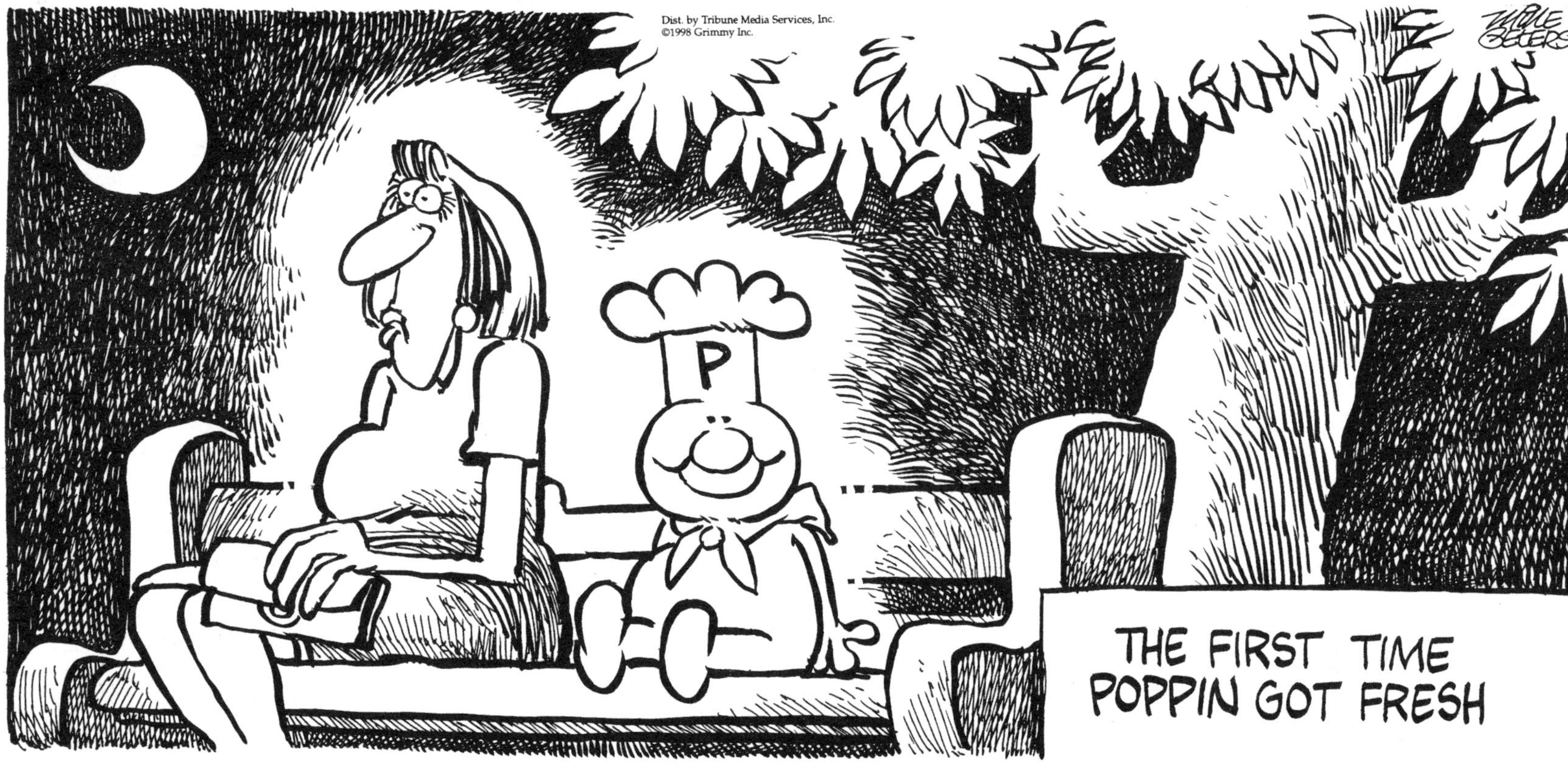

Dist. by Tribune Media Services, Inc.
©1998 Grimmy Inc.
THE FIRST TIME
POPPIN GOT FRESH

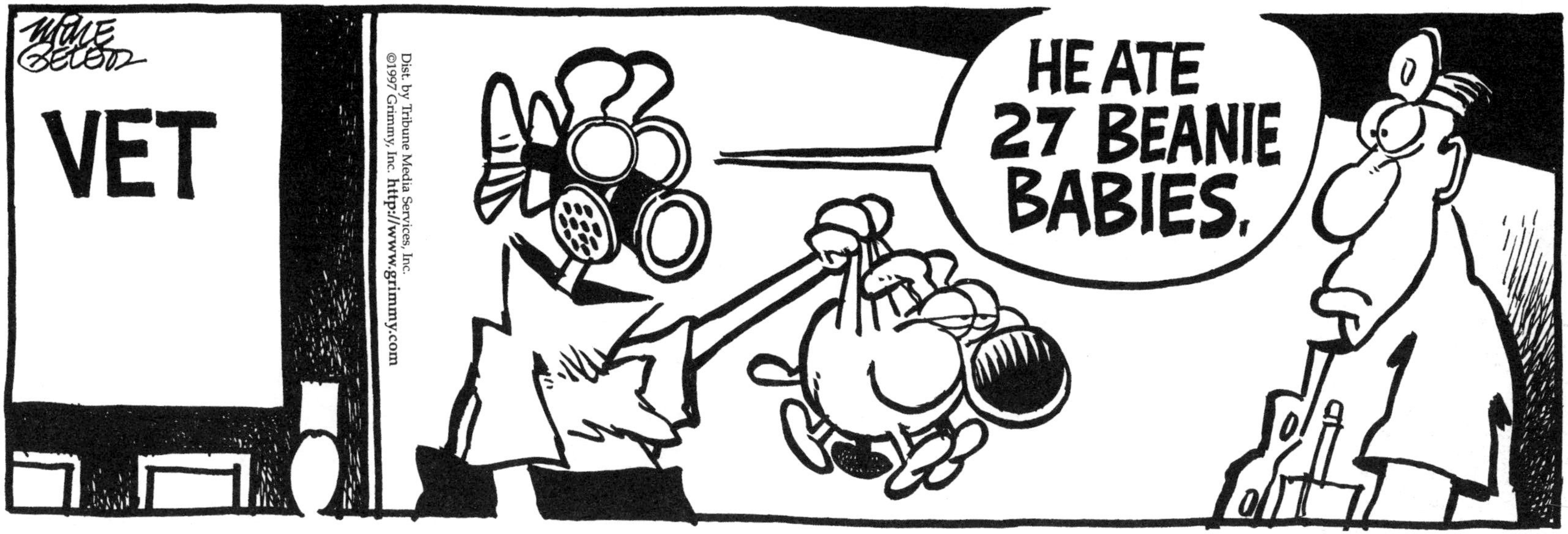
MIKE PETERS
VET
Dist. by Tribune Media Services, Inc.
©1997 Grimmy, Inc. http://www.grimmy.com
HE ATE 27 BEANIE BABIES.

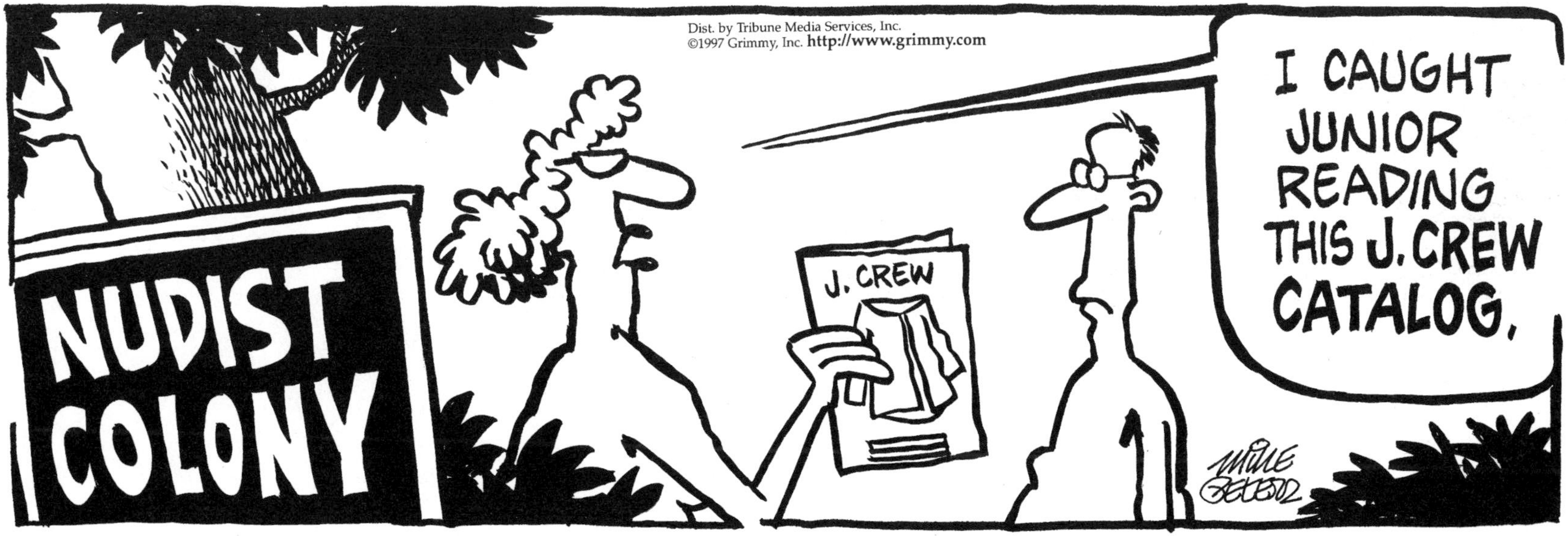
Dist. by Tribune Media Services, Inc.
©1997 Grimmy, Inc. http://www.grimmy.com
NUDIST COLONY
J. CREW
I CAUGHT JUNIOR READING THIS J. CREW CATALOG.
MIKE PETERS

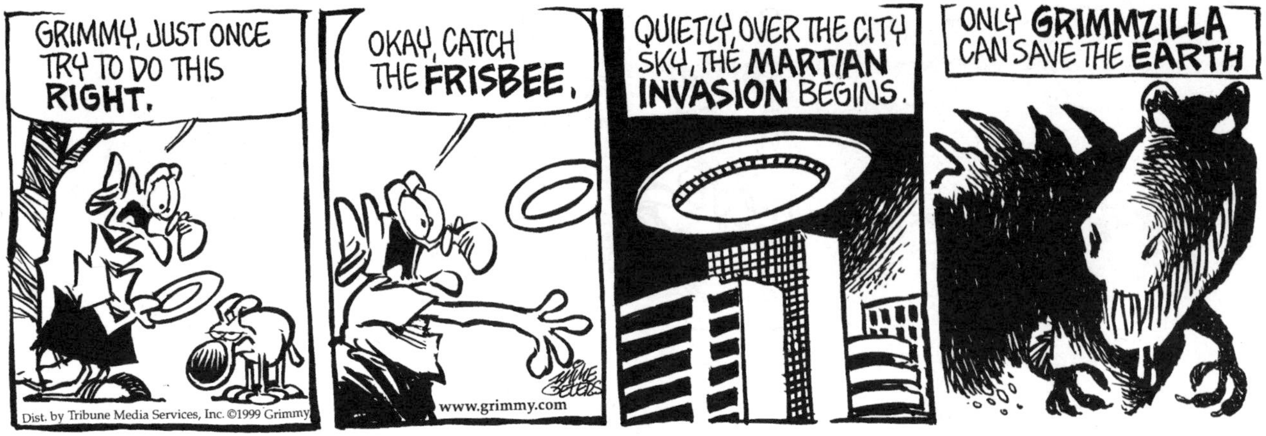
GRIMMY, JUST ONCE TRY TO DO THIS RIGHT.
OKAY, CATCH THE FRISBEE.
QUIETLY, OVER THE CITY SKY, THE MARTIAN INVASION BEGINS.
ONLY GRIMMZILLA CAN SAVE THE EARTH
Dist. by Tribune Media Services, Inc. ©1999 Grimmy
www.grimmy.com

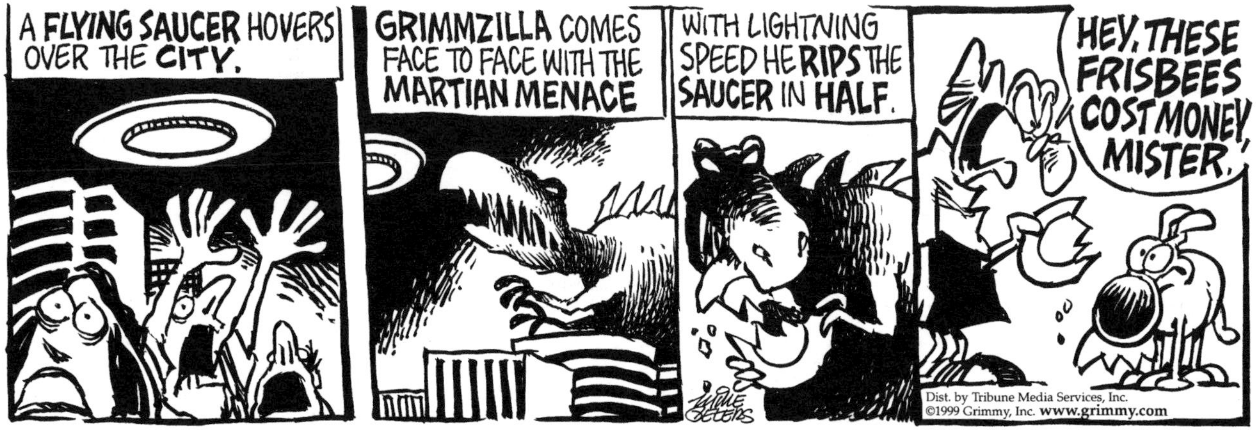
A FLYING SAUCER HOVERS OVER THE CITY.
GRIMMZILLA COMES FACE TO FACE WITH THE MARTIAN MENACE
WITH LIGHTNING SPEED HE RIPS THE SAUCER IN HALF.
HEY, THESE FRISBEES COST MONEY, MISTER.
Dist. by Tribune Media Services, Inc. ©1999 Grimmy, Inc. www.grimmy.com

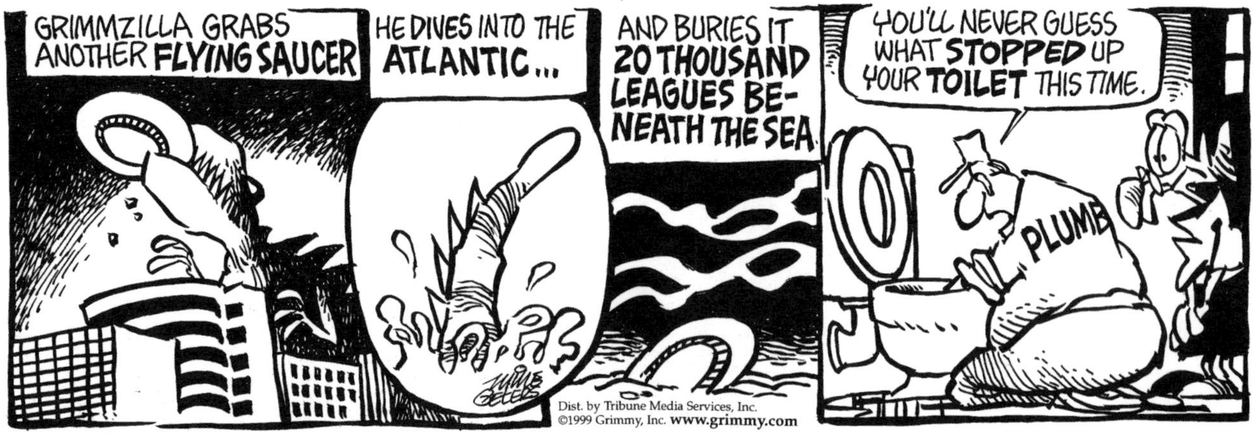
GRIMMZILLA GRABS ANOTHER FLYING SAUCER
HE DIVES INTO THE ATLANTIC...
AND BURIES IT 20 THOUSAND LEAGUES BENEATH THE SEA
YOU'LL NEVER GUESS WHAT STOPPED UP YOUR TOILET THIS TIME.
PLUMB
Dist. by Tribune Media Services, Inc. ©1999 Grimmy, Inc. www.grimmy.com

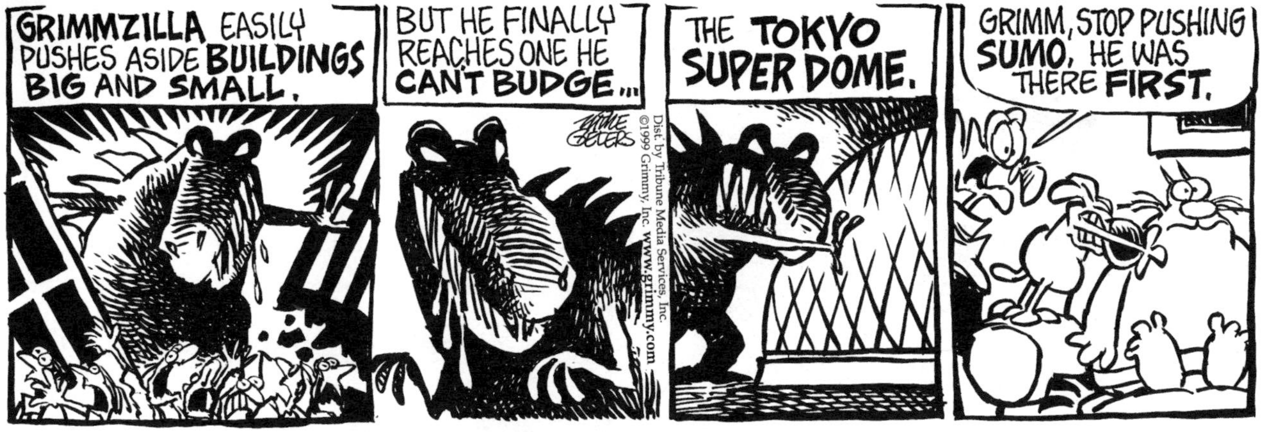
GRIMMZILLA EASILY PUSHES ASIDE BUILDINGS BIG AND SMALL.
BUT HE FINALLY REACHES ONE HE CAN'T BUDGE...
Dist. by Tribune Media Services, Inc. ©1999 Grimmy, Inc. www.grimmy.com
THE TOKYO SUPER DOME.
GRIMM, STOP PUSHING SUMO, HE WAS THERE FIRST.

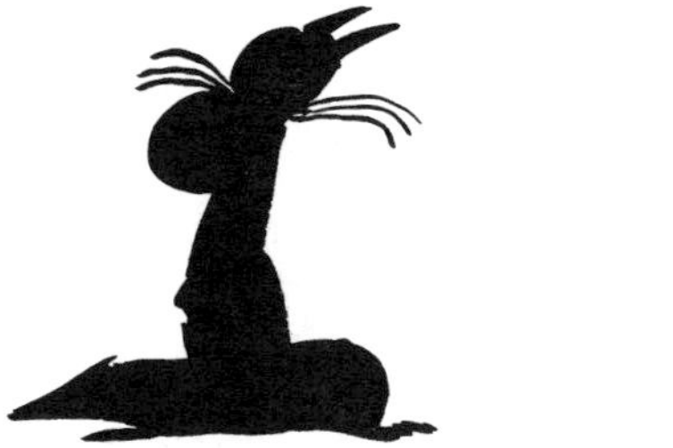

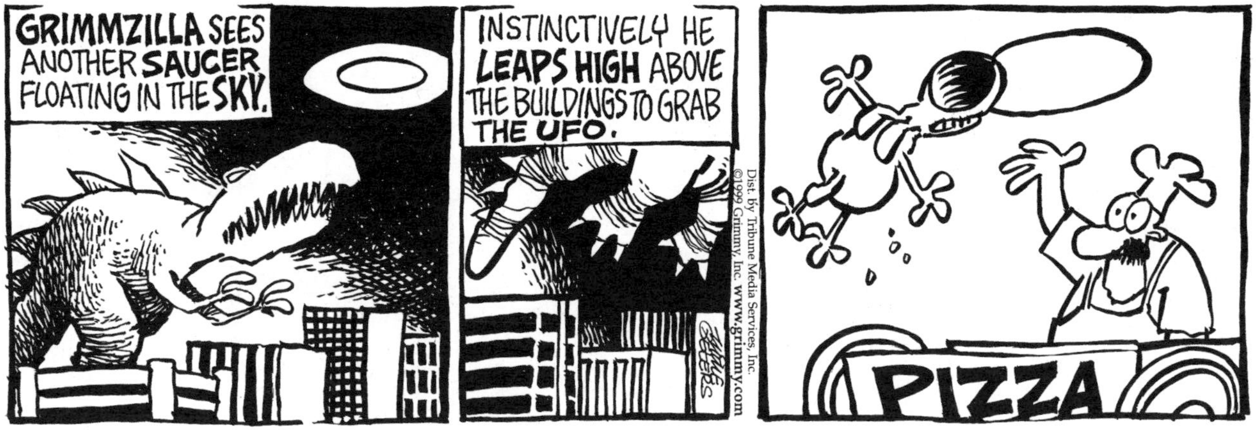
GRIMMZILLA SEES ANOTHER SAUCER FLOATING IN THE SKY.
INSTINCTIVELY HE LEAPS HIGH ABOVE THE BUILDINGS TO GRAB THE UFO.
Dist. by Tribune Media Services, Inc. ©1999 Grimmy, Inc. www.grimmy.com
PIZZA

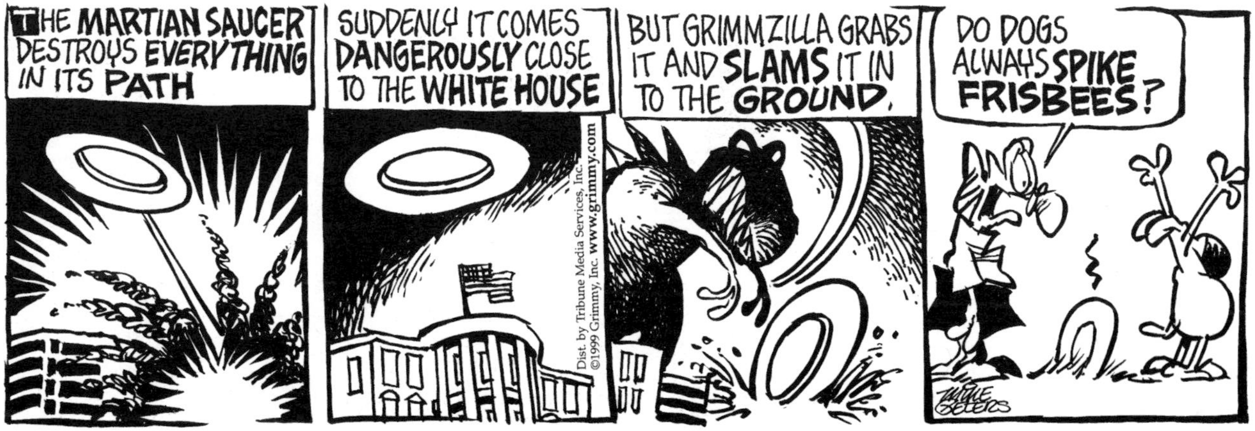
THE MARTIAN SAUCER DESTROYS EVERYTHING IN ITS PATH
SUDDENLY IT COMES DANGEROUSLY CLOSE TO THE WHITE HOUSE
Dist. by Tribune Media Services, Inc. ©1999 Grimmy, Inc. www.grimmy.com
BUT GRIMMZILLA GRABS IT AND SLAMS IT IN TO THE GROUND.
DO DOGS ALWAYS SPIKE FRISBEES?

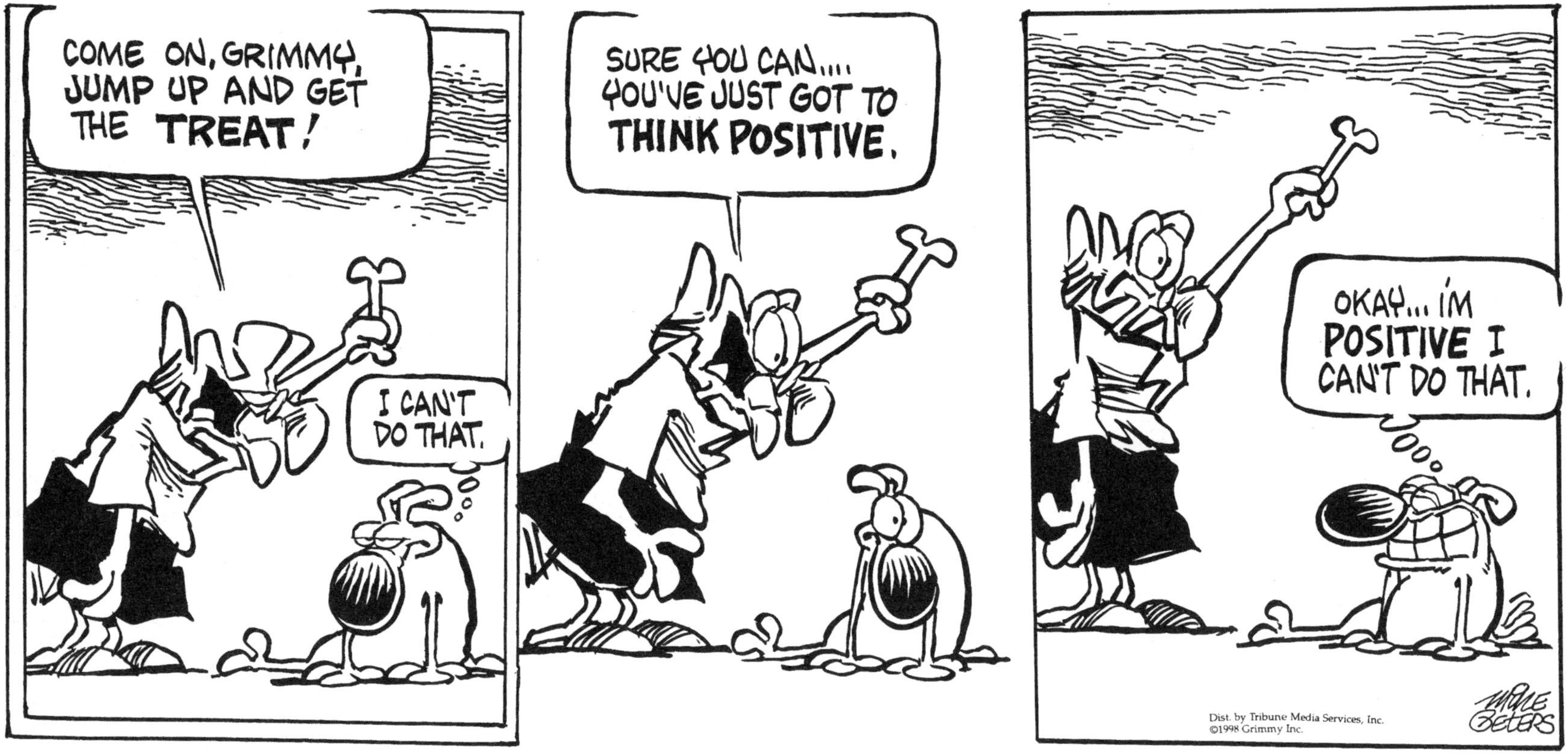
COME ON, GRIMMY, JUMP UP AND GET THE TREAT!
I CAN'T DO THAT.
SURE YOU CAN.... YOU'VE JUST GOT TO THINK POSITIVE.
OKAY... I'M POSITIVE I CAN'T DO THAT.
MIKE PETERS
Dist. by Tribune Media Services, Inc.
©1998 Grimmy Inc.

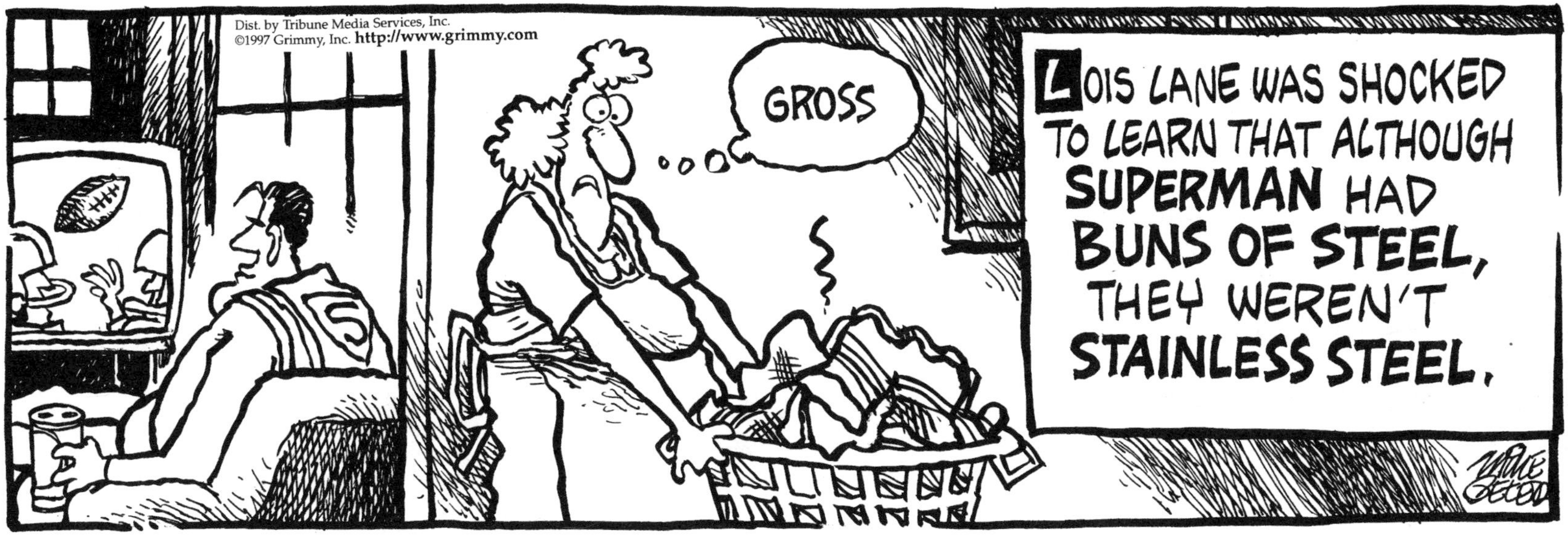
Dist. by Tribune Media Services, Inc.
©1997 Grimmy, Inc. http://www.grimmy.com
GROSS
LOIS LANE WAS SHOCKED TO LEARN THAT ALTHOUGH SUPERMAN HAD BUNS OF STEEL, THEY WEREN'T STAINLESS STEEL.
S

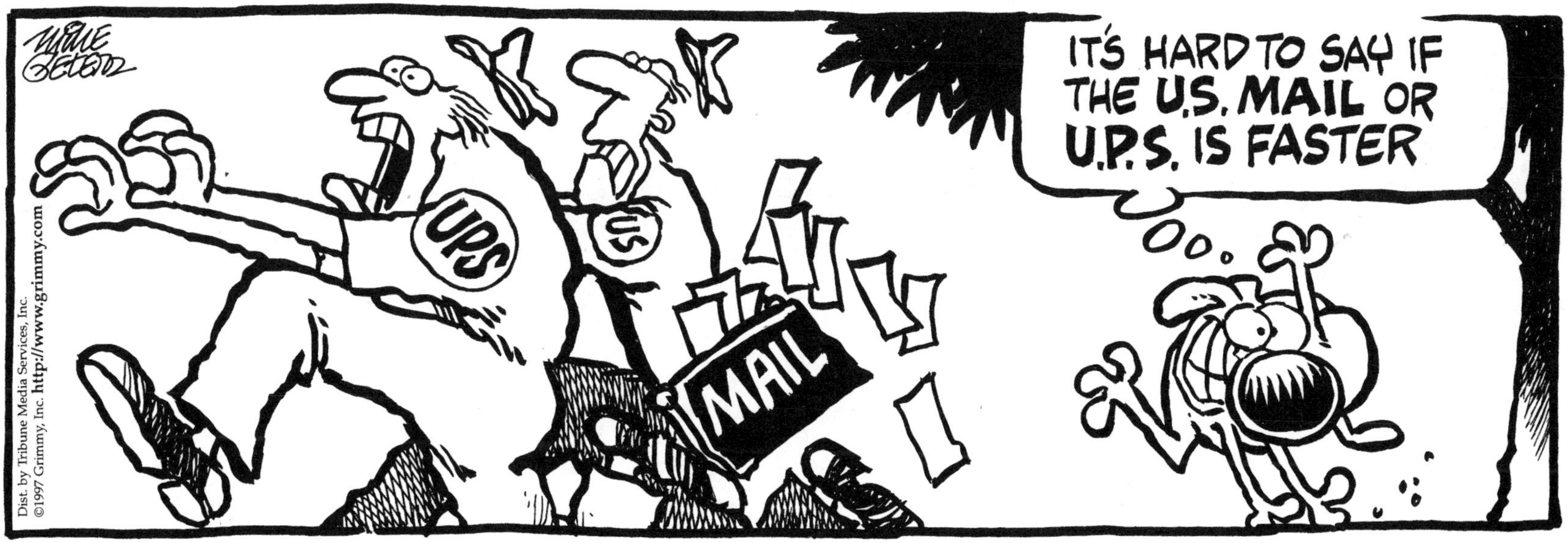
Dist. by Tribune Media Services, Inc.
©1997 Grimmy, Inc. http://www.grimmy.com
IT'S HARD TO SAY IF THE U.S. MAIL OR U.P.S. IS FASTER
UPS
US
MAIL

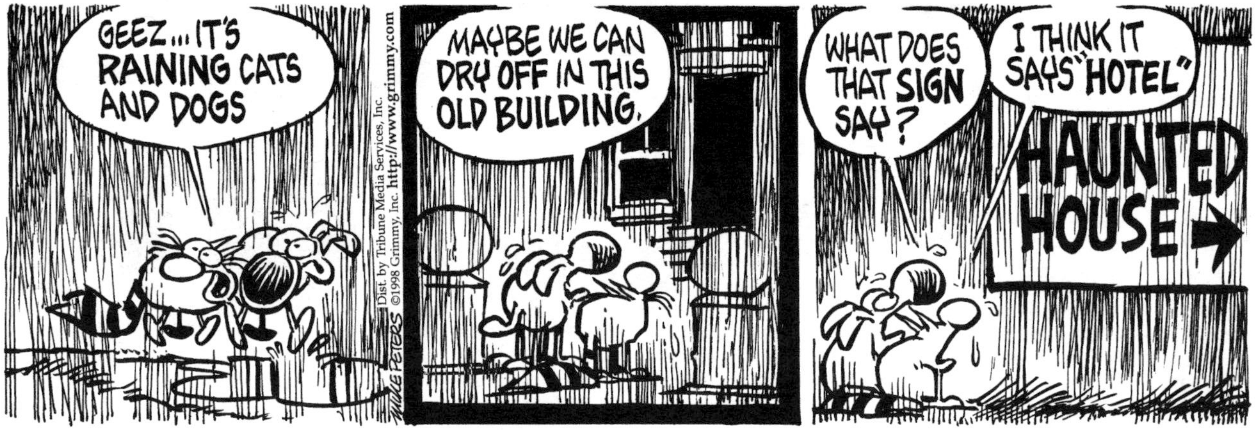
GEEZ... IT'S RAINING CATS AND DOGS
MAYBE WE CAN DRY OFF IN THIS OLD BUILDING.
WHAT DOES THAT SIGN SAY?
I THINK IT SAYS "HOTEL"
HAUNTED HOUSE

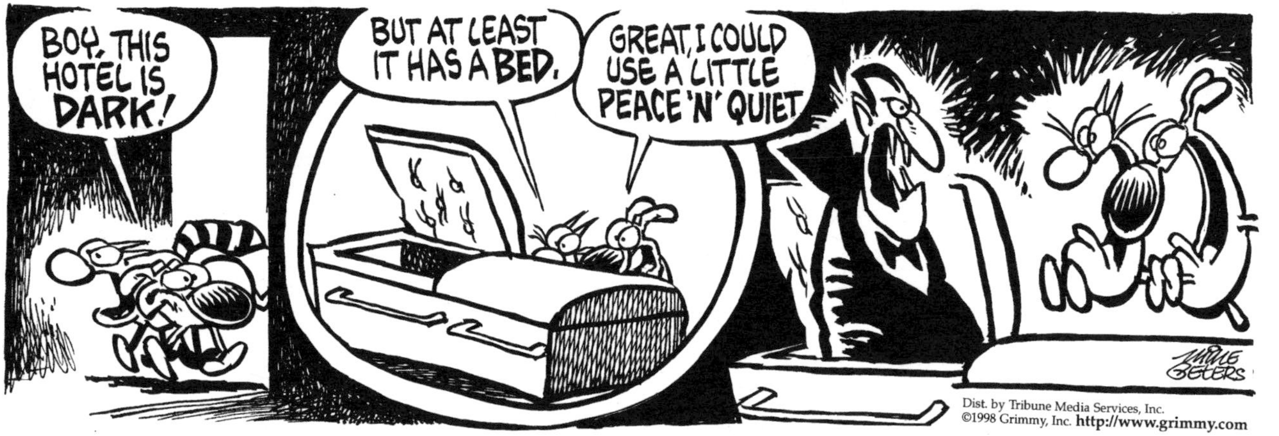
BOY, THIS HOTEL IS DARK!
BUT AT LEAST IT HAS A BED.
GREAT, I COULD USE A LITTLE PEACE 'N' QUIET

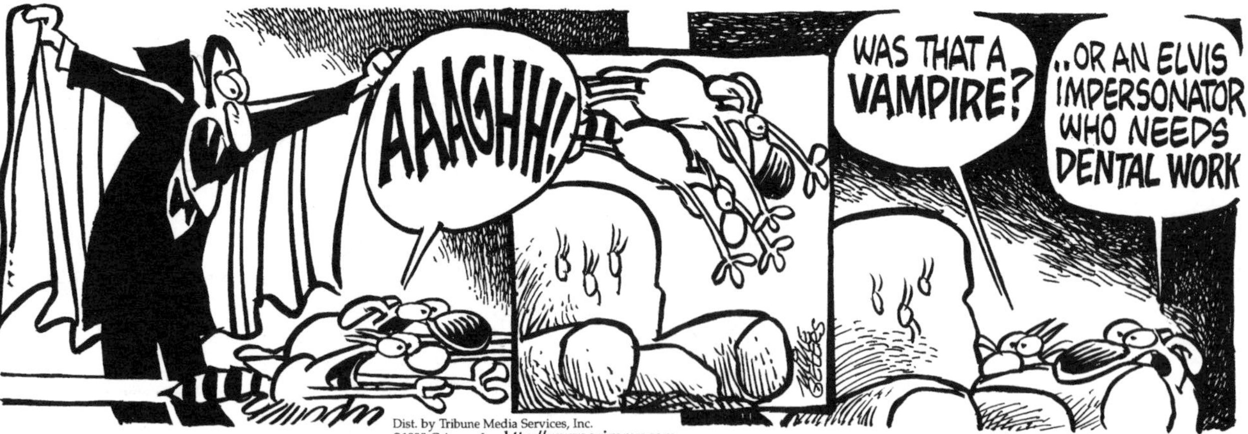
AAAGHH!
WAS THAT A VAMPIRE?
..OR AN ELVIS IMPERSONATOR WHO NEEDS DENTAL WORK

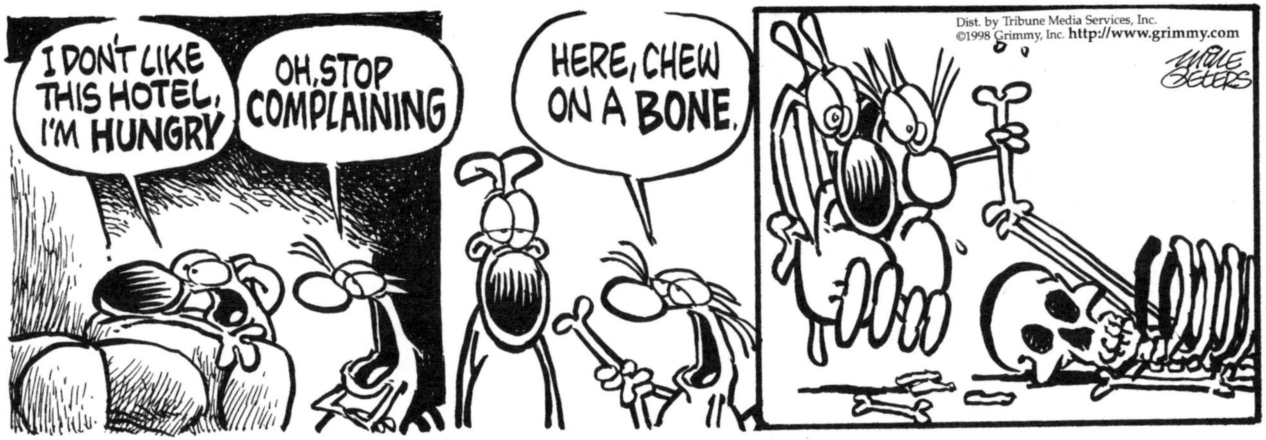
I DON'T LIKE THIS HOTEL, I'M HUNGRY
OH, STOP COMPLAINING
HERE, CHEW ON A BONE.
Dist. by Tribune Media Services, Inc.
©1998 Grimmy, Inc. http://www.grimmy.com
MIKE PETERS

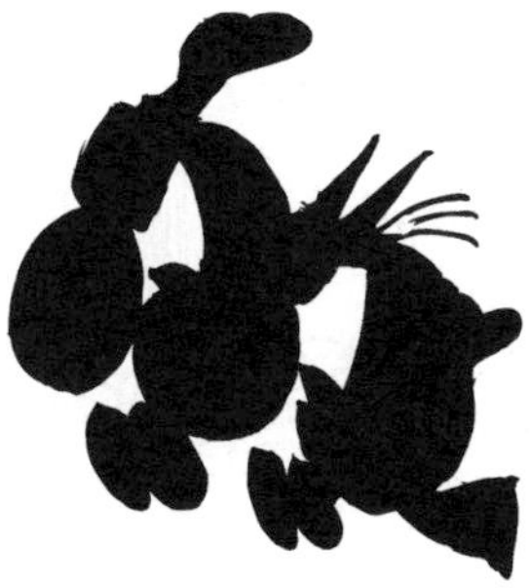

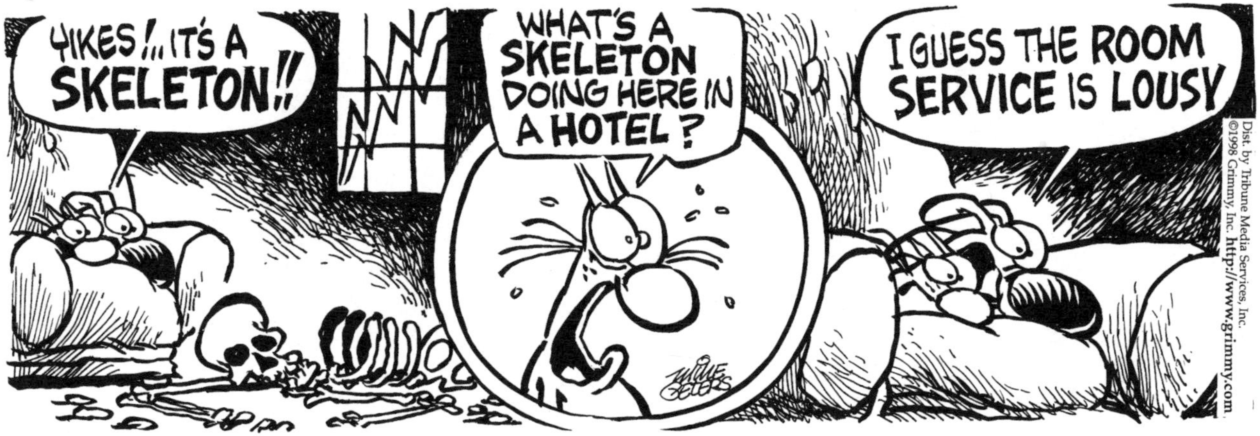
YIKES!... IT'S A SKELETON!!
WHAT'S A SKELETON DOING HERE IN A HOTEL?
I GUESS THE ROOM SERVICE IS LOUSY
Dist. by Tribune Media Services, Inc.
©1998 Grimmy, Inc. http://www.grimmy.com
MIKE PETERS

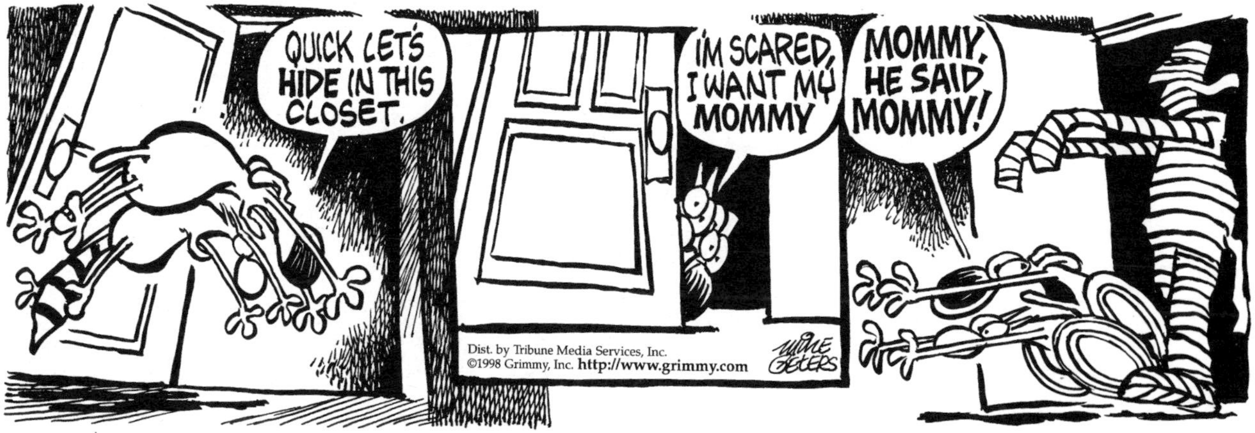
QUICK LET'S HIDE IN THIS CLOSET.
I'M SCARED, I WANT MY MOMMY
MOMMY, HE SAID MOMMY!
Dist. by Tribune Media Services, Inc.
©1998 Grimmy, Inc. http://www.grimmy.com
MIKE PETERS

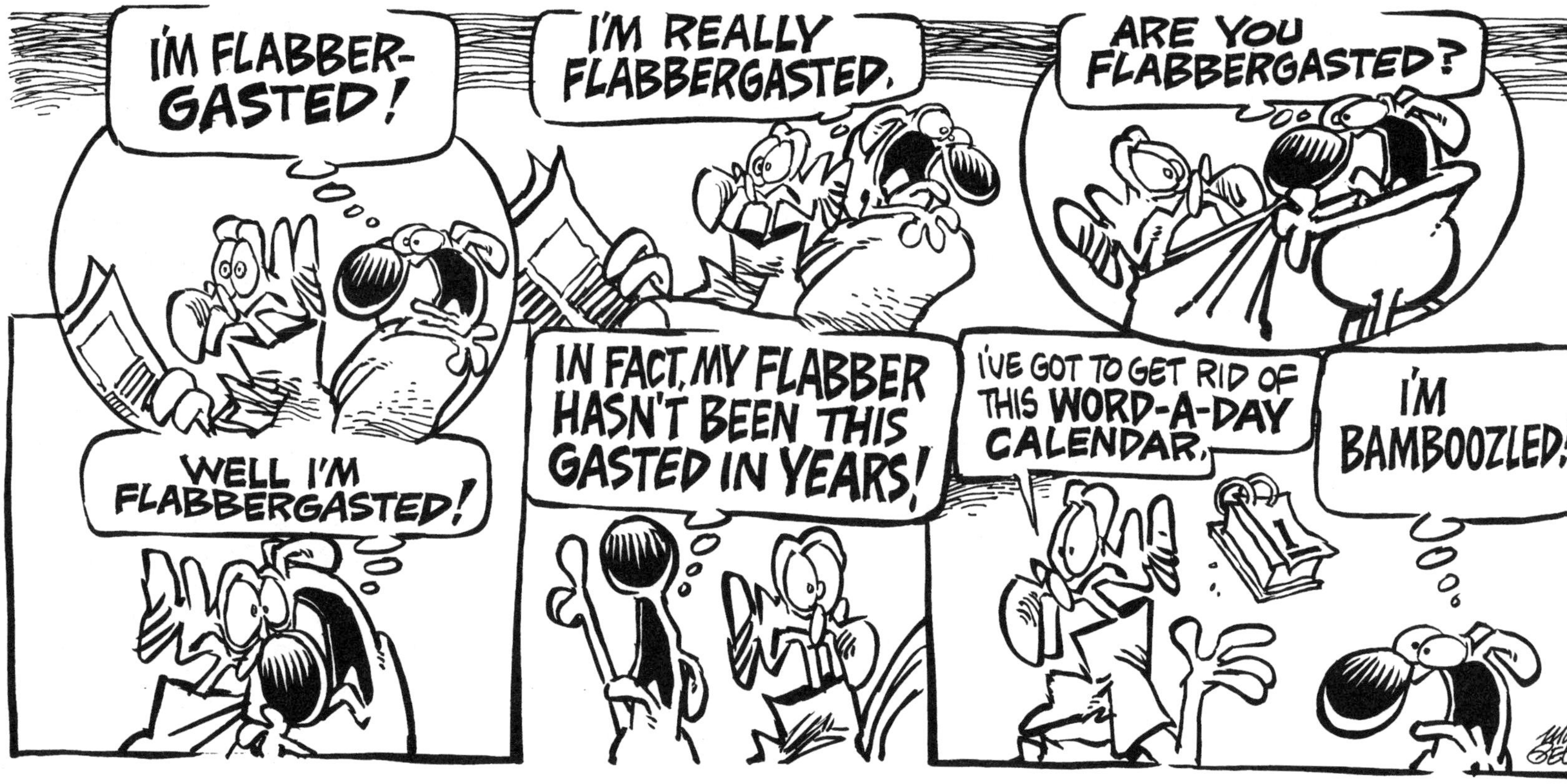
I'M FLABBER-GASTED!
WELL I'M FLABBERGASTED!
I'M REALLY FLABBERGASTED.
IN FACT, MY FLABBER HASN'T BEEN THIS GASTED IN YEARS!
ARE YOU FLABBERGASTED?
I'VE GOT TO GET RID OF THIS WORD-A-DAY CALENDAR.
I'M BAMBOOZLED!
1
MIKE PETERS

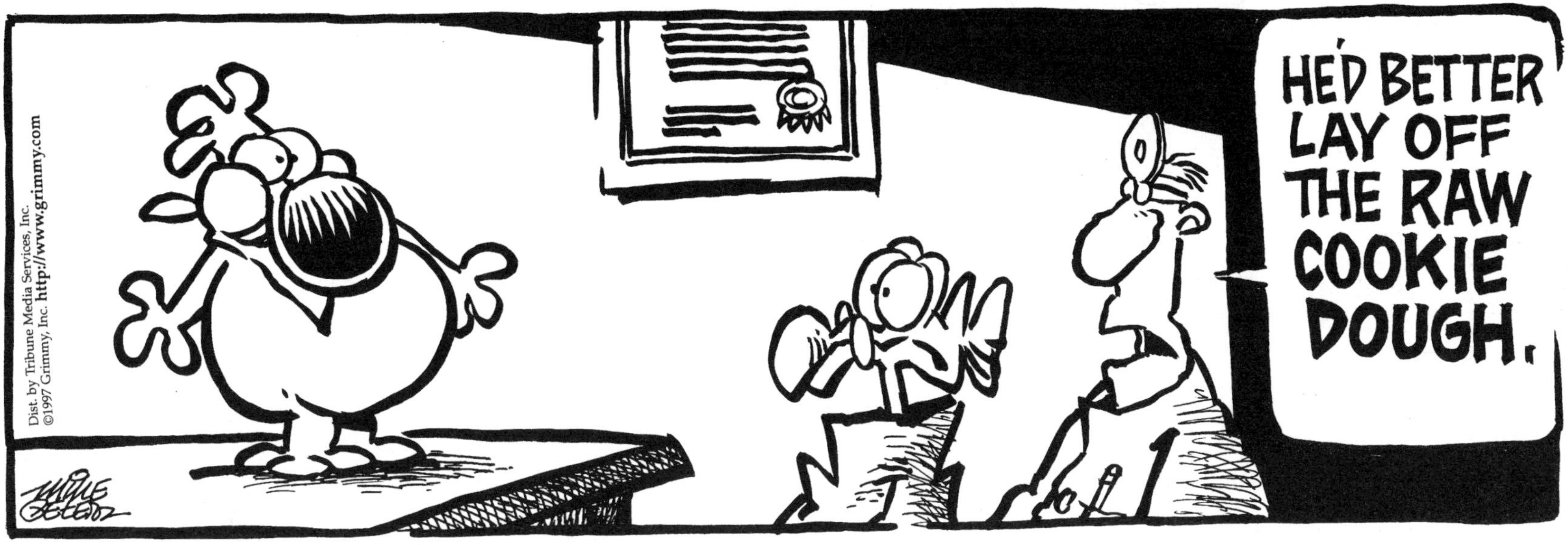
HE'D BETTER LAY OFF THE RAW COOKIE DOUGH.
Dist. by Tribune Media Services, Inc.
©1997 Grimmy, Inc. http://www.grimmy.com

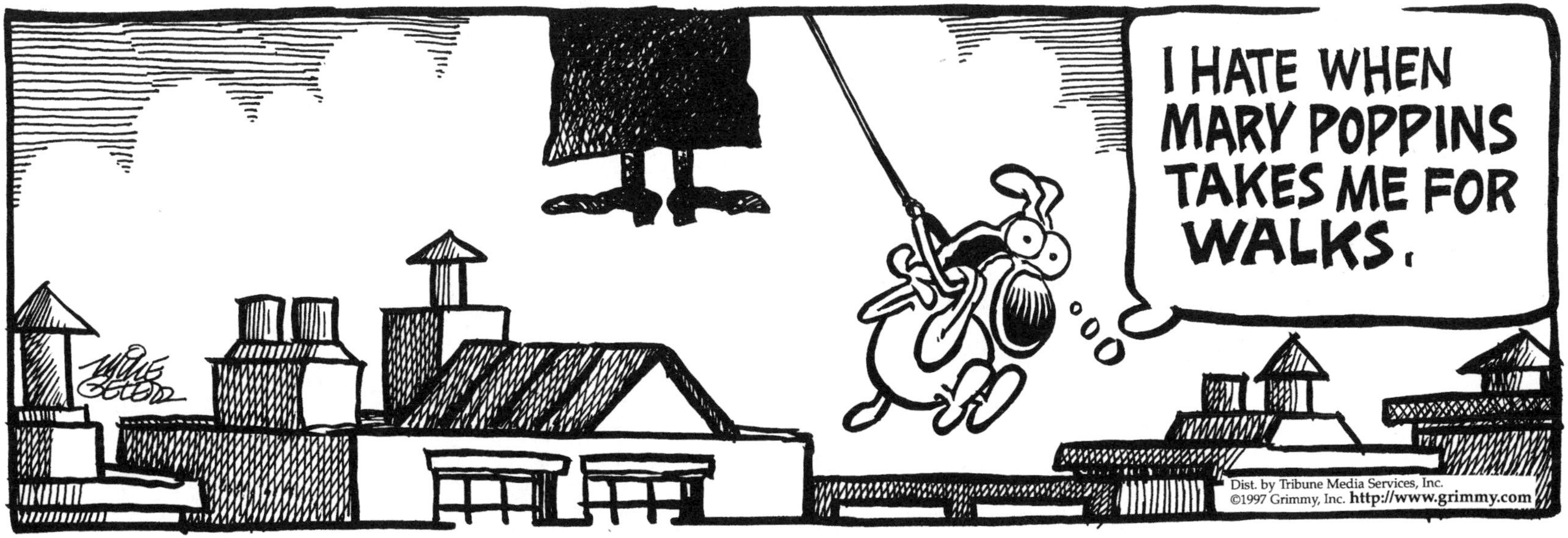
I HATE WHEN MARY POPPINS TAKES ME FOR WALKS.
Dist. by Tribune Media Services, Inc.
©1997 Grimmy, Inc. http://www.grimmy.com

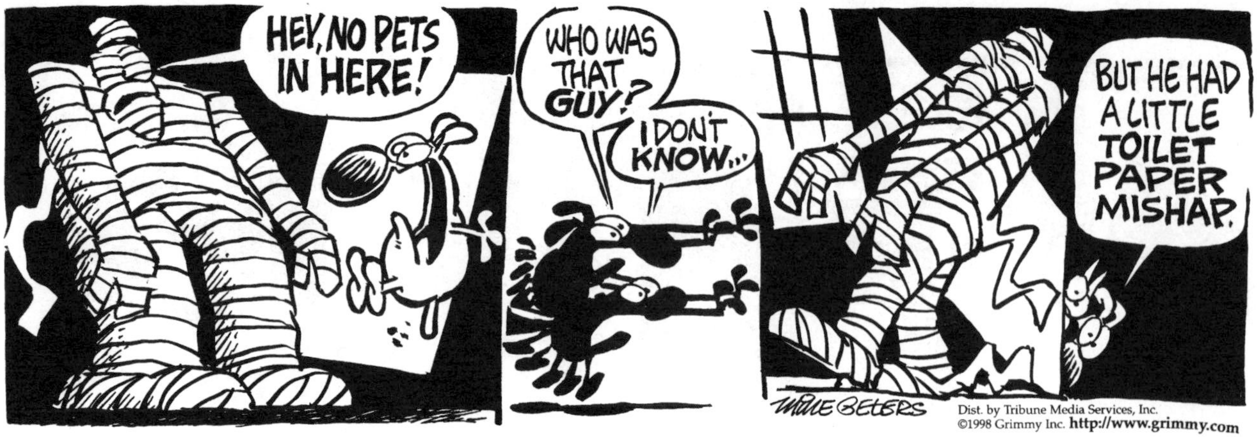
HEY, NO PETS IN HERE!
WHO WAS THAT GUY?
I DON'T KNOW...
BUT HE HAD A LITTLE TOILET PAPER MISHAP.
MIKE PETERS

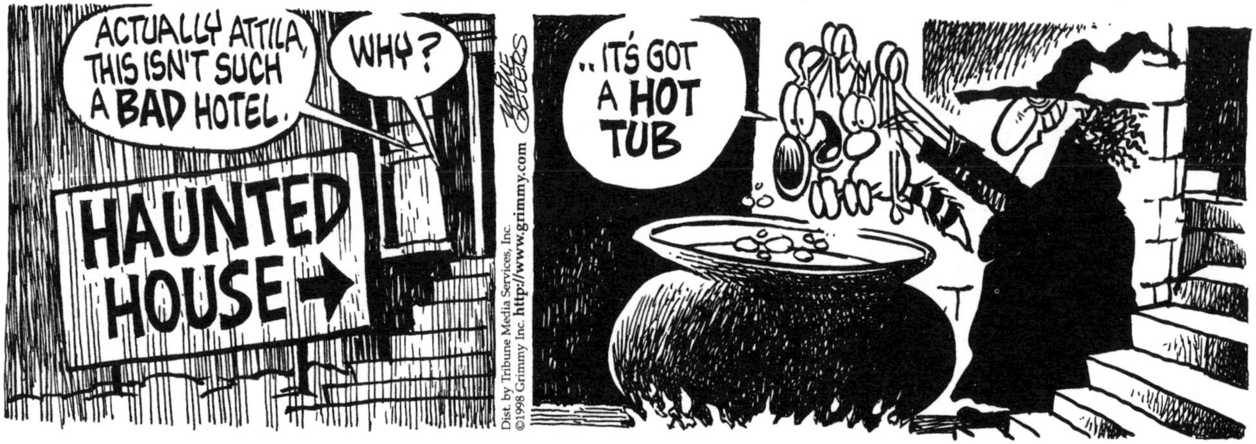
ACTUALLY ATTILA, THIS ISN'T SUCH A BAD HOTEL.
WHY?
HAUNTED HOUSE
...IT'S GOT A HOT TUB
MIKE PETERS

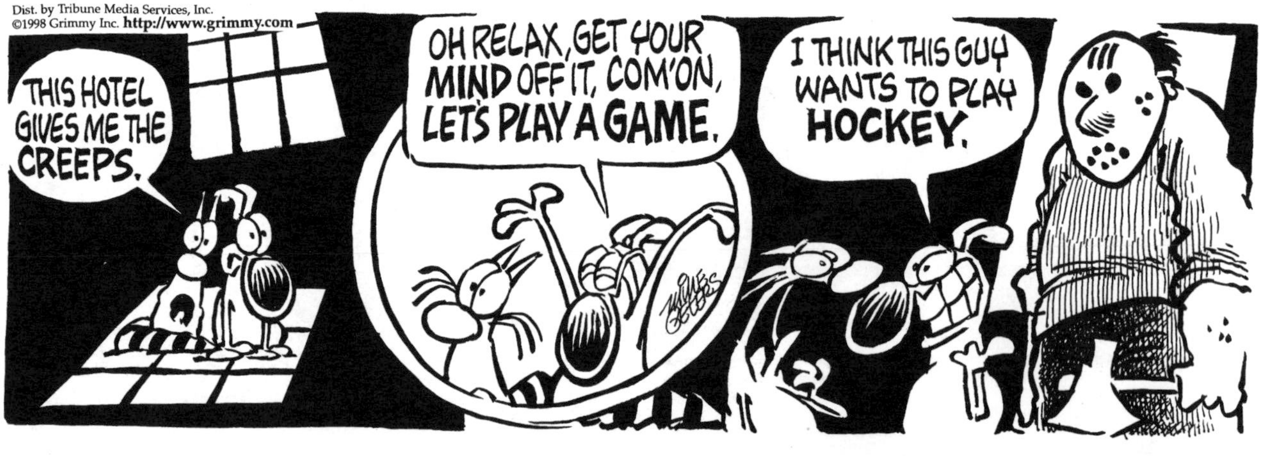
THIS HOTEL GIVES ME THE CREEPS.
OH RELAX, GET YOUR MIND OFF IT, COM'ON, LET'S PLAY A GAME.
I THINK THIS GUY WANTS TO PLAY HOCKEY.
MIKE PETERS

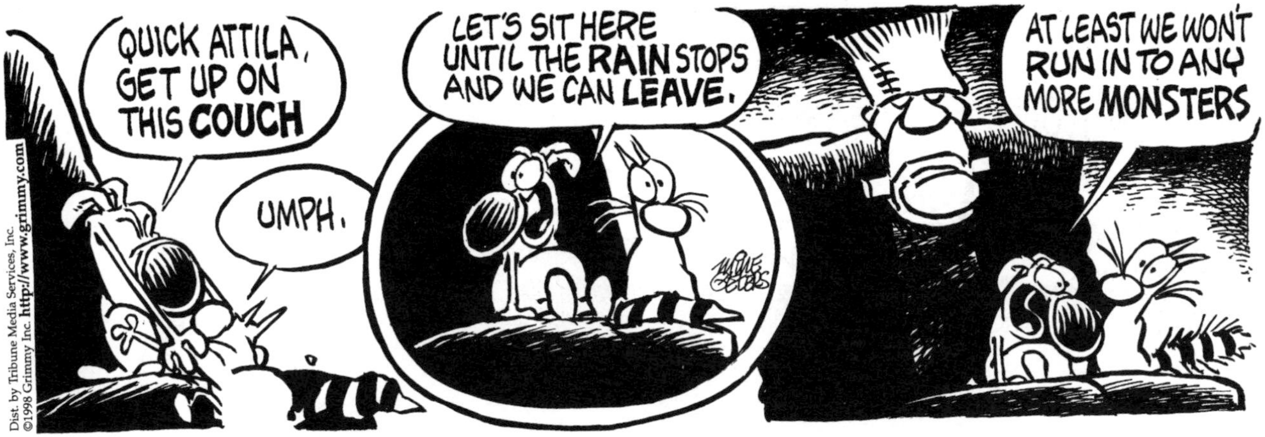
QUICK ATTILA, GET UP ON THIS COUCH
UMPH.
LET'S SIT HERE UNTIL THE RAIN STOPS AND WE CAN LEAVE.
AT LEAST WE WON'T RUN IN TO ANY MORE MONSTERS
Dist. by Tribune Media Services, Inc.
©1998 Grimmy Inc. http://www.grimmy.com

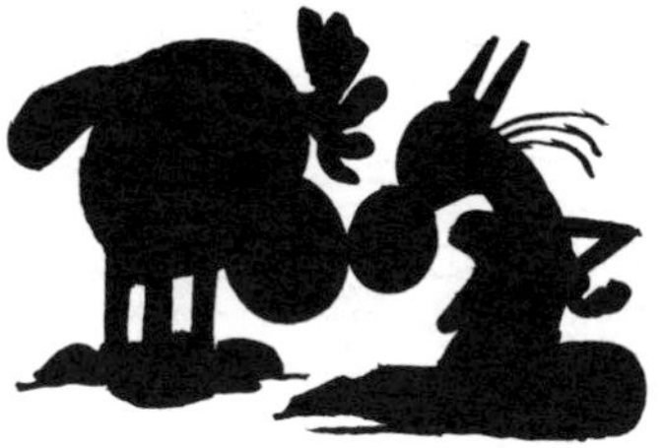

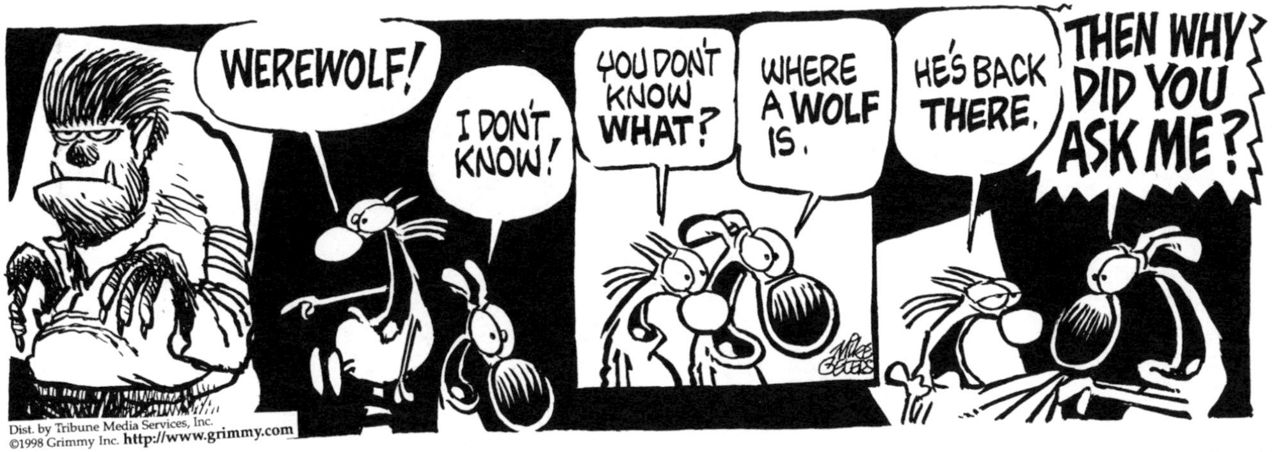
WEREWOLF!
I DON'T KNOW!
YOU DON'T KNOW WHAT?
WHERE A WOLF IS.
HE'S BACK THERE.
THEN WHY DID YOU ASK ME?
Dist. by Tribune Media Services, Inc.
©1998 Grimmy Inc. http://www.grimmy.com

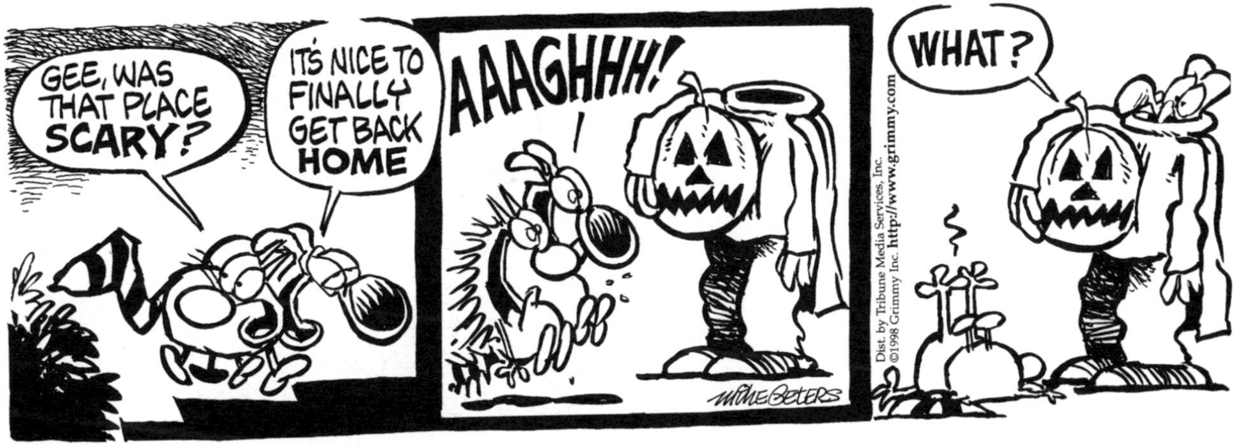
GEE, WAS THAT PLACE SCARY?
IT'S NICE TO FINALLY GET BACK HOME
AAAGHHH!
!
WHAT?
Dist. by Tribune Media Services, Inc.
©1998 Grimmy Inc. http://www.grimmy.com

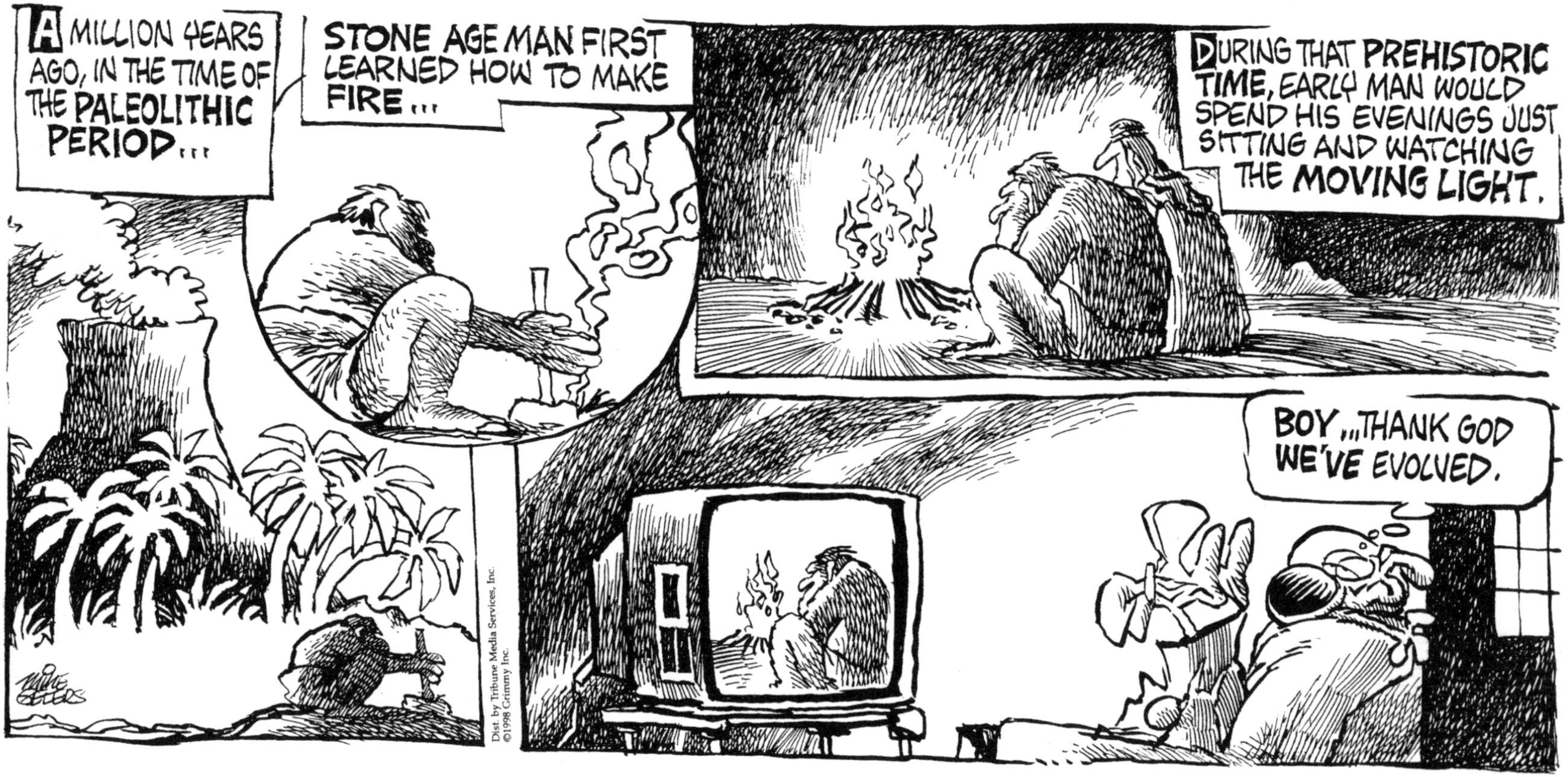
A MILLION YEARS AGO, IN THE TIME OF THE PALEOLITHIC PERIOD...
STONE AGE MAN FIRST LEARNED HOW TO MAKE FIRE...
DURING THAT PREHISTORIC TIME, EARLY MAN WOULD SPEND HIS EVENINGS JUST SITTING AND WATCHING THE MOVING LIGHT.
BOY...THANK GOD WE'VE EVOLVED.
Dist. by Tribune Media Services, Inc.
©1998 Grimmy Inc.

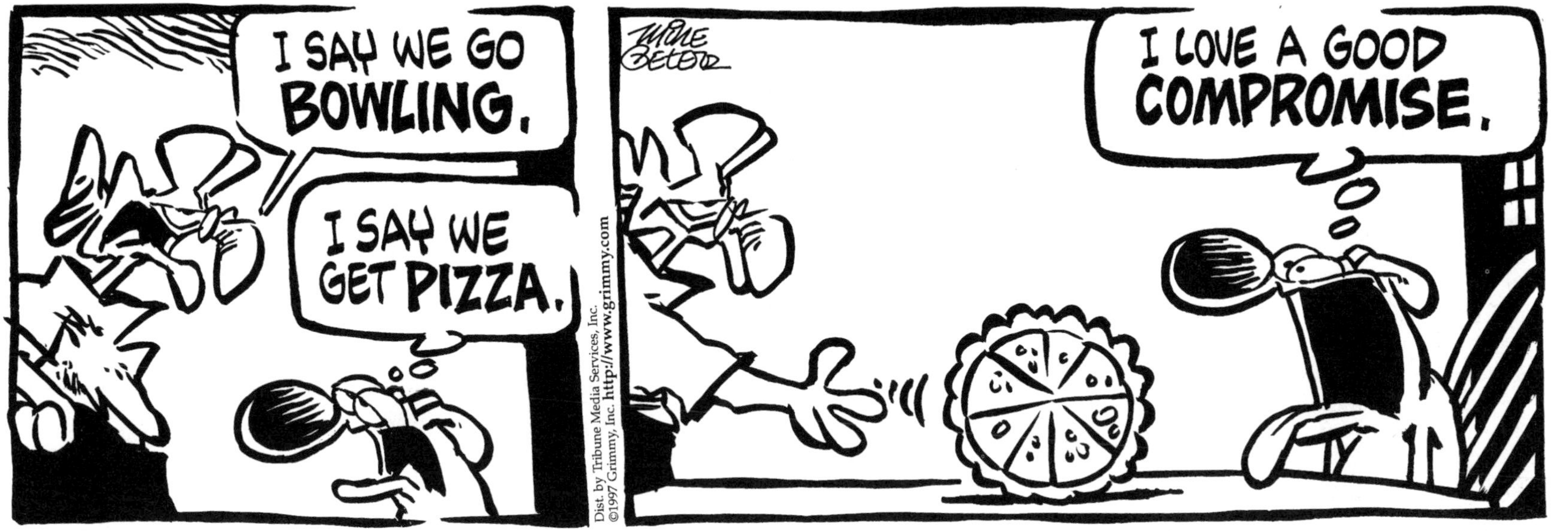
I SAY WE GO BOWLING.
I SAY WE GET PIZZA.
Dist. by Tribune Media Services, Inc. ©1997 Grimmy, Inc. http://www.grimmy.com
I LOVE A GOOD COMPROMISE.

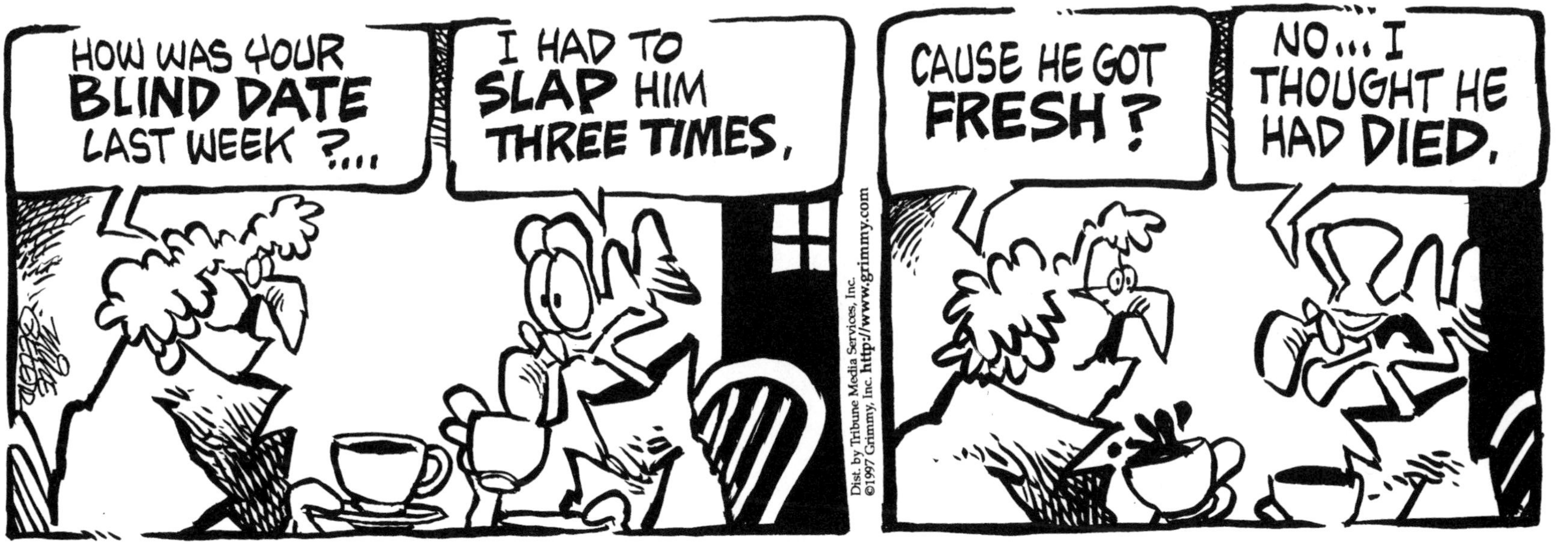
HOW WAS YOUR BLIND DATE LAST WEEK ?...
I HAD TO SLAP HIM THREE TIMES.
Dist. by Tribune Media Services, Inc. ©1997 Grimmy, Inc. http://www.grimmy.com
CAUSE HE GOT FRESH ?
NO... I THOUGHT HE HAD DIED.

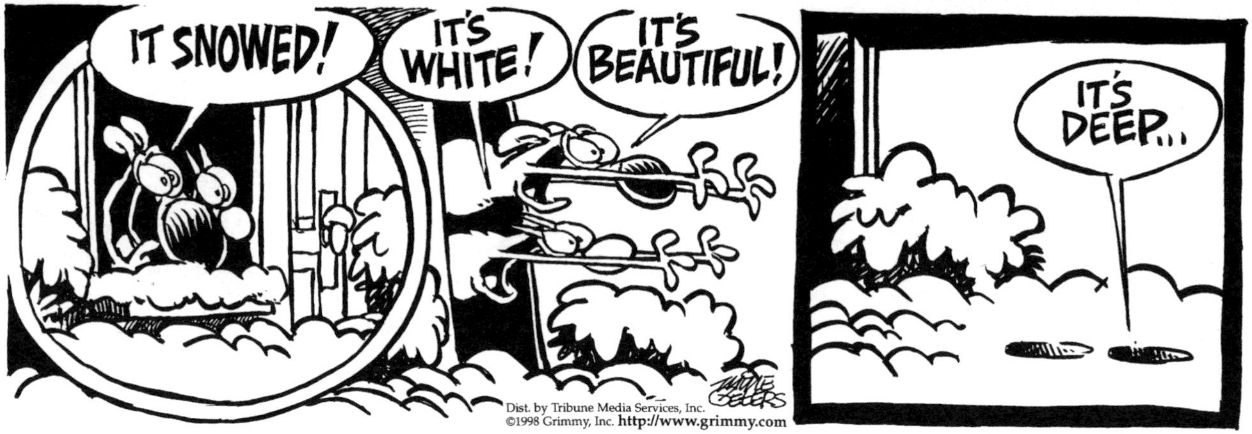
IT SNOWED!
IT'S WHITE!
IT'S BEAUTIFUL!
IT'S DEEP...

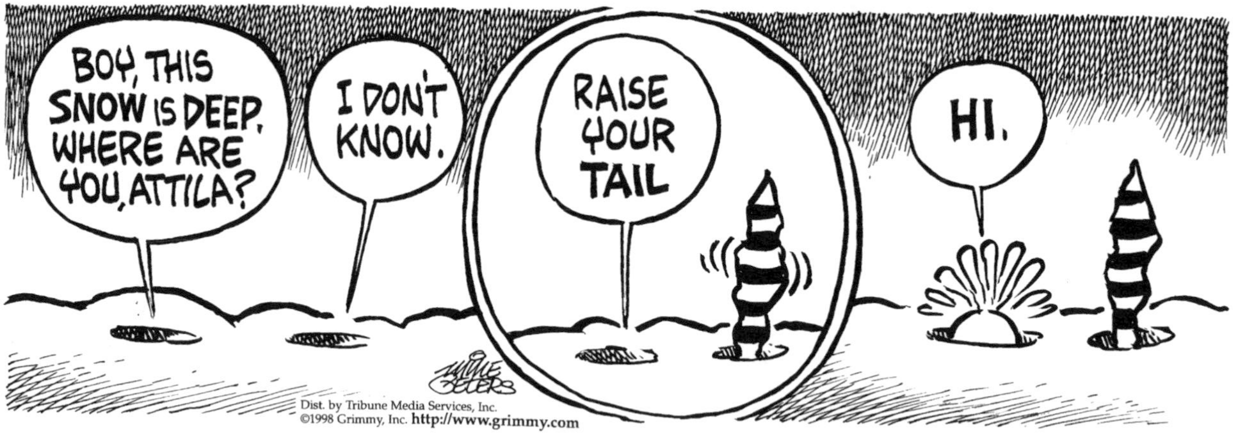
BOY, THIS SNOW IS DEEP. WHERE ARE YOU, ATTILA?
I DON'T KNOW.
RAISE YOUR TAIL
HI.

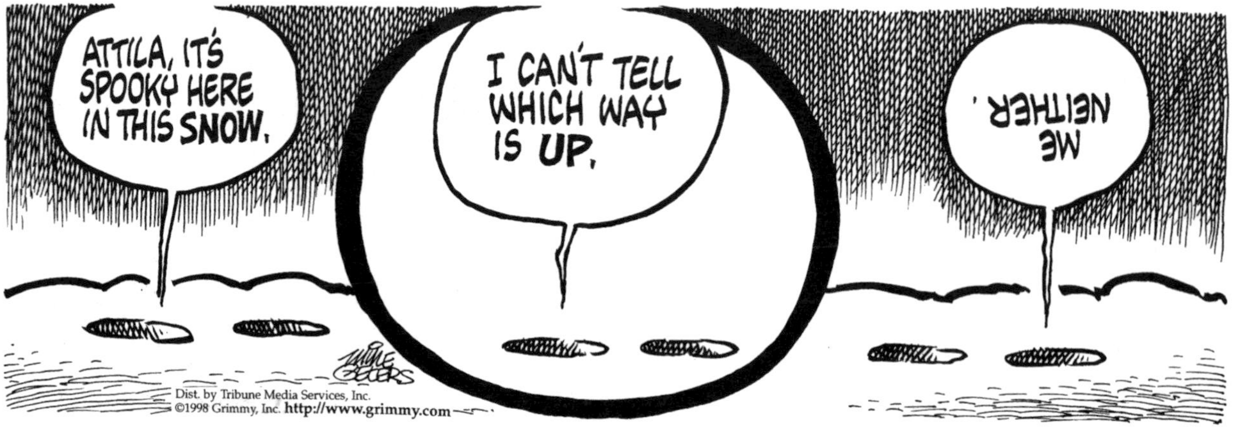
ATTILA, IT'S SPOOKY HERE IN THIS SNOW.
I CAN'T TELL WHICH WAY IS UP.
ME NEITHER.

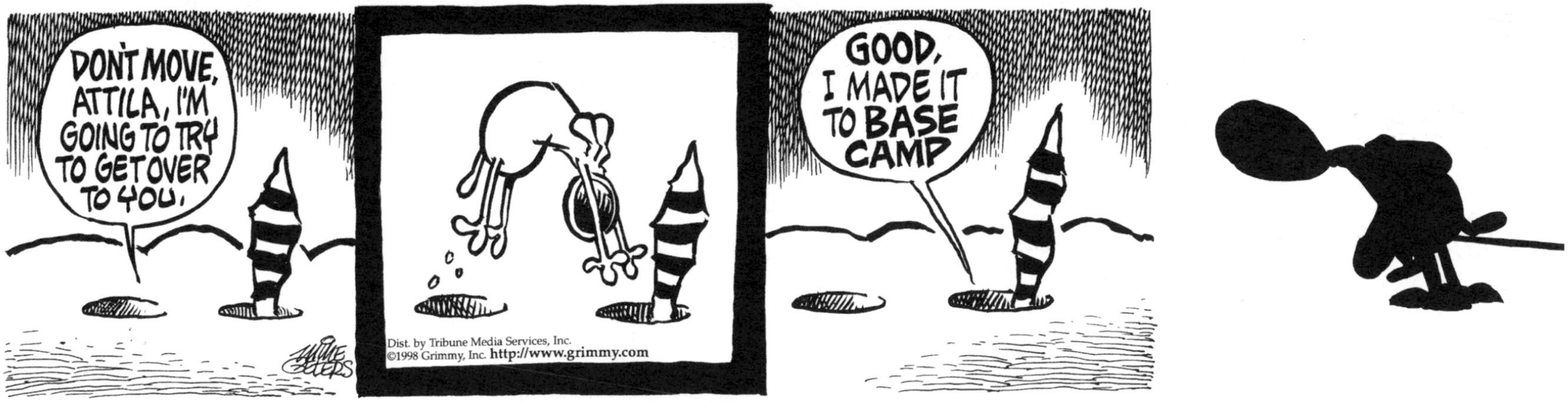
DON'T MOVE, ATTILA, I'M GOING TO TRY TO GET OVER TO YOU.
GOOD, I MADE IT TO BASE CAMP
Dist. by Tribune Media Services, Inc.
©1998 Grimmy, Inc. http://www.grimmy.com

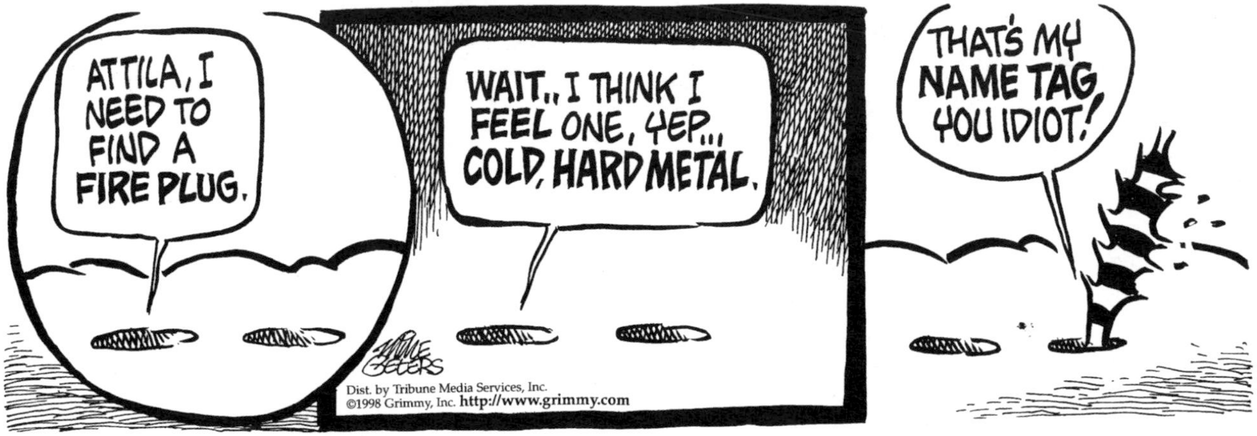
ATTILA, I NEED TO FIND A FIRE PLUG.
WAIT.. I THINK I FEEL ONE, YEP... COLD, HARD METAL.
THAT'S MY NAME TAG, YOU IDIOT!
Dist. by Tribune Media Services, Inc.
©1998 Grimmy, Inc. http://www.grimmy.com

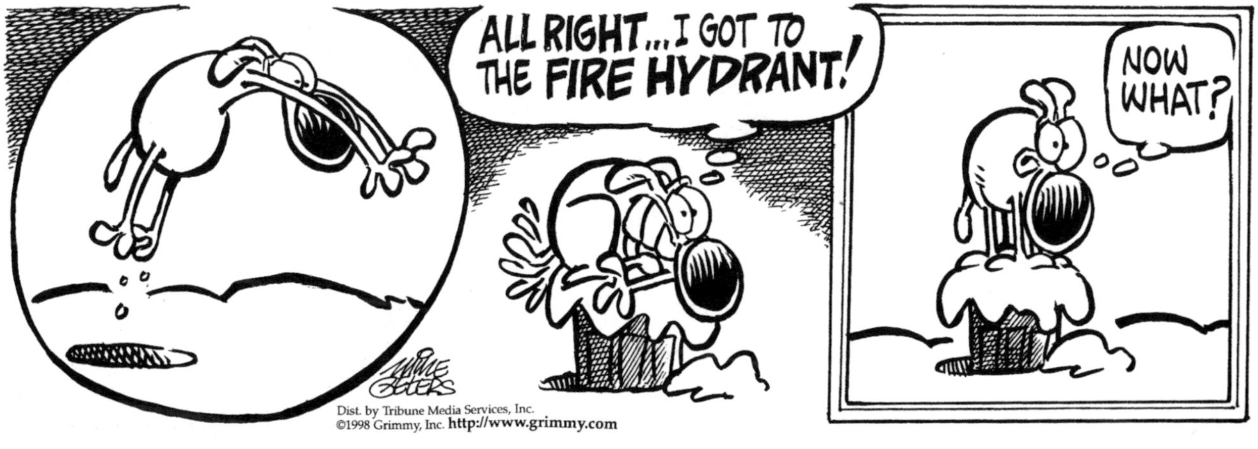
ALL RIGHT... I GOT TO THE FIRE HYDRANT!
NOW WHAT?
Dist. by Tribune Media Services, Inc.
©1998 Grimmy, Inc. http://www.grimmy.com

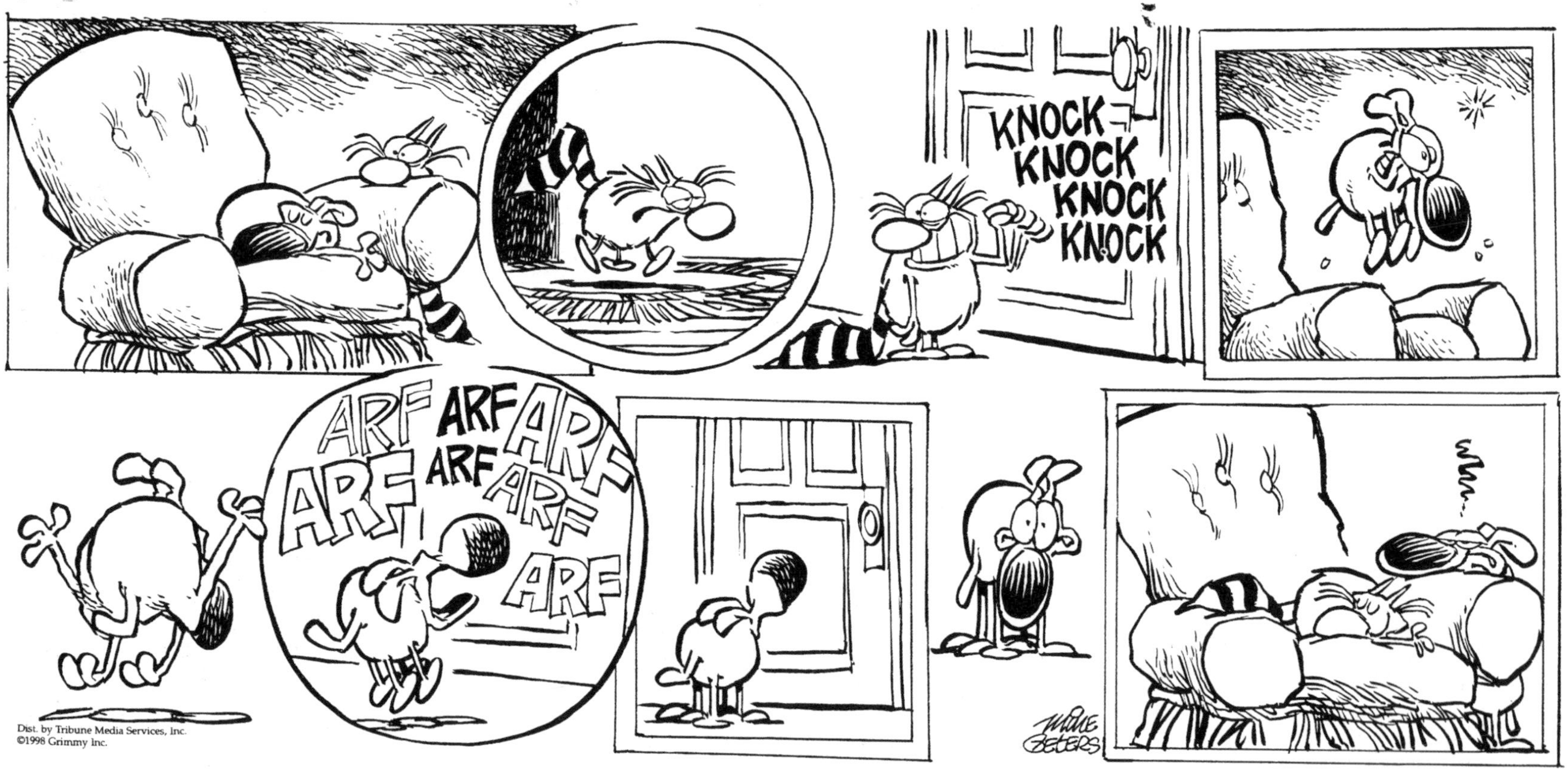
KNOCK
KNOCK
KNOCK
KNOCK
ARF ARF ARF
ARF ARF ARF
ARF
ARF
Mike Peters

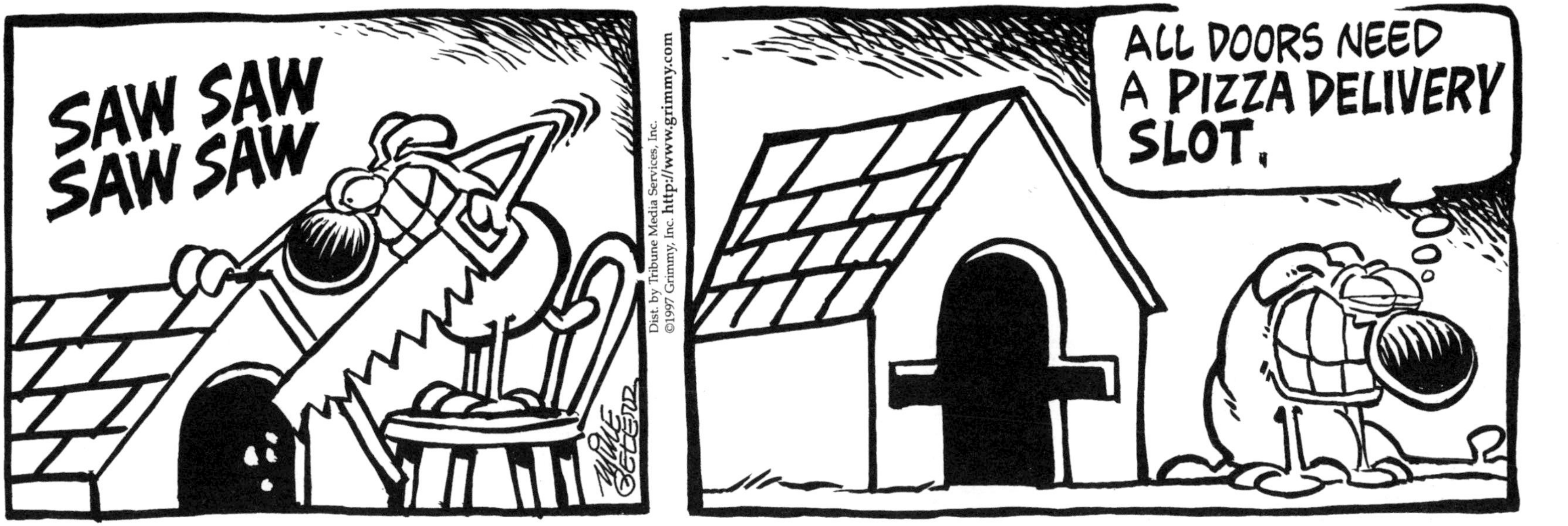
SAW SAW
SAW SAW
Dist. by Tribune Media Services, Inc.
©1997 Grimmy, Inc. http://www.grimmy.com
ALL DOORS NEED A PIZZA DELIVERY SLOT.

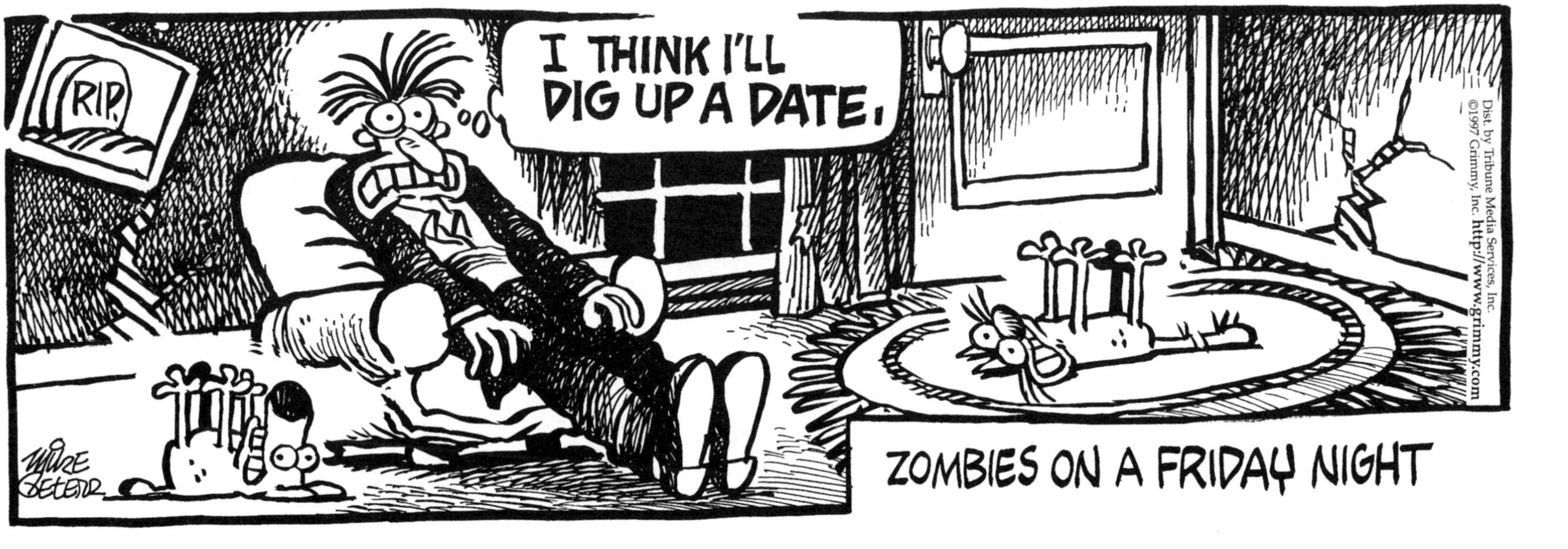
RIP.
I THINK I'LL DIG UP A DATE.
Dist. by Tribune Media Services, Inc.
©1997 Grimmy, Inc. http://www.grimmy.com
ZOMBIES ON A FRIDAY NIGHT

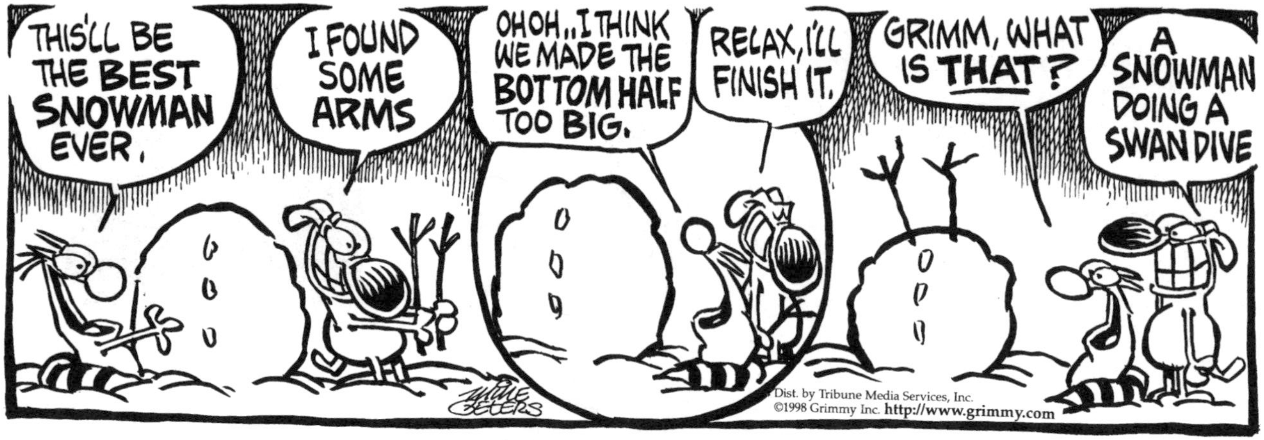
THIS'LL BE THE BEST SNOWMAN EVER.
I FOUND SOME ARMS
OH OH.. I THINK WE MADE THE BOTTOM HALF TOO BIG.
RELAX, I'LL FINISH IT.
GRIMM, WHAT IS THAT?
A SNOWMAN DOING A SWAN DIVE
MIKE PETERS
Dist. by Tribune Media Services, Inc.
©1998 Grimmy Inc. http://www.grimmy.com

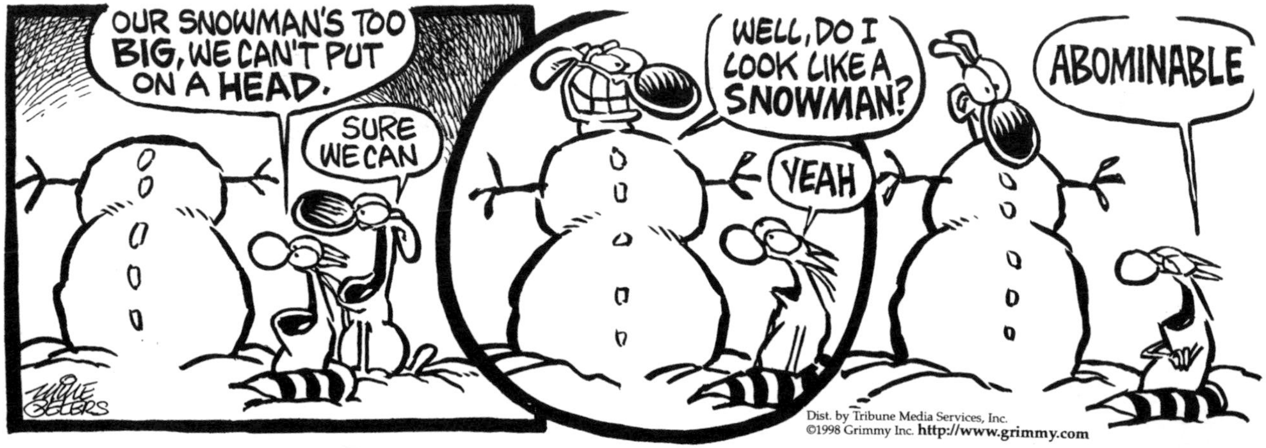
OUR SNOWMAN'S TOO BIG, WE CAN'T PUT ON A HEAD.
SURE WE CAN
WELL, DO I LOOK LIKE A SNOWMAN?
YEAH
ABOMINABLE
MIKE PETERS
Dist. by Tribune Media Services, Inc.
©1998 Grimmy Inc. http://www.grimmy.com

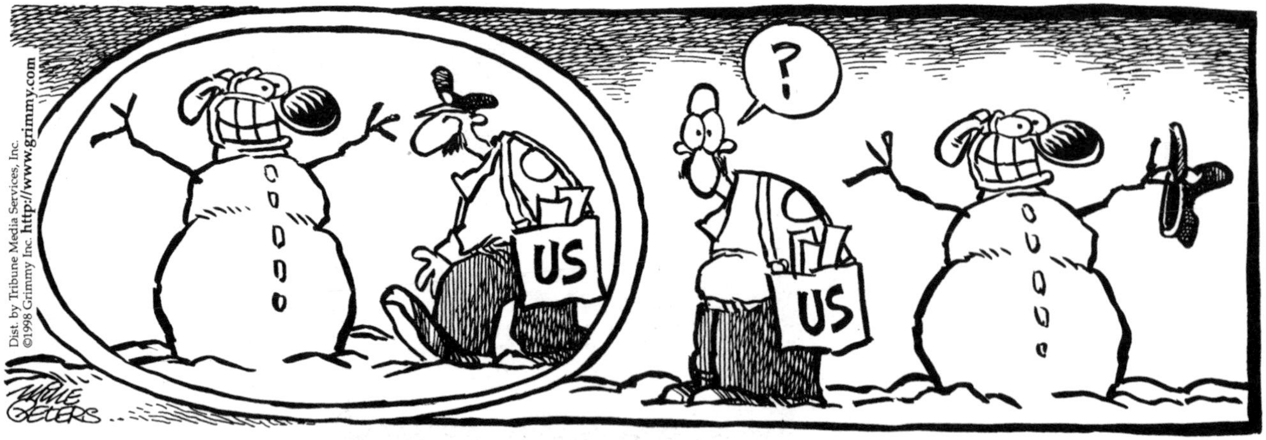
Dist. by Tribune Media Services, Inc.
©1998 Grimmy Inc. http://www.grimmy.com
US
?
US
MIKE PETERS

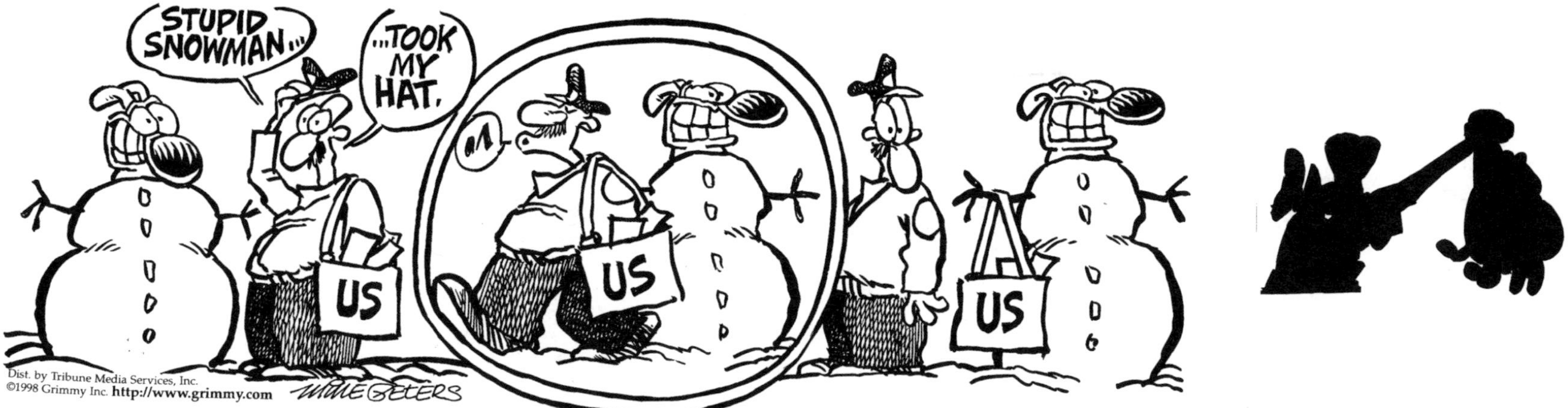
STUPID SNOWMAN...
...TOOK MY HAT.
US
Dist. by Tribune Media Services, Inc.
©1998 Grimmy Inc. http://www.grimmy.com
MIKE PETERS

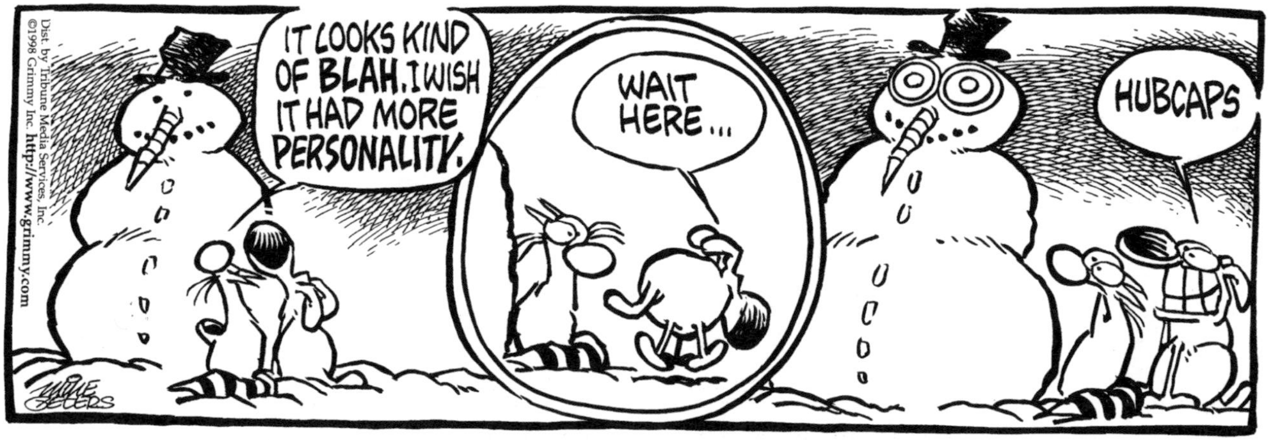
Dist. by Tribune Media Services, Inc.
©1998 Grimmy Inc. http://www.grimmy.com
IT LOOKS KIND OF BLAH. I WISH IT HAD MORE PERSONALITY.
WAIT HERE...
HUBCAPS
MIKE PETERS

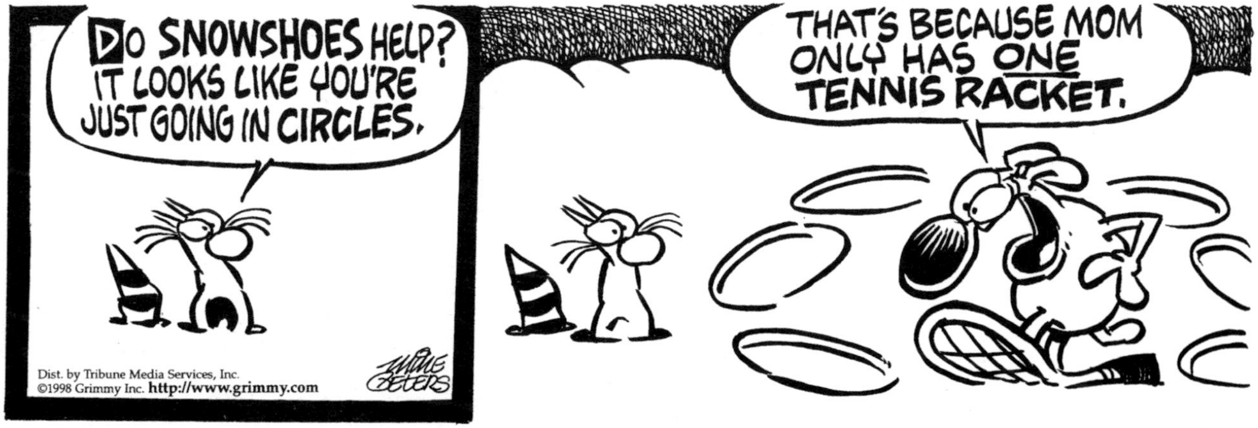
DO SNOWSHOES HELP? IT LOOKS LIKE YOU'RE JUST GOING IN CIRCLES.
THAT'S BECAUSE MOM ONLY HAS ONE TENNIS RACKET.
Dist. by Tribune Media Services, Inc.
©1998 Grimmy Inc. http://www.grimmy.com
MIKE PETERS

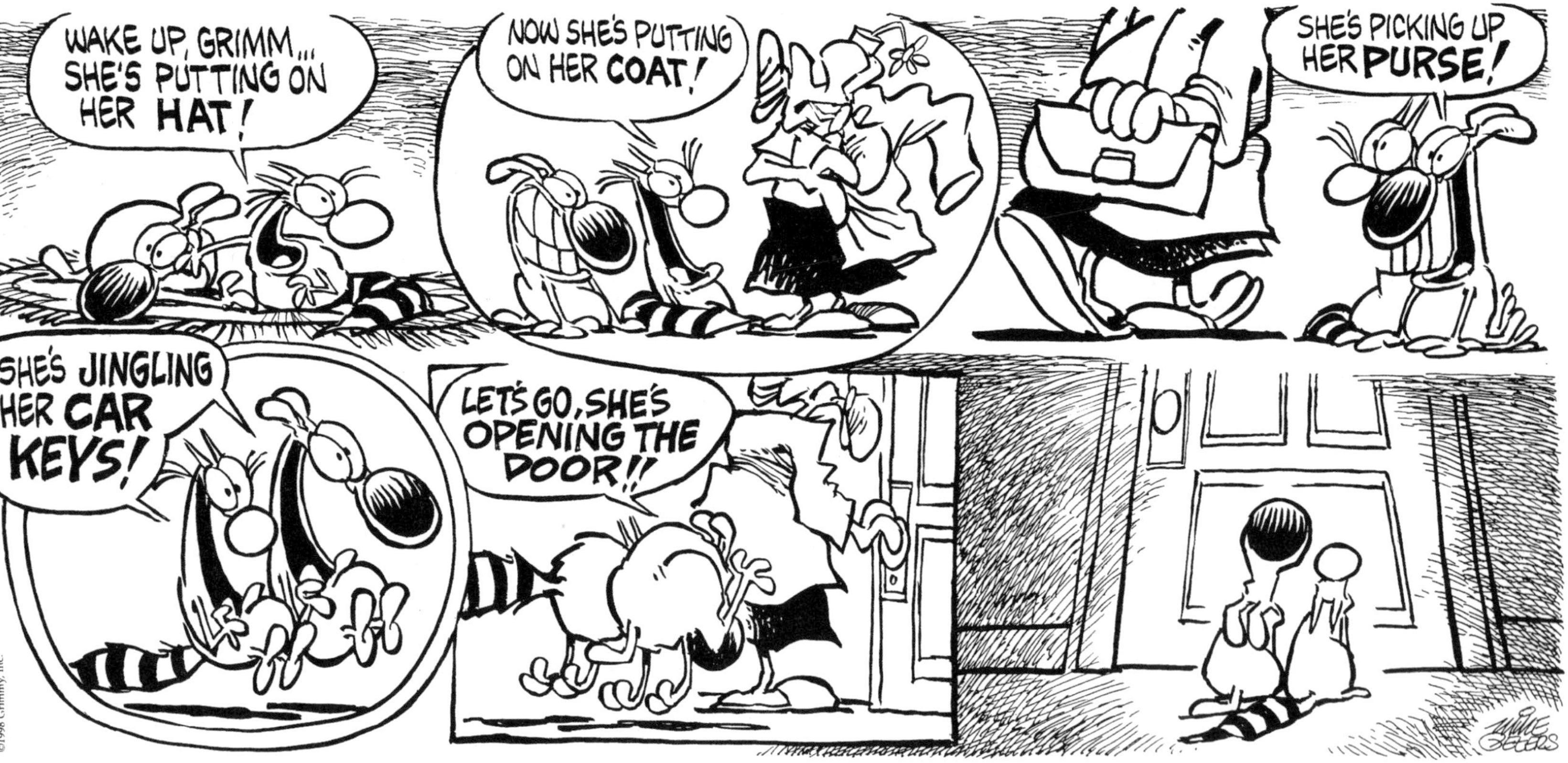
WAKE UP, GRIMM... SHE'S PUTTING ON HER HAT!
NOW SHE'S PUTTING ON HER COAT!
SHE'S PICKING UP HER PURSE!
SHE'S JINGLING HER CAR KEYS!
LET'S GO, SHE'S OPENING THE DOOR!!

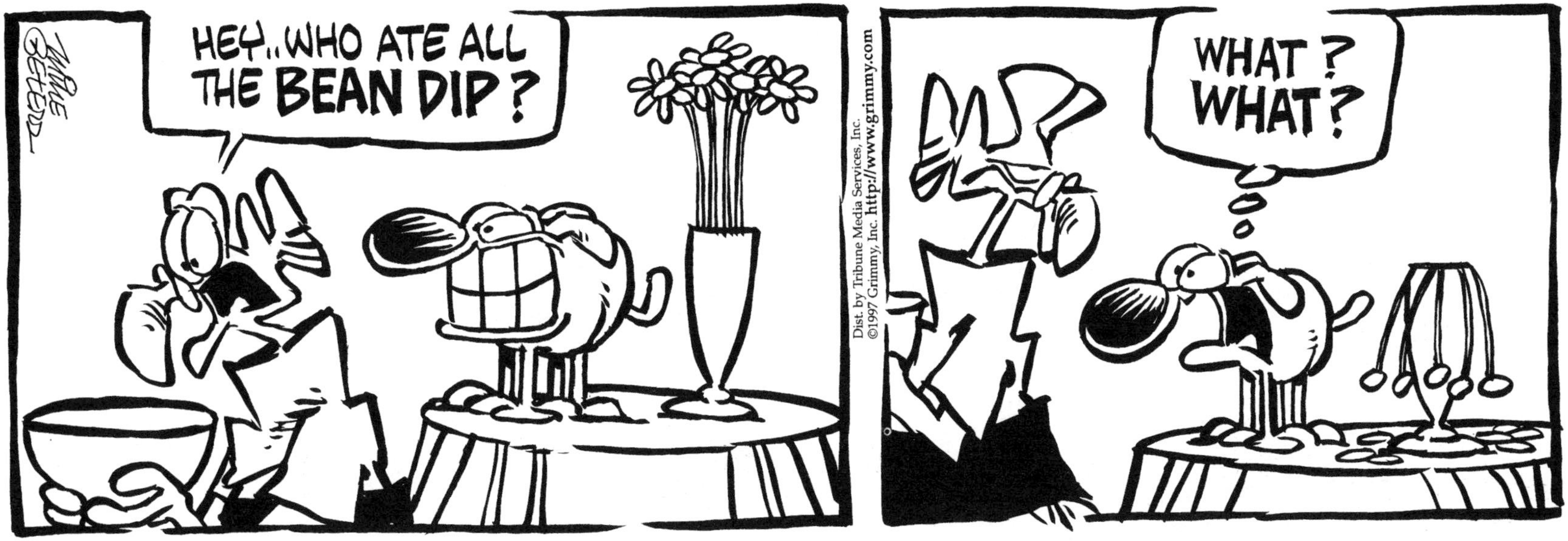
HEY.. WHO ATE ALL THE BEAN DIP ?
Dist. by Tribune Media Services, Inc. ©1997 Grimmy, Inc. http://www.grimmy.com
WHAT ? WHAT ?

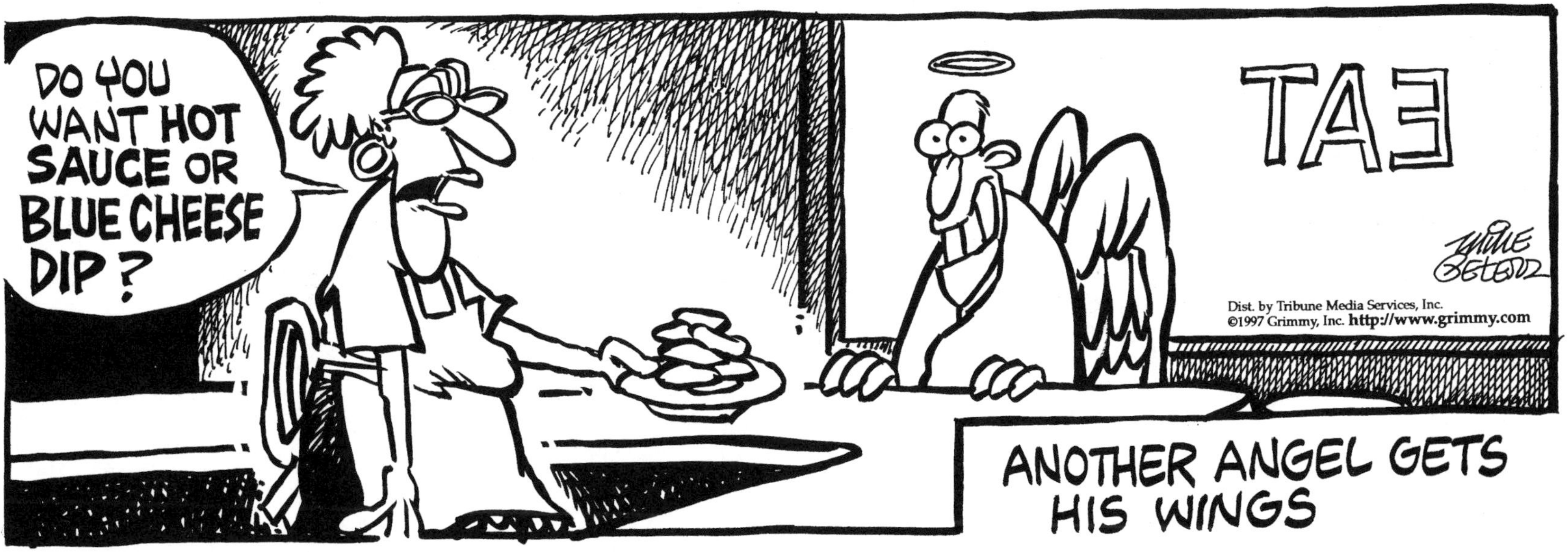
DO YOU WANT HOT SAUCE OR BLUE CHEESE DIP ?
EAT
Dist. by Tribune Media Services, Inc. ©1997 Grimmy, Inc. http://www.grimmy.com
ANOTHER ANGEL GETS HIS WINGS

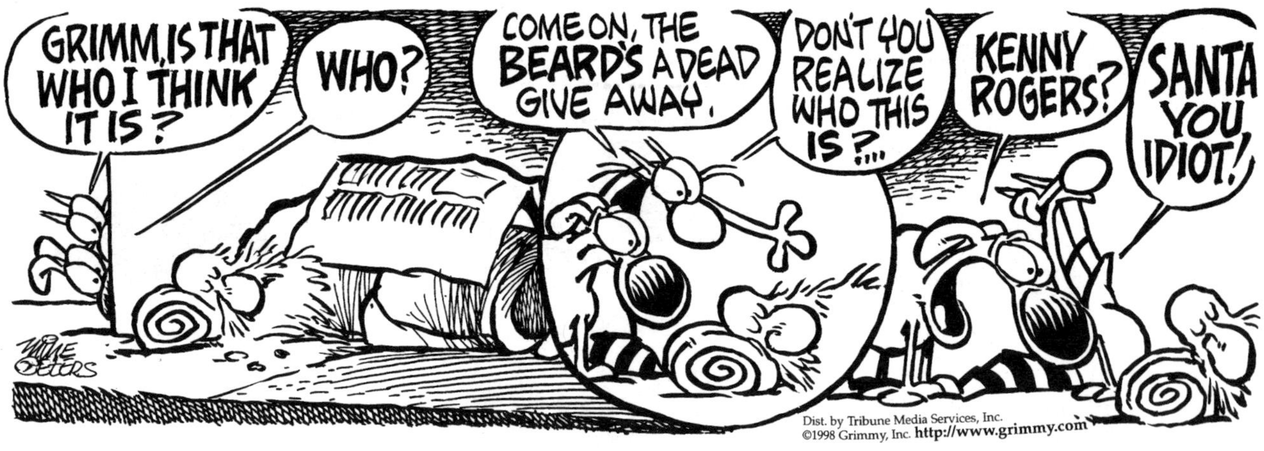
GRIMM, IS THAT WHO I THINK IT IS?
WHO?
COME ON, THE BEARD'S A DEAD GIVE AWAY.
DON'T YOU REALIZE WHO THIS IS?...
KENNY ROGERS?
SANTA YOU IDIOT!
Dist. by Tribune Media Services, Inc.
©1998 Grimmy, Inc. http://www.grimmy.com

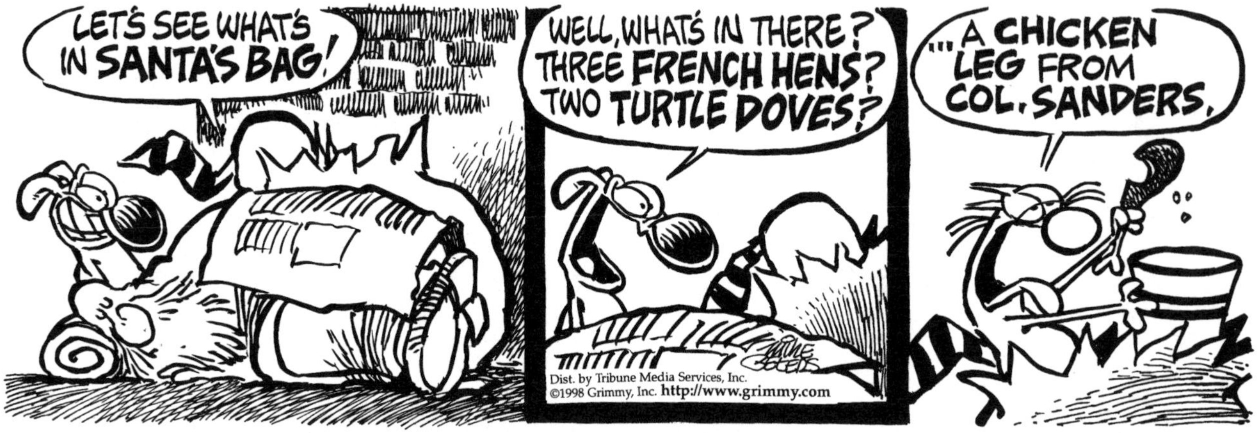
LET'S SEE WHAT'S IN SANTA'S BAG!
WELL, WHAT'S IN THERE? THREE FRENCH HENS? TWO TURTLE DOVES?
Dist. by Tribune Media Services, Inc.
©1998 Grimmy, Inc. http://www.grimmy.com
...A CHICKEN LEG FROM COL. SANDERS.

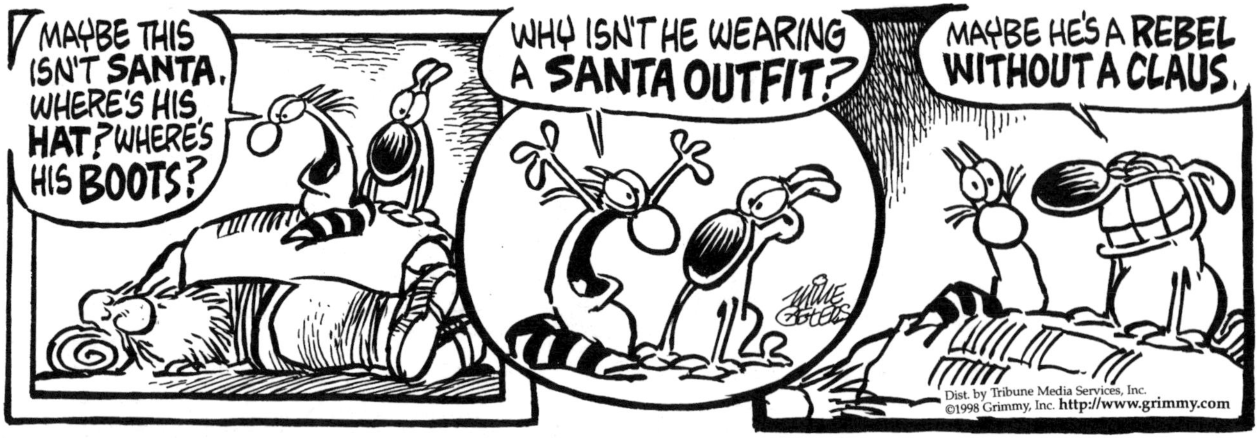
MAYBE THIS ISN'T SANTA. WHERE'S HIS HAT? WHERE'S HIS BOOTS?
WHY ISN'T HE WEARING A SANTA OUTFIT?
MAYBE HE'S A REBEL WITHOUT A CLAUS.
Dist. by Tribune Media Services, Inc.
©1998 Grimmy, Inc. http://www.grimmy.com

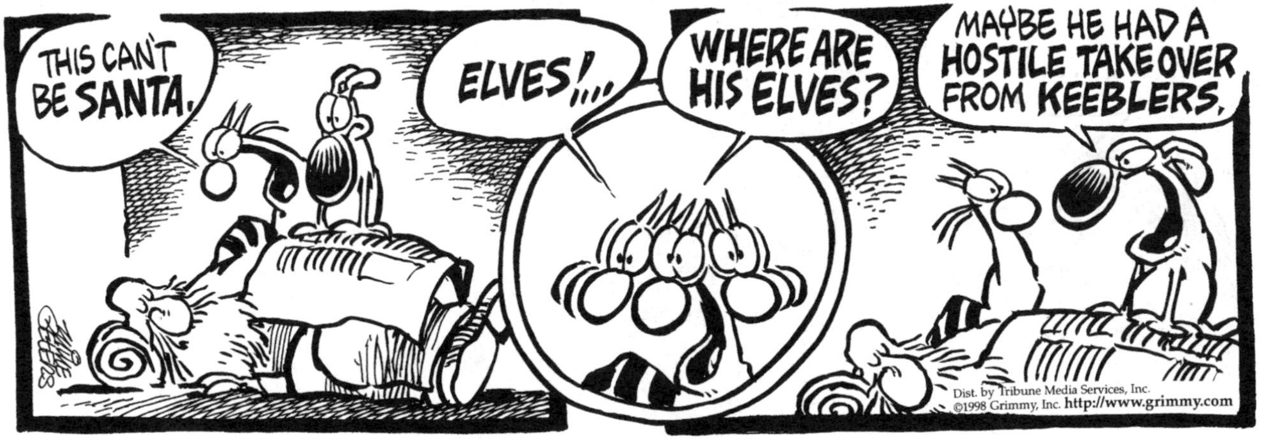

THIS CAN'T BE SANTA,
ELVES!,,,
WHERE ARE HIS ELVES?
MAYBE HE HAD A HOSTILE TAKE OVER FROM KEEBLERS,
Dist. by Tribune Media Services, Inc.
©1998 Grimmy, Inc. http://www.grimmy.com

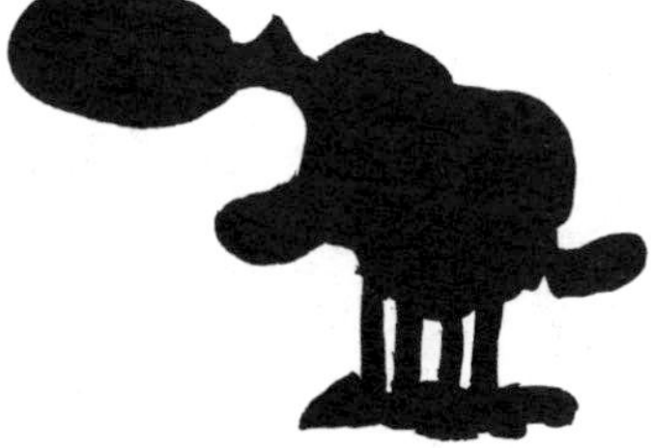

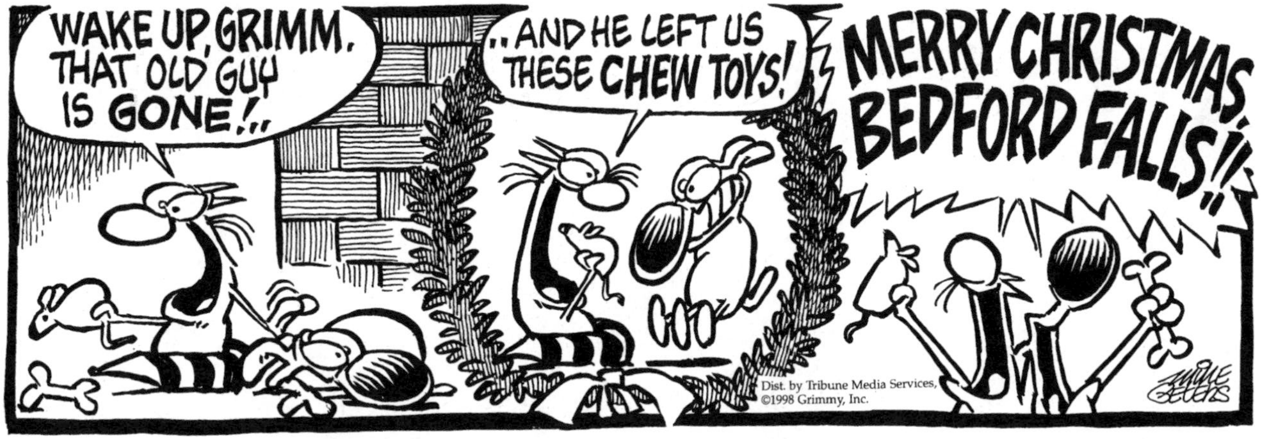

WAKE UP, GRIMM, THAT OLD GUY IS GONE!..
..AND HE LEFT US THESE CHEW TOYS!
MERRY CHRISTMAS, BEDFORD FALLS!!
Dist. by Tribune Media Services,
©1998 Grimmy, Inc.

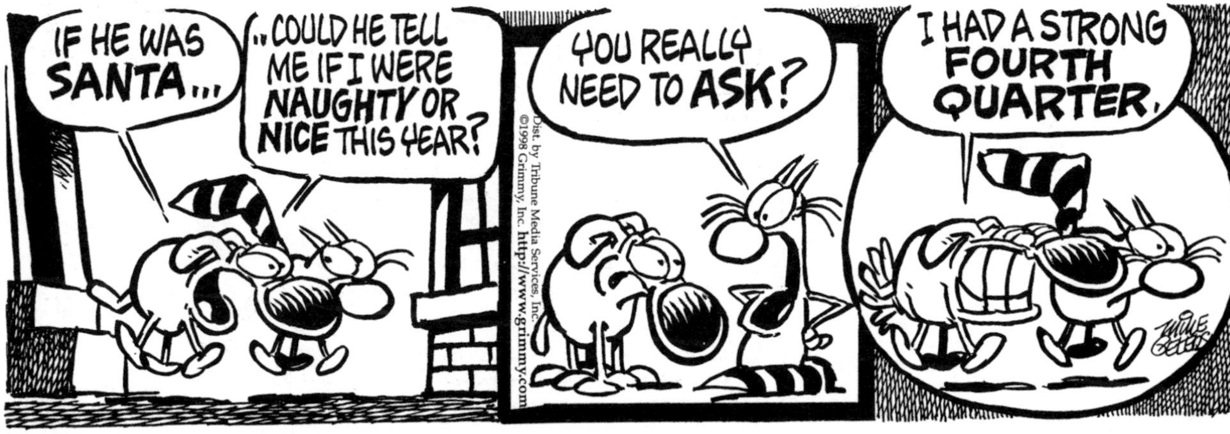

IF HE WAS SANTA...
..COULD HE TELL ME IF I WERE NAUGHTY OR NICE THIS YEAR?
Dist. by Tribune Media Services, Inc.
©1998 Grimmy, Inc. http://www.grimmy.com
YOU REALLY NEED TO ASK?
I HAD A STRONG FOURTH QUARTER,

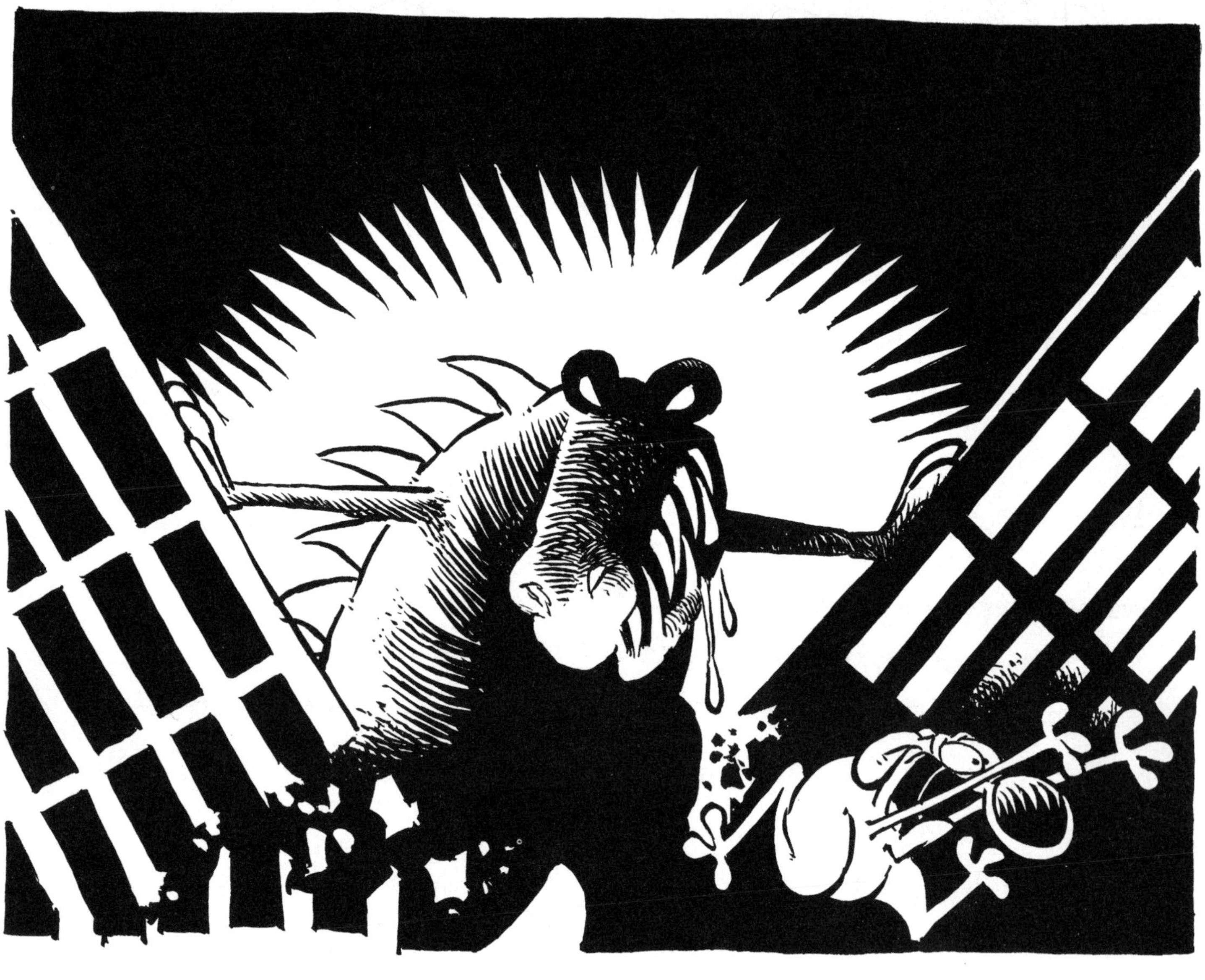

WHERE ARE THE GOODS?

MANY OF OUR READERS ASK HOW THEY CAN BUY GRIMMY MERCHANDISE.

HERE IS A LIST OF LICENSEES IN THE UNITED STATES AND CANADA THAT CARRY GREAT STUFF!

GIVE THEM A CALL FOR YOUR LOCAL DISTRIBUTOR.

WWW.GRIMMY.COM

Avalanche Publishing
1093 Bedmar St.
Carson, CA 90746
PH 800/888-6421
365 Day Box Calendar-Year 2000
www.avalanchepub.com

Classcom, Inc.
770 Bertrand
Montreal, Quebec
Canada H4M1V9
PH 514/747-9492
Desk Art

C.T.I.
22160 North Pepper Rd.
Barrington, IL 60010
PH 800/284-5605
Balloons, Coffee Mugs

Gibson Greetings
2100 Section Rd.
Cincinnati, OH 45237
PH 800/345-6521
Greeting Cards, Party
Papers, Gift Wrap, Egreetings, etc.
www.greetst.com

Linda Jones Enterprises
17771 Mitchell
Irvine, CA 92614
PH 949/660-7791
Cels

MR. TEES
3225 Hartsfield Rd.
Tallahassee, FL 32303
PH 800/833-1428
T-Shirts

Pomegranate
210 Classic Ct.
Rohnert Park, CA 94928
PH 800/227-1428
Wall Calendar-Year 2000
Postcard Booklets
www.pomegranate.com

TOR Books
175 Fifth Ave.
New York, NY 10010
PH 212/388-0100
Paperback Books
www.tor.com

Western Graphics
3535 W. 1st Avenue
Eugene, OR 97402
PH 800/532-3303
Posters

[redacted]

[redacted]